Satellite
Communications
in Europe

Law and Regulation

Lo, soul, seest thou not God's purpose from the first?
The earth to be spann'd, connected by network,
The races, neighbors, to marry and be given in marriage,
The oceans to be cross'd, the distance brought near,
The lands to be welded together.

A worship new I sing,
You captains, voyagers, explorers, yours,
You engineers, you architects, machinists, yours,
You, not for trade or transportation only,
But in God's name, and for thy sake O soul.

Passage to India by Walt Whitman

Satellite Communications in Europe

Law and Regulation

SECOND EDITION

Stewart White
Partner, Ashurst Morris Crisp, Solicitors

Stephen Bate
Barrister, 5 Raymond Buildings, Gray's Inn

Timothy Johnson
Partner, SJ Berwin & Co, Solicitors

LAW & TAX

ISBN 0752 002198

Published by
FT Law & Tax
21–27 Lamb's Conduit Street, London WC1N 3NJ

A Division of Pearson Professional Limited

Associated offices
Australia, Belgium, Canada, Hong Kong, India, Japan, Luxembourg,
Singapore, Spain, USA

A CIP catalogue record for this book is available from the British Library.

ITU material contained herein has been reproduced with the permission of the Union, the copyright holder. The sole responsibility for selecting extracts for reproduction lies with the authors. The complete volume(s) of the ITU material can be obtained from:

International Telecommunication Union
General Secretariat - Sales and Marketing Service
Place des Nations
CH - 1211 GENEVA 20 (Switzerland)

Telephone : +41 22 730 51 11	Telex : 421 000 uit ch
Telegram : ITU GENEVE	Fax : +41 22 730 51 94

X.400 : S = Sales; P = itu; A = Arcom; C = ch
Internet : Sales@itu.ch

Printed and bound in Great Britain by
Bookcraft Ltd

Contents

Foreword to the Second Edition

It is less than two years since I was asked to write the foreword for the first edition of this book. The need for a second edition demonstrates what I described then as 'the extraordinary development of satellite communications'. Much has taken place in that period and I am pleased that the authors have found time in their busy schedules to bring up to date these developments, not only in relation to ITU's Radio Regulations and the important work that has been undertaken by us since 1993, but also the ongoing work of the European Commission in this important sector; the coming closer to reality of satellite delivered personal communications networks; and, of course, the changes that are taking place within the structures of the satellite organisations. All this reflects the changing regulatory environment, which is a complex one.

The second edition is a very useful contribution for those who need guidance and insight in relation to the problems associated with telecommunications generally, and in particular in relation to satellite law.

Dr Pekka Tarjanne
Secretary-General
International Telecommunication Union

Foreword to the First Edition

The extraordinary development of satellite communications has rendered existing regulatory frameworks obsolete. Technical innovations, the multiplication of applications, competition among an increasing number of services geared to a growing demand in the marketplace — all these factors have quickened the pace of regulatory renewal and the process of devising more appropriate regulatory frameworks.

In this complex environment, there is a need for a reference work capable of providing guidance and giving an insight into the problems involved. This is what the authors have done in this very useful contribution which offers a valuable guide to all the important aspects of the law and regulation of satellite communications in Europe.

The appendices to the work contain substantial amounts of information tabulated together for the first time which should be highly useful to people of all vocations working in the satellite field and bring to a conclusion this well-documented volume which will doubtless prove to be a valuable tool for the increasing number of readers interested in the fascinating world of satellites and telecommunications in general.

Dr Pekka Tarjanne
Secretary-General
International Telecommunication Union

The last few years have seen a myriad of different and interesting issues in the field in which the Broadcasting Standards Council operates, many of them generated by the increasingly international scope of television. The boom in satellite broadcasting since 1989 has resulted in difficult questions and taxing issues — it is increasingly clear that a knowledge of the international framework of regulation of satellite communication in the television field is essential if international television services are to continue to be regulated efficiently and harmoniously throughout Europe.

It is, therefore, with great pleasure that I am able to write a foreword to a book which provides an explanation of the way that pan-European regulation of satellite broadcasting has been introduced and also a clear overview of the way in which satellite television services are regulated in the United Kingdom.

Whilst my own field and interests lie mainly in the television sector, I am also interested to see that the scope of this book goes far beyond satellite broadcasting and deals with the complex international regulatory framework for satellite communications of every kind.

I have no doubt that this book will be invaluable for anyone operating not only in the satellite television field but also in the field of satellite communications generally.

Dame Jocelyn Barrow
Deputy Chairman
Broadcasting Standards Council

Acknowledgements

First Edition

We would like to thank all those who assisted with the production of this book. In particular we would like to thank the Secretary-General of the International Telecommunication Union, Dr Pekka Tarjanne, for supplying us with up-to-date information concerning the ITU and also for permission to reproduce various ITU materials. We should also like to thank his staff for answering our many and varied questions. We should also like to thank the Director General of Société Européenne des Satellites, Dr Pierre Meyrat, for his permission to reproduce the footprint maps of the ASTRA Satellite System and Dr Tim Howell, DG XIII of the European Commission for his comments on Chapters 4 and 5.

Thanks are also due to Mr Richard Butler AM, former Secretary-General of the ITU, Mr John Collier, Vice-Master of Trinity Hall, Cambridge, Ian Ellison CBE, Professor Gerald Dworkin and Christopher Vajda for their assistance with various parts of the book.

Furthermore, we should like to thank offices of the Department of Trade and Industry, the Radiocommunications Agency, the Independent Television Commission, DGXIII, INTELSAT, Inmarsat and EUTELSAT for providing up-to-date information and answers to questions, where publicly available.

Lastly, our thanks are extended to those at Denton Hall who provided invaluable assistance to the authors: Askandar Samad (whose offer to read the entire manuscript was above and beyond the call of duty and gratefully accepted), Rupert Lewin-Smith, Amanda Dawson, Vivienne Robinson, Leonie Gordon, Rebecca Holmes-Siedle, Philip Rymer, David Essery and Paula Reidy-Crofts. We also extend thanks to our secretaries for typing the manuscript.

The opinions expressed in this book are ours and should not be attributed to any who have been kind enough to comment on the text in the preparation of this work. Although it has been possible to make some changes before going to press, the law is stated as at 3 June 1993.

Stewart White
Stephen Bate
Timothy Johnson
St Andrew's Day, 30 November 1993

Second Edition

Thanks are due again to Dr Pekka Tarjanne and his staff at the ITU for their ongoing help in updating this publication. The offices of EUTELSAT, INTELSAT and Inmarsat have also been helpful in answering our questions and updating our information, as have the offices of the DTI, the RCA, the ITC and OFTEL in the UK. We are grateful to SES in Luxembourg for their continued permission to reproduce footprint maps.

The preparation of a second edition has involved substantial gathering of material and checking legislation and regulations to ensure that our text has been updated where necessary. We have been helped enormously in this regard by kind colleagues who have been prepared to assist. In particular Seong Sin Han and Prisca Lo at S.J. Berwin & Co and Anthony Palmer, Andrew McMillan and Tom Wheadon at Ashurst Morris Crisp have provided invaluable help. So too has Colin Fraser. We have stated the law as at 1 July 1995.

Stewart White
Timothy Johnson
Stephen Bate

Lammas Day, 1 August 1995

General Introduction

The purpose of this book is to provide an introduction to the law and regulation of satellite communications in Europe. It is not intended to be a comprehensive work, but it is hoped that it will be a useful overview of the subject.

Part 1 deals with the general regulation of satellite services and satellite policy issues which will include an introduction to relevant international laws including international space law. Chapters 2 and 3 cover the International Telecommunication Union (ITU) and the Radio Regulations (RRs) and their relevance to satellite communications. Chapter 4 deals with the public International Satellite Organisations (ISOs) and private satellite organisations providing international services in Europe. Access to space segment capacity is also covered and there is a brief discussion on the development of international regulation. Chapter 5 deals with European satellite policy and Chapter 6 outlines the UK licensing of satellite services.

Part 2 covers legal and regulatory issues relating to satellite television, radio and other services, including regulation of programme content and copyright issues.

Part 3 deals with commercial contracts in the satellite sector; in particular satellite construction contracts, satellite launch contracts, satellite transponder contracts and interconnection and roaming contracts.

Table of Cases

Table of Statutes

Table of Statutory Instruments

Table of EC Legislation

Proposals and drafts

Regulations

Resolutions

Table of International Legislation

Conventions and Treaties

Regulations

I

General Regulation of Satellite Services and Satellite Policy in Europe

1

International Law Background

Introduction

1.1 A satellite is 'a body which revolves around another body of preponderant mass and which has a motion primarily and permanently determined by the force of attraction of that other body'. (International Telecommunication Union, *Radio Regulations* (RRs), Edition of 1994, Volume 1 (ITU Doc No ISBN 92-61-04141-8) RR 171).

The first satellite successfully launched into orbit was Sputnik 1 on 4 October 1957. It was little more than a radio transmitter within an aluminium-coated cylinder 22.8 inches in diameter. It seems amazing that this was less than 40 years ago.

There is a surprisingly large number of satellites presently orbiting[1] the earth. Most are in Geostationary-Satellite Orbit, that is 'whose period of revolution is equal to the period of rotation of the Earth about its axis' (RR 180) where they can provide a 24-hour service at an altitude of 36,000 km. Many are military satellites, with which we need not concern ourselves here.

As will be seen, satellites are used for many peaceful purposes, such as broadcasting, telecommunications (including the fixed-satellite service and land and maritime mobile services), earth exploration, radio and meteorology. In this book, we shall consider those satellites which are used for communication purposes.

1.2 Satellites are extra-terrestrial and extra-territorial and accordingly tend to be regulated in the international sphere by treaties,

3

conventions and international and regional agreements. Both international law and space law are relevant in this regard.

Under international law, government regulation and control of domestic satellite systems are considered to be national matters. As will be seen in Chapter 6 on UK licensing and regulation of satellite services, use of radio frequencies is a matter of domestic licensing. It can be readily appreciated that the introduction of satellite services involves a range of complicated legal, regulatory and policy issues which require international harmonisation (see Chapter 5 in relation to the work of the European Commission in this regard).

Subject to the Constitution and Convention of the International Telecommunication Union (ITU) (currently the 1992 Constitution and Convention of the ITU adopted at the Additional Plenipotentiary Conference, Geneva 1992 (APC Geneva, 1992) (ISBN 92-61-04771-8) and the application of the RRs of the ITU (both of which are dealt with in detail in Chapters 2 and 3), sovereign states have jurisdiction to regulate and control their internal telecommunications and broadcasting systems. This principle applies to the establishment of satellite systems by either public or private commercial operators.

1.3 The RRs clearly indicate that Administrations, which are any 'governmental department or service responsible for discharging the obligations undertaken in the Convention (and Constitution) of the (ITU) and the Regulations' (RR 3), may co-operate in obtaining co-ordination and notification of satellite networks (RR 1042). Although not explicitly stated in the RRs, in common practice jurisdiction lies with the Administration from which a satellite network is controlled. In other words, the country or place where the satellite operator controls its up-link in general terms determines jurisdiction (discussed *below*), although in the case of international satellite organisations there may be control stations in more than one jurisdiction. In essence, a particular Administration will take on the responsibility where, in effect, it is the principal place of business. However, the most important point is that whichever Administration takes the responsibility, it should be in a position to take whatever steps may be necessary to ensure that harmful interference (see *below*) ceases. Administrations may, and sometimes do, delegate this responsibility to recognised agencies. However, art 19 of the Convention (Geneva, 1992) requires an Administration to notify other Administrations where it has authorised an agency to

4

act on its behalf. It is a sad reflection that there are still Administrations, particularly in developing countries, which refuse to recognise private operating agencies even though such agencies have been authorised within the jurisdiction of the Administration to provide new or competitive services.

Administrations, as well as being responsible for the co-ordination of satellite systems (see *below*), are also responsible for reporting cases of harmful interference.

In the field of satellite communications, the importance of international regulation arises primarily because all broadcasting and telecommunication satellites make use of the same resources, namely radio frequency spectrum and orbital positions. The fact that these resources are limited is internationally recognised.[2]

1.4   The possibility of interference to services and the necessity for radio frequency spectrum sharing is at the heart of the international rules concerning the use of this finite asset. Efficiency of use of the radio frequency spectrum is necessary in the hope of introducing as many services as possible. Services should not therefore interfere with each other and to this end, the international community has agreed, through the ITU procedures, to co-ordinate domestic usage of radio frequency spectrum between them so as to avoid harmful interference and to promote efficient usage of radio frequency spectrum. (Co-ordination is discussed in detail in Chapter 3, paras 3.17 and 3.18.)

1.5   RR 160 defines 'interference' as:

> [t]he effect of unwanted energy due to one or a combination of emissions, radiations, or inductions upon reception in a radiocommunication system, manifested by any performance degradation, misinterpretation, or loss of information which could be extracted in the absence of such unwanted energy.

The RRs then divide 'interference' into three types as follows:

> 161.   'Permissible Interference': Observed or predicted interference which complies with quantitative interference and sharing criteria contained in these Regulations or in CCIR Recommendations or in special agreements as provided for in [the RRs].

> 162.   'Accepted Interference': Interference at a higher level than that defined as permissible interference and which has been agreed upon between two or more Administrations without prejudice to other Administrations.

(The terms 'permissible interference' and 'accepted interference' are used in the co-ordination of frequency assignments between Administrations (RRs 161.1 and 162.1).)

> 163.   'Harmful Interference': Interference which endangers the functioning of a radio-navigation service or of other safety services or seriously degrades, obstructs, or repeatedly interrupts a radiocommunication service operating in accordance with [these RRs].

1.6   Use of outer space for communication purposes depends on usage of the radio frequency spectrum. A satellite transmits radio signals (electromagnetic or hertzian waves) sent up to it back to earth. In simple terms, the transmission to a satellite, that is 'up' from earth, is an 'up-link', and the transmission from the satellite 'down' to earth is a 'down-link'. What happens in more technical terms is that a 'radio-communication service'[3] is transmitted from transmitting earth stations or 'stations'[4] to a transponder on a satellite or 'space station',[5] in effect, a receiver, which then amplifies the signal, changes its frequency and retransmits the signal to the receiving earth station.[6] Earth stations can be both transmitting and receiving stations, depending on what services they are designed and authorised to provide (Chapter 6, paras 6.25 *et seq.*).

Because of their short wave characteristics, high frequencies also have the ability to travel long distances (see the discussion of C and Ku Band characteristics *below*). It is a matter of basic physics that higher frequencies travel in straight lines and for this reason satellites are 'in line of sight'. Since the signals are line of sight, they are subject to interference by obstacles such as mountains or officeblocks.

1.7   There are two basic elements to the communication: the 'earth segment', whence signals are transmitted or where signals are received on the ground, and the 'space segment', where signals are received in space on the satellite and retransmitted.

Ground segment, being terrestrial, comes under the national jurisdiction where it is located and for the reasons explained *below* the uses of the relevant transmitting and receiving frequencies are licensed by the national Administration (subject always to international regulation). Likewise, objects in space are generally regarded as governed by the law of the Administration which is, or has been, responsible for the launching of a satellite into outer space (see *below*) and which generally, although not necessarily, will have taken responsibility for the co-ordination of the relevant satellite (RR 1042).

1.8 Article VII of the 1967 Treaty on Principles Governing the Activities of States in the Exploration and Use of Outer Space Including the Moon and Other Celestial Bodies ('the Outer Space Treaty')[7] (see paras 1.29–1.39 *below*), provides that each state which launches an object into space or from whose territory an object is launched, is responsible for any damage which it causes to any other state or its citizens, whether the damage occurs on earth or in space. Article VIII of the Outer Space Treaty also provides that the states retain jurisdiction and control over objects on their registry when they are launched into outer space. The Outer Space Treaty is supplemented by the 1974 Convention on Registration of Objects Launched into Outer Space ('the 1974 Convention'), which requires the registration of objects in space by the 'launching State'. The 1974 Convention defines 'launching State' as 'a State which launches or procures the launching of a space object or a State from whose territory or facility a space object is launched'.

1.9 It is important to note that art XI of the Outer Space Treaty makes no distinction between activities carried out by a state and activities carried out by a private entity, such as a private commercial enterprise, under the jurisdiction of such a state. Under art VI of the Outer Space Treaty, 'the activities of non-governmental entities in outer space, including the Moon and other celestial bodies, shall require authorisation and continuing supervision by the appropriate State'. Furthermore, under art VI, states bear international responsibility for national activities in outer space carried out not only by governmental agencies but also by private nationals and firms.

States are therefore under an obligation to introduce appropriate control and supervision, usually in the form of an authorisation or licensing requirement under domestic legislation (see Chapter 6). The principle of continued jurisdiction and control, contained in art VIII of the Outer Space Treaty, remains unaffected by registration under the 1974 Convention. Thus, states may, by agreement, entrust the task of jurisdiction and control to a state other than the state of registration.

In relation to up-link sites and down-link sites, the RRs provide that there should be no emission of radio waves without a licence by the government of the country where the transmitting station is located, and such licence must be in conformity with the provisions of the RRs (RR 2020).

1.10   Radio waves are not only fundamental to the use of a satellite for communications purposes, but also for control of a satellite, which effectively determines which Administration takes regulatory responsibility for it. This control is generally referred to as TT(M)&C (telemetry, tracking, (monitoring) and command).

Telemetry, in conjunction with tracking, uses radio waves both to and from the satellite to determine its position. Monitoring is just that—how the satellite is functioning in space is carefully monitored 24 hours a day at the control centre of the relevant station. Depending on what is discovered by monitoring it may be necessary to give the satellite commands. Commands are, as their name implies, orders to the satellite from the control centre and can, for example, be used to fire an apogee boost motor if it is necessary to move back a satellite to its correct orbital position.

1.11   A major limitation on the availability of the orbit resource arises from the fact that the so-called Geostationary-satellite Orbit (GSO) is by far the most convenient and practical orbit for satellite broadcasting and telecommunication purposes; it is also relatively inexpensive.

The GSO is the orbit in which a satellite must be placed to be a geostationary satellite (RR 182), and a geostationary satellite (RR 181) is a geosynchronous satellite whose circular and direct orbit lies in the place of the earth's equator and which remains fixed relative to the earth. (RR 180: a geosynchronous satellite is: 'An earth satellite whose period of revolution is equal to the period of rotation of the Earth about its axis'.)

1.12   Some non-geostationary satellites have been in use for many years for military purposes, as have sub-synchronous satellites for gathering weather information. They orbit at about 800 km above the earth. From these applications, commercial private applications have been developed, such as the 'sailor's friend' GPS or Global Positioning Satellites, enabling mariners to fix their positions at sea with a high degree of technical reliability. Increased interest in non-geostationary orbits also arises from proposals for Non-Geostationary Mobile Satellite Telecommunications Systems—the so-called Low Earth Orbiting Satellites, known generally as LEOS or 'satellite personal communication networks' (discussed in Chapter 5, para 5.61 *below*), the name relating to the function rather than the altitude of delivery. Not all present proposals for such mobile satellite systems are for low earth orbits: some are for Medium Earth Orbiting Satellite Systems—up to 10,000 km (known as MEOS) and

others are for Highly Elliptical Orbiting Satellite Systems—
400–3,000 km (known as HEOS). The elliptical orbit requires relatively little energy and, if launched in a non-equatorial plane in a
non-synchronous orbit, it will scan the earth in a way which is very
useful for survey purposes.

1.13 The advantages of GSO satellites, assuming certain technical
characteristics, are that they can 'service' over a third of the earth:
near global communication can be achieved with only three satellites. Also, geostationary satellites are cheaper to operate than satellites in other orbits: fewer satellites are required for uninterrupted
traffic to and from a particular *locus* and trackable antennae are
much less important. GSO satellites, however, have two inherent
disadvantages. First, over Northern Europe and Northern America,
the angle of elevation caused by location of the satellite can be too
acute, with adverse transmission quality consequences: this is also
the case in the Southern hemisphere although of less commercial
importance given the general demography in the affected areas.
Moreover, GSO satellites do not cover the polar regions, because of
their location over the equator (although in population terms this is
hardly important).

1.14 Secondly, transmission delays are experienced resulting from
the long transmission path to and from the satellite, particularly
noticeable in telephone calls via satellite (commonly referred to as
'satellite echo').

Mobile communications have advanced by using GSO satellites.
This has been particularly successful for maritime communications,
under the aegis of the International Maritime Satellite Organisation
(Inmarsat) which is dealt with in more detail in Chapter 4. As
technology has progressed, terminal sizes have been reduced to
more manageable proportions. Inmarsat is now marketing briefcase
size terminals for use on land, at sea and in the air, and has
established its subsidiary trading as I-CO Global Communications
Ltd to market what is known as Inmarsat-P, Inmarsat's entrant to
the global mobile satellite personal communications market. Use of
this equipment raises interesting questions of law, regulation and
policy.

1.15 Similar issues are raised by proposals for LEOS and other
similar satellite systems which aim to achieve global coverage at

much lower altitudes than GSO satellites. They seek to take advantage of developments in cellular telephony and paging technology, using small handsets enabling truly global roaming (see Chapter 12).

LEOS extend services to new outreaches and to specialised needs such as positioning, telemetry, environment, monitoring, remote servicing, traffic management, disaster mitigation and specialised data and information collection and transfer. LEOS also offer 'multipoint to multi-point' potential.

LEOS have already been the subject of international regulatory consideration at the World Administrative Radio Conference (WARC) of the ITU held in Malaga-Torremolinos in early 1992[8] and in respect of LEOS above 1 GHz, subject to negotiated rule-making proceedings of the Federal Communications Commission (FCC) in the USA (where the relevant negotiated rule-making Committee submitted its tentative recommendations to the FCC on 6 April 1993 (Report of the MSS above 1 GHz Negotiated Rulemaking Committee, 6 April 1993)). The European Commission has also been showing an interest in the subject, and organised hearings in Brussels in November 1992 at which various proponents of the LEOS were present[9] (see also Chapter 5, para 5.61).

1.16   In this book, the position with regard to GSO satellites will be highlighted because these are presently the most widely used and most relevant to satellite operators, service providers, regulators and lawyers. However, other satellite proposals will be mentioned where appropriate, especially where the introduction of Global Satellite Communications becomes a reality and raises many of the issues presently relevant to the development of mobile communications, such as interconnection and roaming agreements.

1.17   The most important constraint on the development of any satellite service is the finite number of usable radio frequencies (see *below*). Furthermore, the laws of physics are not affected by the somewhat artificial laws of man because radio-communication signals do not generally respect national borders. This is particularly pertinent to radio-communication services by satellite. While a signal may be 'intended for reception' in one country or countries, it will often be capable of reception elsewhere. This is known as 'spillover'. At the 1977 WARC–BS, which is briefly discussed in Chapter 2 (see para 2.41), a plan for broadcasting satellites with defined national coverage was formulated (see *below*). The state of technological development at the time was such that it was believed that only high powered (100–200 watts) transponders could deliver terrestrial broadcasting quality television signals. Transponders had to be sufficiently far away from each other to avoid harmful interference due to the strength of the signal. This spacing was of the order of about six degrees on the orbital arc.

1.18 Satellites for telecommunication services need much less powerful transponders (approximately 30–60 watts) and can be spaced as closely as three degrees on the orbital arc. In 1977, satellites were thought to be usable only for specialised services and were used primarily by governments or for public telecommunication purposes. Furthermore, they required very large antennae (four to five metres) in order to receive the signal. It was not long, however, before television signals could be transmitted via telecommunication satellites for rediffusion by cable operators. The size of the receiving antenna clearly raised practical, aesthetic and environmental considerations which meant that the possibility of transmitting television signals direct to viewers in their homes was still feasible only with the high powered broadcasting satellites co-ordinated under art 15 of the RRs as Broadcasting-Satellite Services (BSS) (see Chapter 3, para 3.7). The satellites providing this service are known as 'Direct Broadcasting Satellites' or DBS. However, as technology developed it became possible to transmit high-quality television signals on low and medium powered satellites direct to viewers in their homes (DTH) and for such transmissions to be received by antennae which were about the same size as those used for receiving broadcasting satellite signals, but using telecommunication satellites co-ordinated under the RRs as Fixed-Satellite Services (FSS) (see Chapter 3, para 3.8).

The result of this is, as far as the viewer of such services is concerned, legal mummery. What the viewer sees delivered by one type of satellite is generally indistinguishable from what is delivered by the other type. However, from a national/domestic legal point of view, there may be different licensing results (see Chapter 6, paras 6.12 and 6.13) and consequences in copyright law (see Chapter 8, at paras 8.2 and 8.38).

1.19 Usage of telecommunications satellites for DTH created a revolution in the concept of satellite television, because historically broadcasting has been seen as a national prerogative where the spillover of television signals to neighbouring countries is required to be minimised to the greatest extent possible. Sovereign states are concerned with controlling broadcasting for reasons such as, typically, standards of good taste and decency, promotion of indigenous cultural values and various other social and political purposes. Indeed, in the RRs there is a provision whereby any Administration proposing to use a satellite for broadcasting services must ensure that the transmissions are limited 'to the maximum extent practical' from overspilling into other countries (RR 2674).

The 'coverage area' of a satellite is generally referred to as its 'footprint' (see the definition contained in para 1.2 of Annex 5, AP30 (ORB 85) of the RRs). In accordance with the provisions of RR 2674, the coverage area of a satellite must, as far as it is technically possible, 'cover' the satellite's 'service area', but may result 'in an unavoidable transmission over the territory of other countries' (Rules of Procedure 1503.3f). 'Service area' is defined as:

> [t]he area on the surface of the Earth in which the Administration responsible for the service has the right to demand that the agreed protection conditions be provided.

(See para 1.1 of Annex 5, AP30 (ORB 85) of the RR and Chapter 3, para 3.10.)

1.20 This definition emphasises the point, as far as the BSS is concerned, that broadcasting is a national matter and that such services should have a high level of protection against interference by other services.

Set out in Appendix 4 are the footprints of the ASTRA Satellite System operated by Société Européenne des Satellites based in Luxembourg (SES). The covering note explains, in the context of the ASTRA satellites, the relationships between size of the satellite antennae generally available in the market and the EIRP contour. (EIRP or Equivalent Isotropically Radiated Power is defined in RR 155 as '[t]he product of the power supplied to the antenna and the antenna gain in a given direction relative to an isotropic antenna'.)

Thus, footprints are rather like the coverage area contours of terrestrial television or radio transmitters. The level of service quality is directly related to the transmission power received at the particular site of the receiving antenna and its diameter (see *below*).

As noted *above*, to avoid interference between services, the technical parameters of satellites and their use of frequency spectrum is also co-ordinated through the ITU in Geneva (see Chapter 3, para 3.23 *et seq*). This co-ordination extends to the specifications of receiving antennae.

1.21   The ITU is probably the most important organisation concerned with international telecommunications policy and regulation and is dealt with in detail in Chapter 2. It has approximately 190 member countries, that is, sovereign states which are referred to as 'Members of the Union' (art 2 of the Constitution of the ITU (Geneva, 1992) refers to the composition of the ITU). Only sovereign states can be members. The ITU is the oldest of the international bodies concerned with telecommunications, dating back to 1865 when it was founded as the International Telegraph Union. Pursuant to art 50 of its Constitution (Geneva, 1992) the ITU is required to co-operate with international organisations having related interests and activities. The new Constitution and Convention adopted at the APC held in Geneva in 1992 replace the Convention adopted at the Plenipotentiary Conference held in Nairobi in 1982 and the Constitution and Convention adopted at the Plenipotentiary Conference held in Nice in 1989. The general purposes and responsibilities of the ITU are in terms similar to those contained in the Nairobi and Nice Conventions. Both instruments came into force on 1 July 1994. In the interim all the provisions of the new Constitution and Convention relating to the new structure and working methods of the ITU were applied provisionally as from 1 March 1993.

1.22   The United Nations (UN) has been active in the field of satellites, particularly through the General Assembly and its Committee on the Peaceful Uses of Outer Space (COPUOS) (see *below*). The ITU's relationship with the UN is defined by an agreement entered into between the two organisations (Constitution of the ITU (Geneva, 1992), art 49). The ITU provides information on its activities concerning telecommunication and the peaceful use of outer space to the UN annually (see eg 31st Report by the ITU, Booklet No 40 (Geneva, 1992) (ISBN 92–61–04631–2)).

1.23   Two primary functions of the ITU (both concerned with minimising interference) are to:

(*a*)   effect allocation of bands of the radio-frequency spectrum, the allotment of radio frequencies and registration of radio-frequency assignment and any associated orbital positions in the geostationary-satellite orbit . . . in order to avoid harmful interference between stations of different countries; and

(*b*)   co-ordinate efforts to eliminate harmful interference between stations of different countries and to improve the use made of the radio-frequency spectrum and of the geostationary-satellite orbit for radio-communication services. (Final Acts of the Additional

Plenipotentiary Conference (Geneva 1992). Constitution of the International Telecommunication Union, art 1.2(*a*) and (*b*).)

Even with the latest technologies, the physics of the radio frequency spectrum are such that only certain limited frequencies between 390 MHz and 64 GHz are suitable for satellite communications. In addition, regulatory constraints are required to minimise problems of harmful interference which could arise between the various users of the radio frequency spectrum. Other limitations on the use of the GSO and radio frequency spectrum arise from the fact that, eg a particular GSO satellite can be located only in a certain sector of the GSO, if it is to communicate with its service area.

1.24 Another consideration is the size of the antennae necessary to receive signals of a certain strength. These and related technical matters are set out in detail in the RRs (see, eg AP30 (ORB 85)) and in other documents of the ITU. (See, eg the CCIR's publication *Broadcasting Satellite Systems* (Geneva, 1983) ISBN 92–61–01751–7.) For present purposes, FSS frequencies are located primarily in the C Band (4–6 GHz) and Ku Band (11–14 GHz). The lower the frequency, the greater the wavelength. Greater wavelengths have the advantage of being less susceptible to attenuation by rain but have the disadvantage of requiring larger antennae for transmission and reception. In contrast, Ku Band transmissions, because of the higher frequency, have shorter wavelengths and therefore require smaller antennae for transmission and reception.

In addition, the relevant frequency bands for LEOS or satellite personal communication networks, which were the subject of much debate at WARC–92 (see Chapter 2, para 2.43) are the L Band (1610–1626.5 MHz) and S Band (2483.5–2500 MHz). Both these bands have been allocated to Mobile Satellite Services (MSS) (see Chapter 3, para 3.38).

1.25 The International Satellite Organisations (ISOs) are also important and are dealt with in greater detail in Chapter 4. These are international organisations, which enable groups of countries to provide for their own domestic and international telecommunications needs relatively inexpensively and efficiently. However, certain states now have their own domestic systems such as France's TDF1 and TDF2, Germany's DFS Kopernikus 2 and DFS Kopernikus 3 and Spain's Hispasat 1A satellites. Some of these, such as the Luxembourg-based ASTRA Satellite System, Orion and PanAmSat, provide international services for television distribution purposes. Increasingly, with liberalisation in the telecommunication sector, the ISOs are finding that they are having to operate in a very different world from that in which they were founded.

The oldest and largest ISO is the International Telecommunications Satellite Organisation (INTELSAT) (see Chapter 4, para 4.5). More than 133 states are members of INTELSAT and INTELSAT satellites are used by over 200 nations (although only ITU members can be INTELSAT members). INTELSAT is an international corporation which acts on a commercial basis (Preamble to the Agreement relating to the International Telecommunications Satellite Organization 'INTELSAT', Washington 1971, entered into force 12 February 1973 (UKTS 80(1973), Cmnd 5416, 23 UST 3813 TIAS, 7532, 10 ILM 1909)). INTELSAT is mainly concerned with the provision via satellite of international public telecommunication services on a global basis.

1.26 The USSR did not wish to join INTELSAT in 1964 for various reasons, paramount among which was the perception that the USA held a dominant position in INTELSAT. In 1971, INTERSPUTNIK, a separate ISO, was founded by the USSR and eight other— then communist—states. (Agreement on the Establishment of the INTERSPUTNIK International System and Organisation of Space Communications, 15 November 1971, UNTS 862:3). INTERSPUTNIK is an international intergovernmental non-profit making organisation.

1.27 INMARSAT was established in 1979 (Convention on the International Maritime Satellite Organisation, 3 September 1976, 31 UST 1, TIAS 9605, 15 ILM 1051 (which entered into force in 1979)) and is dealt with in more detail in Chapter 4 (see paras 4.18 to 4.20). Inmarsat provides a space segment for maritime and aeronautical communications. It has 77 members and is a dual governmental/ commercial organisation like INTELSAT. However, pursuant to art 7 of the Inmarsat Convention, non-member nations may utilise its space segment on a non-discriminatory basis.

INTELSAT and Inmarsat are global systems. There are also regional systems. The European Telecommunication Satellite Organisation (EUTELSAT) (see Chapter 4, paras 4.14 to 4.17) is a European regional system consisting at present of 44 member countries. The interim EUTELSAT Agreement[10] was signed by 17 European states in 1977. It provides European space segment for international (regional) and domestic public telecommunication services.

1.28 Other regional satellite systems include the Arab Corporation for Space Communications (formed in 1976 by the Arab League states) which provides telecommunication services for the Arab world; PALAPA, which, although owned by Indonesia, also provides domestic and international services to Malaysia, Thailand, the Philippines and Singapore; and OPTUS which provides satellite services for Australia and the Pacific region including television relay services to Hong Kong.

Within Europe, the Commission of the European Communities has been very active in developing its policies regulating the satellite sector, as will be seen in Chapter 5.

As already noted, implementation of these international legal principles is a matter of domestic law. This is considered in Chapter 6.

International space law

1.29   In this book it is not necessary to examine in detail the international law concerning satellites which has been covered by other authors.[11] However, some important milestones are mentioned.

Satellite services are subject to international space law. It is generally agreed that international space law applies to the GSO and to satellites orbiting in medium and low orbits, because the consensus is that these orbits are in 'outer space',[12] although, as discussed *below* (para 1.38), there is no clear agreement as to the boundaries of 'outer space'.

1.30   Space law consists of a body of international agreements relating to the space and matter which are located at and beyond a consensually agreed altitude above the earth. The most important proposition is that outer space is not subject to any kind or means of national appropriation. Despite the Declaration of the First Meeting of Equatorial Countries signed in Bogotá, Colombia on 3 December 1976, by which eight equatorial countries (Brazil, Colombia, Congo, Ecuador, Indonesia, Kenya, Uganda and Zaire) purported to claim sovereignty over parts of the GSO, this claim is not recognised by the overwhelming weight of world opinion.[13] Indeed, it is difficult to see how this could be seriously put forward in light of the non-appropriation principles established at the UN as far back as 1961 (see *below* and para 1.37). However, as late as the World Administration Radio Conference held in Geneva in 1977, these eight equatorial countries pursued this line (see, for example, the somewhat disingenuous Reservation No 51 of the Final Acts (ISBN 92–61–6049–1) and Documents 121, 165 and 400 of the Working Papers).

In any consideration of the international law concerning satellites, one cannot ignore the UN as the foremost institution of the international community, although the ITU has primary responsibility in the international community for telecommunications, as explained in this chapter and in Chapter 2.

1.31 In 1961, the General Assembly of the UN passed Resolution 1721 (XVI) on International Co-operation in the Peaceful Uses of Outer Space.[14] This commended to states the following principles:

(*a*) International law, including the Charter (of the UN), applies to outer space and celestial bodies;

(*b*) outer space and celestial bodies are free for exploration and use by all States in conformity with international law and are not subject to national appropriation.

1.32 It was as a result of the long debates at the UN[15] that the General Assembly passed the 'Declaration of Legal Principles Governing the Activities of States in the Exploration and Use of Outer Space'[16] in 1962. This 'is declaratory of legal principles, and extends their applicability. It declares six principles of law as governing the use of outer space: equality; common use; State responsibility; corporate responsibility; ownership and control; and common humanity'.[17] It also reiterated that outer space was not subject to national appropriation. Relevantly it stated that:

1. The exploration and use of outer space shall be carried on for the benefit and in the interests of all mankind.

2. Outer space and celestial bodies are free for exploration and use by all States on a basis of equality and in accordance with international law.

3. Outer space and celestial bodies are not subject to national appropriation by claim of sovereignty, by means of use or occupation, or by any other means.

4. The activities of States in the exploration and use of outer space shall be carried on in accordance with international law, including the Charter of the United Nations, in the interest of maintaining international peace and security and promoting international co-operation and understanding.

5. States bear international responsibility for national activities in outer space, whether carried on by governmental agencies or by

non-governmental entities, and for assuring that national activities are carried on in conformity with the principles set forth in the present Declaration . . .

6.   In the exploration and use of outer space, States shall be guided by the principle of co-operation and mutual assistance and shall conduct all their activities in outer space with due regard for the corresponding interests of other States . . .

These principles are reflected in the Outer Space Treaty and the Conventions next discussed and also in the constituent instruments of the ISOs which are discussed *below* (Chapter 4, para 4.3 *et seq*).

1967 Treaty on Principles Governing the Activities of States in the Exploration of Outer Space, Including the Moon and other Celestial Bodies

1.33   The principal body of international law relating to the use of outer space is the Outer Space Treaty. Its provisions reflect those of the UN Resolutions referred to in paras 1.31, 1.32 and elsewhere. The treaty establishes the international regime for the peaceful use of outer space for the benefit of all mankind.[18] As stated *above*, it was the work carried out under the aegis of the UN that led to the Outer Space Treaty. The tension between the United States and the former Soviet Union (as the principal users of space at the time) meant that the treaty, like UN Resolution 1962 (XVIII) on which it was largely based, veered away from firm commitments and clearly defined principles. Accordingly, the Outer Space Treaty does not provide any authoritative interpretative principles nor any mechanism for the settlement of disputes relating to its application.

1.34   Peaceful use is embedded in art IV of the treaty, which further provides that the placing 'in orbit around the earth (of) any objects carrying nuclear weapons and any other kinds of weapons of mass destruction' is not permitted. Likewise, in the interests of all mankind, art 1 of the Outer Space Treaty provides that:

> The exploration and use of outer space, including the Moon and other celestial bodies, shall be carried out for the benefit and in the interests of all countries irrespective of their degree of economic or scientific development, and shall be the province of all mankind.

Outer Space, including the Moon and other celestial bodies, shall be free for exploration and use by all States without discrimination of any kind, on a basis of equality and in accordance with international law, and there shall be free access to all areas of celestial bodies.

There shall be freedom of scientific investigation in outer space, including the Moon and other celestial bodies, and States shall facilitate and encourage international co-operation in such investigation.

1.35 This free use of outer space is subject to a number of important limitations arising from its common use by countries and the fact that use is not limited to those countries which are sufficiently developed to exploit it. Outer space is 'the province of all mankind'. All public and private space segment operators, including the ISOs, must operate within these limits.

Use of outer space must be:

(a) in the interests of all mankind (that is, not just countries which have already developed capabilities to exploit outer space) and this is relevant to art IX, for example;

(b) irrespective of the degree of economic and scientific development of any particular country (which is of importance to developing countries and is relevant to the question of 'equitable access' to radio frequency spectrum and orbital positions referred to in Chapter 2, paras 2.19 and 2.39 for example);

(c) without discrimination (which adds to (a) and (b) and is reflected, for example, in art XII);

(d) on a basis of equality (see (b)) and international co-operation (see also arts IX, X and XI); and

(e) in accordance with international law (which is re-emphasised in art III).

Jurisdiction and responsibility for activities in outer space have been discussed briefly above (para 1.8) in relation to arts VII, VIII and XI of the Outer Space Treaty.

1.36 Also relevant to using outer space for placing satellites in orbit are arts V, IX and XI. These articles impose further obligations regarding the use of outer space and deal with states keeping each other informed about activities in space. For example, pursuant to art V: 'States Parties . . . shall immediately inform the other States Parties . . . or the Secretary General of the [UN] of any phenomena they discover in Outer Space . . . which could constitute a danger to life . . .'. Article IX imposes the necessity for states to consult with each other if there is any 'reason to believe that an activity . . . planned by it or its nationals . . . would cause potentially harmful interference with activities of other State Parties in the peaceful . . . use of outer space'. Importantly, art XI provides that 'States Parties . . . conducting activities in outer space . . . agree to inform the Secretary General of the [UN] as well as the public and the international scientific community, to the greatest extent feasible and practicable, of the nature, conduct, locations and results of such activities'.

National appropriation

1.37   Consistent with the principle of free and common use of outer space, the Outer Space Treaty provides that 'Outer Space, including the Moon and other celestial bodies, is not subject to national appropriation by claim of sovereignty by means of use or occupation, or by any other means' (art II). National appropriation, pursuant to which exclusive control or other right of a proprietary type would be assumed, would be incompatible with the free use of outer space for all mankind. While there has been some debate as to whether the treaty's prohibition on 'national appropriation' includes appropriation by individuals, public or private bodies, or by international organisations, it would seem clear that any appropriation is inconsistent with its principles (*pace* Bogotá Declaration). As will be apparent, the Outer Space Treaty supports the principle set out in Resolution 1962 (XVIII) referred to *above* whereby any sort of appropriation in outer space by any entity is inconsistent with the common or free use principle. Consistent with this and the principle of free use, is the principle of the common interests of all mankind, reflected in art 1 of the Outer Space Treaty.

Defining outer space boundaries

1.38   While the term 'outer space' is not defined, it is clear that its outer limit is that of the universe itself. However, there is disagreement over where 'outer space' can be said to begin. There are various views on this issue, but it can be assumed to be somewhere about 80 km above sea level, which, on the one hand, should form an appropriate half way point, 'between the upper limit of the regime of traditional aviation and the lower limit of a satellite regime, and on the other hand, would coincide with the aerological boundary between the lower atmosphere and the outer atmosphere'.[19]

The distinction is important as it has a bearing on the vexed issue of national sovereignty and outer space freedom, and on whether the term 'outer space' includes natural resources situated in outer space.[20]

1.39   Other international agreements concerned with the peaceful use of outer space for all mankind include the Moon Treaty (Title 27 January 1967, 18 UST 2410, TIAS 6347, 610 UNTS 205, Treaty Series No 10 (1968), Cmnd 3519), the 1972 Convention on International Liability for Damage Caused by Space Objects (the 1972 Liability Convention, discussed *below*)[21] the 1974 Convention[22] (discussed *below*) and other bilateral and multi-national treaties. Each of these restrict the ability to use outer space. The ITU's RRs (discussed in Chapter 3) also limit this freedom, particularly in relation to 'equitable access', to radio frequency spectrum and orbital positions.

1972 Convention on International Liability for Damage Caused by Space Objects

1.40   This Convention, like the 1974 Convention (on Registration of Space Objects), supplements the Outer Space Treaty. It entered into force on 1 September 1972.

Primarily, the 1972 Liability Convention establishes strict and fault liability for different kinds of damage caused by space activities, which reflects the provisions of art VII of the Outer Space Treaty.

1.41   Under international law, a state can claim against another state in respect of damage suffered by it or its nationals 'but not that suffered by nationals of some third State or by a Stateless person'.[23] This is generally known as the rule of 'nationality of claims'. Article VIII provides:

1.   A State which suffers damage, or whose natural or juridical persons suffer damage, may present to a launching State a claim for compensation for such damage.

2.   If the State of nationality has not presented a claim, another State may, in respect of damage sustained in its territory by any natural or juridical person, present a claim to a launching State.

3.   If neither the State of nationality nor the State in whose territory the damage was sustained has presented a claim or notified its intention of presenting a claim, another State may, in respect of

damage sustained by its permanent residents, present a claim to the launching State.

1.42   The effect of this is to provide a wider standing for bringing claims against a launching State than is usually recognised under international law. It encompasses claims against the launching State by stateless persons in transit, whom international law currently ignores. It should be noted, however, that the rule of nationality of claims has been retained in art VII of the 1972 Liability Convention which provides that the Convention:

does not apply to damage caused by a space object of a launching State to:

a)   nationals of that launching State;

b)   foreign nationals during such time as they are participating in the operation of that space object from the time of its launching or at any stage thereafter until its descent or during such time as they are in the immediate vicinity of a planned launching or recovery area as the result of an invitation by that launching State.

1.43   Pursuant to art I of the 1972 Liability Convention, 'damage' means 'loss of life, personal injury or other impairment of health; or loss of or damage to property of States or of persons, natural or juridical, or property of international intergovernmental organisations'. By contrast with the position under the 1974 Convention (on the Registration of Objects Launched in Outer Space) 'launching', in the expression 'launching State', here includes 'attempted launching' (see art I). This makes sense, as damage can arise from an attempted launch of a satellite, whereas there is no point registering a satellite which has not been successfully launched.

As to the assessment of compensation for damages, art XII of the 1972 Liability Convention provides that:

The compensation which the launching State shall be liable to pay for damage under this Convention shall be determined in accordance with international law and the principles of justice and equity, in order to provide such reparation in respect of the damage as will restore the person, natural or juridical, State or international organisation on whose behalf the claim is presented on the condition which would have existed if the damage had not occurred.

This Convention does not contain a financial limit of damages. As regards the currency in which compensation is to be paid, art XIII provides that:

> Unless the claimant State and the State from which compensation is due under the Convention agree on another form of compensation, the compensation shall be paid in the currency of the claimant State or, if that State so requests, in the currency of the State from which compensation is due.

1.44   The procedure for making a claim for compensation is set out in art IX and provides that such claims shall be presented to a launching state through diplomatic channels. In general, under art X the time limit for presenting such a claim is not more than a year.

Article XI of the 1972 Liability Convention importantly permits the presentation of a claim to a 'launching State' for compensation for damage under the Convention prior to exhausting any local remedies which might be available to either the claimant state or its nationals. This does not prevent a claim being brought in 'the courts or administrative tribunals or agencies of a launching State'. However, this Convention prevents a claim being brought for the same damage under both methods.

1.45   If no settlement of a claim is achieved through diplomatic channels, art XIV of the Convention provides for the establishment of a 'Claims Commission' at the request of either party. Articles XV to XX detail the composition, membership and procedure for the Claims Commission. In particular, art XIX(2) states:

> The decisions of the Commission shall be final and binding if the parties have so agreed; otherwise the Commission shall render a final and recommendatory award, which the parties shall consider in good faith. The Commission shall state the reasons for its decision or award.

The whole procedure from notification of the claim to final decision should not take longer than two and a half years.

1974 Convention on Registration of Objects Launched into Outer Space

1.46   The 1974 Convention was concluded on 12 November 1974 and entered into force on 15 September 1976 although not all countries have ratified it (see Chapter 6, para 6.32 with respect to the UK). The 1974 Convention goes further than art VIII of the Outer Space Treaty and requires in art II, *inter alia*, that:

(*a*) launching States keep a national register of space objects launched by them; and

(*b*) launching States notify (in accordance with art IV referred to *below*) the Secretary General of the United Nations of the establishment of such a register. (Under art III the Secretary General also keeps a register of notifications which have been received.)

1.47   For the purpose of the 1974 Convention the term 'launching State' has been defined as 'a State which launches or procures the launching of a space object or a state from whose territory or facility a space object is launched'. This is relevant to the question of which country has jurisdiction over the satellite (see para 1.7 *above*). The term 'space object' includes compound parts of a space object, that is, the satellite, as well as the launch vehicle, that is, the booster or space shuttle, as the case may be, and any of its parts.

Article II of the 1974 Convention concerns the registration of an object launched into orbit where there is more than one 'launching State' (as defined by art I):

2.   Where there are two or more launching States in respect of any such space objects, they shall jointly determine which one of them shall register the object in accordance with paragraph 1 of this article . . .

Such determination is also reached in the light of art VIII of the Outer Space Treaty which provides that a state 'on whose registry an object launched into outer space is carried shall retain jurisdiction and control over such object while in outer space . . .'. The determination is also reached without prejudice to bilateral agreements between various states on jurisdiction and control.

The international registry or mandatory registration procedure sought to be established by the UN reinforces art VI of the Outer Space Treaty.

1.48   The basic standard of information which must be submitted to the UN is contained in art IV:

1.   Each State of registry shall furnish to the Secretary-General of the United Nations, as soon as practicable, the following information concerning each space object carried on its registry:

(*a*) name of launching State or States;

(*b*) an appropriate designator of the space object or its registration number;

(*c*) date and territory or location of launch;

(*d*) basic orbital parameters, including:

   (i) nodal period,

   (ii) inclination,

   (iii) apogee,

   (iv) perigee;

(*e*) general function of the space object.

Sections 2 and 3 of art IV respectively allow for additional information to be supplied and oblige each state to notify the Secretary-General of objects which have been, but are no longer, in earth orbit.

1.49 Just as art IV and the provision of information regarding space objects is broad and fairly undemanding, so art V is an equally lax system for marking space objects with a designation or registration number. The system has been criticised in that 'it merely provides that should a marking system exist then the State of Registry is bound to notify the Secretary-General, who must record the notification in the Register. But this does not oblige a State to have a compulsory marking system.'[24] Article V in its entirety reads as follows:

> Whenever a space object launched into earth orbit or beyond is marked with the designator or registration number referred to in Article IV, paragraph 1(*b*), or both, the State of registry shall notify the Secretary-General of this fact when submitting the information regarding the space object in accordance with Article IV. In such case, the Secretary-General of the United Nations shall record this notification in the Register.

1.50 Article VI of the Convention reflects the fact that in 1974 not all signatories thereto [States Parties] had access to space monitoring or tracking services and hence it compels those States possessing such equipment to assist in the tracking of dangerous space objects:

> Where the application of the provisions of this Convention has not enabled a State Party to identify a space object which has caused

damage to it . . . or which may be of a hazardous or deleterious nature, other State Parties, including in particular States possessing space monitoring and tracking facilities shall respond to the greatest extent feasible to a request by the State Party . . . for assistance under equitable and reasonable conditions in the identification of the object.

Article VII of the 1974 Convention has the effect of applying all the foregoing articles:

> . . . to any international inter-governmental organisation which conducts space activities if the organisation declares its acceptance of the rights and obligations provided for in this Convention . . .

This provision is relevant to organisations such as the ISOs.

Conclusion

1.51   Although some of the provisions of the treaties, Conventions and the like discussed above may appear inadequate, the regulatory regimes which now apply to the use of the GSO (as well as other orbits) and to the use of the radio frequency spectrum by telecommunication and broadcasting satellites reflect these general principles of international and space law.

---

1 RR 176 defines 'orbit' to mean '[t]he path, relative to a specified frame of reference, described by the centre of mass of a satellite or other object in space subjected primarily to natural forces, mainly the force of gravity'.

2 Eg, International Telecommunications Convention, Final Protocol, Additional Protocols, Optional Additional Protocol, Resolutions, Recommendations and Opinions, (Nairobi, 1982) (ITU Doc No ISBN 92–61–01651–0), art 33 entitled 'Rational Use of the Radio Frequency Spectrum and of the [GSO]', which is re-stated in art 44 of the 1992 Constitution now entitled 'Use of the Radio-frequency Spectrum and of the [GSO]'.

3 RR 20 defines 'Radio-communication Service' to mean a 'service . . . involving the transmission, emission and/or reception of radio waves for specific telecommunication purposes'.

RR 132 defines 'Emission' to mean '(r)adiation produced, or the production of radiation, by a radio transmitting station'.

'Radiation' is defined as '[t]he outward flow of energy from any source in the form of radio waves' (RR 131), 'radio' being defined as '[a] general term applied to the use of radio waves' (RR 5) which in turn are defined as '[e]lectromagnetic waves of frequencies arbitrarily lower than 3000 GHz, propagated in space without artificial guide' (RR 6).

RR 4 defines 'telecommunication' as '[a]ny transmission or emission or reception of signs, signals, writing, images and sounds or intelligence of any nature by wire, radio, optical or other electromagnetic systems'.

Radio-communication is thus '[t]elecommunication by means of radio waves' (RR 7).

4 RR 58 defines 'Station' as '[o]ne or more transmitters or receivers or a combination of transmitters and receivers, including the accessory equipment, necessary at one location for carrying on a radio-communication service, or the radio astronomy service. Each station shall be classified by the service in which it operates permanently or temporarily'.

'Terrestrial Station' is further defined in RR 59 to be '(a) station effecting terrestrial radio-communication. In these Regulations, unless otherwise stated, any station is a terrestrial station.'

5 RR 61 defines 'Space Station' to be '[a] station located on an object which is beyond, is intended to go beyond, or has been beyond, the major portion of the Earth's atmosphere'.

6 RR 60 defines 'Earth Station' to be '[a] station located either on the Earth's surface or within the major portion of the Earth's atmosphere and intended for communication:

— with one or more space stations; or
— with one or more stations of the same kind by means of one or more reflecting satellites or other objects in space'.

7 Treaty on Principles Governing the Activities of States in the Exploration and Use of Outer Space Including the Moon and Other Celestial Bodies, 27 January 1967, 610 UNTS 206 (1967).

8 Final Acts of the World Administrative Radio Conference for Dealing with Frequency Allocations in certain parts of the Spectrum (WARC-92) Malaga-Torremolinos 1992 ISBN 92–61–04661–4. This is also to be dealt with in part at the World Radio Conference in Geneva in October 1995.

9 See the Rapporteurs Report dated 25 November 1992 on the *Hearings on Non-Geostationary Mobile Satellite Systems* (Low Earth Orbiting Satellite Systems: LEOS), Brussels, 9–10 November 1992, and also a proposal for a draft *Council Resolution on the introduction of satellite personal communications services in the European Community* (COM (93) 171 final).

10 Agreement on the Constitution of a Provisional Telecommunications Satellite Organisation 'INTERIM EUTELSAT'—see N M Matte, *Aerospace Law: Telecommunications Satellites*, (Butterworths 1982) p 155 and Appendix IX.

11 Professor Matte's book on the subject, although published in 1982, remains one of the major works on satellite and aerospace law: N M Matte, *Aerospace Law: Telecommunications Satellites* (Butterworths 1982). See also, eg J E S Fawcett, *International Law and The Uses of Outer Space* (Manchester University Press 1968); D Wadegaonkar, *The Orbit of Space Law* (Stevens & Sons, 1984); and M L Smith, *International Regulation of Satellite Communication* (Martinus Nijhoff Publishers 1990).

12 Fawcett, *op cit* pp 22–23 states '. . . the lower limit of outer space in relation to the Earth must, in the absence of any other agreed limit, constitute the upper limit of the exclusive jurisdiction and control of States . . .'.

13 See, eg the Final Acts of the World Administrative Radio-communication Conference on the Use of the GSO and Planning of Space Services Utilising It (ORB-88) (Geneva, 1988).

14 See below note 15.

15 Resolutions 1721 (XVI) of 20 December 1961: International co-operation in the peaceful uses of outer space (1960–8 UNGS pp 6–7 (XVI)); 32 1802 (XVII) of 14 December 1962: International co-operation in the uses of outer space (1960–8 UNGS (XVII)).

16 Resolution 1962 (XVIII): Declaration of Legal Principles Governing the Activities of States in the Exploration of Outer Space (1960–8 UNGS pp 15–16).

17 Fawcett, *op cit* p 5.

18 Ibid, p. 15

19 Wadegaonkar, *op cit* p 42. See also Convention on the International Maritime Satellite Organisation, 3 September 1976, 31 UST 1 TIAS 9605, 15 ILM 1051 (which entered into force in 1979).

20 See Fawcett, *op cit* pp 20 *et seq*; Smith *op cit* pp 185 *et seq*.

21 Convention on International Liability for Damage Caused by Space Objects, 29 March 1972, 1971 UNJYB (in force 1 September 1972).

22 Convention on Registration of Objects Launched into Outer Space, 12 November 1974 UN General Assembly Resolution 3235 (XXIX), Annex, GAOR, 29th Session Supp 31, 1974 UNJYB 89 (in force 15 September 1976).

23 Wadegaonkar, *op cit* p 23.

24 Ibid, *op cit* p 21.

2

The International Telecommunication Union

An overview

2.1 Following the introductory comments made in Chapter 1, it is necessary to consider the general purposes of the International Telecommunication Union (ITU). These are set out in art 1.1 of the Constitution of the ITU as follows:

(*a*) to maintain and extend international co-operation between all Members of the Union for the improvement and rational use of telecommunications of all kinds;

(*b*) to promote and to offer technical assistance to developing countries in the field of telecommunications, and also to promote the mobilisation of the material and financial resources needed for implementation;

(*c*) to promote the development of new technical facilities and their most efficient operation with a view to improving the efficiency of telecommunication services, increasing their usefulness and making them, so far as possible, generally available to the public;

(*d*) to promote the extension of the benefits of the new telecommunication technologies to all the world's inhabitants;

(*e*) to promote the use of telecommunication services with the objective of facilitating peaceful relations;

(*f*) to harmonise the actions of Members in the attainment of those ends; and (*g*)   to promote, at the international level, the adoption of a broader approach to the issues of telecommunications in the global information economy and society, by co-operating with other world and regional intergovernmental organizations and those non-governmental organizations concerned with telecommunications.

2.2   To these ends, the ITU has certain responsibilities. These are set out in art 1.2 of the Constitution. *Inter alia*, the ITU shall:

(*a*)   effect allocation of bands of the radio frequency spectrum, the allotment of radio frequencies and registration of radio frequency assignments and any associated orbital positions in the geostationary-satellite orbit in order to avoid harmful interference between stations of different countries;

(*b*)   co-ordinate efforts to eliminate harmful interference between stations of different countries and to improve the use made of radio frequency spectrum and of the geostationary-satellite orbit for radio communication services; and

(*c*)   foster international co-operation in the delivery of technical assistance to the developing countries and the creation, development and improvement of telecommunication equipment and networks in developing countries by every means at its disposal, including through its participation in the relevant programmes of the United Nations and the use of its own resources, as appropriate.

The ITU

Role and function

2.3   The ITU has competence to regulate all categories of international telecommunications employing all modes and technologies of transmission. The duties of the ITU which are particularly relevant to satellite operators and users include allocation of the radio frequency spectrum and registration of those allocations and generally organising so as to prevent harmful interference between stations (for the Radio Regulations (RRs) definition of 'station' see Chapter 1, note 4) of different countries. The ITU also introduces regulations designed to optimise the use of the radio frequency spectrum and co-ordinates technical assistance and the development of telecommunication equipment for developing nations. The detailed provisions of the RRs are of the greatest practical importance to satellite operators and users and will be discussed in more detail in Chapter 3.

2.4   The ITU is an international treaty organisation which deals with its members, the sovereign states, and their telecommunication Administrations, which in many cases are still instruments of the states themselves. The growing liberalisation in telecommunications is necessitating rethinking about how such international organisations fit into the modern world and how they should operate. Increasingly, the ITU is taking account of the private sector. This is particularly so in its technical committees. The International Telecommunication Regulations (ITRs) adopted at the World Administrative Telegraph and Telephone Conference in Melbourne in 1988 (WATTC–88), specifically provide that they apply to Administrations 'or recognized private operating agency(ies)'. (Final Acts of the World Administrative Telegraph and Telephone Conference Melbourne, 1988 (WATTC–88) International Telecommunications Regulations (Geneva 1989) (ISBN 92–61–03921–9), arts 1.1, 1.5, 1.7, 3 and 4.2.) Article 42 of the Constitution notes that members can make special arrangements 'for the operating agencies recognized by them and for other agencies duly authorised to do so', provided that those arrangements do not conflict with the Constitution, the Convention or the Administrative Regulations with regard to harmful interference or technical harm which might be caused to services of other members. This was not a new provision. For example, art 13 of the International Telecommunication Convention (Madrid 1932), dealing with 'Special Arrangements' for 'private enterprises' recognised by what were then called 'Contracting Governments', is in substance similar to art 42 of the present Constitution. Indeed, art 19 of the Convention and Resolution 4 in the Final Acts adopted at the Additional Plenipotentiary Conference (APC) in Geneva in 1992 (Geneva APC) specifically deal with participation of entities and organisations other than Administrations in the ITU's activities across all three sections of its work. It is for this reason that greater detail is now given to the workings of the ITU, given the ability of non-Administrations, that is, the private sector, to participate at this high level.[1]

2.5   While there has been criticism of the ITU (generally related to its bureaucratic nature, which is inherent in any multinational organisation), the ITU provides important fora for policy, regulatory, economic and technical issues arising from changes in the political-social and economic milieux shaping international communications operations. The ITU plays a crucial role in protecting and furthering the interests of developing countries in the whole communications sphere.

In recent years there have been huge advances in the development of new communications technologies and part of the ITU's brief is to ensure that access to communications and information networks is made available to developing countries, where communications are often still inadequate. This is obviously true of central and eastern Europe and the CIS. The future development of such countries is in large part dependent on the establishment of good domestic and international communications, aiding political stability, cohesion and economic development. The ITU seeks to promote worldwide provision of basic services as well as the smooth introduction of new services.

More recently, the ITU Council passed Resolution 1081, unanimously welcoming the establishment of 'WorldTel'. This followed the support of the ITU of the Maitland Commission which identified the enormous gap between developed and developing countries in terms of access to basic telephone services (see ITU, *The Missing Link*, Report of the Independent Commission for Worldwide Telecommunications Development, December 1984, the 'Maitland Commission'). WorldTel will operate as a 'hands on' organiser and manager of investment in and operation of telecommunications infrastructure projects in the developing world, where, typically, less than one per cent of the population is serviced by a telephone line, or waiting lists exceed five years.

2.6 Membership of the ITU imposes rights and obligations. These are set out in art 3 of the Constitution and are:

(*a*) to participate in the working of the conferences and to be eligible for election to the Council, as officials of the ITU or a member of the Radio Regulations Board (RRB) (art 3.2(*a*)); and

(*b*) to have one vote at conferences (art 3.2(*b*)) and consultation by post (art 3.2(*c*)).

Execution of the instruments of the ITU imposes upon its members the obligation 'to abide by the provisions of the Constitution the Convention and the Administrative Regulations' and this specifically relates to any services operated 'which are capable of causing harmful interference to radio services of other countries'.[2] 'Members are also bound to take the necessary steps to impose the observance' of these instruments by any operating agencies authorised by them.[3]

Structure

2.7   The basic instrument of the ITU is its Constitution. The Convention of the ITU complements the Constitution. Both instruments are binding on all members of the ITU. Although the Convention, adopted at Nairobi in 1982,[4] was in the process of being superseded by the Constitution and Convention adopted at the Plenipotentiary Conference held in Nice in 1989,[5] both have been superseded by the Constitution and Convention adopted at the Geneva APC which concluded on 22 December 1992.[6] Both the Geneva instruments entered into force on 1 July 1994. It was decided at the APC that the provisions of the Geneva 1992 Constitution and Convention relating to the new structure and working methods of the ITU be applied provisionally as from 1 March 1993 pursuant to Resolution 1 of the APC.[7] The following description is of the organisation as constituted on that date and as affirmed at the Plenipotentiary Conference held at Kyoto on 14 October 1994.[8]

Article 4.1 of the Constitution provides that in addition to the Constitution and Convention, administrative regulations are also 'Instruments of the Union'. The Administrative Regulations, which complement the Constitution and Convention, are binding on all Members and consist of the ITRs and the RRs (art 4.3 of the Constitution). The ITRs were adopted at WATTC–88 to promote the development of telecommunication services and to harmonise the development of worldwide telecommunication facilities. The RRs deal with operational, practical and technical matters and are referred to in para 2.33 *below* and examined in greater detail in Chapter 3.

2.8   The Constitution sets out, *inter alia*, the following:

(*a*)   the purposes of the ITU (as briefly set out above) (art 1);

(*b*)   the composition of the ITU (art 2);

(*c*)   the rights and obligations of members (art 3);

(*d*)   the structure of the ITU (art 7);

(*e*)   the composition of the various organs of the ITU (arts 8, 10–15, 17–18, 21–22);

(*f*)   the legal capacity of the ITU (art 31);

(g)   general provisions relating to telecommunications (arts 33–43);

(h)   special provisions for radio including those relating to harmful interference (arts 44–48); and

(i)   relations with the UN and other international organisations and non-member states (arts 49–51).

Chapter V of the Constitution (arts 25–32) sets out other provisions concerning the functioning of the ITU including, *inter alia*, rules of procedure for world conferences on international telecommunications and provisions relating to languages, finances and the seat of the ITU (Geneva).

2.9   The ITU Convention contains provisions relating to:

(a)   the convening and setting of dates for Plenipotentiary Conferences (art 1)

(b)   elections and related matters (art 2):

(i)   elections to the Council (paras 7–12);

(ii)   the election of officials (paras 13–19);

(iii)   Members of the Radio Regulations Board (RRB) (paras 20–22);

(c)   other conferences (to be held in the period between Plenipotentiary Conferences) (art 3);

(d)   the Council (composed of 43 members elected by the Plenipotentiary Conference) (art 4);

(e)   the General Secretariat (art 5);

(f)   the Co-ordination Committee (to assist and advise the Secretary-General) (art 6);

(g)   the structure and duties of the Radiocommunication Sector (arts 7–12):

(i)   World Radiocommunication Conferences (art 7);

(ii)   Radiocommunication Assembly (art 8);

(iii)   Regional Radiocommunication Conferences (art 9);

(iv)   RRB (art 10);

(v)   Radiocommunication Study Groups (art 11); and

(vi)   Radiocommunication Bureau (art 12);

(*h*)   the structure and duties of the Telecommunication Standardization Sector (arts 13–15):

(i)   World Telecommunication Standardization Conferences (art 13);

(ii)   Telecommunication Standardization Study Groups (art 14); and

(iii)   Telecommunication Standardization Bureau (art 15);

(*i*)   the structure and duties of the Telecommunication Development Sector (arts 16–18):

(i)   Telecommunication Development Conferences (art 16);

(ii)   Telecommunication Development Study Groups (art 17); and

(iii)   Telecommunication Development Bureau and Advisory Board (art 18);

(*j*)   relations between Sectors and with International Organisations (art 22);

(*k*)   conferences in general (Chapter II, arts 23–31);

(*l*)   the rules of procedure for conferences and other meetings (Chapter III, art 32);

(*m*)   finances and languages (Chapter IV, arts 33–35); and

(*n*)   arbitration and amendment (Chapter VI, arts 41–42).

The ITU collates information provided by all members in order to draw up technical standards, plans and regulations so as to discharge its duty to maximise efficiency in international communications.

The major components of the ITU

2.10   Pursuant to art 7 of the Constitution, the ITU comprises:

(*a*)   a Plenipotentiary Conference, which is the supreme authority of the ITU;

(b)   the Council, which acts on behalf of the Plenipotentiary Conference in the period between conferences;

(c)   a world conference on international telecommunications;

(d)   the Radiocommunication Sector (which includes World and Regional Radiocommunication Conferences, Radiocommunication Assemblies and the RRB);

(e)   the Telecommunication Standardization Sector (which includes World Telecommunication Standardization Conferences);

(f)   the Telecommunication Development Sector (which includes World and Regional Telecommunication Development Conferences); and

(g)   the General Secretariat.

It is now appropriate to consider each of these organs in more detail.

The Plenipotentiary Conference

2.11   Articles 8 and 9 of the Constitution and art 1 of the Convention deal specifically with the Plenipotentiary Conference.

The Plenipotentiary Conference is the policy-making body of the ITU and meets every four years. It is the only body empowered to revise the Convention which it does in order to reflect new advances in telecommunications and technological developments. The emphasis is on long-term policy decisions. It is made up of delegations from all ITU member countries. It formulates the general policy of the ITU and the framework to be followed by the other ITU bodies between Conferences. The Plenipotentiary Conference also elects the Council which shall not exceed 25 per cent of the members from all regions of the world (currently 43 members).

The Council

2.12   Article 10 of the Constitution and arts 2 and 4 of the Convention deal with the Council (previously called the 'Administrative Council'). It meets once a year and its function is to act as the policy-making body during the periods between Plenipotentiary Conferences. The Council submits draft strategic plans covering the aims, work programmes and anticipated outcomes for each constituent part of the ITU until the following Plenipotentiary Conference.

The General Secretariat

2.13   The General Secretariat is governed by art 11 of the Constitution and art 2 of the Convention. It carries out administrative functions implementing administrative and financial regulations made by the Council. It is directed by a Secretary-General, who is elected by the Plenipotentiary Conference for four years until the next Plenipotentiary Conference.   ·

World conferences on international telecommunications

2.14   These replace the former World Administrative Telegraph and Telephone Conferences. They are convened to discuss matters specific to telephone and telegraphic services. The category of delegates entitled to participate in them is analogous to that for the Radiocommunication Conferences outlined *below*.

The Radiocommunication Sector

2.15   Chapter II (arts 12–16) of the Constitution and Section 5 (arts 7–12) of the Convention specifically deal with the Radiocommunication Sector.

The 1994 Plenipotentiary Conference at Kyoto confirmed the ITU organisational structure adopted by the APC of 1992. The IFRB is to continue to assist, for example, in the ongoing work on the simplification of the RRs (see Chapter 3, para 3.3). Under the same resolution, the present staff of the CCIR, the Consultative Committee on International Telegraphy and Telephony (CCITT) and the IFRB were assigned to the new Bureaux by the Secretary-General in consultation with the Directors of those Bureaux.[9] In essence the functions of the IFRB have been divided into two. The 'board' functions of the IFRB have now been transferred to the RRB, and the 'secretarial' functions have been transferred to the Radiocommunication Bureau (RCB) (see arts 14 and 16 Constitution and arts 10 and 12 Convention (Geneva 1992)).

2.16   In particular, the Sector consists of :

(*a*)   World and Regional Radiocommunication Conferences;

(b)   Radiocommunication Assemblies which are associated with World Radiocommunication Conferences;

(c)   the RCB, headed by an elected Director, whose election is deemed to have taken place at the 1989 Nice Plenipotentiary Conference;[10]

(d)   Radiocommunication Study Groups; and

(e)   the RRB (art 12, Constitution (Geneva, 1992)).

The work of this Sector encompasses the following elements:

(a)   the examination and registration of all notices for frequency assignments which are deemed liable to cause interference outside the territory of the country in which the station is located;

(b)   examination of all notices for the orbital positions of geostationary satellites;

(c)   the performance of the necessary calculations to ensure transmissions are free of interference;

(d)   ensuring that the provisions of the RRs are properly applied by the ITU member countries;

(e)   providing assistance and advice to developing countries to facilitate their access to the spectrum-orbit resource; and

(f)   the general management of the radio frequency spectrum in an efficient and equitable manner.

Some of the internal structures of the Radiocommunication Sector are discussed in more detail *below*.

World and Regional Radiocommunication Conferences

2.17   World Radiocommunication Conferences are to be held every two years to dovetail with meetings of the World Radiocommunication Assembly. The next is to take place in Geneva in October 1995. These conferences replace the former World Administrative Radio Conferences (WARCs). The main function of World Radiocommunication Conferences is to review and revise the RRs on the basis of the agenda adopted by the Council following consultation with the membership. This is obviously an important step, as amendment of the RRs has been both cumbersome and slow.

The first World Radiocommunication Conference was held in Geneva from 15–19 November 1993 and made recommendations to the ITU Council for the agenda of the 1995 World Radiocommunication Conference. These have now been adopted by resolution of the Council and will include a review of the RRs based on the report of the Voluntary Group of Experts (VGE) and a review of the use of frequency bands allocated to the Mobile-Satellite Service (MSS) (see Chapter 3, para 3.38). Additionally, recommendations for the preliminary agenda for the 1997 World Radiocommunication Conference will be made (see para 2.45 *below*).

Regional Radiocommunication Conferences are to be convened from time to time to deal with specific regional radiocommunication issues and replace the former Regional Administrative Radio Conferences (RARCs).

Radiocommunication Assemblies

2.18   Radiocommunication Assemblies will formulate the technical basis for the World Radiocommunication Conferences, finalise and approve the work programmes of the various Radiocommunication Study Groups and decide on the priority and urgency of various studies. The Study Groups consist of experts (including radiocommunication Administrations and public and private sector entities) which study technical questions relating to radiocommunication issues and adopt recommendations. In particular, the Study Groups will consider distress and safety aspects of radiocommunications, the use of the radio frequency spectrum and GSO in terrestrial and space radiocommunications, the operation of stations and the characteristics, specifications and performance of radio systems.

The Radiocommunication Assemblies consider the reports of the Study Groups and approve, modify or reject their recommendations. The Assemblies also decide on which Study Groups to maintain, set up or abolish and on the work allocation among them. All these functions were carried out by the CCIR prior to March 1993.

The Radio Regulations Board

2.19   The RRB took over part of the work of the former IFRB in 1993. The RRB consists of nine members elected by the Plenipotentiary Conference. The RRB members serve, in effect, as custodians of an international public trust, not as representatives of their respective member states or regions (art 14.3 of the Constitution).

Members of the RRB cannot participate as members of their national delegations at any meetings or conferences of the ITU where they have a duty to advise as representatives of the RRB.

In the case of Plenipotentiary Conferences the chairman and vice-chairman of the RRB, (or their nominated representatives) have a duty to participate in an advisory capacity.[11]

The duties of the RRB include the following:

(*a*) consideration and approval of the Rules of Procedure to be employed in the registration of frequency assignments (art 14.2a of the Constitution);

(*b*) deliberation on any question which cannot be resolved by the application of the Rules of Procedure (art 14.2b);

(*c*) all duties concerned with the equitable assignment and utilisation of frequencies and the GSO (art 121.1(1)); and

(*d*) consideration of reports from the Director of the RCB which are the result of investigations of cases of harmful interference. Such investigations are made at the request of one or more ITU members and the RRB makes recommendations after reviewing the report (art 10.2 Convention).

With regard to its duties concerning equitable access, see further the reference to the debate concerning this usage in para 2.39 *et seq, below*.

The Radiocommunication Bureau (RCB)

2.20 Article 12.1 of the Convention (Geneva 1992) empowers the Director of the RCB 'to organise and coordinate the work of the Radiocommunications Sector'.

The Bureau has the responsibility for:

(*a*) provisions of the RRs and various regional agreements;

(*b*) processing the information received from Administrations, such as notices (eg concerning co-ordination) (and preparing that information for publication (art 12.2(2)(b));

(*c*) keeping relevant records concerning frequency assignments and orbital positions, and updating the Master International Frequency Register (art 12.2(2)(e)); and (*d*)   investigating complaints concerning harmful interference and where necessary making investigations and preparing reports, together with draft recommendations to the affected Administration, for consideration by the RRB.

The Bureau also provides technical support for the Telecommunication Development Sector (see *below*).

The Telecommunication Standardization Sector

2.21   Chapter III (arts 17–20) of the Constitution and Section 6 (arts 13–15) of the Convention regulate this Sector.

Following the 1994 Plenipotentiary Conference at Kyoto, the Telecommunication Standardization Sector takes over the standardisation activities of the former CCITT and CCIR.

The functions of this Sector are, *inter alia*, to study technical, operating and tariff issues and to formulate recommendations to facilitate the standardization of telecommunications worldwide. This includes making recommendations on the interconnection of radio systems in public telecommunication networks and the specifications required therefor. Questions relating specifically to technical and operational issues in the radiocommunications field are dealt with by the Radiocommunication Sector.

2.22   The Sector consists of:

(*a*)   World Telecommunication Standardization Conferences (held every four years);

(*b*)   Study Groups; and

(*c*)   a Bureau headed by an elected Director, whose election is deemed to have taken place at the 1989 Nice Plenipotentiary Conference.[12]

The conferences consider the reports of the Study Groups and approve, modify or reject the recommendations made. They will also set the subjects to be studied and allocate them among the various Study Groups. Like the Development Conferences they will not produce 'Final Acts' binding on all members, as do the other ITU World Conferences (although there is a view that recommendations can be more than that, by their inclusion by reference in the RRs— see para 2.35 *below*).

There is provision for an accelerated approval procedure whereby if a Study Group decides unanimously that a recommendation is urgent, it can be approved before the next Plenary Conference by correspondence. The recommendation is sent to all Administrations, which have three months to indicate their approval or otherwise. If a majority approves the recommendation, it is put into effect.

2.23   The first World Telecommunication Standardization Conference and the first Radiocommunication Assembly will review this procedure. The purpose of the review is to set a definite number of replies which are to be required for the approval of recommendations, and to institute a procedure that will afford members the right to request a Standardization Conference to reconsider a particular recommendation if they feel themselves to be adversely affected by its application.

2.24   An Advisory Group was established in 1993 to advise on the following issues:

(*a*)   priorities and strategies in the ITU's standardisation activities;

(*b*)   the progress achieved in implementing the work programme;

(*c*)   the provision of guidelines for the Study Groups' work; and

(*d*)   measures aimed at improving co-operation and co-ordination with other ITU bodies and non-ITU standardisation organisations.

The Telecommunication Development Sector

2.25   The Telecommunication Development Sector is made up of World and Regional Development Conferences and a Bureau headed by an elected Director. The most important function of this Sector is to assist developing countries by advising them on and explaining the policy and structural options aimed at producing greater resources for the development of telecommunications.

Pursuant to Resolution 1 of the APC, the appointment of the Director of the Telecommunication Development Bureau (BDT) at the APC did not count as a first election to that post so he is eligible to have two terms of office under the Constitution of Geneva, 1992.

Development Conferences are convened at regular intervals to foster international co-operation in order to harmonise and enhance the development of telecommunication services and facilities. They make resolutions, decisions, recommendations and reports but not Final Acts (which are binding on members). These have to be consistent with the Constitution, Convention and the Administrative Regulations.[13] The conferences will also decide on development priorities and plan the activities of the Sector. They have in addition, set up Development Study Groups and Working Groups to carry out studies on specific issues. These issues will include development policy and financing, network planning, operation and new services. The Study Groups replace the Special Autonomous Groups of the CCITT. In the near future, particular attention is to be given to measures aimed at increasing the participation of developing countries in the standardisation activities of the ITU.

It should be noted that the Telecommunication Development Sector has as members both Administrations (as of right) and any other 'entity or organisation authorized in accordance with the relevant provisions of the Convention'.[14]

A Telecommunication Development Advisory Board has been established to advise the Director of the Bureau on priorities and strategies in the development field and to make recommendations on co-ordination and co-operation with other organisations engaged in telecommunications development (art 18 of the Convention (Geneva, 1992)).

The Administrative Regulations

2.26   As indicated in para 2.3, the RRs are one of the basic legal instruments of the ITU. However the ITU also formulates ITRs. We will now consider both these regulations in more detail.

The International Telecommunication Regulations

2.27   The ITRs apply to the extent that the RRs do not otherwise provide.[15]

As noted above at para 2.7, the current ITRs were adopted at WATTC–88. They are expressed to supplement the then Convention, and while they recognise the sovereign right of the members to regulate their telecommunications, they are adopted to promote 'the development of telecommunication services and their most efficient operation while harmonising the development of facilities for worldwide telecommunications'.[16]

This theme is apparent in art 1:

1.1 (*a*)   These Regulations establish general principles which relate to the provision and operation of international telecommunication services offered to the public as well as to the underlying international telecommunication transport means used to provide such services. They also set rules applicable to Administrations or recognized private operating agency(ies).

(*b*)   These Regulations recognise in Article 9 the right of Members to allow special arrangements.

. . .

1.2 In these Regulations, 'the public' is used in the sense of the population, including governmental and legal bodies.

1.3 These Regulations are established with a view to facilitating global inter-connection and interoperability of telecommunication facilities and to promoting the harmonious development and efficient operation of technical facilities, as well as the efficiency, usefulness and availability to the public of international telecommunication services.

2.28   It should be noted pursuant to art 1.2 that public 'is used in the sense of the population, including governmental and legal bodies'.

The increasing role of the private operating agencies and the freedom of members in certain jurisdictions to pursue development of international services through mutual agreement and with the private sector are clearly recognised—see arts 1.5 and 1.7, for example.

The main provisions of the ITRs relevant to satellite services concern:

(*a*)   the international network (art 3);

(*b*)   international telecommunication services (art 4);

(*c*)   charging and accounting (art 6); and

(*d*)   special arrangements (art 9).

2.29   *International network and telecommunication services*   The service obligations of members are set out in art 3.

Members are obliged to ensure that Administrations and recognised operating agencies co-operate in the establishment, operation and maintenance of the international network to provide:

(*a*)   'quality of service' (art 3.1);

(b)   'sufficient telecommunication facilities to meet the requirements of and demand for international telecommunication
services' (art 3.2);

(c)   'international routes or choice of routes by mutual agreement'
(art 3.3); and

(d)   'users with rights to send traffic' (art 3.4).

The level of satisfactory quality of service referred to in art 3.4 is that
corresponding 'to relevant CCITT Recommendations'. Compliance
'to the greatest extent practicable' with CCITT recommendations is
also required by art 4, which relates to the services carried on the
international networks (see also art 9). Importantly, art 4.1 requires
members to promote international telecommunication services and
to make such services generally available to the public in the
members' national networks.

2.30   *Charging and accounting*   Article 6 sets out the specific provisions relating to charging and accounting for international telecommunication services. General provisions, such as the establishment, revision and settlement of balances of account, which need to
be taken into account by Administrations or recognised private
operating agency(ies) in determining accounting rates, are set out in
Appendices 1 and 2 of the ITRs.

Appendix 3 sets out the charging and accounting principles applicable to service and privileged telecommunications. Such classes of
telecommunications may be provided free of charge and accordingly are not included in international accounting.

Service telecommunications are public international telecommunications exchanged among Administrations, recognised private operating agencies and various representatives or authorised officials
of the ITU set out in art 2.4. Privileged telecommunications are
telecommunications exchanged during sessions of the ITU Council,
conferences and meetings and relating either to matters under
discussion therein or to public international telecommunications.
The charging and accounting principles applicable to these services
must take into account relevant CCITT recommendations.

2.31   Administrations and recognised operating agencies establish
the charges to be collected from their customers. The level of charges
is a national matter and is therefore subject to national law. However 'too great a dissymmetry between the charges applicable in
each direction of the same relation' should be avoided.[17]

Generally, where a national tax is levied on international tele-communication service charges, the tax is collected only in respect of international services billed to customers in that country.[18]

Accounting rates are established and revised by mutual agreement between Administrations or operating agencies. However, as mentioned previously, such agreement must be reached in accordance with the provisions of Appendix 1 and relevant CCITT recommendations. Relevant cost trends are also taken into account.

The monetary units to be used in the composition of accounting rates for international telecommunication services are set out in art 6.3.1 as follows:

- either the monetary unit of the International Monetary Fund (IMF), currently the Special Drawing Right (SDR), as defined by that organisation;

- or the gold franc, equivalent to 1/3.061 SDR.

It should be noted, however, that this provision, in accordance with the ITU Convention, does not prevent 'bilateral arrangements for mutually acceptable coefficients between the monetary unit of the IMF and the gold franc'.[19]

2.32   *Special arrangements*   This is the provision of most relevance to satellite services, particularly for the development of satellite-based networks using Very Small Aperture Terminals (VSATs) (see Chapter 5, para 5.53 and Chapter 6, para 6.29 for a more detailed discussion of VSATs).

While 'by-pass' is probably the most contentious word in the international telecommunications vocabulary at the moment, art 9 of the ITR has set in place the regime for 'special arrangements' using 'special telecommunication networks, systems and services, in order to meet specialised international telecommunication needs within and/or between the territories of the Members concerned'.[20] Subject to the necessity that such special arrangements 'avoid technical harm'[21] to the services of developing countries and to national laws[22] this is an important step in the advance of services to areas currently not served or badly served. This is especially relevant to developing countries in Europe.

The Radio Regulations

2.33   The RRs, like the Constitution and Convention, have the status of an international instrument and bind all members.[23] As noted (Chapter 1, para 1.3), they are a restriction on members' rights to use certain frequencies in outer space. However, no sanctions are provided for breach of any obligation or responsibilities under these instruments.

The RRs consist of extremely detailed provisions covering the assignment and use of frequencies and the associated orbital positions for space stations, which are currently the subject of simplification by the ITU (see Chapter 3, para 3.4). They include the important Table of Frequency Allocations (the Table) which governs the use of radio frequency bands between 9 kHz and 400 GHz for all the various radio services. The Table is dealt with in more detail in Chapter 3, para 3.15. The RRs also lay down rules for the coordination, notification and registration of frequencies. The present version of the RRs came into force in 1990 (International Telecommunication Union, Radio Regulations, edition of 1990 (ITU Doc No ISBN 92–61–04141–8)) as revised in 1994 and will be discussed in more detail in Chapter 3.

2.34　The RRs are created or revised at World Radiocommunication Conferences held every two years. They were formerly revised at WARCs which were held on a worldwide basis. Those relevant to satellites are referred to *below*. Radio Conferences were also held at a regional level at RARCs in respect of the relevant ITU region: Europe and Africa (ITU Region 1), The Americas (ITU Region 2) and Asia and Oceania (ITU Region 3)—at RARCs. A world map (Fig. 3.1) showing the demarcation of these regions is provided in Chapter 3, para 3.15. RARCs could deal only with regional telecommunications issues and conference decisions had to be consistent with the RRs and could not amend the RRs. Amended or new regulations were, of course, binding on members although, as with other international instruments, reservations may be made to the Final Acts of any particular Conference. By such reservations, members of the Union 'purport to exclude or to modify the legal effect of (the provision so reserved) in their application to that (member)' (art 2(1)(*d*) Vienna Convention on the Law of Treaties (UN Doc A/Conf 39/27)). As Milton Smith points out, 'for any nation that takes [*sic*] a Reservation, all ITU members are relieved of obligations to that nation in accordance with the Reservation taken' (*op cit* p 25f).

2.35　WARCs and RARCs could also adopt recommendations and resolutions expressing the views of the Conference on matters which it considered should be the subject of studies and the convening of further conferences or procedures which should be adopted. On the face of it, recommendations and resolutions are not of the same legally binding character as the RRs; however, they do reflect policy and, by being referred to in the RRs, can arguably become part of them (see Smith *op cit* p 25). Even so, it should be noted that some resolutions have the force of the treaty (depending on their wording) when they are referred to in the treaty.

Development of satellite regulation through the ITU

2.36   A limited number of WARCs and Plenipotentiary Conferences are relevant to the contemporary regulation of satellites. These are (in chronological order): the 1927 International Radio Telegraph Conference of the International Radiotelegraph Union (as the ITU was then called) (the 1927 Washington Conference); the 1947 International Telecommunications and Radio Conference (1947 Atlantic City); 1959 Administrative Radio Conference Geneva 1959; the Radio Conference Geneva (1963 EARC); the 1971 WARC for Space Telecommunications (Geneva 1971) (WARC–ST); the 1973 Plenipotentiary Conference (Malaga-Torremolinos 1973); the 1974 World Maritime Administrative Radio Conference Geneva 1974; the 1977 WARC for the planning of the Broadcasting Satellite Service in frequency bands 11.7–12.2 GHz (in Regions 2 and 3) and 11.7–12.5 GHz (in Region 1) (Geneva 1977) (WARC–BS–77) (Geneva 1977 (ISBN 92–61–00491–1)); the 1979 WARC Geneva (ISBN 92–61–00861–5) (WARC–79); the 1982 Plenipotentiary Conference (Nairobi) (ISBN 92–61–01651–0); the 1983 RARC for Broadcast Satellite Service in Region 2 (ISBN 92–61–01802–5) (SAT–83); the two sessions of the WARC on the Use of the Geostationary-Satellite Orbit and the Planning of Space Services Utilising It 1985 (ISBN 92–61–02611–7) and 1988 (ISBN 92–61–03931–6) (often alternatively cited as the WARC–ORB 85 and WARC–ORB 88); the 1992 WARC Dealing with Frequency Allocations in Certain Parts of the Spectrum (ISBN 92–61–04661–4) (WARC–92); and the WRC concerning the Agenda for the 1995 WRC, including the review of the Radio Regulations based on the report of the VGE (ISBN 92–61–05021–2). There were no other WARCs or Plenipotentiary Conferences relevant to contemporary satellite regulation between 1988 and mid-1992.

However, the 1995 World Radiocommunication Conference (WRC–95) will review the final report of the Voluntary Group of Experts in undertaking a revision of the RRs, and formulate a timetable for the implementation of any recommended actions. For those seeking detailed consideration of those various Conferences prior to 1990, reference should be made to N M Matte, *Aerospace Law: Telecommunications Satellites* (Butterworths 1982) p 87 ff and to M L Smith, *International Regulation of Satellite Communication* (Martinus Nijhoff Publishers 1990) Chapters 4, 6 and 8. For present purposes, it is appropriate to note some of the more significant developments.

2.37 As with other aspects of international law, the development of satellite regulation through the ITU has been evolutionary. Although satellites were not even contemplated at the time of the 1927 Washington Conference, certain fundamental principles were laid down which have been developed for the purposes of regulation of satellites. These included a recommendation on the division of the radio frequency spectrum for use by particular services and an initial Frequency Allocation Table (art 5). This was the beginning of what has now become art 8 of the RRs, namely the Table of Frequency Allocations (see Chapter 1, para 1.4 and Chapter 3, paras 3.5 and 3.15). This reflected that 'the increased use of radio was causing harmful interference'.[24] The work of the 1927 Washington Conference was greatly added to by the work carried out at the two conferences held in Atlantic City after the Second World War at the 1947 WARC and the 1947 Plenipotentiary Conference. Basically, these 1947 Conferences created the structure of the ITU, which was not altered until 1992 (see *above* para 2.1 *et seq*).

2.38 Importantly, from the point of view of regulation of satellites, the IFRB was established in 1947, the International Table of Frequency Allocations was revised and detailed provisions were provided for the notification and registration of services by Administrations (see, for example, art 3, International Telecommunications Conventions, Atlantic City 1947 (Berne issue, 1948)). Because of the importance of avoiding harmful interference (referred to *above*, Chapter 1, para 1.4) members' obligations pursuant to the ITU Convention and the RRs were clearly stated and recognition of frequency assignments and related technical matters became part of the international regulatory regime.

Whilst the 1959 WARC dealt specifically with space services (admittedly for research purposes only), increasingly the usage of and access to the radio frequency spectrum and orbital positions were debated (see, for example, Chapter II of the RRs adopted in 1959 (RRs Geneva 1959)). The 1963 EARC particularly had to deal with the sensitive issue of access to necessary radio frequency spectrum bands and orbital positions. This Conference laid down the procedure for the obligatory prior co-ordination of services, whether terrestrial or space, using the same radio frequency bands (see, for example, Revision of art 3 of the RRs (Annex 2, Final Acts, EARC, ITU (Geneva 1963)). That principle has been adopted for the sharing of radio frequency bands by different space services, which was relevant to the proceedings of WARC–92.

2.39   The 1927 Washington Conference recognised the 'first come, first served' basis for the registration of frequencies granting protection to the user first registered from harmful interference by those seeking later registration. This approach was favoured by those ready to develop or exploit new technology, mainly the developed countries. However, concern as to the fairness of such a rule (particularly among less developed countries lacking the technology to exploit these scarce resources immediately) led to Recommendation No 10A of the Final Acts of the 1963 EARC, which was to the effect 'that the utilization and exploitation of the frequency spectrum for space communications be subject to international agreements based on principles of justice and equity permitting the use and sharing of allocated frequency bands in the mutual interest of all nations' (which was specifically recognised at the 1971 WARC–ST). Resolution 9A of the 1963 EARC recognised that there had been great progress in the space field and that 'this progress depends upon efficient and orderly space communications' involving 'rational use of frequency bands'. This, together with Resolution 10A, led to the development of international principles for the allocation of these scarce resources on a worldwide basis which is presently entrenched. Recommendation No 10A of the 1963 EARC referred to Resolution 1721 (XVI) and 1802 (XVII) of the UN General Assembly (see Chapter 1 para 1.31) and recognised the principle of 'equitable access' and further that 'principles of justice and equity' should govern the sharing of the radio frequency spectrum. Given the free use of outer space principle laid down in treaties such as the Outer Space Treaty (see Chapter 1, para 1.37) and the fact that radio frequency spectrum and orbital positions are finite, it seems hardly surprising that many nations seeking to use such scarce resources sought a fair or equitable approach to that use, especially when their technological development was behind that of those promoting the 'first come, first served' principle. Those supporting the equitable approach wanted to have laid down general principles which were transparent and could be applied fairly.[25]

2.40   The issue of equitable access underlay the next two conferences, namely the 1971 WARC–ST and the 1973 Plenipotentiary Conference. The 1973 Plenipotentiary Conference entrenched 'equitable access' in the ITU Convention (Malaga-Torremolinos) itself which reflected the principles that were established at the 1971 WARC–ST. In particular, art 33 of the 1973 ITU Convention, which reflects Resolutions 9A and 18A of the 1963 EARC, stated:

Rational Use of the Radio Frequency Spectrum and of the Geostationary Satellite Orbit

1   Members shall endeavour to limit the number of frequencies and the spectrum space used to the minimum essential to provide in a satisfactory manner the necessary services. To that end they shall endeavour to apply the latest technical advances as soon as possible.

2   In using frequency bands for space radio services Members shall bear in mind that radio frequencies and the geostationary satellite orbit are limited natural resources, that they must be used efficiently and economically so that countries or groups of countries may have equitable access to both in conformity with the provisions of the Radio Regulations according to their needs and the technical facilities at their disposal.

At the same time the role and function of the IFRB was increased specifically to include the regulation of the geostationary orbit.

2.41   Perhaps somewhat surprisingly, in view of art 33 of the 1973 ITU Convention, subsequent conferences continued the debate between those supporting the 'first come, first served' method of allocation (favoured by developed countries) against those who argued for general principles to be laid down as to the future allocation of orbital positions and radio frequency spectrum (see Resolution No 2 of WARC–79 and Chapter 3, para 3.47). This was accompanied by the development of broadcasting satellite services (BSS) (see *above*, and Chapter 1, para 1.18) globally at the WARC–BS–77 and the development of fixed satellite services in C and Ku bands. Importantly, in relation to the question of 'equitable access', WARC–79 passed Resolution No 3 calling for an administrative conference specifically 'to guarantee in practice for all countries equitable access to the geostationary satellite orbit and the frequency bands allocated to space services'. This resulted in the two sessions of the Space WARC of 1985 and 1988 referred to *above* and known as WARC–ORB 85 and WARC–ORB 88.

It should be noted that arising out of the WARC–BS–77 and WARC–79 was the plan for the development of BSS which allocated orbital positions and related frequencies to all members of the ITU. Importantly, from the point of view of the 'equitable access' debate, art

12.12 of the Final Acts of the WARC–BS–77 did not necessarily recognise in Region 2 (ie the Americas—see Chapter 3, para 3.15) that already planned services would be protected or given priority when establishing the plan for that region. The regulations adopted at WARC–BS–77 and WARC–79 differed greatly in their approaches to the development of 12 GHz services in Regions 1 and 3 and to the development of those services in to Region 2 (reflecting the equitable access approach versus the 'first come, first served' approach). While there continued to be this different approach between Regions 1 and 3 and Region 2, Resolution No 2 of WARC–79 (see Chapter 3, para 3.47) declared in the Final Acts that, all delegates having signed them, if any Administration were to 'make reservations concerning the application of one or more of the provisions of the [RRs], no other Administration shall be obliged to observe that provision . . . in its relations with that particular Administration' (see *above* concerning Reservations). SAT–83 then dealt with the plan for Region 2 for services in the 12.2–12.7 GHz band. This was generally consistent, subject to fairly flexible guidelines, with the plan for Regions 1 and 2.

2.42   As will be apparent from the discussion referred to in Chapter 1, technological advances have somewhat overtaken the work that the ITU has carried out in relation to the development of both BSS and FSS bands. WARC–ORB 85 carried out crucially important work in relation to the planning of services and providing guidelines for regulatory procedures for services where frequency bands had not been selected for planning (see Smith, *op cit*, p 87). It concentrated on the developments in the FSS band and, in particular, usage of the C and Ku bands as well as dealing with the development of frequency bands for BSS. WARC–ORB 85 led to the development of art 15 (RR 1656, see also the important RR AP30 (ORB–85) and Chapter 3, para 3.39) which dealt with the process for regulating the usage of the frequencies allocated for BSS. WARC–ORB 88 continued the work of WARC–ORB 85 and established an allotment plan for FSS and laid down the lengthy consultation procedures that are not contained in the RRs (see *below*, Chapter 3, paras 3.18–3.32) in relation to the usage of the FSS band. WARC–ORB 85 arguably has laid to rest the 'first come, first served' issue. Certainly, as noted in para 12, the equitable approach is enshrined in the Constitution (Geneva 1992), art 12.1(1).

Since the work carried out at WARC–ORB 85 and WARC–ORB 88, the next conference to deal with space related issues was WARC–92.

The WARC–92 (Malaga-Torremolinos)[26]

2.43   This conference partially revised the RRs, the revisions coming into force on 12 October 1993.[27] Certain modifications to the definitions in the RRs were effected in the Final Protocol. A large number of additions to the RRs were made with respect to the detailed allocation of frequencies, and amendments were made to the control of interference to geostationary-satellite systems (see generally, Chapter 3, and in particular, para 3.44). The conference also reviewed and revised certain existing resolutions and recommendations in accordance with its agenda and adopted a number of new resolutions and recommendations. Certain frequency bands previously allocated to fixed and mobile services were reallocated to broadcasting services. Some existing fixed and mobile assignments of frequencies therefore must be moved from those reallocated bands and reaccommodated in other appropriate frequency bands. The conference also resolved to assist developing countries in implementing the changes in frequency band allocations necessitating the transfer of existing assignments. Provision was also made for regulating frequency assignments relating to non-GSO networks, recognising that there is increasing interest in the use of systems using such non-GSO networks. Further detail on the provision for non-GSO networks appears in Chapter 3. Other resolutions included provisions for:

(a)   the establishment of standards for the operation of LEOS—the conference invited the organs at the ITU to carry out studies aimed at establishing standards governing the operation of LEOS so as to ensure equitable and standard conditions of access for all countries and to guarantee proper protection for existing services and systems in the telecommunication network. Affected Administrations were also invited to participate;

(b)   the allocation of frequencies to the FSS in the band 13.75–14 GHz;

(c)   use by the Mobile Service of the frequency bands 2025–2110 MHz and 2200–2290 MHz. The Conference invited the Consultative Committee on International Radiocommunications (CCIR) (as it then was) to study appropriate methods of protecting space services operating in the bands 2025–2110 MHz and 2200–2290 MHz from harmful interference from stations of the mobile service;

(*d*)   the implementation of Future Public Land Mobile Telecommunication Systems (FPLMTS);

(*e*)   the development of an arrangement for the allocation of frequencies for the Aeronautical Mobile (OR) Service in certain exclusive bands; and

(*f*)   convening a World Administrative Radio Conference for the planning of HF bands allocated to the Broadcasting Service.

In the European context it is important to note that the members of the European Union have agreed to apply the partial revisions of the RRs in accordance with their obligations under the Treaty of Rome (Final Protocol: Statement No 20), and thus recognise that the RRs apply as part of the international obligations of member states, but are subjected to reservation where there may be any inconsistency with the Treaty of Rome (see Chapter 4, para 4.28).

The WRC–93 (Geneva)[28]

2.44   The main purpose of this WRC was to establish a WRC in late 1995 in Geneva to review the Final Report of the VGE to facilitate a review of the RRs, and to set a timetable for the implementation of outstanding recommended actions. The agenda for WRC–95 is to deal with matters relating to mobile satellite services, including:

(*a*)   protection of space services in 2,025–2,110/2,200–2,290 MHz ranges;

(*b*)   earth-exploration satellite service in 401–403 MHz, 13.4–13.75 GHz and above 50 GHz;

(*c*)   allocation of other unplanned space services;

(*d*)   spurious emissions, wind profiler radars, multiservice satellite networks;

(*e*)   examination of the use of the HF bands allocated to broadcasting;

(*f*)   issues related to the implementation of the Global Maritime Distress and Safety System;

(*g*)   use of AP18 (transmitting frequencies for stations in the Maritime Mobile Service); and

(*h*)   revision of AP30/30A for Regions 1 and 3 taking account of the need to ensure that the integrity of the Region 2 Plans and their associated provisions is preserved (Region 1 covers Europe (including the whole territory of the ex-USSR and Mongolia) and Region 2 comprises the Americas and Region 3, Asia and Australasia).

2.45   It also set a preliminary agenda for WRC–97, which is to include consideration of the following matters:

(*a*)   review of technical constraints associated with allocations and associated provisions for Mobile-Satellite Services (MSS) below 3 GHz with a view to facilitating the use of those frequency bands;

(*b*)   review of the date of entry into force of allocations of certain bands allocated to MSS (1,980–2,010/2,170–2,200 MHz in Regions 1 and 3 as well as 1,970–2,010/2,160–2,200 MHz in Region 2). Entry into force for the use of these bands by MSS is presently 1 January 2005, except in the United States where the date is 1 January 1996;

(*c*)   allocation and regulation feeder links for MSS;

(*d*)   review of power limits for earth stations in earth-exploration satellite space research and space operation services in 2,025–2,110 MHz;

(*e*)   EIRP (equivalent isotropically radiated power) limits for earth stations in the Fixed-Satellite Service in 13.75–14 GHz and on compatibility of primary and secondary allocations in this band;

(*f*)   preparatory work carried out in relation to AP30 and 30A (regulatory provisions for the Broadcasting-Satellite Service and BSS feeder links in certain bands) to enable WRC 97 to take action;

(*g*)   space service allocations in bands between 8–35 GHz;

(*h*)   use of HF bands newly allocated to broadcasting.

2.46   Has the issue of first come, first served finally been laid to rest? At present the plans for the radio frequency spectrum and orbital positions set out in the RRs as a result of the various WARCs referred to have set in place a system which is frozen in time and based on technology at that particular time. Given that there are always technological advances, if certain radio frequencies are not being used for a particular service or an orbital location is not being utilised, those in a position to do so, will want to do so. This is an inherent tension in the ITU regulatory regime—how to balance 'justice and equity' (whatever that may mean in this context) on the one hand against rational, efficient and economic usage of these scarce resources (see art 12 of the Convention (Geneva, 1992)—also Chapter 3, para 3.47) on the other hand.

As noted *below*, it is not certain that the equitable access debate has concluded because, by setting aside frequencies for satellite personal communications, the fact is that once the Federal Communications Commission in the USA assigns those frequencies, that assignment will use all those frequencies available globally and hence will become assignments on a first come, first served basis.

Conclusion

2.47   It will be obvious from the foregoing that the development of satellite services in Europe is consistent with general international developments. The work of the ITU, in particular, in the case of the radio frequency spectrum, cannot be underestimated or ignored. As the international forum, it has laid down the framework, for example, for the development of satellite personal communication networks. However, implementation of these remains a domestic matter or one for co-operation between members of the ITU and their Administrations or recognised operating agencies. There is obviously scope for differing levels of commitment and implementation of the principles of the ITU. Despite the differing implementation in different countries, it is not being suggested that the ITU should act as a regulator on a global level. It is correct to state that private entities can do very little to enforce the obligations of the members, especially when the members themselves do not seek compliance with other members' obligations in the International Court of Justice (ICJ) or under the arbitration procedure laid down in the Constitution of the ITU (see Chapter 3, para 3.43). However, the reality of international law is that nation states can disregard international treaties if they are minded to do so and, in the absence of Governmental will, very little can be done to prevent it. This problem in relation to the use of frequency assignments and orbital slots is particularly acute in the Asian-Pacific region where there is a high demand for orbital slots in respect of which a number of Administrations are making competing claims or claims which indicate that there are likely to be significant amounts of harmful interference with other satellite systems, either because of insufficient angular separation or otherwise.[29] There also remains the tension between the developed and developing world: between, for example, equitable access to radio frequency spectrum and the GSO, and a rational, efficient and economic use of those resources, an argument of particular importance when technology advances rapidly and can often be constrained by regulation, especially by *a priori* planning which sets aside large amounts of scarce resources for possible future development which in fact may not happen.

---

1 Article 19.1 of the Convention of the ITU states:
 . . . The Secretary-General and the Directors of the Bureaux shall encourage the enhanced participation in the activities of the Union of the following entities and organisations:
 (*a*) recognized operating agencies, scientific or industrial organizations and financial or development institutions which are approved by the Member concerned;
 (*b*) other entities dealing with telecommunication matters which are approved by the Member concerned;
 (*c*) regional and other international telecommunication, standardization, financial or development organizations. (See also para 2.14.)
2 See art 6.1 of the Constitution of the ITU. With respect to installations for national defence services Article 48 of the Constitution provides that 'members retain their entire freedom with regard to military radio installations . . . nevertheless, these installations must, so far as possible, observe . . . the provisions of the Administrative Regulations concerning the types of emission and the frequencies to be used . . . '
3 *Above*, note 2; art 6.2.
4 International Telecommunication Convention. Final Protocol, Additional Protocols, Optional Additional Protocol, Resolutions, Recommendation and Opinions (Nairobi 1982), ITU Geneva. (ISBN 92–61–01651–0).
5 Final Acts of the Plenipotentiary Conference (Nice 1989), Constitution and Convention of the International Telecommunication Union, Optional Protocol, Decisions, Resolutions, Recommendations and Opinions (ITU Geneva) (ISBN 92–61–04131–0).
6 Final Acts of the Additional Plenipotentiary Conference (Geneva 1992) (APC), Constitution and Convention of the International Telecommunication Union, Declarations and Reservations, Optional Protocol, Resolutions, Recommendation (ITU, Geneva). All references throughout this Guide to the ITU's Constitution, Convention or Articles therein will be to those appearing in the Final Acts of the APC.
7 Final Acts of the Additional Plenipotentiary Conference (Geneva 1992) (APC), Resolution 1, deals with the provisional application of certain parts of the Constitution and the Convention of the ITU.

8 Final Acts of the Plenipotentiary Conference (Kyoto, 1994), Constitution and Convention of the International Telecommunication Union, Signatures, Declarations, Reservations, Decisions, Resolutions and Recommendations (ITU, ISBN 92–61–05521–4).

9 APC, note 17; Resolution 2, deals with the Allocation of Work of the Radiocommunication Sector and the Telecommunication Standardization Sector.

10 APC Resolution 1.

11 APC art 10(3).

12 APC Resolution 1.

13 APC art 22(4).

14 APC art 21(4).

15 WATTC–88 art 1.8.

16 *Ibid*, Preamble.

17 *Ibid*, art 6.1.1.

18 *Ibid*, art 6.1.3.

19 *Ibid*, art 6.3.2.

20 *Ibid*, art 9.1.

21 *Ibid*, art 9.1(*b*).

22 *Ibid*, art 9.1(*a*) (see also Chapter 1).

23 *Above*, note 3; art 54.

24 Matte, *op cit*, p 80.

25 See discussion in Matte, *op cit*, pp 96 *et seq* and Smith, *op cit*, Chapter 5. The 'first come, first served' approach is sometimes referred to as the *a posteriori* approach, and the equitable access approach is sometimes described as the *a priori* approach.

26 Final Acts of the World Administrative Radio Conference for Dealing with Frequency Allocations in Certain Parts of the Spectrum (WARC–92) (Malaga-Torremolinos, 1992) (Geneva, 1992) (ISBN 92–61–04661–4).

27 *Ibid*, Preamble.

28 Final Acts of the World Radiocommunication Conference (WRC–1993) (Geneva, 1993); ITU, ISBN 92–61–05021–2.

29 Angular separation is the angle of elevation from the earth station to the horizontal plane. It is insufficient when the degree of elevation falls below the prescribed limits set out in the RRs, namely RRs 2549–2551; see generally, Chapter 3, para 3.44.

3

The Radio Regulations

Introduction

3.1 Given that the radio frequency spectrum is a limited natural resource, its usage is regulated in order to maximise the efficiency of such usage and to minimise the possibility of harmful interference (see Chapter 1, para 1.4). Concurrent with this is the concept that any usage of the radio frequency spectrum should be on an equitable basis (see Chapter 2, para 2.39 *et seq*).

The Radio Regulations (RRs) deal with all matters touching on the emission and reception of radio waves. Thus, there are provisions relating to maritime mobile services, radio astronomy, land mobile services, nautical mobile services, radio navigation services, space research services, meteorological services and of course all forms of other satellite services. There are also important provisions dealing with the regulation of safety and distress signals.

3.2 As mentioned (in Chapter 2, para 2.34 *et seq*) the RRs have been developed at the various WARCs. Development of regulation and plans for broadcasting and fixed services were the subject of a number of WARCs (referred to in Chapter 2, para 2.34 *et seq*). In particular, the debates on the use of the fixed satellite service were initiated at the 1971 WARC–ST and were finalised during WARC–ORB 85 and WARC–ORB 88. WARC–ORB 88 also saw the finalisation of the allocation of orbital slots and related radio frequencies for the broadcasting-satellite service. The shape of the existing RRs is a result of these various WARCs and the Additional Plenipotentiary Conference (APC) held in Geneva in 1992. 1995 is a significant year for the RRs, as the Final Report of the Voluntary Group of Experts (VGE) is to be considered at the WRC to be held in Geneva in October 1995, in respect of which the agenda was put forward at the WRC–93 (see Chapter 2, para 2.36).

This chapter is concerned mainly with the detail of the co-ordination, notification and registration of frequency procedures for geostationary satellite services.

3.3   Pursuant to arts 12 and 14 of the Constitution and arts 10 and 12 of the Convention as adopted by the APC (Geneva) 1992, the International Frequency Registration Board (IFRB) is now replaced by the Radio Regulations Board (RRB) and the Radiocommunication Bureau (RCB), the former discharging the 'Board' functions of the IFRB and the latter discharging its secretarial functions (see Chapter 2, para 2.15). Until the date specified at the next Plenipotentiary Conference, the members of the IFRB shall discharge the duties of the RRB (Resolution 1, Final Acts, APC (Geneva) 1992). All references in this chapter are to 'the RRB' or 'RCB' as the case may be, as the functions of the new body will be very similar to those of its predecessor. Originally, the IFRB dealt only with the 'Administration' which had been designated by the relevant member of the International Telecommunication Union (ITU) to deal with the IFRB and had been charged with the responsibility of notifying frequency assignments to the IFRB in accordance with the provisions of the RRs. As a consequence, the RRs were for a long time outside the work of private practitioners. The interpretation and application of the RRs were mainly the concern of civil servants within the national Administrations and the IFRB. However, as indicated in Chapter 2, since the emergence of private commercial satellite operators which are often in competition with the Administrations, the ITU has recognised the need for such operators, if recognised to do so, to have direct access to the ITU and the RRB. Thus, the World Administrative Telegraph and Telephone Conference (WATTC–88) recognised the existence of these private operating agencies by applying the rules of the ITRs to such entities (WATTC–88, International Telecommunication Regulations, art 1.7(*a*)) (see Chapter 2, para 2.4). In addition, the Convention specifically directs the Secretary-General and the Directors of the Bureaux to 'encourage the enhanced participation' of recognised operating agencies in the activities of the ITU (Convention of the ITU (Geneva, 1992), art 19 and see also Resolution entitled 'Participation of Entities and Organizations other than Administration of the Activities of either Union'.)

3.4   The RRs have developed into a cumbersome three-volume looseleaf edition which incorporates all the revisions to previous editions in the form of appendices and all the resolutions and recommendations made pursuant to the various World Administrative Radio Conferences (WARCs). Fortunately, as already noted (see Chapter 2, para 2.33) the ITU has embarked on a programme of simplification of the RRs; the work is being undertaken by the VGE[1] and is to be considered at WRC–95.

Helpfully, the RCB has published, with the approval of the RRB, Rules of Procedure on the provisions of the RRs and related topics, which provide guidance on the interpretation of these matters by the RRB.[2]

The importance of the RRs can be gauged by the fact that, as part of an international treaty, they stand behind all national legislation which deals with the usage of radio waves.[3] For example, art 24 of the RRs provides that there should be no emission of radio waves without a licence by the government of the country where the transmitting station is located and such licence must be in conformity with the provisions of the RRs (RR 2020).

As was briefly mentioned in Chapter 2, WARC–92 introduced interim procedures for the co-ordination and notification of frequency assignments to non-geostationary satellite networks as a result of the allocation of frequency bands for the purposes of bringing into operation Low Earth Orbiting Satellites (LEOS),[4] but it is likely that these procedures will be further simplified in line with the work which is currently being carried out by the VGE (see below at para 3.33).

Terms and definitions

3.5   Before analysing the articles dealing with the co-ordination, notification and registration of frequencies with the RRB, it is necessary to understand some of the basic terms used in the RRs.

As mentioned in Chapter 2, the purpose of various WARCs has been, *inter alia*, to 'allocate' frequencies. 'Allocation' refers to the entry in the Table of Frequency Allocations (Table) in the RRs (see para 3.15) of a given frequency band which can be 'assigned' (see *below*) by an Administration for the service specified in the Table (RR 17). The term 'allotment' (RR 18) refers to the entry of a designated frequency channel in an agreed plan, to be adopted by conference and used by one or more Administrations in certain countries or geographical areas. This term is used when frequency bands are allotted by a bilateral or multi-lateral agreement or pursuant to a Regional Administrative Radio Conference (RARC). The term 'assignment' (RR 19) means the authorisation given by an Administration for a station to use a radio frequency or radio frequency channel. It is the assignments made by any Administration which are the subject of the co-ordination, notification and registration procedures.

3.6   For the sake of convenience, set out below is the full text of RRs 17, 18 and 19:

Section II. Specific Terms Related to Frequency Management

17   2.1   Allocation (of a frequency band): Entry in the Table of Frequency Allocations of a given frequency band for the purpose of its use by one or more terrestrial or space radiocommunication services or the radio astronomy service under specified conditions. This term shall also be applied to the frequency band concerned.

18   2.2   Allotment (of a radio frequency or radio frequency channel): Entry of a designated frequency channel in an agreed plan, adopted by a competent conference, for use by one or more Administrations for a terrestrial or space radiocommunication service in one or more identified countries or geographical areas and under specified conditions.

19   2.3   Assignment (of a radio frequency or radio frequency channel): Authorization given by an Administration for a station to use a radio frequency or radio frequency channel under specified conditions.

These three terms are specifically relevant to the concept of radio frequency management. First, radio frequency management requires the analysis of the most appropriate frequency band to be allocated or allotted to particular services and secondly, to the maximisation of efficiency and minimisation of possible harmful interference resulting from use of radio frequencies which are contiguous.

3.7   There are two other terms which should be understood at the outset. The first is 'Broadcasting Satellite Service' (BSS) which is defined as:

A radiocommunication service in which signals transmitted or retransmitted by space stations are intended for direct reception by the general public.[5]

Article 15 (discussed *below*) deals with the co-ordination of the BSS and this is relevant to the service provided by Direct Broadcasting Satellites (DBS).

3.8 The BSS satellites are to be contrasted with telecommunication satellites, which are co-ordinated under the provisions of art 11 of the RRs. As explained in Chapter 1, this is known as the 'Fixed-Satellite Service' which is defined as:

> A radiocommunication service between earth stations at given positions, when one or more satellites are used; the given position may be a specified fixed point or any fixed point within specified areas; in some cases this service includes satellite-to-satellite links, which may also be operated in the inter-satellite service; the fixed satellite service may also include feeder links for other space radiocommunication services. (RR 22)[6]

Harmful interference

3.9 As has been noted *above* (see Chapter 1, para 1.4 and Chapter 2, para 2.3) one of the fundamental purposes of the ITU and of its RRs is to give protection from harmful interference to services which operate in accordance with the RRs. Article 1.2 of the Constitution (Geneva 1992) states that the responsibilities of the ITU cover the allocation of frequencies in order to avoid harmful interference and to co-ordinate efforts to 'eliminate harmful interference'.

Article 45 of the Constitution also relates to harmful interference and states that:

> . . . all stations, whatever their purpose, must be established and operated in such a manner as not to cause harmful interference to the radio services or communications of other Members or of recognised operating agencies, or of other duly authorised operating agencies which carry on a radio service, and which operate in accordance with the provisions of the [RRs].

Each member undertakes to ensure that the operating agencies it recognises and the other duly authorised operating agencies observe the provisions of art 45 and further recognise the need to take all practicable steps to prevent the operation of electrical apparatus and installations of all kinds from causing harmful interference to the radio services or communications referred to *above*.

3.10   But what is 'harmful interference'? As noted in Chapter 1, para 1.5, it is defined in art 1 of the RRs as:

> Interference which . . . seriously degrades, obstructs or repeatedly interrupts a radiocommunication service operating in accordance with [the RRs]. (RR 163)[7]

The RRB has considered the issue of determining whether 'harmful interference' exists. In the Rules of Procedure (1047 5/6), it is stated that such a determination will be based on technical characteristics as notified by the relevant Administrations. In the event of disputes between Administrations as to whether or not a territory should be excluded from the 'service area' (see Chapter 1, para 1.19) of a particular Administration, the RRB will note that there is a dispute which has not been resolved and which it, the RRB, has no power to resolve.

Chapter 5 of the RRs contains provisions designed to help identify harmful interference and to deal with it. Article 20 (RRs 1872–1886) sets up a system of international monitoring whereby Administrations agree to assist in monitoring the radio waves to ensure efficient and economical use of the radio frequency spectrum and to help in the prompt elimination of harmful interference. The Secretary-General nominates monitoring stations across the world which conduct monitoring as may be required of them by the RRB or by the Designated-Monitoring Station (DMS) of other Administrations.

3.11   Further, art 21 (RRs 1915–1917) provides that infringements of the Convention or the RRs are to be reported to the Administration of the country having jurisdiction over the station committing the infringement. There is a duty on such Administration to '. . . ascertain the facts, fix the responsibility and take the necessary action' (RR 1917). The lack of any express provision as to what action the Administration is to take is very much in line with the lack of enforcement powers possessed by the RRB and the ITU under the RRs. In other words, enforcement is a national obligation under appropriate domestic law.

3.12   In this context, art 22 sets out the procedures to be used in cases of harmful interference. The reliance on agreement between the parties, evidenced by the wording of art 22, further emphasises the consensual nature of treaty arrangements. In particular RR 1943 which is contained in art 22 states:

> It is essential that Members exercise the utmost goodwill and mutual assistance in the application of the provisions of Article 35 of the

Convention and of this Article to the settlement of problems of harmful interference.

The consensual nature of the RRB is further reinforced by the subsequent sections, which encourage Administrations to deal with harmful interference by agreement. The only obligation of the Administration is to provide the necessary information to help establish the extent and nature of the interference. If the concerned Administrations agree, harmful interference can also be dealt with by the DMS (RR 1946).

3.13   Harmful interference is of particular concern when it affects safety services. ('Safety service' means 'any radiocommunication service used permanently or temporarily for the safeguarding of human life and property' (RR 56).) Article 22 therefore provides in RR 1957 the following:

> . . . recognising that transmissions on the distress and safety frequencies (see Article 38) require absolute international protection and that the elimination of harmful interference to such transmissions is imperative, Administrations undertake to act immediately when their attention is drawn to any such harmful interference. (RR 1957)

In cases of harmful interference occurring as a result of emissions from space stations, the Administration which has jurisdiction over the stations experiencing the interference may request from the Administration which controls the space stations the necessary data to allow determination of the positions of such space stations (RR 1955). If rapid action is required, the RRs permit information to be exchanged directly between the DMS subject to the authorisation of the relevant Administrations (RR 1956).

If harmful interference persists, the Administration having jurisdiction over the transmitting station whose service is being interfered with may address to the Administration having jurisdiction over the interfering station a report of the irregularity or infraction in accordance with art 21 (RR 1959). It is only after all these steps have been taken that an Administration can forward details to the RCB for its information.

3.14   The relevant Administration may also request the RCB to provide technical support by conducting a study and the RRB can then make recommendations (based on a report from the RCB) for the solution of the problem (RRs 1576–1584 and 1962).

Once the RRB reaches its conclusions it makes recommendations, a copy of which is forwarded to the Administration reporting the harmful interference. The conclusions and report are also forwarded by telegram to the Administration believed to be responsible for the source of harmful interference together with the request for prompt action (RR 1966). It is clear that the RRB has no power to impose sanctions against the Administration whose station is causing the interference. This goes to the very heart of the international regulatory regime. Enforcement is a matter of domestic law. The members have not yet granted any regulatory powers to the RRB concerning enforcement of the RRs. Furthermore, the principles of international public law do not enable enforcement through the RRB. The question therefore remains whether the RRB will continue to be confined to making recommendations and to have no regulatory powers, or whether the development of telecommunications will ultimately require that the ITU should be given such power, in the absence of the members of the ITU having recourse to enforcement of international obligations by other members (and their Administrations or recognised operating agencies) in the ICJ (see Chapter 2, para 2.47). It is outside the scope of this book to comment on this other than to point out that if the members actually fulfilled their obligation to the ITU by having appropriate domestic law to reflect their obligations, there is really little point in arguing for the ITU to become a 'super' regulator.

Table of Frequency Allocations

3.15   As briefly mentioned in Chapter 2, para 2.37, art 8 of the RRs contains the Table which sets out the allocation of frequency bands which have resulted from various WARCs. Due to differing regional requirements, in some cases services are allocated differently in each of the regions. As indicated in the world map *below*, the world is basically divided into three regions to which allocations are made as follows.

> *Region 1*   Region 1 includes the area limited on the east by line A (lines A, B and C are defined below) and on the west by line B, excluding any of the territory of Iran which lies between these limits. It also includes that part of the territory of Turkey and the [former] Union of Soviet Socialist Republics (USSR) lying outside of these limits, the territory of the Mongolian People's Republic, and the area to the north of the [former] USSR. which lies between lines A and C.

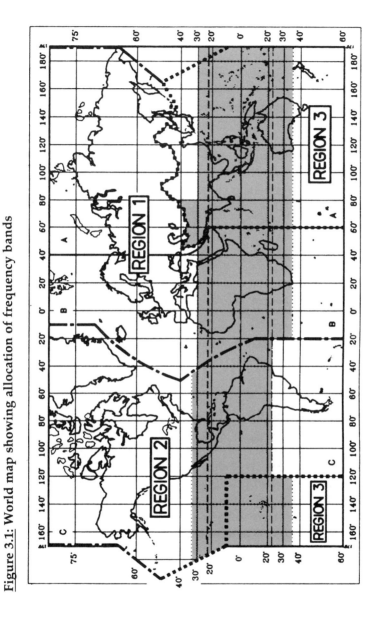

Figure 3.1: World map showing allocation of frequency bands

The shaded part represents the Tropical Zone

Reproduced with the kind permission of the ITU.

Region 2 Region 2 includes the area limited on the east by line B and on the west by line C.

Region 3 Region 3 includes the area limited on the east by line C and on the west by line A, except the territories of the Mongolian People's Republic, Turkey, the territory of the former USSR and the area to the north of the [former] USSR. It also includes that part of the territory of Iran lying outside of those limits.

The lines A, B and C are defined as follows:

Line A Line A extends from the North Pole along meridian 40° East of Greenwich to parallel 40° North; thence by great circle arc to the intersection of meridian 60° East and the Tropic of Cancer; thence along the meridian 60° East to the South Pole.

Line B Line B extends from the North Pole along meridian 10° West of Greenwich to its intersection with parallel 72° North; thence by great circle arc to the intersection of meridian 50° West and parallel 40° North; thence by great circle arc to the intersection of meridian 20° West and parallel 10° South; thence along meridian 20° West to the South Pole.

Line C Line C extends from the North Pole by great circle arc to the intersection of parallel 65° 30' North with the international boundary in Bering Strait; thence by great circle arc to the intersection of meridian 165° East of Greenwich and parallel 50° North; thence by great circle arc to the intersection of meridian 170° West and parallel 10° North; thence along parallel 10° North to its intersection with meridian 120° West; thence along meridian 120° West to the South Pole.

(The preamble to the RRs (RR 1) states that 'the application of the provisions of [the RRs] . . . does not imply the expression of any opinion whatsoever on the part of the ITU concerning the sovereignty or the legal status of any country, territory or geographical area'.)

3.16 The Table not only allocates different services to the different regions as a result of the decisions of the relevant WARCs, but also provides for frequency bands to be shared by different services. These are further distinguished as 'primary', 'permitted' and 'secondary' services (RRs 413–425). Primary and permitted services have equal rights, except that in the preparation of frequency plans, the primary services have prior choice of frequencies (RR 419). Stations of secondary services must not cause harmful interference to stations of primary or permitted services whether the assignment to the primary or permitted service takes place before or after the assignment to the secondary service. Furthermore, stations of the secondary services cannot claim protection from harmful inter-ference from stations of a primary or permitted service.

The Table also has footnotes which set out the procedure for alloca-tions in areas which are smaller than the three regions. The footnotes also contain what are known as 'additional' allocations for that smaller area or particular country. If there is no further restriction in the footnote on the service then the stations of that area or country for that service have an equal right to operate with stations of other primary services indicated in the Table (RRs 427–428). The addi-tional allocation, as its name implies, is in addition to that indicated in the Table for that area or country. The footnotes also contain provisions for 'alternative' allocations. These are also provided where one or more services are allocated in an area smaller than a region or in a particular country and which for that area or partic-ular country replace the allocation indicated in the Table. The same provision as to equality of right for operating stations applies as for additional allocations.

Co-ordination, notification and registration of frequencies

3.17   Before proceeding to analyse the details of the co-ordination, notification and registration procedures, the functions of the RCB, as set out in art 10 of the RRs, are briefly noted. The following are some of the more important functions:

(a)   the processing of frequency assignment notices, including in-formation about any associated orbital locations of geosta-tionary satellites;

(b)   the processing of information received from the adminis-trations in accordance with the procedures of the RRs, and the provision of assistance to the Administrations in these mat-ters;

(c)   the computation for publication in suitable form of frequency lists reflecting the data recorded in the MIFR (see para 3.30 *below*), as well as other material relating to the assignment and use of frequencies;

(d)   the review of entries in the MIFR with the view to amending or eliminating, as appropriate, those which do not reflect actual frequency usage, subject to the agreement of the Administrations which notified the assignments;

(e)   the long term study of the usage of the radio frequency spectrum to maximise efficiency; and

(f)   the investigation at the request of one or more of the interested Administrations into cases of harmful interference and the formulation of recommendations to eliminate such interference (RRs 990–1006).

The RCB is also entrusted with the duty to provide technical assistance to countries in special need of it and to train members of Administrations in the field of radio frequency spectrum management, where such training is not readily available.

Article 11

3.18   This article deals with the co-ordination of radio frequency assignments to stations in space radiocommunications service except stations in the Broadcasting Satellite Service. The process can be divided into four distinct steps:

(a)   advance publication;

(b)   co-ordination;

(c)   notification; and

(d)   registration.

The flowcharts

3.19   The RRs have developed into three cumbersome looseleaf volumes which incorporate all the revisions to previous editions in the form of appendices, and all the Resolutions and Recommendations made pursuant to the various WARCs.

To try and simplify the RRs, flowcharts are given in the following pages. These are extracted from those published with the RRs by the ITU.

Flowchart No 1 outlines the advance publication procedure applicable to stations in geostationary or non-geostationary satellite networks (para 3.20). Flowchart No 2 outlines the co-ordination procedure applicable to space or earth stations in a geostationary satellite network.

The flowcharts are intended by the ITU to act as an aid to understanding and they do not form part of the Rrs. There are at least two reasons for this, first the Rrs contain much more detail than the flowcharts and, second, the Rrs can, in certain circumstances, be more flexible than the flowcharts suggest.

References in the paragraphs below to 'boxes' are references to the box numbers on the relevant flowchart.

Advance publication

3.20   Requirements are imposed on any Administration which wishes to bring into use a satellite network within a satellite system (which includes any network not owned by that Administration but of which, for the purpose of the ITU, that Administration is the 'representative', for example, in the case of the ISOs, the USA for INTELSAT and France for EUTELSAT and similarly with regard to private satellite systems, Luxembourg for the ASTRA Satellite system and the USA for PanAmSat). Such an Administration must, no earlier than six years and no later than two years before the date of bringing into service a proposed satellite network, provide the information which is required by the RCB (RRs 1041–1044 and boxes 1 and 2).

The Rules of Procedure have confirmed that in relation to RR 1042 any publication notice more than six years in advance is to be returned to the responsible Administration; this also applies to notices in respect of mobile-satellite networks to which Recommendation No 2 of WRC–95 applies. Importantly, the Rules of Procedure also make clear that the maximum validity of any advance publication is nine years (Rule of Procedure 1042.2.1). Failure to bring any network into service within that nine-year period, 'irrespective of the regulatory status of the network', will lead to cancellation of any entry in the Master Register of advance publication or co-ordination, as the case may be (Rule of Procedure 1042.3.1).

The information which is sent is known as the 'advance publication' information. Once the RCB has received it, it reviews it in accordance with the technical standards set out in the RRs (boxes 3 and 6). When the information is in proper form, the RCB publishes it in a document called the *Weekly Circular*. The *Weekly Circular* (box 4) is received by all Administrations and puts them on notice of any

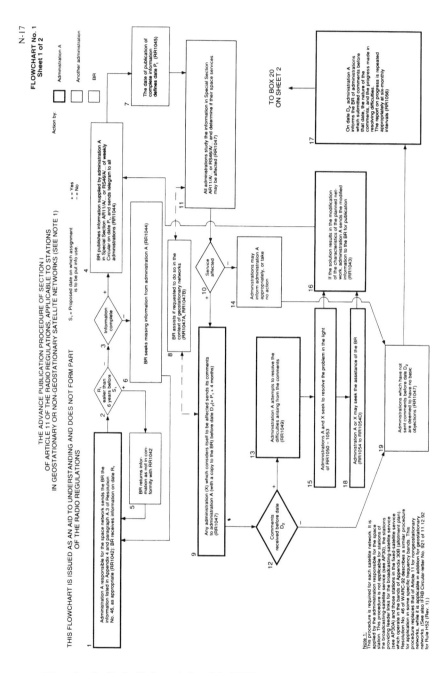

[*Reproduced with the kind permission of the ITU.*]

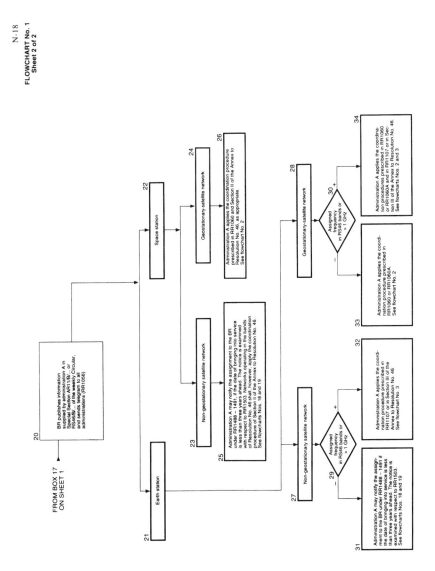

FROM BOX 17
ON SHEET 1

20
BR publishes information
supplied by administration A in
Special Section AR11/B/... or
RS46/B/... of the weekly Circular,
and sends telegram to all
administrations (RR1056)

21
Earth station

22
Space station

23
Non-geostationary satellite network

24
Geostationary-satellite network

25
Administration A may notify the assignment to the BR
under RR1488 – 1491, if the date of bringing into service
is less than three years ahead. The notice is examined
with respect to RR1503. Networks operating in the bands
of Resolution No. 46 shall, however, apply the coordination
procedure of Section II of the Annex to Resolution No. 46.
See flowcharts Nos. 18 and 19

26
Administration A applies the coordination procedure
prescribed in RR1060 and Section II of the Annex to
Resolution No. 46, as appropriate.
See flowchart No. 2

27
Non-geostationary satellite network

28
Geostationary-satellite network

29
Assigned
frequency
in RS46 bands or
> 1 GHz

+

–

30
Assigned
frequency
in RS46 bands or
> 1 GHz

+

–

31
Administration A may notify the assignment to the BR under RR1488 – 1491 if
the date of bringing into service is less
than three years ahead. The notice is
examined with respect to RR1503.
See flowcharts Nos. 18 and 19

32
Administration A applies the coordi-
nation procedure prescribed in
RR1107 or in Section III of the
Annex to Resolution No. 46
See flowchart No. 3

33
Administration A applies the coordi-
nation procedure prescribed in
RR1060 or RR1060A
See flowchart No. 2

34
Administration A applies the coordination procedures prescribed in RR1060
or RR1060A and in RR1107 or in Section III of the Annex to Resolution No. 46.
See flowcharts Nos. 2 and 3

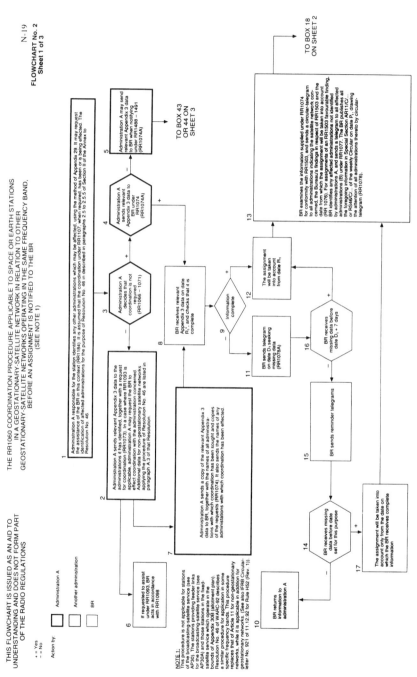

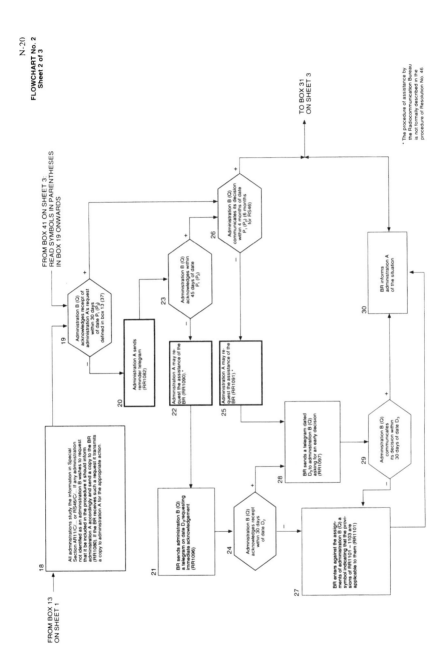

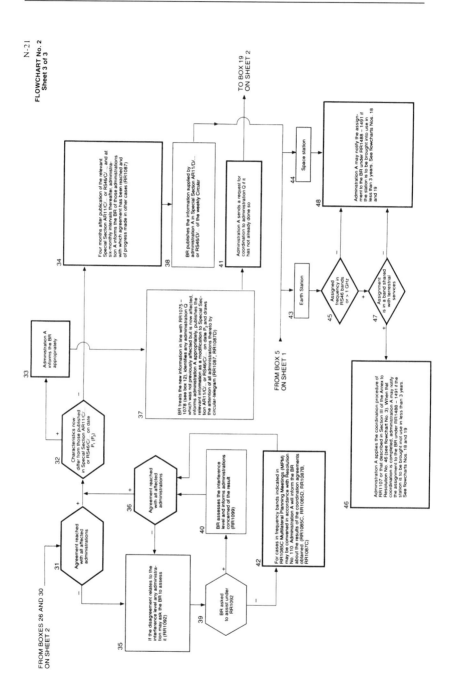

proposed satellite network. The RCB can request further information if the information supplied is incomplete (RR 1044 and Box 6).

3.21 Under RR 1042, modifications to any advance publication notice which 'significantly change' the characteristics of the network may require the whole advance publication procedure to be recommenced. Under the Rules of Procedure, the RRC has opined that changes in frequency would likewise require recommencement (Rule of Procedure 1043.2).

If modifications to the proposed network are subsequently made, such that its character is significantly changed, the advance publication procedure may be recommended (box 16).

Within four months of the date of publication in the *Weekly Circular* any Administration which believes that unacceptable interference may be caused by the proposed assignments to an existing or planned satellite network, must send to the Administration proposing the new satellite network its comments on such anticipated interference (boxes 9, 10, 11, 12 and 19). RR 1047 states that:

> If, after studying the information published . . . any Administration is of the opinion that interference which may be unacceptable may be caused to assignments of its existing or planned satellite networks, it shall, within four months after the date of the weekly circular . . . send the Administration concerned its comments on the particulars of the interference to its existing or planned satellite systems. A copy of these comments shall also be sent to the [RRB]. If no such comments are received from an Administration within the period mentioned above, it may be assumed that the Administration has no basic objections to the planned satellite network(s) of that system on which details have been published.

3.22 Provision is made for resolution of any difficulties which may have been identified as a result of advance publication (boxes 13, 15 and 19). When the RRs were redrafted following WARC–71 there appeared to be an order of priorities whereby the onus of resolving difficulties was placed initially upon the Administration proposing the new satellite network. The Administration had to explore all possible solutions without considering the possibility of adjusting other networks (RR 1051). It is only after this process has been completed that a request can be forwarded, to the Administration whose satellite network is likely to be affected, to investigate any modifications to its system which may resolve the problem (RR 1052). Finally, the Administrations should seek to work together to resolve the difficulties identified as a result of advance publication by mutually acceptable means.

As a result of various disputes which were not resolved and the absence of any powers of sanction available to the RRB, the RRB (then the IFRB) issued on 26 February 1993 a rule of procedure (Rule H40) regarding priority of dates in the application of arts 11 and 13 of the regulations (Radio Regulation Board Rules of Procedure, rule no H40 (Rev 1)). Pursuant to rule H40, no Administration now obtains any particular priority as a result of being the first to start either the advance publication phase or the request for the co-ordination procedures. The RRB has further clarified this in the Rules of Procedure, and status, with regard to RR 1060.

The RRB can be requested to assist in resolving any such disputes (box 18). Once relevant problems have been resolved, the RRB publishes in the *Weekly Circulars* the results of the advance publication procedures (RR 1056 and boxes 17 and 20).

If all necessary arrangements have been made, the Adminstration intending to bring the network into use may then proceed to co-ordination of the frequency assignments pertaining to the network (box 26).

Co-ordination

3.23   When an Administration sends the information for advance publication, it may at the same time, or thereafter, request the RCB to forward to any Administration which it thinks would be affected by the proposed satellite network (RR 1058) technical details of its proposed satellite network. Frequency assignments which are to be taken into account (boxes 1 and 3) in the application of co-ordination procedures are those in the same frequency bands as that of the planned assignment and which belong to the same service or to any other service which has that band allocated to it with equal rights or higher category allocation (that is, a secondary service assignment must be co-ordinated with a permitted or primary service but not *vice versa*) (RR 1061). The further qualification is that the only frequency assignments to be taken into account in the co-ordination procedures are those which are in conformity with the RRs and which are either recorded in the MIFR or co-ordinated under the provisions of the RRs or, where co-ordination is not required, have been notified to the RCB (RRs 1061–1065). The RRB has provided detailed clarification of these RRs, in particular RR 1063 (Rules of

Procedure) and has tabulated the way in which the RCB may take into account assignments in accordance with that RR as follows:

	Assignments to be taken into account in accordance with RR1063	
Assignments under consideration	Recorded in the MIFR (or Article 13 notification received)	received for publication in a Special Section AR11/C
primary/ permitted	primary/permitted with: –a favourable finding RR1503 and –a favourable finding RR1504 or –a favourable finding RR1506 or –an unfavourable finding RR1506 without having caused harmful interference	–primary/permitted with a favourable finding RR1503
secondary	a) any primary/permitted assignment as above b) any secondary assignment with: –a favourable finding RR1503 and –a favourable finding RR1504 or –a favourable finding RR1506 or –an unfavourable finding RR1506 without having caused harmful interference	–primary/permitted –secondary with a favourable finding RR 1503
RR435	a) any primary/permitted assignment as above b) any secondary assignment as above c) RR435 with: –a favourable finding RR1503 and –a favourable finding RR1504 or –a favourable finding RR1506 or –an unfavourable finding RR1506 without having caused harmful interference	–primary/permitted –secondary –RR435 with a favourable finding RR1503
RR342*	none	none

* Frequency assignments with reference to RR342 which are submitted for publication in AR11/C special section series are included in this publication for information only.
Reproduced with the kind permission of the ITU.

Co-ordination is not required when it is proposed that a satellite network will use a typical earth station and its technical specifications suggest that it is unlikely to cause any interference of a level greater than that caused by the typical earth station (RRs 1066–1071 and RR Appendix 29).

3.24   Once the Administrations with which co-ordination will be required have been identified the Administration proposing the new satellite network must forward all relevant data to the Administrations which are affected with copies to be supplied to the RCB (RR 1073 and boxes 2 and 7).

As with advance publication, the RRB can request further information (boxes 9, 10, 11, 14, 15, 16 and 17). When full information has been provided, the RRB examines the information supplied for conformity with the RRs and sends the information to affected Administrations, together with the result of the examination. The RRB will then publish the information in the special section of the *Weekly Circular* (box 13).

If modifications are subsequently made to the information that has been published in the *Weekly Circular*, the co-ordination procedure may have to be recommended (boxes 19, 32, 33, 37 and 41).

There are detailed provisions relating to time limits within which the Administrations must forward their comments to the Administration proposing the new satellite network (boxes 19–31). Within four months of the publication of the *Weekly Circular* any Administration which has any objection to the technical specifications of the proposed satellite network must forward its objections to the Administration proposing the new satellite network. It also has to provide the RCB with copies of any suggestions or solutions to the problem. In practice, however, Administrations do not always manage to meet the four month deadline. In the past there has been political opposition to accepting objections outside the period. When notifying the Administration proposing the new satellite network that there are objections, the technical details upon which the disagreement is based must be identified. The objecting Administration should also make suggestions for resolving such problems (RR 1084).

3.25   The RRs also state that the affected Administrations shall make all possible mutual efforts to overcome the difficulties in a manner acceptable to the parties (RR 1085A). This is the principle behind rule H40, and Rules of Procedure clarification of RR 1060 referred to above, whereby there is no priority and the onus on resolving any difficulty is shared equally between those Administrations which control satellite systems and which have already been co-ordinated, and the Administration proposing the new satellite system. Once the co-ordination procedure has begun, after the four month period, the Administration proposing the new satellite system informs the RRB of the Administrations with which agreement has and has not been reached (box 34). Thereafter, it reports to the RRB at six-monthly intervals on progress in securing the consent of other relevant Administrations (RR 1087).

If the disagreement cannot be resolved, the RRB is requested to provide assistance to try and resolve the difficulties. There are specific instances when the RRB's assistance may be sought. These include where the Administration identified under the advance publication procedures as being affected by the proposed satellite system does not acknowledge receipt of the co-ordination data (box 22), or, if it does acknowledge receipt, does not provide an answer as to whether or not it has agreed to the proposed satellite system (box 25). The RRB also assists where there is a continued disagreement between the Administration seeking co-ordination and the Administration with which the co-ordination is sought, or if co-ordination is not possible for any other reasons (RRs 1088–1094 and boxes 35, 39, 40 and 42).

3.26 Once the RRB becomes involved, it takes all necessary steps to facilitate reaching an agreement, including setting up meetings between the relevant Administrations (box 42). It also assesses the extent of interference and evaluates the technical grounds on which the Administration is objecting to the new proposed satellite network (box 35).

In essence, there is a 30-day 'cure' period, during which the Administration with whom co-ordination is sought must announce its decision (box 29). If that Administration fails to act within this period (box 27), the Administration with which co-ordination was sought is deemed to have undertaken that:

(*a*)   no complaint will be made in respect of any harmful interference affecting the services rendered by its space radiocommunication stations which may be caused by the use of the assignment to a station of the satellite network for which co-ordination was requested; and

(*b*)   its space radiocommunication stations will not cause harmful interference to the satellite network assignment for which co-ordination was requested.

The RRB lacks any powers of sanction to deal with failure to respond. In practice, to avoid this deemed undertaking, the objecting Administration can simply provide unhelpful responses (RRs 1095–1103).

3.27 A recent resolution of the ITU Plenipotentiary Conference held in Kyoto[8] instructed the Director of the RRB to initiate a review of issues concerning satellite network co-ordination with the objectives of ensuring:

(*a*)   equitable access;

(*b*)   that co-ordination procedures meet Administrations' needs; and

(*c*)   efficient use of the radio frequency spectrum.

A preliminary report is to be made to WRC–95 with a final report to WRC–97. Thus, the position on co-ordination may change to reflect the stated objectives.

There are similar provisions for the co-ordination of frequency assignments for earth stations operating as part of a geostationary satellite network. The procedures are the same, but the technical detail is of course different, as are the instances where co-ordination is not required (RRs 1106–1144).

Notification and registration in the Master International Frequency Register

Notification

3.28 Frequency assignment must be notified to the RRB in the following circumstances:

(*a*)   if use of the frequency is capable of causing harmful interference to the services of any other Administration; or

(*b*)   if the frequency is to be used for international radiocommunications; or

(*c*)   if it is desired to obtain international recognition of the use of the frequency (RRs 1488–1491).

The RRB is then under an obligation to publish the notification in the *Weekly Circular* within 40 days of receiving this notice. The *Weekly*

Circular has to contain all particulars of the notice received. The publication in the *Weekly Circular* amounts to notification to all Administrations of the complete notice. There are of course provisions for the RRB to request further information if the information provided is not complete (RRs 1498–1500).

3.29   The RRB is under an obligation to examine each notice to ensure its conformity with the Table and with other provisions in the RRs (RRs 1502–1512). Apart from a few technical exclusions, the RRB must examine the proposed notification against all the existing co-ordinated or notified frequency assignments which are likely to be affected. There are different standards against which the notice must be examined, depending on whether there has been a complete co-ordination procedure or whether co-ordination was not required (see para 3.23). If the RRB arrives at an unfavourable finding based upon the possibility of harmful interference with an assignment which has been entered in the MIFR for a space station which it believes is not in use, the RRB can consult the Administration responsible for the assignment; if it is discovered that the recorded assignment has not been in use for two years it can disregard such recorded assignment. In such a case, the recorded assignment becomes suspended and if it is brought back into use, it must go through the co-ordination procedure once again.

Registration

3.30   Once the review of the notice is complete, the RRB can proceed to make an entry in the MIFR. If the review of the RRB is favourable, the RRB enters it as such in the MIFR.

Any registration can also include a reference to the fact that the assignment will operate in accordance with the provisions of RR 342, whereby the Administration agrees that the assignment is made on the basis that it will operate only so long as harmful interference is not caused, and as soon as such harmful interference is caused to a service which is operating in accordance with the RRs, the assignment must cease (see volume 2 of the Radio Regulations, Appendix 30 (Orb 85), art 5, 'Notification, Examination and Recording in the Master Register of Frequency Assignments to Space Stations in the Broadcasting Satellite Service').

3.31   When the RRB makes an unfavourable finding on the notice of an Administration, the RRB will return the notice for it to be changed and resubmitted, if appropriate (RRs 1506 and 1542). Even though an Administration then resubmits a notice with insufficient changes to permit a favourable finding (RR 1543), nevertheless, pursuant to rule H40, the notice may be recorded in the MIFR:

(*a*)   'provisionally' (RRs 1544 and 1556) where an earlier notified assignment which was at the origin of the unfavourable finding is not in operation; or

(*b*)   'definitely' (RR 1544) where both assignments have already been in operation for at least four months without any harmful interference being reported.

Both the above cases are subject to the general provision of RR 1559 which stipulates that stations using frequencies recorded with a finding under RR 1544 must immediately cease interference on receipt of a complaint of harmful interference caused to stations which have been recorded with favourable findings (see Rule of Procedure 1544 *passim*).

3.32   It is clear that what is being sought is an elimination of unnecessary obstruction of the radio frequency spectrum by Administrations that record frequencies and then do not or cannot use them. This creates a delicate political problem relating to the very disparate state of technological advancement between different countries. The developing countries fear that if they do not protect both their orbital slots and their frequency assignments, the developed countries, by continued use over the years, may be able to claim a proprietary interest in them. This is arguably inconsistent with the 'non-appropriation' principle set out in the Outer Space Treaty (see Chapter 1, para 1.33).

Co-ordination and agreement in accordance with the footnotes to the Table, are also required for assignments. As for the co-ordination procedure set out above, there are strict time limits, and the RRB can be requested to intervene and assist in the reaching of an agreement.

It will be obvious that the above outline and the flowcharts do not include all the detail of the various procedures provided for by the RRs which are exceptionally complicated and make distinctions for different services. It is for this reason that it is very much hoped that the simplification which the Voluntary Group of Experts (VGE) is carrying out will be put into effect as soon as possible. The burden of responsibilities on the RRB is so vast that there is an enormous backlog of co-ordination to be effected especially as more and more

Administrations are requesting frequency assignments to be recorded in the MIFR.

Work of the Voluntary Group of Experts

3.33   As referred to in para 3.2 *above*, the VGE was assigned the task of reviewing the RRs at the WRC–93, to be considered at WRC–95 in October 1995.[9] Accordingly, the VGE considered alternative methods of allocating the radio frequency spectrum in a manner which would permit additional flexibility to Administrations in the allocation process and, where possible, would simplify the regulatory provisions. The VGE concluded that the current approach (block allocation methodology with footnotes) remains the best method.

The VGE then made the following recommendations concerning frequency allocation:

(*a*)   to retain the present concepts of 'allotment' and 'assignment' (see para 3.5);

(*b*)   to retain both primary and secondary categories of service (see para 3.16). However, the 'permitted' category should be deleted from art 8 of the RRs and any existing allocation with this status should become primary;

(*c*)   to retain the concepts of additional allocation, alternative allocation and different category in the allocation footnotes (other formulations of allocation footnotes should be avoided);

(*d*)   WRCs should, where possible, allocate frequency bands to the most broadly defined services to provide maximum flexibility to administrations in spectrum use, taking into account technical, operational, economic and other relevant factors;

(*e*)   WRCs should also allocate frequency bands on a worldwide basis, to the same services, within the same category of service and with aligned frequency band limits, taking into account technical, operational, economic and other relevant factors;

(*f*)   to confine footnotes to the Table of Frequency Allocations, wherever possible, to altering, limiting, or otherwise changing the relevant allocations rather than dealing with the operation of stations, assignments of frequencies or other matters;

(*g*)   to include as footnotes to the Table only those which have international implications for the use of the radio frequency spectrum;

(*h*)   to adopt new footnotes to the Table only if they:

(i)   improve flexibility; or

(ii)   protect existing use where the relevant allocations are changed; or

(iii)   introduce transitional or permanent restrictions on a new service to achieve compatibility; or

(iv)   provide for the specific requirements of a country or region where it is impracticable to do so otherwise in the Table;

(*i*)   to write footnotes serving a common purpose in a common format and, whenever possible, to group them into a single footnote with appropriate references to the relevant frequency bands.

3.34   The VGE was also entrusted to review the regulatory provisions and procedures of the RRs with a view to developing recommendations to simplify them. With respect to the regulatory provisions and procedures, the VGE concentrated on:

(*a*)   Articles 11, 12, 13, 14, 14A, 15, 15A, 16 and 17 of the RRs;

(*b*)   Appendices 1, 2, 3, 4 and 5, all of which specify the information to be provided under procedures referred to in the above articles; and

(*c*)   Appendices 25, 26, 27, 30, 30A and 30B, all of which contain worldwide frequency allotment of assignment plans with associated procedures and technical data.

In reviewing the regulatory procedures, the VGE agreed that the major features of existing procedures, such as advance publication (for space services), prior co-ordination, plan modification, notification and recording of frequency assignments in the Master International Frequency Register (MIFR), should be retained and, where possible, existing wording should be preserved. The VGE identified the need to restructure the procedures in a simple and consistent way and to eliminate unnecessary complications, excessive repetitions, unnecessary detail, over-use of cross-references and over-regulation. The VGE also identified material which is not appropriate for inclusion in an international treaty. Accordingly, certain of the present procedures should be transferred to the Rules of Procedure.[10]

3.35   The VGE also proposed that the parallel procedures for terrestrial and orbital services should be replaced by an integrated procedure. This procedure would have the following features:

(*a*)   a new art S9 containing a standardised procedure for effecting 'co-ordination' with or obtaining 'agreement' of other Administrations whose services may be affected by a proposed frequency usage (the VGE recognised that, at present, arts 11, 14 and 14A, and Resolutions 33, 46 and 329 have many common features and could be integrated into a single article which could also be used where the interests of all affected Administrations are to be safeguarded before assignments are notified);

(*b*)   a new art S10 containing a standardised procedure for modifying a frequency allotment or assignment plan;

(*c*)   a new art S11 containing a consolidated set of regulations for the notification of frequency assignments to the RCB, the various examinations of those notices by the RCB, the entries to be made in the MIFR and various associated provisions;

(*d*)   a new art S12 containing a simplified version of part of the present art 17 procedure relating to high frequency broadcasting.

3.36   The VGE concluded that most of the existing operational, technical and administrative provisions should be maintained with the same force (eg mandatory, optional or provisional). This is particularly important in relation to radiocommunication services, operational procedures and technical material, which involve broad international use of equipment and practices and for which there is no obvious alternative. The VGE considered that it was appropriate and desirable to transfer a significant amount of material from articles and appendices of the RRs to ITU-R Recommendations, with appropriate provisions being incorporated by reference.

Non-geostationary satellites

3.37   WARC–92 introduced interim procedures for the co-ordination and notification of assignments of frequencies for non-geostationary satellite networks. The procedures are very similar to the simplified procedures which the VGE is proposing for geostationary satellites. These are contained in Resolution No 46 of

WARC–92[11] and cover *inter alia* the recent developments relating to LEOS previously referred to (see Chapter 1, para 1.12; Chapter 2, para 2.43).

Following advance publication, if co-ordination procedures are not commenced within six years, the advance publication information is cancelled. Co-ordination procedures can commence at the same time as advance publication information is provided.

The interim provisions make it clear that bringing into use radio frequency assignments prior to co-ordination and notification does not afford any priority to such usage. The co-ordination procedures require that any assignment should be co-ordinated with assignments in the same band (with equal rights or a higher category of allocation) and in accordance with the Table recorded in the MIFR or must be in the process of being co-ordinated.

There are provisions dealing with co-ordination with terrestrial stations for assignments to earth stations for non-geostationary satellite networks and *vice versa*.[12] Following co-ordination, a very simplified notification procedure applies.

Mobile-Satellite Service

3.38   The frequency assignments for LEOS applications are indicated in the Table of Frequency Allocations as 'Mobile-Satellite Service' (MSS). However, this service covers a number of other applications. These include FPLMTS and any service which is:

- between mobile earth stations and one or more space stations, or between space stations used by [MSS]; or

- between mobile earth stations by means of one or more space stations.[13]

Where non-geostationary satellites are involved, amendments to the Table made at WARC–92 make it clear where MSS entries are limited for usage by non-geostationary systems, in which case the procedures of Resolution 46 apply. Alternatively, where geostationary satellites are involved, the co-ordination procedures in art 11 (discussed *above*) apply.

Given that several additional frequency bands were allocated to MSS, concerns were expressed relating to compatibility with GSO satellite systems where LEOS were used for MSS. Additionally, because of serious sharing problems with existing terrestrial services, the newly allocated bands are subject to power flux density limitations, have a lower category of allocation or require the mandatory application of additional co-ordination procedures, not only with other space services but also with respect to the terrestrial services.

Broadcasting Satellite Service

3.39   The Space–WARC (1985–1988), in its second session (ORB–88), completed the planning for BSS. Accordingly, each country had both an orbital slot and an allocated frequency band which it could use for the purposes of providing BSS.

Article 15 deals with the assignment of frequencies for BSS (the details are set out at length in volume 2 of the RRs, Appendix 30). When an Administration wants to bring such a service into use, it must notify the RCB not earlier than three years, and not later than three months, before the date on which it is to be brought into use. Such notification is entered into the MIFR. When the RCB receives the particulars, the date of receipt is published in a *Weekly Circular*, which contains all particulars of all such notices received since the publication of the previous *Weekly Circular*. Publication in the *Weekly Circular* constitutes acknowledgment of receipt of the notice. At the same time, the RCB must examine the conformity of the notice with the RRs, except where the services are being provided under a Regional Plan or where for certain technical reasons it is not necessary. This is usually where harmful interference is not likely to occur (see Appendix 30). Upon examination, the RCB can then enter a favourable or unfavourable finding in the MIFR. If the finding is unfavourable, it can notify the relevant Administration with suggestions as to how to resolve the problem. If a favourable finding has been entered into the MIFR before the frequency comes into use, this is recorded as a provisional entry which diminishes its status in terms of any future co-ordination which might be required. When a modification is requested in respect of the Regional Plan under which the BSS is operating detailed co-ordination procedures apply. They are much simpler than those in art 11 (see volume 2 of the RRs, Appendix 30 (Orb 85), art 5 'Notification, Examination and Recording in the Master Register of Frequency Assignments to Space Stations in the Broadcasting Satellite Service'). Article 6 of Appendix 30 also sets out the co-ordination procedures which are required in respect of assignments to terrestrial stations and which affect broadcasting-satellite frequency assignments in the frequency bands 11.7–12.2 GHz (in Region 3), 11.7–12.5 GHz (in Region 1) and 12.2–12.7 GHz (in Region 2). These co-ordination procedures are subject to the same simplified rules which are set out above in respect of the work currently being carried out by the VGE.

3.40   Article 8 of Appendix 30 provides that the RCB shall use all appropriate means at its disposal to conduct studies of cases of alleged contravention or non-observance of the procedural provisions in the RRs or of harmful interference.

When the RCB makes recommendations for the solution of a problem and does not receive a response within three months, it will consider that such suggestions or recommendations are unacceptable. The RCB will discontinue the study and no further action will be taken.

Miscellaneous provisions

Service documents

3.41   The Secretary-General is under an obligation to publish certain documents, the most important of which is that known as List A/List B, now called the 'List of Geostationary and Non-Geostationary Space Stations'. On 22 September 1992, the first of these new lists was published. It consists of three sections:

(*a*)   Section 1—a list of geostationary space stations for which information has been received by the RRB in the application of the procedures of art 11 and/or art 13, as appropriate (space stations in the BSS are not included).

(*b*)   Section 2—the list of non-geostationary space stations for which information has been received by the RRB in application of Resolution No 46 of WARC–92 or which are recorded in the MIFR using frequencies in the bands referred to in that resolution.

(*c*)   Section 3—the list of geostationary space stations for which information has been received by the RRB in application of Resolution No 46 of WARC–92 or which, using frequencies in the bands referred to in that resolution, are either recorded in the MIFR or are in the co-ordination phase of art 11.

Secrecy

3.42   Another important provision of the RRs is art 23, which deals with secrecy. It provides that the Administrations each agree to take the necessary measures to prohibit and prevent:

(*a*)   the unauthorised interception of radiocommunications not intended for the general use of the public;

(*b*)   the divulgence of the contents, simple disclosure of the existence, publication or any use whatever, without authorisation, of information of any nature whatever obtained via the interception of any radiocommunication not intended for the general use of the public. (RRs 1992–1994)

Domestic laws of members give effect to this obligation in different ways; for example, in the UK, see s 5 of the Wireless Telegraphy Act 1949 (WTA) and s 1 of the Interception of Communications Act 1985 (both referred to in Chapter 6 *below*).

Optional Protocol

3.43   In view of the problems which the RRB has encountered in resolving difficulties between Administrations, during the APC Geneva, 1992, an Optional Protocol to the Constitution of the ITU and the Convention of ITU (Geneva, 1992) was added whereby members of the Union which ratify the Optional Protocol agree to disputes concerning the interpretation or application of the Constitution, the Convention or the Administrative Regulations being submitted for compulsory arbitration. (Final Acts of the Additional Plenipotentiary Conference (Geneva, 1992) Optional Protocol on the Compulsory Settlement of Disputes Relating to the Constitution the Convention of the ITU and to the Administrative Regulations.) This applies provided that one of the methods of settlement listed in art 56 of the Constitution has not already been chosen by common agreement. The compulsory arbitration will be possible in accordance with art 41 of the Convention, para 5, which is to be amplified as follows:

5.   Within 3 months from the date of receipt of the notification of the submission of the dispute to arbitration, each of the two parties . . . to the dispute shall appoint an arbitrator. If one of the parties has not appointed an arbitrator within this time limit, this appointment shall be made, at the request of the other party, by the Secretary-General who shall act in accordance with Nos 509 and 510 of the Convention.

Curiously, art 4 of the Optional Protocol envisages the possibility that any member party to the Protocol may denounce it by notification addressed to the Secretary-General, and such denunciation takes effect after a period of one year from the date of receipt of this notification by the Secretary-General. This does, however, give a one-year period during which disputes can be resolved.

Sharing of services

3.44   Part B of the RRs (Chapter VIII) contains provisions relating to the choice of site and to frequency and power limits, where groups of services share the same frequency bands. In particular, it deals with instances where terrestrial radiocommunication services share frequency bands with space radiocommunication services above 1 GHz (arts 27 and 28).

There are also provisions for the control of interference to geostationary satellite systems (RR 2613). Non-geostationary space stations are required to cease or reduce their emissions to a negligible level, and their associated earth stations are prohibited from transmitting to them whenever there is insufficient angular separation between non-geostationary satellites and geostationary satellites which results in unacceptable interference (in accordance with the relevant Consultative Committee on International Radiocommunications (CCIR) recommendations) to geostationary Fixed-Satellite Services (FSS) satellite space systems operating in accordance with the RRs. This provision, as modified by WARC–92,[14] makes it clear that it is insufficient angular separation causing the unacceptable interference which is sought to be controlled. There are also provisions for the cessation of emissions by earth exploration satellite services when emissions are directed towards the GSO (RRs 2613–2614).

Distress and safety communications

3.45   Article 37 of the RRs deals with distress, urgency and safety calls and messages.[15] These are of great importance and largely relate to maritime mobile services. Article 37 also applies in respect of aeronautical mobile services except in the case of special arrangements between the governments concerned. The provisions of art 37 do not prevent the use by stations, in exceptional circumstances, of any means at their disposal to assist a mobile station or a mobile earth station in distress. Thus, stations on board aircraft or ships engaged in search and rescue operations, or indeed land stations or coast earth stations, can, in exceptional circumstances, make use of any means available to assist a mobile station or mobile earth station in distress. Chapter 10 also includes a provision for aeronautical mobile-satellite service safety and distress provisions. This sets out the responsibilities, priorities and general procedural rules whereby safety and distress signals are given utmost priority and assistance. Article 67 (Chapter 12) deals with the conditions to be observed by land mobile-satellite services. These basically provide for power levels to be at their minima, and that they should not cause any harmful interference to the services of stations which are operating in accordance with the RRs (RRs 5136–5137).

Resolutions and recommendations

3.46   At WARC–79 two important resolutions were passed, namely, Resolution 1 which relates to the notification of frequency assignments, and Resolution 2 relating to the equitable use by all countries, with equal rights, of the GSO and of frequency bands for space radiocommunication services.

Resolution 1 replaced Resolution 5 of the Administrative Radio Conference held in Geneva in 1959 and Resolution 2 replaced Resolution Spa 2–1 of the WARC for Space Telecommunications in Geneva in 1971.

In essence, Resolution 1 was to the effect that unless specifically stipulated by special arrangements communicated to the ITU by Administrations, any notification of a frequency assignment to an earth station shall be made by the Administration of the country on whose territory the station is located.

This is not to be confused with the responsibility of Administrations in obtaining co-ordination and notification of satellite networks. In the latter case, Administrations may co-operate in obtaining the required co-ordination and notification (see Chapter 1, para 1.3).

3.47   As noted in Chapter 2, para 2.41, WARC–79 saw the development of the principle of 'equitable access' which replaced the earlier 'first come, first served' utilisation of radio frequency and orbital slots.

Resolution No 2 of WARC–79 states:

(1) that the registration with the [RRB] of frequency assignments for space radiocommunication services and their use should not provide any permanent priority for any individual country or

groups of countries and should not create an obstacle to the establishment of space systems by other countries;

(2)   that accordingly, a country or a group of countries having registered with the [RRB] frequencies for their space radio communication services should take all practical measures to realise the possibility of the use of new space systems by other countries or groups of countries so desiring;

(3)   that the provision contained in paras 1 and 2 of this Resolution should be taken into account by the Administration and permanent organs of the [ITU].

This resolution is self-explanatory (see also M L Smith, *International Regulation of Satellite Communication* (Martinus Nijhoff Publications 1990) and Chapter 2, para 2.39 *et seq* for more detailed discussion concerning the 'equitable access' debate and these resolutions).

Conclusion

3.48   The foregoing outline of the RRs is indicative of the complex areas covered by them. They are a cumbersome set of rules, originally directed to the members and their Administrations. As noted, the ITU is presently working on their simplification, and WRC–95 should see progress on the final report of the VGE. With the development of private commercial operators it is to be hoped that the RRs will become less burdened by bureaucratic procedures and address the needs of the private operators, in particular, the streamlining of procedures and simplification of the rules. As mentioned in the introduction to this chapter, private operators will have to be increasingly aware of the regulatory pitfalls, which may impair the ability of a satellite operator to establish its proposed system. There is also the need to co-ordinate proposed satellite systems with the satellite treaty organisations—the ISOs and private satellite networks—which are dealt with in the next chapter.

---

1   Final Acts of the Additional Plenipotentiary Conference (ITU, Geneva, 1992), Resolution 8.
2   Rules of Procedure approved by the Radio Regulations Board for the application by the Radiocommunications Bureau (ITU, Geneva, 1995; ISBN 92–61–05491–9).

3 'Radio Waves' or 'Hertzian Waves' mean 'Electromagnetic waves of frequencies arbitrarily lower than 3000 GHz, propagated in space without artificial guide' (RR 6).

4 Final Acts of the World Administrative Radio Conference for Dealing with Frequency Allocations in Certain Parts of the Spectrum (ITU WARC–92) Malaga-Torremolinos, 1992, Resolution 46.

5 Radio Regulation 37: 'Radiocommunication service' means 'a service involving the transmission, emission and/or reception of radio waves for specific telecommunication purposes' (RR 20).

'Space Station' means 'a station located on an object which is beyond, is intended to go beyond, or has been beyond, the major portion of the Earth's Atmosphere' (RR 61).

6 'Earth Station' means 'a station located either on the Earth's surface or within the major portion of the Earth's atmosphere and intended for communication: with one or more space stations; or with one or more stations of the same kind by means of one or more reflecting satellites or objects in space' (RR 60).

'Inter-satellite service' means 'a radiocommunication service providing links between artificial earth satellites' (RR 24).

'Space Radiocommunication' means 'any radiocommunication involving the use of one or more space stations or the use of one or more reflecting satellites or other objects in space' (RR 9).

'Feeder Links' means 'a radio link from an earth station at a given location to a space station, or *vice versa*, conveying information for a space radiocommunication service other than for the fixed satellite service. The given location may be at a specified fixed point, or at any fixed point within specified areas' (RR 109).

7 'Interference' means 'the effect of unwanted energy due to one or a combination of emissions, radiations, or inductions upon reception in a radiocommunication system, manifested by any performance degradation, misinterpretation, or loss of information which could be extracted in the absence of such unwanted energy' (RR 160).

8 See footnote 8, Chapter 2.

9 See footnote 8, Chapter 1.

10 See Rules of Procedure approved by the RRB for the application, by the RCB, of the provisions of the RRs, Regional Agreements and Recommendations of World and Regional Radiocommunication Conferences (1994 Edition), ITU, Geneva, 1995.

11 See note 2.

12 RR 2613 gives priority to geostationary-satellite space systems in the FSS over non-geostationary space stations whenever there is insufficient angular separation between non-geostationary and geostationary satellites resulting in unacceptable interference to geostationary-satellite space systems in the FSS.

13 RR 27.

14 See note 2, art 29.

15 RR 2930 provides that:

'The provisions specified in [Chapter IX of the RRs] are obligatory (see Resolution 331(MOB-87)) in the maritime mobile service for stations using the frequencies and techniques prescribed in this Chapter and for communications between these stations and aircraft stations. However, stations of the maritime mobile service, when additionally fitted with any of the equipment used by stations operating in conformity with the provisions specified in [Chapter IX of the RRs] shall, when using that equipment, comply with the appropriate provisions of that Chapter. The provisions of this Chapter are also applicable to the aeronautical mobile service except in the case of special arrangements between the governments concerned.'

4

International Satellite Service Providers

Introduction

4.1 Although the International Satellite Organisations (ISOs) IN-TELSAT, Inmarsat and EUTELSAT (referred to in Chapter 1, paras 1.14, 1.25–1.27) were until recently the major international providers of space segment, they are no longer the sole providers. In Europe, there has been increasing liberalisation and competition in the provision of space and earth segments. (For descriptions of what constitutes 'space segment' and 'earth segment', see Chapter 1, para 1.7.) Specialised Satellite Service Providers (SSSPs) are making inroads into the traditional businesses of the ISOs and the Public Telecommunications Operators (PTOs), utilising very small aperture terminals (VSATs) for services such as satellite news gathering (SNG) and fixed multipoint private networks for data, audio and / or video. These SSSPs resell satellite capacity to their customers and are generally value added service providers. Such services are not yet uniformly available in Europe, though there are signs of innovation and increasing competition in the market place, but not at the pace desired by many of the SSSPs. These events have raised interesting legal and regulatory issues, both domestically and at the European level, which are considered below in paras 4.35 *et seq.*

4.2 While the ISOs are important, consideration will also be given to privately owned satellite systems currently providing international services in Europe, namely the ASTRA satellite system (Société Européenne des Satellites (SES)) based in Luxembourg and PanAmSat (Alpha Lyracom) based in the USA. For the reasons explained in Chapter 1 (see para 1.26), neither the other ISO, INTER-SPUTNIK nor the regional systems, such as ARABSAT, and other government-owned domestic satellite operators are dealt with in this work.

To understand the present market in earth and space segment capacity and the ability to provide new satellite services, it is necessary first to consider the ISOs and their present structures. Consideration will then be given to regulatory issues that have been raised by bodies such as the European Commission with regard to access to space segment and the ISOs' 'co-ordination procedures' (both 'economic' and 'technical') (see para 4.21 *below*) and which may affect competition in, and availability of, satellite services. In the light of these matters, reference will then be made to some of the ISOs' proposals for reform to meet these concerns. The present procedures for obtaining space segment from the ISOs, eg through the Signatory Affairs Office in the UK, will be explained. Finally, the somewhat complicated way of obtaining space segment capacity from the ISOs rather than from the private operators referred to *above* will be discussed.

INTELSAT, EUTELSAT and INMARSAT

Introduction

4.3 All three ISOs have essentially similar tripartite structures[1] consisting of:

(1)   the parties: that is, the sovereign states which have entered into the formative treaties of each ISO. The bodies made up of the parties to the INTELSAT, Inmarsat and EUTELSAT treaties are known as the 'Assemblies of Parties';

(2)   the signatories: the telecommunications entities designated by the parties, which invest in the ISO and are responsible for its operation. The signatories operate through the Meetings of Signatories in INTELSAT, the Council of Inmarsat and the Board of Signatories of EUTELSAT; and

(3)   the Executive: this is the management arm of the ISO at its relevant headquarters. In the case of EUTELSAT, for example, its headquarters and executive are in Paris.

Funding of the ISOs is effected by the signatories under the relevant operating agreement. The signatories make a contribution to the ISOs' requirements and receive a return on their respective investment. The size of each signatory's 'investment share' in the relevant ISO is determined by reference to its usage of the system. For example, the INTELSAT Operating Agreement provides:

> ... [e]xcept as otherwise provided in this Article, each Signatory shall have an investment share equal to its percentage of all utilization of the INTELSAT space segment by all Signatories. (art 6.)

4.4   To access the space segment of the ISOs, earth stations have traditionally been owned and operated by the monopoly (state-owned) Post Telegraph and Telephone (PTT)[2] signatory of each party. Under the constituent instruments, access to space segment by any person who has ground segment capacity in the territory of a party is through the signatory of that party (see EUTELSAT Operating Agreement, art 16; INTELSAT Operating Agreement, art 15; and Inmarsat Operating Agreement, art XV). Although strict compliance with this is to some extent being waived by signatories or modified by the ISOs (see paras 4.43–4.54 *below*), the fact remains that the signatories are the gateways to such space segment. In addition to the signatories, certain operators (called, in the case of INTELSAT, for example, 'Authorised Customers'), are recognised as able to deal directly with the ISOs (this is similar to the 'Recognized Operating Agencies' under the ITU procedures referred to in Chapter 2, para 2.4). In EUTELSAT's case, the European Broadcasting Union (EBU) has always been given direct access to that ISO.

Each ISO is recognised as an 'international institution' and is accorded certain immunities appropriate to that status under international law (see, for example, art XVII of the EUTELSAT Convention). Immunity from suit is a somewhat complicated matter and is touched on briefly in paras 4.39–4.43 *below*. This is particularly relevant today in considering whether the ISOs are acting in their regulatory capacity or their 'commercial' capacity.

As will be apparent from this chapter, the ISOs, born in a different telecommunications age, have a regulatory and an operational function. This means that, at times, the legitimate 'regulatory' aims of the ISOs may conflict with their commercial interests. This apparent conundrum is of concern to the user of satellite services and has been the subject of some regulatory and judicial consideration (see *below* para 4.41 *et seq*). It has also resulted in substantial pressure (to which the ISOs are gradually responding) to change and modernise the ISO's structures and practices (see paras 4.43 to 4.53 *below*). There is also some movement towards the alteration of the ISOs themselves into more commercial entities (for example at the INTELSAT Assembly of Parties meeting in November 1994, a Working Party was established to report to INTELSAT as to possible future structures by the end of 1995). Before considering these questions and developments, however, it is necessary to understand the present basic structures of the individual ISOs.

INTELSAT

INTELSAT general description and purpose

4.5   In 1962 the US Congress enacted the Communications Satellite Act. This Act provided in s 102, *inter alia*:

> . . . that it is the policy of the United States to establish, in conjunction and in co-operation with other countries, as expeditiously as practicable a commercial communications satellite system, as part of an improved global communications network, which will be responsive to public needs from national objectives, which will serve the communication needs of the United States and other countries, and which will contribute to world peace and understanding.

The establishment of INTELSAT followed in 1964, led by the USA which was joined by ten other nations under an interim arrangement (Agreement Establishing Interim Arrangements for a Global Commercial Communications Satellite system and the related Special Agreement 15:2 UST 1705 (1964)) reflecting the underlying principles of resolution 1721 (XVI) of the General Assembly of the United Nations that 'communication by means of satellites should be available to the nations of the world as soon as practicable on a global and non-discriminatory basis' (see Chapter 1, para 1.32). Its membership now consists of over 122 countries including all the EU member states and all the EFTA countries. Over 175 nations currently use INTELSAT satellites. INTELSAT provides almost two-thirds of the world's public international telecommunication services. It currently has 24 satellites in orbit with another 9 on order.

4.6   INTELSAT is presently constituted by two definitive international instruments: the Agreement (Agreement Relating to the

International Telecommunications Satellite Organisation 'INTEL-SAT') and the Operating Agreement (Operating Agreement relating to the International Telecommunications Satellite Organisation 'IN-TELSAT'). Both documents were signed on 20 August 1971 and entered into force on 12 February 1973. The parties to the INTELSAT Agreement are sovereign states (the 'parties') and the Operating Agreement is signed either by governments or by their designated public or private telecommunications entities (the 'signatories').

INTELSAT's purpose is to 'continue and carry forward on a definitive basis the design, development, construction, establishment, operation and maintenance of the space segment of the global commercial telecommunications satellite system' (INTELSAT Agreement, art II(*a*)). INTELSAT earth stations are owned and operated by the local entities, such as PTOs, but INTELSAT formulates the detailed specifications and operating rules. The IN-TELSAT space segment is made available to other domestic public telecommunications services on a non-discriminatory basis, so long as INTELSAT's main objective is not impaired (INTELSAT Agreement, art XIV).

Members of INTELSAT accept some restrictions when joining IN-TELSAT. Before establishing their own satellite facilities, the parties must undertake extensive consultation procedures with INTELSAT. These are the so-called co-ordination procedures, which are discussed *below* in paras 4.21 and 4.22.

INTELSAT's structure

4.7 Pursuant to art VI of the INTELSAT Agreement, INTELSAT is organised into four distinct parts or organs: the Assembly of Parties; the Meeting of Signatories; the Board of Governors and an Executive Organ responsible to the Board of Governors.

The Assembly of Parties consists, as its name implies, of the parties to the INTELSAT Agreement, and is the supreme organ of IN-TELSAT (INTELSAT Agreement, art VII).

The Meeting of Signatories consists of the signatories to the Operating Agreement. It meets annually and considers commercial matters of interest to the signatories as investors in the INTELSAT system (INTELSAT Agreement, art VIII).

INTELSAT is managed by the Board of Governors. The Board of Governors meets at least four times a year and has responsibility for the 'design, development, construction, establishment, operation and maintenance of the INTELSAT space segment' (INTELSAT Agreement, art X). It is made up of a governor from each signatory that has a minimum investment share in INTELSAT (ie the signatories who are the major users of INTELSAT capacity). Finally, there is the Executive Organ which is headed by the Director General (INTELSAT Agreement, art XI).

4.8 The INTELSAT Agreement also sets out, *inter alia*, rules on the following:

(*a*) the scope of INTELSAT activities (art III);

(*b*) procurement of satellites (art XIII);

(*c*) co-ordination (both economic and technical) of other satellite systems (art XIV) (see paras 4.21 and 4.22 for a discussion of these co-ordination procedures);

(*d*) the withdrawal of a party or signatory from INTELSAT (art XVI); and

(*e*) the settlement of disputes between the parties (art XVIII).

The Operating Agreement sets forth, as its name implies, rules regarding more operational matters of day-to-day importance including the following:

(*a*) the ceiling on the capital contributions of the signatories (art 5);

(*b*) the financial adjustments between the signatories (art 7);

(*c*) utilisation charges and revenues (art 8);

(*d*) paying due consideration to the relevant regulations, recommendations and procedures of the ITU's constituent bodies (art 13);

(*e*) applications for approval of earth station to utilise the INTELSAT space segment (art 14);

(*f*) the procedure for allotment of space segment capacity (art 15);

(*g*) settlement of disputes (art 20); and

(*h*) withdrawal of a signatory from INTELSAT (art 21).

4.9 There is provision in art XVII of the INTELSAT Agreement for any party to propose amendments to the agreement and in art 22 of the Operating Agreement for amendments to be made to it in response to proposals by any signatory, the Assembly of Parties or the Board of Governors.

As regards amendment of the INTELSAT Agreement itself, any party may propose an amendment and submit it to the Executive Organ which then distributes it to all parties and signatories. The Assembly of Parties must consider the proposed amendment at its first ordinary meeting following the distribution (or at an extraordinary meeting, if convened), provided that the distribution is at least 90 days before the meeting. The Assembly of Parties then makes a decision and, if approved, the amendment enters into force 90 days after the depository (the government of the USA) has received notice of approval, acceptance or ratification of the amendment from either:

(*a*)   two-thirds of the parties or their designated signatories who, at the date of approval held at least two-thirds of the total investment shares; or

(*b*)   85 per cent of the total number of parties at the date of approval regardless of investment shares.

In November 1994, the Assembly of Parties decided to delete the provision in Art XVII that an amendment shall not enter into force less than eight months nor more than 18 months after the date it has been approved by the Assembly of Parties. This amendment is awaiting ratification. It will streamline the process for amendments to the constitutive documents.

4.10   As regards amendment of the Operating Agreement, any signatory, the Assembly of Parties or the Board of Governors may propose amendments, which must be submitted to the Executive which must then distribute them to all parties and signatories. The Meeting of Signatories must then consider the proposed amendment at its first ordinary meeting following its distribution (or earlier at an extraordinary meeting, if convened) provided that the distribution is at least 90 days beforehand. An amendment that has been approved by the Meeting of Signatories shall enter into force after the depository has received notice of approval of the amendment from either:

(*a*)   two-thirds of the signatories who, at the date of approval by the Meeting of Signatories, held at least two-thirds of the total investment shares; or

(*b*)   85 per cent of the total number of signatories at the date of the approval by the Meeting of Signatories regardless of investment share.

The amendment then enters into force 90 days after the depository has notified the signatories that it has received the appropriate approval. As with the Convention, the Meeting of Signatories in April 1995 decided to remove the rule in art 22 of the Operating Agreement that an amendment shall not enter into force later than 18 months after the date of approval by the Meeting of Signatories.

INTELSAT's space segment

4.11   INTELSAT is a major supplier of international communications services including telephony, television, data, videoconferencing, telex and facsimile. Its global satellite network is used by countries worldwide for international communications and by a number of countries for domestic communications. A large proportion of all international telephone calls and trans-oceanic television transmissions are carried by the INTELSAT system.

INTELSAT may, on request and under appropriate terms and conditions, provide satellites or associated facilities separate from the INTELSAT space segment for certain specialised purposes, provided that the efficient and economic operation of the INTELSAT space segment is not unfavourably affected in any way (INTELSAT Agreement, art III(*e*)). Though the main purpose of INTELSAT is to provide international public telecommunication services, its facilities are also to be made available for domestic public telecommunication services on a non-discriminatory basis, so long as its ability to achieve its prime objective is not impaired (INTELSAT Agreement, art III(*c*)). The INTELSAT facilities may also be used for other non-military 'specialised telecommunications services' which are not public telecommunication services, provided that the public services are not thereby adversely affected and there are no unfavourable effects on the provision of public telecommunication services and satisfactory technical arrangements are made (INTELSAT Agreement, art III(*d*); see also art XIV on co-ordination of other space segments and the discussion contained in paras 4.21 and 4.22 of this chapter).

4.12   The Operating Agreement governs the way that signatories proceed to allot INTELSAT space segment capacity in the following terms:

> . . . [a]ny application for allotment of INTELSAT space segment capacity shall be submitted to INTELSAT by a Signatory or, in the case of a territory not under the jurisdiction of a Party, by a duly authorised telecommunications entity. (INTELSAT Operating Agreement, art 15(*a*).)

The Board of Governors is responsible for adopting criteria and procedures for the approval of earth stations for access to and utilisation of the INTELSAT space segment. The signatories must ensure that any allotment of space segment capacity to any applicant complies with these terms and conditions. Any entity wishing to use an earth station in connection with the INTELSAT space segment must submit an application for approval of that station to INTELSAT. The actual approval must be given by the signatory in whose territory the earth station is to be used. That signatory is then responsible for the compliance of that earth station with INTELSAT's rules and regulations. In Europe, ETSI deals with the specifications for usage with INTELSAT (see Chapter 5, para 5.93).

4.13   INTELSAT's charges for the use of its space segment by its signatories are fixed by the Board of Governors guided by such general rules as may be established by the Meeting of Signatories. Such charges are set with the objective of covering the operation, maintenance and administration costs of INTELSAT, the provision of such 'operating funds' as the Board of Governors may determine to be necessary, the amortisation of signatories' investments and compensation for use of the capital of the signatories (INTELSAT Operating Agreement, art 8).

Recent developments in respect of access to INTELSAT space segment are examined in para 4.44 *et seq below*.

EUTELSAT

EUTELSAT general description and purpose

4.14   The origins of EUTELSAT date back to the authorities given by the European Space Agency (ESA) in 1977. On 13 May 1977 17 European PTTs signed the interim EUTELSAT Agreement, which was modelled on that of INTELSAT. EUTELSAT was permanently established by signature of the EUTELSAT Convention (Convention establishing the European Telecommunications Satellite Organisation, 'EUTELSAT', current version entered into force 1 September 1985), and Operating Agreement (Operating Agreement relating to the European Telecommunications Satellite Organisation, EUTELSAT, current version entered into force 1 September 1985). EUTELSAT's Convention was entered into by parties (being sovereign states) and its Operating Agreement is entered into by signatories (being states or their designated telecommunications entities). There are currently 44 member countries of EUTELSAT including all the EU member states and countries which have entered into co-operation agreements with the EU.

EUTELSAT's main objective is constructing, establishing, operating and maintaining the European space segment and providing the space segment required for international public telecommunication services in Europe (EUTELSAT Convention, art III(*a*)). As with INTELSAT, the EUTELSAT Convention provides that as long as the ability of EUTELSAT to achieve its main objective is not impaired, EUTELSAT space segment may also be made available for other domestic or international public telecommunication services (EU-TELSAT Convention, art III(*c*)). In the implementation of its activities, EUTELSAT applies the principle of 'non-discrimination as between Signatories' (EUTELSAT Convention, art III(*d*)).

Likewise, EUTELSAT's space segment capacity may be used for other non-military specialised telecommunication services with the same proviso as with INTELSAT (EUTELSAT Convention, art III(*e*)).

EUTELSAT's structure

4.15   EUTELSAT is structurally similar to INTELSAT, having an Assembly of Parties (composed of all the parties), Board of Signatories (amalgamating the roles of INTELSAT's Meeting of Signatories and Board of Governors) and an Executive, headed by a Director General (EUTELSAT Convention, art VI). In general terms, these organs meet on a basis similar to those of INTELSAT.

The Convention also sets out rules on, *inter alia*, the following:

(*a*)   the scope of EUTELSAT activities (art III);

(*b*)   the composition, procedure and functions of the Assembly of Parties (arts VIII and IX);

(*c*)   the composition, procedure and functions of the Board of Signatories (arts X–XII);

(*d*)   the Executive (art XIII);

(*e*)   procurement (art XIV);

(*f*)   the rights and obligations of the parties and signatories (art XV);

(*g*)   the co-ordination (both economic and technical) of other satellite systems (art XVI);

(*h*)   the withdrawal and suspension of parties or signatories (art XVIII); and

(*i*)   the settlement of disputes (art XX).

4.16   The Operating Agreement sets forth regulations covering the following areas, *inter alia*:

(*a*)   the capital contributions of signatories (art 4);

(*b*)   the capital ceiling on contribution of the signatories (art 5);

(*c*)   the investment shares of signatories (art 6);

(*d*)   the utilisation charges and their determination (art 8);

(*e*)   the application of EUTELSAT's revenues (art 9);

(*f*)   the requirement that EUTELSAT take account of the relevant recommendations of the Conférence Européenne des Administrations des Postes et des Télécommunications (CEPT) (art 14);

(*g*)   procurement (art 17); and

(*h*)   the settlement of disputes (art 20).

There is provision in art XIX of the Convention for any party to propose amendments to the Convention and there is provision in art 22 of the Operating Agreement for amendments to be made to it in response to proposals by any signatory or by the Assembly of Parties. The amendment procedures are similar to those of INTELSAT (see para 4.9 *above*). At the EUTELSAT Assembly of Parties meeting in May 1995, similar modifications were made to these procedures as for INTELSAT.

EUTELSAT's space segment

4.17   EUTELSAT operates satellites for fixed and mobile communications. EUTELSAT satellites are used for telephony, EBU Eurovision transmissions, television and radio distribution to cable network head-ends and domestic reception systems, business communications and the Euteltracs land mobile service.

Article XII of the EUTELSAT Convention provides that one of the functions of the Board of Signatories is to adopt terms and conditions governing the allotment of EUTELSAT space segment capacity and to establish terms and conditions for access to the EUTELSAT space segment by telecommunications entities which are not under the jurisdiction of a party.

Allotment of space segment capacity by signatories is dealt with in art 16 of the Operating Agreement. Applications for allotment of EUTELSAT space segment capacity may be submitted only by signatories or, in the case of a territory not under the jurisdiction of a party, by a duly authorised telecommunications entity. The Board of Signatories will authorise allotment of space segment capacity in accordance with the terms and conditions established by it under the Convention.

Each entity to which an allotment is made is responsible for compliance with all the terms and conditions set by EUTELSAT for such allotment except where the signatory has assumed such responsibility.

Articles 15 and 14, respectively, of EUTELSAT and INTELSAT's Operating Agreements make similar provision in respect of earth station approvals (applications for approval to be made by signatories and compliance being the responsibility of the signatory in each respective territory—see Chapter 5, para 5.93 with regard to the work of ETSI). As to utilisation charges, arts 8 of both Operating Agreements are also very similar and provide for such charges to be fixed by the Board of Signatories (in EUTELSAT's case and the Board of Governors in INTELSAT's case).

Recent developments in respect of access to EUTELSAT space segment are examined in para 4.50 *et seq below.*

INMARSAT

INMARSAT general description and purpose

4.18   The Convention (Convention on the International Maritime Satellite Organisation (INMARSAT)) and Operating Agreement (Operating Agreement on the International Maritime Satellite Organisation (INMARSAT)) establishing INMARSAT entered into force on 16 July 1979. Membership of INMARSAT is open to all nations. At present, 79 countries including the USA and all member states of the EU (apart from the Republic of Ireland, Austria and Luxembourg) and EFTA are members. Although originally established to provide maritime services, INMARSAT now provides global satellite communications at sea, in the air and on land. It provides a wide variety of services for commercial and safety applications, including telephony, telex, fax and data, connections for maritime applications, flight data, voice and data, automatic position and status reporting, fleet management for land transport, and emergency communications in disaster situations. INMARSAT uses its own INMARSAT-2 satellites and leases capacity on a number of others, to provide a global network, configured according to four regions (Atlantic (N), Atlantic (E), Indian and Pacific). It has contracted for an INMARSAT-3 series of four larger satellites, the first of which was launched in 1994, and is currently investigating satellite systems for the 21st century under its Project 21 initiative. (For more information about INMARSAT see *Facts about INMARSAT*, a fact sheet updated regularly by INMARSAT.)

In December 1994, INMARSAT's Assembly passed a resolution to modify the Convention and Operating Agreement so as to change its name from the International Maritime Satellite Organisation (INMARSAT) to the International Mobile Satellite Organisation (Inmarsat).

Inmarsat's structure

4.19   The Inmarsat Convention was entered into between the various nations party to it, being the 'parties' and together forming the 'Assembly' (the current versions of the Convention and Operating Agreement were last amended in 1989). The Inmarsat Parties appoint signatories who are also the parties to the Operating Agreement. Pursuant to art 13 of the Convention, the main decision-making body of Inmarsat is the Council which is made up of the 18 signatories holding the largest investment shares and four other signatories elected by all the signatories. Inmarsat also has an Assembly (Inmarsat Convention, art 10) and an executive organ headed by a Director General (Inmarsat Convention, art 10).

The Inmarsat Convention sets out detailed rules covering similar areas to those covered by the EUTELSAT Convention and the INTELSAT Agreement. According to art 1(*c*) of the Inmarsat Convention, a signatory to the Convention can be either a party, which means a state in respect of which the Convention has entered into force, or a competent entity designated in accordance with art 2(3) subject to the jurisdiction of that state. In this case relations between the party and the signatory are governed by the applicable domestic law. The party must provide guidance and instructions to ensure that the signatory fulfils its responsibilities. A party is not liable for obligations arising under the Operating Agreement, but the party is responsible for ensuring that the signatory does not violate obligations which the party has accepted under the Convention or related international agreements (Inmarsat Convention, art 4(*c*)).

Article 7 of the Inmarsat Convention relates to access to space segment, and art 8 deals with co-ordination procedures. Article 34 provides for amendment of the Convention and art XVIII of the Operating Agreement deals with amendment of the Operating Agreement (the procedures for amendments of the Inmarsat Convention and Operating Agreement set out in art 34 of the Convention and art XVIII of the Operating Agreement are very similar to the procedures in the INTELSAT Agreement and EUTELSAT Convention and the INTELSAT and EUTELSAT Operating Agreements).

Inmarsat's space segment

4.20   Article 7(1) of the Inmarsat Convention states that the Inmarsat space segment is open for use by ships and aircraft of all nations and by mobile earth stations on land on conditions to be determined by the Council. Access is also permitted for land-based earth stations located on structures operating in the marine environment other than ships.

Allotment of space segment capacity is achieved, as with INTELSAT and EUTELSAT, by submission to the organisation of an application to use the space segment by a signatory or, in the case of a territory not under the jurisdiction of another party, by an authorised telecommunications entity. The signatory in question is then responsible for compliance by the user of such space segment with Inmarsat's rules and regulations. The regime for the application of approval of earth stations is similar to that of INTELSAT and EUTELSAT (art 14 of INTELSAT's Operating Agreement and art 15 of EUTELSAT's Operating Agreement, see paras 4.12 and 4.17, *above*). Pursuant to art 19 of the Convention, utilisation charges are established by the Council.

Recent developments in respect of access to Inmarsat space segment are examined in para 4.54 *below*.

Co-ordination procedures

4.21   Reference has been made to the ISOs' co-ordination proce-dures. Some background is needed to set in context the changes which are now being made in the area to meet some regulatory and other concerns about potentially anti-competitive practices by the ISOs.

As noted above in the introductory remarks to this chapter (see para 4.1), there are a number of privately owned satellite operators of satellite systems, such as ASTRA or PanAmSat, which are independent of the ISOs. The EUTELSAT and Inmarsat Conven-tions and the INTELSAT Agreement all contain provisions which prescribe procedures for co-ordination by any party or signatory, which proposes to establish a system separate from the space segment provided by the relevant ISO (see Inmarsat Convention, art 8.1, EUTELSAT Convention, art XVI(*a*) and (*b*), and INTELSAT Agreement, art XIV(*c*) and (*d*)). All these procedures are broadly similar, involving 'economic co-ordination', based on the concept of potential 'significant economic harm' to the ISO's own system, and 'technical co-ordination' based on the concept of technical compati-bility with the relevant ISO's own usage of space segment and radio frequency spectrum. This is obviously consistent with the reasoning of the International Telecommunication Union (ITU) and the Radio Regulations (RRs) that new services should not be introduced if they will cause 'harmful interference'—see Chapter 1, para 1.4, Chapter 2, para 2.2 and Chapter 3, para 3.1.

4.22   For example, the EUTELSAT Convention provides in art XVI that:

(*a*)   Any Party or Signatory which intends, or becomes aware that any person within the jurisdiction of that Party intends, in-dividually or jointly, to establish, acquire or utilize space seg-ment equipment separate from the EUTELSAT Space Segment in order to meet the requirements of international public tele-communications services within the EUTELSAT Space Segment service area to provide services in accordance with paragraphs (*a*) and (*b*) of Article III of the Convention shall, before such establishment, acquisition or utilization, furnish all relevant in-formation to the Assembly of Parties through the Board of Signatories which shall establish whether there is likely to be any *significant economic harm* to EUTELSAT. The Board of Signatories shall submit its report and conclusions to the Assembly of Par-ties. The Assembly of Parties shall give its views within six months from the start of the foregoing procedure. An extraordinary meeting of the Assembly of Parties may be convened for this purpose.

(b)   The Board of Signatories shall draft and submit to the Assembly of Parties, as a matter of priority, the guidelines to be considered by any party or Signatory which intends, or becomes aware that any person within the jurisdiction of the Party intends, individually or jointly, to establish space segment equipment separate from the EUTELSAT Space Segment in order to meet its requirements for domestic or international public or specialized telecommunications services, *to ensure technical compatibility of such separate equipment* and its operation with the use of the radiofrequency spectrum and orbital space by an existing or planned EUTELSAT Space Segment. (Emphasis added.)

In both cases, detailed information is required to be furnished by the party/signatory intending to introduce such new services. With regard to 'economic harm', the information required includes material that could in other circumstances be regarded at the very least as 'commercially sensitive' by the proposed service provider. Information that can be required with regard to technical co-ordination can be very detailed.

While one cannot disagree that there is a need for new systems to be technically compatible (and presumably avoid harmful interference), it is not difficult to appreciate that lengthy technical co-ordination of potential competitors to an ISO may be in the interest of the ISO (by delaying the introduction of any new competitive services). Such issues have caught the attention of a number of regulators which, for the purpose of this book, can be usefully confined to the European Commission and OFTEL in the UK. This has now resulted in certain of the ISOs addressing the 'co-ordination' problem (see paras 4.44 and 4.50 *below*).

Legal and regulatory issues concerning satellite services

4.23   The 1990 Satellite Paper, *Towards Europe-wide systems and services—Green Paper on a common approach in the field of satellite communications in the European Community* (COM(90) 490) recognised the implications of the dramatic changes due to new technologies, particularly in the area of earth stations, on increasing the diversification of satellite services and service providers. This, in turn, has raised important questions relating to competition policy as an increasing number of satellite service providers seek to compete with existing providers of 'traditional' satellite services. In the 1990 Satellite Paper, the Commission foresaw that:

> ... [w]hile traditional telephony services and entertainment broadcast services still account for 90% of satellite communications revenues in the Community, the new business services such as point-to-multipoint one-way and interactive two-way systems and the satellite news gathering (SNG) systems—the collection of news and data from multiple points—show major growth potential if regulatory conditions are adjusted to allow their development. (1990 Satellite Paper (English Version), p 35.)

Two aspects of this competition, namely competition in the earth segment and in the space segment, are examined next.

4.24   As to the earth segment, advances in earth station equipment, particularly in developing more efficient antennae and more sensitive receivers, have led to a dramatic decrease in their size and cost, be it for telephony, television distribution or business communications. Such developments have led, in particular, to the emergence of VSATs. These are small earth stations, usually with an antenna diameter below 3.5 metres, which can be installed at the user's own premises and used for one-way or two-way voice and data communications. In addition, whereas direct broadcasting by satellite was originally capable of being delivered only from high powered Direct Broadcasting Satellites (DBS), due to the increased sensitivity of receivers this can now be delivered from medium power satellites such as ASTRA and EUTELSAT directly to domestic receiving dishes with diameters as low as 60 cm. As noted in Chapter 1, para 1.18, this has led to a blurring of the distinction between Broadcasting Satellite Services (BSS) and Fixed Satellite Services (FSS) satellites.

With these technological advances in earth station equipment, a variety of new services become available, mostly directed at specific large businesses rather than the general public, and offering a range of services including: special voice and data services; videoconferencing and satellite news gathering (SNG). This has naturally led to the growth in satellite business service providers who provide value added services using space segment leased from one of the satellite operators on private leased VSAT networks. The 1990 Satellite Paper concluded that:

. . . [t]he introduction/expansion of major new satellite service lines—such as wide-area VSAT networks to serve the European-wide communications requirements of specific user groups—will depend on the development of a regulatory framework which will allow it to happen on a Europe-wide basis. (1990 Satellite Paper (English version), p 55.)

In Europe, the level of liberalisation of such services differs between different countries.

4.25   The potential for the development of such services and service providers in competition with services provided by the PTOs is the basis for a debate concerning the question of competition in this sector and was the subject of particular attention by the European Commission in the 1990 Satellite Paper. Some of the main points of contention concern the ISOs, in particular their co-ordination procedures (both economic and technical) and the provision of access to their space segment generally.

As regards co-ordination, as discussed at para 4.21 *above*, the procedures relating to 'significant economic harm' may be seen as a potential limitation on competition which could prevent other space segment providers from entering the market. As currently drafted, the economic co-ordination and harm provisions of the ISOs' constituent instruments give power to the ISOs to decide whether potential competitors are likely to provide an unacceptable level of competition to the services provided by the ISOs, that is, to cause 'any significant economic harm to [the ISO]' and if the Assembly of Parties decided that it would, co-ordination can be refused (see, eg, the EUTELSAT Convention, art XVI).

4.26   In the 1990 Satellite Paper, the Commission pointed out that the current regulation of the space segment reflects the situation which existed in the 60s and 70s, when the ISOs were created, where the only economically and technically feasible application of satellite communications was as additional transmission paths to carry international or national long-distance traffic for telecommunication organisations. The structure of the ISOs was that the state-owned PTTs were designated as signatories to the Operating Agreements and were thus in the delicate situation, over the question of access to space segment, of being referee and player at the same time. Over time, some parties have, to a greater or lesser extent, liberalised their telecommunications regimes—in many instances the PTTs have been replaced by PTOs, some of which, such as BT, have been privatised, others of which, such as France Télécom, have been corporatised with a view to privatisation in the medium term.

4.27   The European PTOs have been the subject of close scrutiny by the Commission (which is discussed in more detail in Chapter 5). Suffice it to say that one principal concern of the Commission was to ensure that there was a separation of operational and regulatory functions once the PTT was reformed and corporatised/privatised. The lack of separation between regulatory and operational functions can lead to growing conflicts of interest. The Commission stated that:

> ... in order to ensure that conflicts of interest do not lead to legal uncertainty, the principle of the separation of regulatory and operational functions requires that the independent regulatory authorities of the Member States rather than the telecommunications organisations decide about the authorisation of competing space segment providers, taking account of Community Law. In cases of doubt, it will be for the Commission to decide whether the conditions of Article 90(2) are fulfilled and competition from a competing space segment provider could be limited. (1990 Satellite Paper (English Version), p 106.)

The reference to art 90(2) of the Treaty of Rome should be noted, as it is an indication of the Commission's concern about potentially anti-competitive practices and of the powers the Commission could use to overcome those concerns.

To bring the regulation of access to and provision of space segment in line with general EU telecommunications policy, the 1990 Satellite Paper emphasised the following consistent 'ONP' (open network provision) principles (see, eg, Chapter 5, para 5.45):

- the principle of open and efficient access, based on objective, transparent and non-discriminatory procedures;

- clear separation of regulatory and operational functions;

- full application of the provisions of the Treaty, in particular competition rules.

(1990 Satellite Paper (English version), p 101.)

The Commission went on to propose that: tariffs should be cost-oriented; the co-ordination procedures of the ISOs should be reviewed and rendered less cumbersome; there should be more open access; users could be given direct access to space segment capacity, including facilities up-link subject to compliance with licensing conditions; and all providers could be given the right to market space segment capacity directly to users. (A useful review of the Commission's position is contained in pp 130–133 of the 1990 Satellite Paper, English version.)

4.28   In the 1990 Satellite Paper, the Commission deals with the question of whether or not the ISO constituent instruments are consistent with the member states' obligations under art 5 in conjunction with arts 59, 85, 86 and 90 of the Treaty of Rome. The Commission believes that the provisions of the ISOs' constituent instruments do not represent essential requirements for the protection of the public interest, which might warrant limiting the freedom to provide services under art 59 of the Treaty, since the provisions in question are of an economic nature. The Commission states that the ISO constituent instruments will have to be applied in conformity with the requirements of the Treaty of Rome competition rules which:

> . . . means that the basic decision of the Treaty of Rome to institute a system of undistorted competition and guarantee the freedom to provide services has to be respected by the Member States in applying these provisions. In particular, a *systematic rejection* of competing providers of space segment or a *systematic limitation* of their capability to compete with satellite organisations would not be in conformity with Member States' obligations under Articles 5 and 90 in conjunction with Articles 59, 85 and 86 of the Treaty. (1990 Satellite Paper (English Version), p 105.)

In brief, the Commission in the 1990 Satellite Paper emphasises that member states should ensure objective, transparent and non-discriminatory procedures, in particular with regard to the procedures concerning co-ordination under the RRs and administered by the Radio Regulations Board (RRB), and full separation of regulatory and operational functions as regards access to the orbital resource for the provision of space segment.

4.29   The 1990 Satellite Paper goes on to state that the best solution to avoid distortion of competition and to allow full use and best allocation of the existing space segment would seem to be to give users direct access to space segment capacity and give space segment providers the right to market space segment capacity directly to users. Member states should also facilitate more open access to the space segment provided by the ISOs, via the signatories, and pay special attention to the implementation of the principle of cost-orientation of tariffs.

The Commission believes that, to create a favourable environment for the development of satellite policy within the EU, a number of adjustments need to be made within the ISOs and in particular EUTELSAT. While the Commission recognised that the member states' percentages within both INTELSAT and Inmarsat were much smaller than in EUTELSAT, it noted that 'Member States play an influential role in these global satellite organisations' and therefore requested that steps be taken to bring the obligations of the member states within those organisations into line with the member states' obligations under the Treaty of Rome (see 1990 Satellite Paper (English version), p 139).

4.30   Since the 1990 Satellite Paper, the Commission has been active in implementing the policies set out in it. Many of these are dealt with in detail in Chapter 5 *below*, but it is useful to note here that, in the context of access to ISO space segment, the Commission issued a communication to the Council and the European Parliament in June 1994 (COM (94) 210 final, 10 June 1994) stating that it intended to use all the available powers under the EU competition rules to eliminate restrictions relating to access, and called for steps to be taken to liberalise fully the arrangements for access to space segment of the ISOs. This position was adopted by the EU Council (Council Resolution 94/C 379/04 of 22 December 1994 on *Further development of the Community's satellite communications policy, especially with regard to the provision of, and access to, space segment capacity*), which called on member states to provide non-discriminatory access to space segment capacity at a national level and for member states to collaborate closely in the reforms being considered by the ISOs and in managing orbital frequency resources.

Another important step, following the 1990 Satellite Paper, to deal with one of the major obstacles to increased competition and access to ISO space segment capacity, was Directive 94/46/EC on the Liberalisation of Satellite Services and Equipment of 13 October 1994. This directive requires member states to abolish all 'special and exclusive' rights which have the effect of restricting the ability of other undertakings from entering the market. Member states are required to ensure that any fees imposed on providers of services as part of authorisation procedures be based on objective, non-discriminatory criteria; 'any regulatory prohibitions or restrictions on the offer of space segment capacity to any authorised satellite earth station network operator' be abolished; and to authorise 'any space segment supplier within their territory to verify that the satellite earth station network for use in connection with the space segment of the supplier in question is in conformity with the published conditions for access to its space segment' (art 2(6)(*b*) of the directive).

4.31   However, it must be recognised that amendment to the constituent instruments of the ISOs is not straightforward. Reference has been made *above* (see paras 4.9, 4.10 and 4.16) to the steps required to be taken with regard to formal amendment of these instruments, which are treaties. As far as the member states are concerned, arts 5 and 234 of the Treaty of Rome pose interesting questions for them with regard to their Treaty obligations and any inconsistency between those obligations and their ISO obligations. This adds a dimension wider than the EU (assuming all member states agree with the Commission's programme) which brings into play international political and bureaucratic dimensions, all of which bodes badly for the speedy resolution of these issues. Nevertheless, the position of the Commission and of other European regulators is having its effect on the reform moves within the ISOs (see para 4.44 *et seq below*).

To take one example, the desirability of amendment of the ISO constituent instruments expressed by the Commission has been echoed by others, such as the former UK Director-General of Telecommunications, Sir Bryan Carsberg. In *Review of British Telecom's Arrangements for the Provision of Space Segment*, he noted:

> 9.   A promising way to eliminate the potential conflict of interest [between the regulatory and operational side of British Telecom] would be for the executive organs of the satellite consortia to deal directly with all users of space segment in those countries which had liberalised the provision of satellite services. However, this is not something which the UK can bring about unilaterally as it would require amendments to the international treaties. The use of satellites for innovative services is still in its infancy in Europe. But we can expect significant developments as competition in the UK and elsewhere stimulates innovative satellite services and as EC proposals stemming from the Commission's [1987] Green Paper lead to liberalisation throughout the Community. As competition grows in this way there is bound to be increasing pressure, not only in the UK but also elsewhere, to look again at the provisions of the Operating Agreements which prevent users of space segment dealing directly with the organisations. I believe that when a suitable opportunity arises and taking account of the development of liberalisation elsewhere, the UK Government should encourage the amendment of the relevant instruments.

10.   Until the Operating Agreements can be amended to permit or require INTELSAT and EUTELSAT to deal directly with those seeking to make use of space segment, I need to ensure that the Signatory function in the UK is carried out in a way which prevents the potential conflict of interest from distorting competition. I have therefore examined thoroughly the way that BT fulfils its role as Signatory and as a result BT has introduced new arrangements. If these arrangements are strictly adhered to, BT's competitors should not be at a disadvantage in using space segment provided by the international consortia. (Statement of 28 November 1989 of Sir Bryan Carsberg, Director-General of Telecommunications in the UK; *Review of British Telecom's Arrangements for the Provision of Space Segment*, p 4.)

In the UK, therefore, where the commercial and regulatory functions were separated, following a consideration of the issue by the Office of Telecommunications in 1989, it became possible to deal with the Signatory Affairs Office (SAO), rather than with BT, the relevant signatory. Other Administrations have established, or are in the process of establishing, their own signatory affairs offices. Although this was the position in 1989, it should be noted that a long-awaited review of the SAO was published in July 1993 as a Consultative Document (*The Operation of BT's Signatory Affairs Office and Competition in the Satellite Service Sector* (OFTEL 12/93)). This was followed in February 1994 by an OFTEL statement (*The Future of the Signatory Affairs Office: Statement by the Director General of Telecommunications*), setting out proposals for the continued operation of the SAO (see para 4.55 *et seq below* and Chapter 6).

Competition law

4.32   In the wider context, the European Commission will keep a close eye on the development of competition in space and ground segment services. The competition guidelines of DG IV make this clear (see *Guidelines on the application of EEC competition rules in the telecommunications sector* (91/C233/02) pp 22–23 (OJ 6.9.91 C233)), as do two recent matters that have come before the Commission's competition law enforcement arm, DG IV. The first is the *ASTRA* case (Commission Decision of 23 December 1992 relating to a proceeding pursuant to art 85 of the Treaty of Rome (IV/32. 745–Astra) (93/50/EEC OJ 28.1.93 L20/23)). The second is *INTRAX* (Notice pursuant to art 19(3) of Council Regulation No 17 concerning a request for negative clearance or an exemption pursuant to art 85(3) of the Treaty of Rome (Case No IV 34–282–*Intrax*, OJ 28.4.93 C117/4)).

4.34   In *ASTRA*, the Commission decided that an agreement between SES and BT, under which the two companies co-operated in the joint provision of satellite distribution services to television companies, constituted an infringement of art 85(1) of the Treaty of Rome and did not qualify for exemption under art 85(3). The arrangement was terminated by the parties and later declared by the Commission to be contrary to its competition rules.

Under the agreement a 50/50 joint venture company, BT ASTRA, was set up. SES undertook to lease transponders to the joint venture company which, in turn, offered operators of UK-originated television programmes a packaged service consisting of a BT up-link in the UK and transponder space on ASTRA 1A. One of the principal reasons why the agreement was found to contravene art 85(1) was that customers who wished to transmit their programmes via the ASTRA 1A satellite were not given the choice of concluding separate contracts for, on the one hand, up-link services (ground segment) and, on the other, the lease of transponder capacity (space segment). In other words, the earth and space segment services were 'bundled'.

This case is the subject of an appeal by BT. Nevertheless, the decision is important and confirms the Commission's power to examine arrangements for co-operation between companies operating in the satellite sector for compatibility with the competition rules. Any agreement on satellite services may be examined critically, regardless of whether the satellite services are public or private sector offerings. However, where art 85(1) applies, the parties may apply for an exemption from that prohibition.

Also of significance in *ASTRA* was the Commission's decision to require BT and SES to allow those programme providers who had already signed long-term agreements with BT for the 'bundled' service, a four-month period in which to renegotiate or terminate those contracts. The Commission took the view that although the BT/SES joint venture had been terminated by the parties, the continued existence of these contracts for services could perpetuate the restrictive effects of the joint venture.

4.33   The second matter to come before the Commission relatively recently concerning competition policy in the satellite sector involves the *INTRAX* arrangement in respect of which an application was made for negative clearance or exemption under art 85(3) of a co-operation agreement in the field of SNG services. The co-operation agreement is between PTT Telecom BV (the EUTELSAT and INTELSAT signatory in The Netherlands) and Nederlands Omroepproduktie Bedrijf NV (NOB) (a provider of television facilities) and concerns the setting up of a joint venture SNG company called INTRAX.

In giving its consent (see OJ 28.4.93 C117/3) and clearing the arrangement, the Commission had to decide whether PTT Telecom BV's position as signatory would result in a *de facto* monopoly for INTRAX because competing SNG service providers would not have the benefit of the PTTs partnership. The Commission's reasoning was that:

(*a*)   the up-linking of signals to satellites was liberalised in the Netherlands in 1991 as far as SNG is concerned;

(*b*)   PTT Telecom BV assured the Commission that as signatory to the ISOs it will deal with INTRAX on the same footing as other companies;

(*c*)   with respect to space segment capacity, companies competing with INTRAX in the Netherlands will have access to EUTEL-SAT capacity via at least three EUTELSAT signatories, other than PTT Telecom (because of the multiple access arrangement referred to at para 4.53); and

(*d*)   they will have access to satellites belonging to organisations other than EUTELSAT.

The Commission's decision in response to the INTRAX application appears to demonstrate that the Commission will not automatically disapprove of arrangements between signatories or related companies.[3]

It is clear that the Commission will scrutinise the ISOs and, in particular, their signatories, as well as other space segment providers, to ensure that their practices comply with the competition laws of the Treaty of Rome.

4.35   Thus, in the current climate of liberalisation of telecommunications services around the world, the potentially anti-competitive provisions of the ISO constituent instruments are coming under closer scrutiny and criticism by users and regulators. This is particularly so because a signatory is often the PTO of the relevant party and, therefore, unless operational and regulatory functions are clearly separated, there is concern that commercially sensitive or confidential material may pass from the signatory/regulatory side of the operator to the commercial/operational side (see *above* at para

4.27). It is not possible here to examine this issue in detail, but a few points should be borne in mind when considering the separation of operational and regulatory functions in the ISOs. While the term 'undertaking' is not defined in the Treaty of Rome nor in the Commission's secondary legislation, the term has always been given a wide meaning by both the Commission and the European Court of Justice (ECJ).

4.36 State-owned corporations, bodies entrusted by the state with particular tasks and quasi-governmental bodies may all be 'undertakings' if they carry on economic or commercial activities related to the supply of goods and services. In *Sacchi* (case 155/73) [1974] ECR 409, the ECJ held that the Italian state television monopoly, RAI, was an entity the activities of which were subject to the prohibitions on discrimination in the Treaty of Rome. To the extent that these comprised economic activities they fell within art 90 of the treaty concerning public undertakings. The Commission relied on *Sacchi* in its decision in *Re German TV Films* (Commission Decision 89/536/EEC OJ 3.10.89 L284/36), when it found that German public television broadcasting organisations were undertakings for the purposes of art 85(1) of the Treaty of Rome, notwithstanding that they were charged with the task of providing programmes in the public interest. The Commission said that:

> ...this applies notwithstanding the fact that the ARD broadcasting organisations are public institutions charged under national law with the task of providing programmes in the public interest. The functional concept of undertaking in Article 85(1) covers any activity directed at trade in goods or services irrespective of the legal form of the undertaking and regardless of whether or not it is intended to earn profits. Accordingly, the Court of Justice ruled in [the *Sacchi* case] that public television broadcasting organisations are undertakings within the meaning of Article 85(1) in so far as they exercise separate activities of an economic nature. (*Re German TV Films* OJ 3.10.89 L284/36, para 38.)

4.37 In *Italian Republic* v *Commission of the European Communities* (case 41/83) [1985] ECR 873, Italy argued that the competition rules applied solely to the activities of business concerns carried out under private law and not to rule-making activities carried out pursuant to statute by a public body functioning in conformity with conditions laid down by central government. The ECJ held that the management by a nationalised industry of public telecommunications equipment and charging users a fee for the use of it amounted to a business activity which was subject to the obligations imposed by art 86 of the Treaty of Rome. It found that UK statute law empowered BT to establish the charges and conditions subject to which such services were offered and that, therefore, they performed the same function as contractual terms which were freely adopted by BT pursuant to the powers vested in it and without intervention on the part of the UK authorities. The ECJ said:

> It should be noted . . . that . . . despite BT's status as a nationalised industry, its management of public telecommunications equipment and its placing of such equipment at the disposal of users on payment of a fee do indeed amount to a business activity which as such is subject to the obligations imposed by Article 86 of the Treaty. (*Italian Republic* v *Commission of the European Communities* [1985] ECR 873, at para 18.)

The UK legislature did not predetermine the content of the charges and conditions, which were freely determined by BT. The ECJ held that, in such circumstances, the schemes must, therefore, be regarded as an integral part of BT's business activity. However, this case leaves open the question of whether BT's activities would still have been considered commercial had BT not been free itself to determine the fees and conditions.

4.38 *LTU Lufttransportunternehmen GmbH & Co KG* v *Eurocontrol* [1976] ECR 1541 (the *Eurocontrol* case) concerned the European Organisation for the Safety of Air Navigation (Eurocontrol), an international organisation established by treaty, and was a decision on the interpretation of the Convention of 27 September 1968 on Jurisdiction and the Enforcement of Judgments in Civil and Commercial Matters. The action concerned the recovery of charges payable by a person governed by private law to the international body governed by public law for the use of equipment and services provided by the international body where such use was obligatory and exclusive. The ECJ held that a judgment given in an action between a public authority, in this case Eurocontrol, and a person governed by private law, in which the public authority acted in the exercise of its powers, is excluded from the area of application of the convention on the basis that it is not a 'civil and commercial matter'.

This case was later relied upon in an action before the English courts (*Irish Aerospace (Belgium) NV* v *European Organisation for Safety of Air Navigators and Another* (1991) *The Times*, 18 July) in which it was decided that Eurocontrol, a regulatory body established by international convention performing the function of a public authority with the power to levy charges, was not thereby a commercial organisation and, therefore, was not subject to art 86 of the Treaty of Rome. The fact that Eurocontrol covered its expenses by levying charges did not convert its essentially regulatory activities into commercial ones. This is of interest in relation to the discussion relating to immunity from suit set out *below*.

Immunity from suit under English law

4.39   Each of the ISOs has immunities. For example, the UK's EUTELSAT (Immunities and Privileges) Order 1988 (SI No 1299), made under the International Organisations Act 1968, reflects art XVII of the EUTELSAT Convention. The order confers immunity from suit on EUTELSAT in respect of transactions effected in the exercise of its 'official activities', which are defined as the activities carried out by it in the framework of its objectives as defined in the EUTELSAT Convention. There are exceptions to this immunity, none of which is relevant here. Further, the organisation is granted immunity generally from search, restraint, requisition, seizure, confiscation, expropriation, sequestration or execution in relation to the EUTELSAT space segment and all other property of the organisation wherever it is located or by whomsoever held. The Director General and the Assembly of Parties may waive the immunity.

Representatives of parties, the Director General and staff members of EUTELSAT also enjoy certain immunities but these are not relevant for present purposes. The representatives of signatories enjoy immunity from suit and legal process in respect of acts done in the performance of their official functions. Their immunities may be waived by the government of the party or by the signatory of the party they represent. Immunity is withheld from representatives of the UK or the signatory designated by the UK.

4.40   The immunity of parties in the UK is regulated by the State Immunity Act 1978. The immunity of signatories may depend on whether they are departments of government. There is no immunity in respect of commercial transactions by undertakings. Signatories which are private (that is non-governmental) bodies have no immunity at all. The *Alpha Lyracom* case (referred to *below*) would support this. However, it is possible that, in certain circumstances, where signatories are acting as members of the Board of Signatories rather than as entities in their own right, they may seek to invoke the immunity of the EUTELSAT organisation.

If the Commission were to take proceedings against a signatory for recovery of a fine (imposed for a breach of EU competition law) in the relevant national courts (either after the ECJ found in favour of the Commission on an appeal, or in circumstances where the signatory may try and claim immunity from suit), the success of this argument would, of course, depend on national law. In the UK, it is possible (if the relevant circumstances pertained) that the courts might find that the signatory was indeed acting as part of EUTEL-SAT in the matter complained of and not in its own right and, therefore, accept the immunity plea. However, this would be applied very strictly and it would have to be clear beyond doubt that the circumstances related to the activities of the signatory solely as a component of the EUTELSAT organisation.

Therefore, the critical question in any proceeding against a signatory would be: was the action complained of carried out as part of the 'official activity' of EUTELSAT? That is a question of fact and law, which must be resolved in each particular case. It is thought that the ECJ and national courts would take a very strict view of what constitutes the 'official activity' of EUTELSAT or of any ISO.

4.41   Of relevance in this context is the *Alpha Lyracom* case (*Alpha Lyracom Space Communications Inc and others* v *Communication Satellite Corporation*, United States District Court, Southern District of New York, judgment dated 13 September 1990, at first instance and on appeal, United States Court of Appeal Second Circuit 946 F 2d 168; and *Alpha Lyracom Space Communications Inc and others* v *Communication Satellite Corporation*, United States District Court, Southern District of New York, judgment dated 30 March 1993) in the USA. Alpha Lyracom Space Communications Inc and others, as operators of the PanAmSat satellite system, have brought several actions against Communication Satellite Corporation (COMSAT), the US signatory to INTELSAT, basically claiming that it has acted to exclude them from the satellite business. The case has not been decided, but the interlocutory proceedings in which COMSAT sought to have the claims dismissed gives an interesting assessment of immunity of signatories.

Obviously, cases in the United States, especially interlocutory proceedings, are not binding on European courts. However, the approach of the US courts in the *Alpha Lyracom* cases is of relevance in the present context. In the particular matter, COMSAT moved the court to dismiss a complaint by Alpha Lyracom and sought to deny Alpha Lyracom's request that COMSAT give discovery. COMSAT argued that the complaint made by Alpha Lyracom failed:

(*a*)   to distinguish between COMSAT's signatory conduct and its common carrier role; and

(*b*)   to plead an anti-trust claim (and then went on to name five other grounds, which do not concern us here).

The court considered the fundamental issue of COMSAT's role as signatory versus its role as a common carrier. To make its point, COMSAT argued that the present action was very similar to a previous action which had been rejected for failing to distinguish between the two forms of conduct.

The court rejected COMSAT's contention:

> . . . that all of the actions alleged by the Plaintiffs (Alpha Lyracom) are either performed as a signatory or are so intertwined with its signatory duties that they are indistinguishable. (p 10, judgment of 30 March 1993.)

4.42   The court referred to the fact that Alpha Lyracom had amended their complaint so that they sought redress against COMSAT only in its role as common carrier and referred to the fact that Alpha Lyracom only needed to make reference, by way of a short statement of claim, to the anti-trust complaints. The court stated that it did not need to consider further the distinction between COMSAT's roles as common carrier and as INTELSAT signatory.

With regard to the second point, the anti-trust claim under US law, COMSAT had argued that:

> . . . a firm with monopoly power has no general duty to help its competitors, whether by holding a price umbrella over their heads or otherwise pulling its competitive punches. (p 14, judgment of 30 March 1993.)

It was held, however, that (under US law):

> COMSAT may not, however, exercise its monopoly power to maintain its monopoly (p 14, judgment of 30 March 1993).

It was then held that Alpha Lyracom had sufficiently pleaded their conspiracy claims on the anti-trust grounds against COMSAT and therefore declined to find for COMSAT on this point. Having dealt with the other points the court then ordered discovery to proceed.

While only in relation to a judgment on a motion to dismiss, the important feature of the decision is the clear statement rejecting the proposition that the fact that signatory duties and common carrier duties are intertwined should entitle COMSAT to immunity. (The corollary, of course, is that signatory duties are in themselves immune.)

As an epilogue, following the discovery process, the plaintiffs sought to amend their claim by adding 15 other INTELSAT signatories (and two parent companies) as defendants for conspiring with COMSAT to exclude the plaintiffs from the satellite business, again emphasising that the claim was against the relevant entities as common carriers, not as INTELSAT signatories. The request was refused on the basis of excessive delay (*Alpha Lyracom Space Communications Inc v Communications Satellite Corporation*, United States District Court for Southern District of New York, judgment dated 7 June 1994) and unfair prejudice to COMSAT. The judge made it clear that if the plaintiffs wished to pursue the other entities, they would have to file a new suit (which could not be consolidated with the existing case).

Bearing in mind those points regarding competition law and immunities from suit, it is convenient to consider what steps the ISOs are taking to reform themselves.

Recent changes by the ISOs

4.43 Criticism by the Commission and others, together with the policy statements and initiatives taken by the Commission, have generated momentum for change within the ISOs themselves. All the ISOs have taken or are taking steps to modify and modernise their 'economic harm' co-ordination procedures and the arrangements for non-signatory access to their space segment capacity. They are even considering a complete review of their structures with a view to becoming quasi-commercial operating companies. These steps are discussed in paras 4.44–4.52 *below*.

Before considering the action taken or considered by each of the ISOs with regard to access to their space segments, it is worth reviewing the issues common to all the ISOs that are of particular importance in resolving the 'direct access' problem and which have proved stumbling blocks to date:

(1) Earth station approval and allotment of space segment capacity: all applications for approval of an earth station to utilise the

ISOs' space segment and for access to space segment are made through the signatory in whose territory the earth station is, or will be, located (see, for example, arts 14 and 15 of the INTELSAT Operating Agreement).

(2)   Liability: the responsibility for ensuring compliance by the earth station with the rules and standards set out in the approval document for the earth station and for ensuring compliance with the terms and conditions for the allotment of space segment capacity lies with the signatory through whom the application was processed (ie the signatory might be liable for the default of the person who has obtained access).

(3)   Investment share: The investment share of a signatory in an ISO is calculated according to the volume of use by that signatory, including use by any entity obtaining access to space segment capacity through that signatory (see para 4.3 *above*). In other words obtaining access to ISO capacity by a non-signatory may generate a financial burden for the relevant signatory.

The ISOs have consistently made it clear that any alteration to the position in (1) must be coupled with a modification of the positions in (2) and (3).

INTELSAT

4.44   The INTELSAT parties are considering fundamental changes to their methods of operation, including changes to procedure to make it easier for signatories to authorise other entities to use INTELSAT facilities. Between March 1993 and September 1994, a series of decisions have been taken by the INTELSAT Board of Governors and the INTELSAT Assembly in an attempt to address both the co-ordination issue and the 'direct access' issue.

While any party may propose amendments to the INTELSAT Agreement, which must be submitted to the Executive Organ in accordance with the detailed provisions set out in art XVII of the INTELSAT Agreement (similar provisions governing the procedure for amending the Operating Agreement are set out in art 22), it is obviously difficult, particularly with the spread of membership—not just in terms of geography but also in terms of the level of telecommunications deregulation/liberalisation—to obtain the requisite agreement to amend the constituent instruments of IN-TELSAT. The steps that have been taken recently have the benefit of not requiring amendments to INTELSAT's constitutive documents (although formal constitutional changes may still be proposed in the future).

4.45 As regards 'economic' co-ordination, INTELSAT's procedures now differ according to whether or not the systems are connected to the PSN (see INTELSAT press release dated 6 November 1992). In cases where systems are not connected to the PSN, the Assembly has determined that no system shall be deemed to cause 'significant economic harm', although it should be noted that this decision has to be reviewed at each ordinary Assembly. For such economic co-ordination, the consulting party (that is, the party seeking co-ordination) or signatory provides complete technical information covering: network information such as orbital locations and tolerances, types of transmission for each type of service; details of earth to space transmissions such as frequency bands including those for space operations, radiation patterns for antennae, television parameters, EIRP figures (for a definition of EIRP see Chapter 1, para 1.20); details of space to earth transmissions such as frequency bands for each type of service including space operations, antenna gain patterns and television parameters. The consulting party or signatory also provides an identification of the traffic planned to be carried by the separate system which is included in INTELSAT's traffic database. The Board of Governors is authorised by the Assembly to determine, on the basis of this information, whether the proposed services are public switched or non-switched, and reports accordingly. The Board is not required to make such a finding in cases of requests for associations with previously concluded consultations where the Director General is authorised by the Assembly to make the determination.

4.46 Where systems are connected to the PSN, the Assembly has determined a threshold below which the use of a separate system would be automatically deemed not to cause significant economic harm. The present threshold (set in November 1994) is 8,000 equivalent 64 kbit/s circuits per satellite, connected to the PSN. This is part of a four- to six-year transition period during which a higher threshold will be set in 1996. It is the intent of the Assembly progressively to increase this threshold and to consider eliminating all economic harm considerations altogether at the end of the transitional period. In the cases of requests for association with previously concluded consultations, the Director General is authorised by the Assembly to make the determination. Any request for consultation concerning the proposed utilisation of a separate system above the threshold would be referred through the Board to the Assembly. Except for requests for consultation concerning the proposed utilisation of a separate system above the threshold, the Assembly has delegated authority to the Board to make findings in respect of the technical consultation requirements under art XIV.

The new procedure for economic co-ordination outlined *above*, including, where necessary, consideration by the Assembly, should be completed within six months of commencement. The procedure for technical co-ordination, however, remains as before.

4.47 With regard to direct access to space segment, the major stumbling block for INTELSAT has been the issue of signatories' liability for non-payment by entities who have obtained access through them and mis-operation of earth stations by such entities (see para 4.43 *above*).

With regard to these issues, the INTELSAT Board of Governors agreed at a meeting in March 1993 that direct access would be permitted on the following basis:

(1) Any signatory can authorise other entities to deal directly with INTELSAT.

(2) Such authorised entities will be held directly liable for non-payment of utilisation charges. INTELSAT management will examine creditworthiness and impose conditions where it deems this appropriate. The signatory will have no liability.

(3) If utilisation charges are not paid, additional service will be denied after 30 days, and all service suspended after 150 days.

(4) If requested, the signatory will not be liable for mis-operation of earth stations by the operator provided the relevant party assumes responsibility (but not financial liability) for operation of the earth stations.

4.48 In the most recent meeting of the Board concerning the 'direct access' issue, it was decided that INTELSAT, on the request of a signatory, would refrain from holding the designated signatory liable for payment of investment share financial adjustments and capital contributions attributable to the use of the INTELSAT system by its authorised entities. Instead, the INTELSAT management will deal directly with an authorised entity in connection with the billing and payment of capital contributions, repayments of capital, compensation for use of capital, and financial adjustments relating to investment share changes. The authorised users are to be primarily liable for such payments, and appropriate steps may be taken to obtain payment, including using the authorised entities' investment share as collateral. Only actual users of the INTELSAT system may be authorised by the signatory to invest; the investment may be withdrawn, while the entity is still a user, only with the signatory's agreement.

As a corollary to allowing authorised entities to invest in IN-TELSAT, it was also decided by the Board that authorised entities may be permitted by their signatories to participate in 'investment trading'. Under art 6(d) of the Operating Agreement, the signatories have always been able to swap investment shares, so that a signatory whose usage is substantial (and is therefore liable for a large investment share) may dispose of part of its investment share to another signatory who would like a greater investment in IN-TELSAT than its usage requires. Year-end investment trading between signatories has long been a feature of INTELSAT and there has traditionally been an excess of demand over supply. With the introduction of non-signatory entities as investors in INTELSAT, the system now in place provides for a first round of investment share trading restricted to signatories, followed by a second round open to all investors. It is understood from INTELSAT that some non-signatory entities have taken investments in the organisation and certain of them have successfully participated in investment share trading. The only restriction is that an investor must retain a minimum investment. This minimum investment is calculated (see art 6(h) of the Operating Agreement) at 0.05 per cent of the total investment shares and has been redefined to take into account the independent investment by authorised entities, in that it is the combined investment share of a signatory and the authorised entities within its country. In addition, at a signatory's request, IN-TELSAT management will apportion the national investment share between the signatory and its authorised entities. The INTELSAT management will, however, play no part in any financial settlements or adjustments between the signatory and its authorised entities, except where such adjustment arises solely from the annual adjustment of investment shares comprising part of the general INTELSAT-wide settlement process.

4.49   As a result of the changes described *above*, an entity designated to have direct access to INTELSAT is termed an 'Appointed Customer', with four ascending and cumulative levels of access available to a non-signatory entity:

(1) *Operating technical access*: participation in global Traffic and Operations Representatives meetings, access to published capacity availability and assignment information and INTELSAT's information systems, receipt of operational and technical materials.

(2) *Commercial and service matter access*: meetings with INTELSAT management staff on commercial and capacity availability, receipt of the INTELSAT Service Guide and Tariff Manual, access to Occasional Use Video capacity availability information through the INTELSAT ESTA/TV-MAX.

(3) *Contractual access*: direct ordering of all, or specified, INTELSAT services, including the declaration of long-term commitments, submission of earth station and antenna applications, devolution of billing liability for satellite utilisation charges to the service ordering entity.

(4) *Investment*: see *above*.

A signatory is able to authorise either some or all of the services available under the first three of the above levels, although signatories are encouraged to authorise all the services in the particular level of access to be granted.

As has been mentioned, these arrangements have and will require no re-wording of the constitutive agreements of INTELSAT and are already in place and functioning. However, their effectiveness in providing direct access will be dependent on the particular party and signatory for the relevant country. The appointment of an authorised entity is still through the signatory and the devolution of liability for those entities will be at the discretion of the party. Needless to say, with the different parties to INTELSAT being at different stages of economic development, many of them have different priorities and policies. For example, the UK, which is strongly in favour of full liberalisation, has submitted a blanket approval for all UK telecommunication operators to have full service and investment access to INTELSAT. It may be that other parties will consider the development of a single national PTO of greater importance.

EUTELSAT

4.50 Like INTELSAT, EUTELSAT has recently changed the procedure under art XVI(*a*) for 'economic harm' co-ordination but will continue to apply the requirements of technical co-ordination. At the twelfth meeting of the Assembly of Parties held in May 1992, a resolution was adopted changing the application of the procedures under art XVI(*a*). In the case of 'non-reserved services' the procedure is considerably simplified. (Non-reserved services are services which do not fall into the category of reserved services. Reserved services comprise: 'international telecommunications via satellite which are or are to be routed through at least two international exchanges located respectively in the countries of origin and destination.' Such international exchanges corresponding to the definition are given in CCITT Recommendation E.100 para 5 (see Attachment No 2 AP 14–8E, BS41–22E).)

The new procedure (see Attachment No 2 AP14–8E, BS41–22E) will consist simply of the issue by the relevant party or signatory of a declaration giving broad general information on the intended utilisation including the number of satellites planned for the system, the number of transponders per satellite, the orbital positions, the operating frequencies and bands; the EIRP contours of relevance for the purpose; and a general description of the services to be provided. The issued information is then forwarded to the Assembly of Parties on behalf of the Board of Signatories. The Director General determines that he has all the necessary information and confirms to the consulting party or signatory that the proposed utilisation falls outside the reserved services area. The Assembly is informed of the completion of such consultations, in due course, by letter to individual parties.

In cases concerning the provision of reserved services, the consulting party or signatory provides all relevant information including, but not limited to: orbital positions, operating frequencies and bands; EIRP contours; proposed date of commencement and duration of operation of the facilities; available in-orbit capacity; number of satellites and transponders per satellite; number of transponders for each type of service; plans for follow-on system; identification of projected traffic or services; and identification of any such traffic presently carried or planned to be carried by EUTELSAT. The Director General is authorised to reach a view on behalf of the Assembly for short-term and urgent utilisation. EUTELSAT is now considering a proposal to amend the Convention to delete art XVI altogether.

4.51 The current thinking within EUTELSAT is to encourage flexibility in the interpretation of the articles in the Operating Agreement dealing with earth station approval and reservation and allotment of space segment capacity. The signatories which are responsible for ensuring compliance with EUTELSAT's rules, procedures, and technical characteristics *vis-à-vis* earth station operation hope to improve the efficiency of the use of the system made by themselves and the operators licensed in their territories.

Although space segment capacity must be requested via a signatory pursuant to the Operating Agreement, there is nothing in the EUTELSAT constituent instruments to prevent the actual agreement from being signed directly by the end user and EUTELSAT.

Also, as outlined *above*, the signatory or party in whose territory an earth station is being used must submit technical and operational data to EUTELSAT to obtain approval of that earth station. However, signatories are now responsible only for the initial compliance of the earth station at the time of approval. Thereafter, it is the operator that is liable for non-compliance. Proposals are being submitted by signatories to amend art 15 of the Operating Agreement to bring EUTELSAT's provisions relating to earth station approvals in line with the EC Directive of October 1994 (see para 4.30 *above*) and remove signatories from the process completely.

4.52   EUTELSAT has recognised that, in the light of the Commission's harmonisation measures and liberalisation proposals in the field of satellite telecommunication services and equipment, there is a need to improve access for non-signatory entities to the EUTELSAT space segment and to adapt EUTELSAT's regulatory regime to a new regulatory and political environment. (See paper given by Birgitta Näslund at the International Bar Association Conference, 21 September 1992, p 7.) EUTELSAT decided in December 1994 to allow non-signatory entities to have access to EUTELSAT provided they invest in EUTELSAT (with a minimum share of at least 0.05 per cent) and subject to national arrangements (to deal with the above-mentioned issues) being notified to EUTELSAT. To date, no such measures have been notified, but EUTELSAT expects such notifications by the end of 1995. The question of whether any such non-signatory entities who thereby acquire an investment share should then be able to take part in investment share trading (as with INTELSAT, see para 4.48 *above*) is still under consideration by EUTELSAT.

These arrangements may resolve some of the issues of conflict of interest, but the direct nature of the arrangement does not extend fully to all the areas of concern such as liability for investment share and compliance with EUTELSAT's terms and conditions. While the non-signatory entity will have primary responsibility for meeting its investment requirement, and although EUTELSAT has said that it will use strenuous efforts to recover such sums from the non-signatory entity directly, ultimate liability will remain with the signatory. Likewise, responsibility for compliance with terms and conditions will also, ultimately, remain with the signatory. It is to be hoped that these issues will be dealt with within the so-called 'national arrangements', but there remains the possibility of signatories being responsible for entities over which they have no control, which might make signatories more reluctant to countenance such arrangements.

4.53 In addition, a so-called 'multiple access' arrangement has been entered into by the UK, The Netherlands, Germany, France and Switzerland (the arrangement is open to all EUTELSAT members who wish to join). This is a system which allows individual users to avoid having to deal directly with their local signatory, which may well be their most immediate competitor, and to approach the signatory in any of the other countries in the arrangement to acquire space segment. It also allows the possibility of competition between signatories for that business. It has been necessary for the five signatories concerned to agree cross-indemnities with one another to mitigate the effects this arrangement could have on the liabilities which may arise under the Convention and Operating Agreement. Such agreements are apparently now in place between all five signatories. Given the terms of the EC Directive of October 1994 (see para 4.48 *above*), it is to be hoped that multiple acess arrangements of this nature will be extended to other countries.

Finally, signatories and parties are also considering the idea of a 'controlled access arrangement' where a Signatory Affairs Office would be established in each country and all requests from users licensed to operate in the given country would be channelled through these. Another suggestion is the establishment of a common European Signatory Affairs Office. EUTELSAT is also considering a proposal by one of its parties to allow more than one signatory per country.

It will still be the case that requests for utilisation of the EUTELSAT space segment can be made directly by any operator licensed as a duly authorised telecommunications entity by the government of a country which is not a member country of EUTELSAT.

Inmarsat

4.54   Inmarsat's Assembly established an Intersessional Working Group (IWG) in October 1991 to review the appropriateness of its co-ordination article, art 8 of the Inmarsat Convention (which applies only to maritime services). The IWG has now concluded its report and recommended to the Assembly that no system which falls within the scope of art 8 and has been notified should be deemed to cause significant economic harm. However, this recommendation must be adopted by the Assembly before it results in any change to Inmarsat's co-ordination procedures.

Inmarsat is a rather different creature from EUTELSAT and IN-TELSAT in that it does not lease space segment to users. Instead it provides what might be called a space segment service, to mobile users who operate land earth stations (LES) which are owned and operated by entities other than Inmarsat itself.

Those other entities are generally Inmarsat signatories, though not always, and only a minority of signatories operate LES. The result of this is that demand for better access comes from a completely different quarter, that is, newly licensed public operators who wish to run large land earth stations to provide public maritime mobile services.

As regards access by non-signatories, there are currently three countries where non-signatories have varying degrees of access to Inmarsat: Australia where OPTUS has the same degree of access as the signatory; the USA where IBD has some rights of access; and the UK where Cable & Wireless forms part of the BT signatory delegation to the Council and other Inmarsat committees.

The IWG established by the Assembly has made some progress in this area and two or three minor amendments to the legal instruments which would facilitate better technical and operational access to Inmarsat by non-signatory LES operators. The IWG concluded that arts VII, XII and XIV of Inmarsat's Operating Agreement should be amended so as to facilitate technical and operational access to Inmarsat by non-signatory LES operators. The IWG further recommended that a new working group should be formed to study matters relating to access to the Inmarsat system. Work on access has continued after the October 1993 Assembly but as of July 1995, access to Inmarsat remained through the signatories only.

Gaining access to space segment in the United Kingdom

4.55   Access to Inmarsat differs from access to EUTELSAT and INTELSAT, reflecting the different nature of the organisations.

As regards access to Inmarsat space segment, once Inmarsat terminals are bought or leased, then the applicant must commission the terminal through a routing organisation, which is usually the PTO (in the UK's case, the BT Inmarsat Product Group). The routing organisation used depends on the country in which the terminal is to be used, the flag of the vessel in the case of maritime users, or in certain circumstances, the country of residence of the applicant. The commissioning form is provided to the applicant once his equipment is acquired. Once the commissioning application is approved, the routing organisation will issue the applicant with an Inmarsat Mobile Number (IMN). The IMN will be allocated to a terminal rather than a particular vehicle.

The commissioning procedure ensures that:

(*a*)   permission to transmit, according to national and international regulations is given;

(*b*)   satisfactory billing arrangements have been made;

(*c*)   the user agrees to operate his terminal according to the terms and conditions set out by Inmarsat; and

(*d*)   the terminal equipment has been tested to ensure it is operating correctly (this is done through the initial 'logging-on' procedure).

When commissioning is complete, the mobile user can select any land earth station within the assigned region through which to communicate.

Access to INTELSAT and EUTELSAT space segment in the UK may be obtained via BT's Signatory Affairs Office (the SAO). Alternatively, access to INTELSAT and EUTELSAT may be obtained through BT's Commercial Division by commercial negotiation, or in the case of EUTELSAT space segment, via another EUTELSAT signatory with whom 'multiple access' arrangements have been agreed (see para 4.53 *above*).

The SAO was established in response to the UK government's decision to liberalise satellite telecommunications. Potential operators are invited to discuss their requirements and the SAO will explain its function, that is, of arranging, where necessary, for ISO approval of earth stations and ordering space segment capacity as required. If a potential operator wishes to proceed, it must enter into contractual arrangements with BT. Once the 'enabling agreement' has been signed, the SAO is also able to assist in the provision of operational and tariff information and will keep the Satellite Service Operator (SSO) up to date with ISO information relevant to operational matters. The SAO is not a commercial entity, and has standard contractual arrangements with all SSOs. The current enabling agreement covers the principles of the relationship between BT (as signatory to INTELSAT and EUTELSAT) and the licensed SSO.

Each time an SSO wishes to reserve space segment capacity or request approval for an earth station, a subsidiary agreement must be completed assigning the specific capacity or registering a given earth station. In the case of the reservation of capacity, a bank guarantee must be provided by the SSO for the full amount of the financial exposure to BT.

The 1993 SAO Review (see para 4.31 *above*) was a detailed review by OFTEL of the operations of the SAO since its inception and included a number of important observations regarding the proposed reforms to the ISOs (discussed *above*) and some interesting proposals as to how the SAO might be altered in the light of experience. Comments were requested from interested parties and, following this consultation process, the 1994 SAO Statement was published by OFTEL, setting out the conclusions reached. These are summarised *below*.

4.56   *OFTEL's comments on the activities of the SAO*   In the 1993 SAO Review OFTEL drew a number of conclusions on how access to space segment had worked since the establishment of the SAO, which included:

— . . . the independent sector is still however in its infancy and to this extent there is a continuing responsibility for the regulatory authorities to ensure that BT does not misuse its dominant market position in the supply of satellite services or its role as a dominant provider of space capacity;

— access to the right space capacity, at the right time and on reasonable terms, is the life blood of the SSOs [Satellite Service Operators]; . . .

— even though the SAO is nominally independent from BT, BT is the SSOs' major competitor and there remains potential scope for conflict of interest. Even if the currently proposed changes within the EUTELSAT and INTELSAT become a working reality BT will still be a dominant player in the market, and as long as the SAO has a role to play the potential for conflict of interest will remain;

— BT's role as Signatory to the international consortia gives it advantages over the SSOs; currently BT's voice rather than the SSOs' is heard at consortia meetings, BT plays a part in setting prices for capacity that both it and its competitors will have to pay on a non-discriminatory basis and is closely involved in the approval process for SSOs' earth station (para 3.4.1).

OFTEL then enumerated the oft-voiced complaints of those who had had dealings with the SAO (such as excessively bureaucratic procedures; SAO staff lacking flexibility; potential for 'Chinese walls' within BT not being effective; lack of sufficient information about dealing with the ISOs; excessive signatory charge or mark-up (7 per cent); SAO unwilling (or unable) to deal with problems encountered with the ISOs (para 4.2). OFTEL commented:

> . . . understandable though they are, it is disappointing that many of the concerns voiced at the time of the previous review . . . are still current. This reflects the nature and structure of the SAO, and the inherent conflicts of interest they give rise to . . . (para 4.3.)

BT made a number of proposals, having conducted its own evaluation of the SAO, in three main areas:

(*a*)   investment share contribution;

(*b*)   indemnity insurance;

(*c*)   an administration charge.

These can be summarised as follows:

(1)   Each SSO should contribute to the UK's investment share in respect of the ISOs or compensate BT for the investment that it has made on the SSO's behalf.

(2)   Each SSO should obtain indemnity insurance to cover any liabilities it may occasion through its use of ISO capacity.

(3)   BT should be entitled to a fixed amount from any applicant registering with the SAO who did not proceed to obtain space capacity from BT.

4.57   *OFTEL's conclusions regarding the SAO*   In the 1994 SAO Statement, OFTEL's proposals, upon which the 1993 SAO Review had invited comments were restated (in slightly modified form) as formal recommendations as to the continued operation of the SAO and a modification to BT's licence conditions, as follows:

(*a*)   That BT should not be allowed to demand investment share contributions at this stage.

SSOs may choose to pay to BT an amount equal to the investment share contribution occasioned by their usage and so become ISO investors, but they cannot be obliged to do so.

(*b*)   That BT be allowed to require independent operators to have adequate indemnity insurance arrangements to meet liabilities that might otherwise fall on BT as Signatory.

This would require SSOs to obtain insurance before being able to obtain space segment through the SAO, to cover BT for any liability deriving from the activities of a SSO.

(*c*)   That BT should be allowed to charge reasonable costs of copying documentation supplied in response to a request for information that does not lead to the acquisition of space capacity.

BT's complaint is that in order to service the requirements of every enquiry, it is put to substantial expense.

(*d*)   That BT's main operating licence should be modified to bring its activities relating to the provision of satellite capacity within its ambit.

(*e*)   That BT should establish appropriate arrangements for the preparation and publication of separate financial statements for all of the Signatory functions, including those relating to BT's acquisition of space capacity for its own business, on a basis to be agreed by OFTEL.

(*f*)   That the licence modification should include a provision to the effect that it would be a licence breach for BT staff involved in the SAO to reveal confidential information to those not directly employed in SAO activities.

(*g*)   That OFTEL and BT should explore the scope for greater separation between the SAO and the remainder of the Company and especially its Visual and Broadcast Services business.

(*h*)   That the DTI presses ahead within EUTELSAT towards the objective of direct access and works to ensure the moves within INTELSAT to enable direct access become a practical reality.

(*i*) That the SAO should process INTELSAT earth station approvals following mandatory testing supervised by operators themselves or by third parties.

With the introduction of direct access to INTELSAT, this recommendation becomes redundant.

(*j*) That BT should be allowed to operate a regime that recognises the different risks associated with different SSOs, and continue to seek bank guarantees or other forms of security, on the basis that it is willing to make detailed changes to tighten procedures to meet legitimate concerns.

But OFTEL made it clear that this is subject to the *caveat* that BT and OFTEL will explore the scope for building more flexibility into the arrangements for seeking securities.

(*k*) That the SAO considers the scope for streamlining its range of contractual agreements within a reasonable timescale. OFTEL would expect draft contracts to be the subject of discussion with the SSOs and to be publishable.

(*l*) That in future OFTEL would expect significant changes to the contractual documents issued by the SAO to be made only after agreement has been reached by both sides.

(*m*) That the SAO draw up a concise and comprehensive outline of its duties and responsibilities including where appropriate its contractual obligations, for circulation to both the SSOs and potential market entrants.

(*n*) That BT's offer of further discussions on the distribution of consortia information be pursued, with the aim of achieving the widest possible distribution of such information to the SSOs.

BT's proposals for improving its system of document distribution are annexed to the 1994 SAO Statement.

(*o*) That OFTEL should consider with the SAO the arrangements for the SSOs' attendance at certain consortia meetings, particularly the Traffic Planning meetings.

(*p*) That OFTEL should consider with the SAO arrangements to ensure that the views of the SSOs be taken into account by the UK Signatory at consortia meetings.

(*q*) That the DTI considers strengthening its own arrangements to ensure that the views of the SSOs are more directly taken into account in formulating the UK position at consortia meetings.

(*r*)   That the SAO be required to agree with OFTEL, publish and adhere to a code of confidentiality with regard to customer information.

This is effectively subsumed by recommendation (*f*) (see *above*).

(*s*)   That the SAO should agree to make tariff information available on demand to both operators and potential operators.

(*t*)   That the SAO commences the preparation of financial statements, beginning with the forthcoming financial year, on a basis to be agreed with OFTEL; the information that is produced should be freely available to the independent operators.

This effectively replicates recommendation (*e*) and so OFTEL agreed it should lapse.

(*u*)   That it should be made clear to all those who are active in the satellite market that there are no regulatory inhibitions to the sub-leasing of reserved space capacity to third parties.

(*v*)   That the SAO review its internal challenge procedures in order to ensure that they provide complete independence in the allocation of capacity . . . The procedures would then be published, in a manner to be agreed with OFTEL. As part of any revised challenge procedure, [OFTEL] would expect to see a reference to an independent arbitrator as the final step in any unresolved dispute. (1994 SAO Statement, para 17)

4.58   In the 1994 SAO Statement, OFTEL welcomed the changes that have been made by INTELSAT (see para 4.47 *above*) with regard to direct access and endorsed the proposals agreed between BT and the DTI regarding new arrangements applicable in the UK whereby:

(a)   independent operators would be authorised to approach [INTELSAT] directly for the acquisition of satellite capacity; such operators will be liable to INTELSAT for their own acquisition charges and for any investment share liability;

(b)   independent operators would deal directly with INTELSAT on operational matters including earth station approvals;

(c)   BT would not seek indemnities for any residual liabilities that accrued to it as Signatory for such use of INTELSAT capacity, or contributions to the costs of the Signatory function which it performs on behalf of all UK consortium users.

OFTEL pointed out that these proposals remove the need for the SAO as regards INTELSAT.

OFTEL commented that the position with EUTELSAT is less clear and that accordingly it expected the SAO to continue to be required to administer EUTELSAT space segment in the medium term.

In the 1994 SAO Statement, OFTEL also accepted the principle that the revised arrangements applying to the SAO should extend to Inmarsat, where applicable. OFTEL did, however, point out that the 1993 SAO Review focused almost exclusively on INTELSAT and EUTELSAT and that accordingly further discussion would be necessary to determine the extent to which arrangements should apply to Inmarsat.

OFTEL expressed the hope that, with the ISOs moving towards direct access, there would be no need for a further review of the SAO, and that the SAO would eventually become unnecessary. It made it clear that it did not intend to review the SAO arrangements until at least three years following the 1994 statement.

Conclusion

4.59   It would be foolish to believe that the ISOs are now creatures of the past, shortly to be made extinct by the privately owned operators such as SES, PanAmSat and Orion. All are showing signs of greater commercial awareness and, indeed, are actively competing not only with the private operators (for example, EUTELSAT with SES in the commercial DTH market in Europe, or Inmarsat's subsidiary ICO-P's planned mobile service against the Low Earth Orbiting Satellites LEOS proposals—see Chapter 1, para 1.14) but also with each other (for example, EUTELSAT's Euteltracs Service against the fleet management for land transport offered by Inmarsat).

However, competition in earth and space segment capacity is of paramount importance. Various regulatory concerns about the ISO constituent instruments have been mentioned. The European Commission will monitor the reforms of the ISOs and their practices as commercial entities. Likewise, the Commission will continue to keep an eye on the private operators.

The private sector may express concern about the extent and speed of reform of the ISOs; perhaps the statements of the parties and signatories need to be tested against their actions.

Indeed, in the 1993 SAO Review, while acknowledging 'substantive changes within INTELSAT . . . which have brought direct access close to being a reality,' OFTEL regarded EUTELSAT's proposals as 'tentative' (para 3.3.4 of the Review) and expressed the view that 'there remains the possibility of an art 90(3) Directive requiring EC Member States to work actively within EUTELSAT to bring about necessary changes.'

If there is to be reform, reform should be 'transparent', to adopt terminology from the European Commission, not 'opaque'.

---

1 INTELSAT has four organs, as listed in para 4.7. However, the role of the INTELSAT Meeting of Signatories and Board of Governors has been amalgamated in the case of EUTELSAT and Inmarsat.

2 Under UK law a 'PTO' or 'public telecommunications operator' is a 'person authorised by a licence to which s 8 (of the Telecommunications Act 1984) applies to run a public telecommunications system' (s 9(3) Telecommunications Act 1984). In other words, it is a private operator which has been licensed under s 7 of the Telecommunications Act 1984 to run a public telecommunications system which has been so designated by the Secretary of State. Such a 'PTO' licence will include conditions such as the requirement to provide specified telecommunications services and to permit interconnection. 'PTO' has come to be a term of general use to describe a privatised telecommunications operator as opposed to a state-owned telecommunications utility Administration.

'PTT' is the acronym used for a 'Post Telegraph and Telephone', public utility, usually a state-owned and non-corporatised monopoly, running a country's public telecommunications network and providing telecommunication services under special or exclusive rights.

A 'TO' is simply a general term for a telecommunications operator ie any operator who is licensed to run a telecommunications system. This term is frequently used in EU documentation.

3 Article 85(3) of the Treaty of Rome provides that the provisions of art 85(1) of the Treaty may be declared inapplicable in the case of 'any agreement or category of agreements between undertakings; . . . which contributes to improving the production or distribution of goods or to promoting technical or economic progress, while allowing consumers a fair share of the resulting benefit, and which does not:

(*a*)   impose on the undertakings concerned restrictions which are not indispensable to the attainment of these objectives;

(*b*)   afford such undertakings the possibility of eliminating competition in respect of a substantial part of the products in question.'

5

European Policy and Regulation

Introduction

5.1 Since the Treaty of Rome (Treaty Establishing the European Economic Community signed at Rome on 25 March 1957 (UK Treaties 15 (1979) Cmnd 7480, considered in Chapter 4, paras 4.28 and 4.38)), there has been a movement of the European Union (EU) member states towards a much closer union. This is evidenced by the Single European Act (OJ 29.7.87 L169/1) and, of course, the Maastricht Treaty (Treaty on European Union, OJ 31.7.92 C224) which is to be the subject of revision in 1996. This is not, as yet at least, the United States of Europe once much vaunted by General de Gaulle, but the treaties do require member states to take steps towards harmonisation of their domestic laws as agreed in EC legislation in order to ensure the creation of a single market and the free flow of goods and services within the EU. International law has been considered briefly in Chapter 1, as has the relationship between the international legal obligations of the member states and their obligations under the Treaty of Rome.

The EU has, in recent years, been active in formulating policy and regulation in the field of telecommunications, especially in the satellite and mobile communications sectors. As will be apparent, in the last two years, many of the matters that had been in the process of formulation have come to fruition and a clear timetable for full liberalisation has been established, first by *Council Resolution 93/C213/01 of 22 July 1993 on the review of the situation in the tele-communications sector and the need for further development in that market* (OJ 6.8.93 C213/1) ('the July 1993 Resolution') which set the date of

1 January 1998 for the full liberalisation of voice telephony services to the public;[1] and, secondly, by *Council Resolution 94/C 379/03 of 22 December 1994 on the principles and timetable for the liberalisation of telecommunications infrastructure* (OJ 31.12.94 C 379/4) ('the December 1994 Resolution') which has similarly set 1 January 1998 as the date for liberalisation of telecommunication infrastructure.[2]

These goals must now also be seen in the context of the 'global information society', especially as encapsulated in the *Communication from the Commission to the Council and the European Parliament and to the Economic and Social Committee and the Committee of the Regions, Europe's way to the information society: an action plan,* COM(94) 347 final, 19 July 1995 ('the Information Society Action Plan'), adopted following the Council meeting in Corfu on 24–25 June 1994, at which the Recommendations to the European Council, *Europe and the Global Information Society,* chaired by Commissioner Martin Bangemann (the so-called Bangemann Report), were endorsed. This is inextricably linked with the Commission's continuing work in relation to infrastructure liberalisation in the *Green Paper on the liberalisation of telecommunications infrastructure and cable television networks* (Part 1: COM(94) 440 final, 25 October 1994 and Part 2: COM(94) 682 final, 25 January 1995) ('the Infrastructure Green Paper') and the *Green Paper on a common approach in the field of mobile and personal communication in the European Union,* COM(94) 145 ('the Mobile Green Paper'). The consultation on the Infrastructure Green Paper has now been completed and the results communicated to the Council and European Parliament (*Communication from the Commission to the Council and the European Parliament on the consultation on the Green Paper on the liberalisation of telecommunications infrastructure and cable television networks,* COM(95) 158 final, 3 May 1995). The Information Society Action Plan is now being considered with a view to a methodology for the implementation of information society applications, and a *Proposal for a European Parliament and Council Decision on a series of guidelines for trans-European telecommunications networks* (COM(95) 224 final, 31 May 1995) ('the TENs Methodology Guidelines Proposal').

5.2 There are presently 15 member states of the EU (Austria, Belgium, Denmark, Finland, France, Germany, Greece, Republic of Ireland, Italy, Luxembourg, The Netherlands, Portugal, Spain, Sweden and the UK). In accordance with the European Economic Area (EEA) Agreement (OJ 3.1.94 L1/1), members of the EEA (which now includes members of the Union, the European Coal and Steel Community, the European Community and the EFTA (European Free

Trade Area) members) are now bound by all art 90(3)[3] Directives and all amendments as from 1 July 1994 (Competition Annex (xiv)). This widening of the jurisdictional scope of art 90(3) is also relevant to the Europe Agreement and the Interim Agreements signed with Romania, Hungary, Bulgaria, Poland and the Slovak and Czech Republics.[4]

Although this chapter is principally concerned with EU matters, the role of other bodies in Europe, such as the Council of Europe (see para 5.84 *below*) and the European Telecommunications Standards Institute (ETSI) (see para 5.93 *below*) should not be discounted. Obviously, the EU's work in telecommunications must take into account the wider international issues arising, for example, from membership of the International Telecommunication Union (ITU) and the international satellite organisations (ISOs) (see Chapters 1, 2 and 4). The work being carried out on satellite personal communications networks (referred to in para 5.61 *below*) specifically recognises that, whatever the EU wishes to achieve, requires close co-operation between a number of institutions including ETSI and the ITU. Indeed, in the 1992 *Review of the situation in the telecommunications sector* (SEC 92/1048 of 2 October 1992 ('the 1992 Services Directive Review'), discussed at 5.29 *below*, the Commission noted that it was willing to consider taking action at the wider international level, particularly through the ITU or the European Conference of Post and Telecommunications (CEPT), rather than simply at the EU level. Furthermore, its work in the satellite sector cannot be reviewed in isolation as the telecommunications and broadcasting sectors converge.

This chapter is devoted principally to the issues of liberalisation and competition in the general field of satellite systems and services and does not (except in passing) examine directives or proposals in the broadcasting field relating to programme content, copyright and related rights, which are dealt with in Chapters 7 and 8; nor does it cover in much detail the Commission's work in the important area of mobile communications, except in relation to satellite/personal communications.

5.3 The principal institutions of the EU are the Council, which is the primary policy and legislative body, and the Commission, which is responsible for, *inter alia*, developing policy and drafting legislation. In addition, the European Court of Justice (ECJ) and, increasingly, the European Parliament, play significant roles. The ECJ has made some important decisions in the telecommunications field and the Parliament has proved an important forum for debate.

In general, the European Parliament is consulted on EU legislation only, but its participation in the legislative process was recently extended under art 189b of the Treaty on European Union. This is a negative assent procedure and similar to the co-operation procedure which was adopted under the Single European Act, whereby the Parliament may propose amendments to legislation before the Council. The new feature of this so-called 'co-decision' procedure is that a Conciliation Committee, mediating between the two institutions, will try to settle an agreed text, which, if successful, should be adopted by both. If agreement is not reached, then the Council can proceed to adopt its text, but faces the risk of its being rejected by the European Parliament which cannot introduce amendments at that stage. If it is rejected by an absolute majority, the measure fails.

Day-to-day work for the Council is carried out by the Committee of Permanent Representatives of the Member States (COREPER), which is a permanent body made up of representatives of the member states. It carries out such tasks as may be requested by the Council and comprises working parties to investigate or prepare matters for the Council.

The EU Commission consists of 20 Commissioners, as well as a large supporting civil service. The present Commission took office on 25 January 1995, following the admission of the new member states (see para 5.2 *above*). The President of the Commission is nominated by the member states (through the Council) and must, like the Commissioners, be a citizen of a member state. The President is elected by the European Parliament. Each Commissioner is responsible for one or more Directorates-General (DGs). At present there are 24 DGs covering the administrative and policy matters in the EU. One of the most important functions of the Commission is to see that the provisions of the Treaty of Rome are complied with by the member states and that regulations, directives and decisions, promulgated for the purpose of implementing the Treaty of Rome, are enforced by the member states. As indicated, a further important function of the Commission is to make proposals for legislative measures to be considered and, if thought fit, adopted by the Council.

5.4   Before dealing specifically with the development of EU policy, it is convenient to consider the two principal DGs responsible for communications and competition policy respectively, namely DG

XIII (Telecommunications, Information Markets and Exploitation of Research) and DG IV (Competition). While DG XIII is the Directorate most involved in the development of satellite policy, the research and development side of the space dossier is also co-ordinated by DG XII (Science Research and Development). Other Directorates General concerned include DG III (Industry), because of the importance of space to European industry; DG X (Information, Communication, Culture, Audiovisual), because of its role in the development of audiovisual policy, which is relevant to communications development generally; DG XI (Environment, Nuclear Safety and Civil Protection), which is concerned with environmental issues;[5] and DG XV (Internal Market and Financial Institutions), which deals with issues such as copyright and databases.

Directorate-General XIII

5.5 DG XIII is responsible for telecommunications, postal services policy, including liberalisation and regulation, interconnection and interoperability of networks and services, and communication security.

DG XIII also has a research and development role in the areas of advanced communications and telematics applications. It provides support for the practical implementation of these programmes. On the research and development side, DG XIII was once solely concerned with information technology, telecommunications, telematic networks and services and computer languages. However, following restructuring, responsibility for some of these areas, including such matters as High Definition Television (HDTV) (see para 5.66 *below*), has moved to DG III (Industrial Policy) and DG X (Audiovisual Policy).

One of the important research and development functions of DG XIII is its contribution to the RACE Programme (Research and Development in Advanced Communications technologies in Europe). The RACE Programme was started in 1985 and will run to the end of 1995. Its purpose is to create a strong EU market for Internal Broadband Communications (IBC) and a competitive market for telecommunications equipment and services with uniform standards and specifications throughout Europe. The programme, now drawn to its close, has largely achieved its goal for the introduction of IBC in Europe of Community-wide services through the implementation of the results of its research projects.

Following the European Commission's White Paper, *Growth, competitiveness, employment: The challenges and ways forward into the 21st century* COM(93) 700 final, December 1993, the focus of DG XIII's work will be on supporting the development of European information highways, including both network infrastructure and general applications (eg e-mail).

DG XIII is also responsible for developing international relations with respect to telecommunications between the EU and other international organisations, such as the CEPT (see para 5.87 *below*).

Directorate-General IV

5.6   DG IV is responsible for competition policy. It investigates complaints of anti-competitive conduct under arts 85 and 86 of the Treaty of Rome and monitors state aid to industry, including aid in the field of telecommunications.

DG IV has issued important guidelines concerning its policy in applying the competition rules of the Treaty of Rome and these are discussed in more detail in paras 5.40 to 5.43 and paras 5.48 and 5.49 *below*. DG IV was responsible for the review of the Services Directive. The preface to the *Communication by the Commission to the European Parliament and the Council on the status and implementation of Directive 90/388/EEC on competition in the markets for telecommunications services* (COM(95) 113, final, 4 April 1995 ('the Services Directive Review') makes clear the inter-relationship of various aspects of the Commission's work in the context of the 'global information society' (see *below*). It also highlights the failure of certain member states to implement, or implement effectively, current EU law into domestic law.

Exercise of art 90 by the Commission (see para 5.2 *above*) basically originates in DG IV; see paras 5.7 and 5.9 *below*.

Development of European Policy and Regulation

5.7   As will be apparent from the discussion in Chapter 4 (see paras 4.23–4.38), the Commission's satellite policy has been developed in the light of the economic importance of satellite communications and communications generally in the EU. The policy has, in particular, been one of combining liberalisation and harmonisation to bring about an internal market in telecommunications for the benefit of all citizens of the EU. These policies are aimed at creating greater competition and hence greater consumer choice in a sector which was previously subject to the hegemony of national public telecommunications operators and state owned broadcasters. The Commission has emphasised, *inter alia*, the importance of separating the regulatory and operational functions of the former monopoly telecommunications operators in the satellite and telecommunications fields (see Chapter 4) so that no operator is in the position of being both a competitor and a regulator in relation to its undertakings and those of its fellow competitors.

As noted *above*, the thrust of the Commission's work to date has been to adopt policies in respect of the three basic constituent elements of the telecommunications business of the PTTs, whether satellite or terrestrial, namely:

(*a*)   the networks themselves (in other words, the telecommunications infrastructure);

(*b*)   the services provided on, or using part of, those networks; and

(*c*)   the equipment which can be attached to those networks.

Hitherto, the PTTs enjoyed monopolies over all three areas. While there has been a gradual erosion of those monopolies at the 'edges', like the exclusive supply of terminal equipment by the PTTs or the provision of value added services, the PTTs' monopolies over the network infrastructure, and the right to provide basic voice telephony, generally has remained in their exclusive domain. In a number of important developments in the course of 1994 and 1995, however, reforms have been taken to the heartland of the continued preserves of the dominant telecommunications operators (TOs) (especially about what constitutes 'voice telephony' (see the Services Directive Review, p 13 *et seq*).[6] The Commission has been active, not only in Directorate General XIII, but also in Directorate General IV, and there has been high profile personal involvement by Commissioners Bangemann and Van Miert. These developments are referred to *below* (para 5.9).

The main preserve under concerted attack is the continuing monopoly in the provision of 'voice telephony', whether under 'exclusive rights' or 'special rights'. The EC Treaty does not prevent member states from granting exclusive or special rights or having public undertakings. However, there is an important distinction for the purposes of art 90 between 'special rights', where the right is granted to more than one undertaking but the number of undertakings is limited, and 'exclusive rights', where a single undertaking is granted the sole right.

Article 90(2) stipulates that these rights can be exercised only if the undertakings concerned respect other provisions of the treaty and, in particular, the competition rules (see paras 5.48 and 5.49 *below*). The Treaty of Rome makes it clear that public undertakings, such as the TOs themselves, are subject to the Treaty, but only in so far as compliance with those rules does not obstruct their performance of the particular tasks entrusted to them, and only if the development of trade is not affected to such an extent as would be contrary to the interests of the EU (Treaty of Rome, art 90(2)). Article 90(3) of the Treaty of Rome requires the Commission to ensure the application of the provisions of art 90 and, where necessary, to address 'appropriate directives or decisions to member states'.

5.8   Although it is the Council which is the institution primarily empowered to pass legislation, art 90(3) gives the Commission an express power to adopt directives, that is to legislate, in certain circumstances without the prior approval of the Council (see *above*, para 5.3). This important and substantial power of the Commission was formally upheld by the ECJ in 1991 in the case of *French Republic (and Others)* v *Commission of European Communities* (Case C-202/88) [1992] 5 CMLR 552. The case was brought by France, supported by Italy, Belgium, Germany and Greece, which applied for the annulment of certain provisions in the Terminal Equipment Directive adopted by the Commission under art 90(3) (Commission Directive 88/301/EEC of 16 May 1988 on Competition in the Markets in Telecommunications Terminal Equipment, OJ 27.5.95 L131/73) (the 'Terminal Equipment Directive') (see para 5.23 *below*). The ECJ confirmed that art 90(3) of the Treaty of Rome empowered the Commission to specify general obligations with which member states must comply under the Treaty by the implementation of directives. Directives generally impose no obligations on private individuals.

In broad terms, the general principle followed by the Commission in drafting its directives and other proposals for legislation is that a market economy will be a generally more efficient way of introducing competition, and will lead to reduced prices for the consumer and to the provision of a wider range of goods and services. In this regard, those that have followed the Commission's somewhat interventionist proposals with regard to High Definition Television

(HDTV) and the history of Directive 92/38/EEC will readily agree (see para 5.66 *below*). The principal barriers to competition in the telecommunications sector occur in the areas of standards, interconnection, restrictive trade practices, abuses of a dominant market position and the scarcity of radio frequency spectrum.

There is no doubt that, since 1987, there has been a considerable increase in the range of services available to consumers. Competition and liberalisation have had obvious benefits for all users. However, it is still discernible that the TOs or former PTTs have the largest share of the telecommunications market in Europe. This is hardly surprising given their privileged and entrenched positions with which newcomers have to contend. This is as true in the UK, where arguably liberalisation is furthest advanced, as it is in the less liberalised member states. Regulations are usually aimed at establishing a 'level playing field', but this can too often favour the incumbent TO. In many cases, to encourage competition, there may need to be positive discrimination against the incumbent while the newcomer is given special treatment. While it might be contended by the UK government that this was what the duopoly policy did, that is, to foster Mercury Communications Limited (Mercury) in its early days in competition with British Telecom plc (BT), it might also be said that Mercury still needs more positive assistance from the government to compete against BT. Furthermore, it is said by those who wish to compete against both, such as the post-duopoly licensed PTOs (eg Ionica L3 Ltd), that they need to be given assistance to compete.

5.9   Recent types of regulatory assistance are given by or arise from, *inter alia*:

(a)   the July 1993 Resolution, following the 1992 Services Directive Review, by laying down 1 January 1998 as the date for full liberalisation of voice telephony services for the general public within the EU (subject to certain derogations for Spain, Portugal, Greece and Ireland until 1 January 2003, and for Luxembourg until 1 January 2000);

(b)   the December 1994 Resolution, by setting out the principles and timetable for liberalisation of telecommunications infrastructure and the establishment of open competition by 1 January 1998;

(c)   the Information Society Action Plan, by calling for directives on:

(i) the establishment of a European-level authority on the information society (to be submitted by January 1996),

(ii) standardisation of activities and services,

(iii) interconnection of networks and interoperability of services and the updating of the ONP framework;

(d) the Mobile Green Paper, by recommending the:

(i) abolition of exclusive and special rights in the mobile telecommunications sector (except where licensing agreements are essential);

(ii) removal of all restrictions on the provision of pan-European mobile services by independent service providers or mobile network operators (allowing the combination of different services under various licences throughout the member states);

(iii) full liberalisation for network operators to develop and operate networks offering an unrestricted combination of services via fixed and mobile networks;

(iv) establishment of a European-wide system to facilitate access to resources comprised in numbering and frequency spectrum;

(e) (following on from (d)), a *draft Commission Directive 95/ ... /EEC of 21 June 1995 amending Directive 90/388/EEC with regard to mobile and personal communications based on art 90(3) of the Treaty* ('the Article 90 Mobile Draft Directive') which extends the operation of Directive 90/388/EC (Commission Directive 90/388/EEC of 28 June 1990 on Competition in the Markets for Telecommunications Services (OJ 1990 L192/10; item (a) above)) by way of amendment so as to introduce full competition in the EU mobile and personal communications market by 1 January 1996. This is being pursued by Commissioner Van Miert, in co-operation with Commissioner Bangemann, following a meeting of the Telecommunication Council of 13 June 1995.

Also of importance was the review of the Services Directive carried out post-1992, which led to the Services Directive Review. In the context of interoperability and the principles of open network provision, the Commission has proposed a *European Parliament and Council Directive on interconnection in telecommunications ensuring universal service and interoperability through application of the principles* of open network provision (ONP) (COM(95) 379, 19 July 1995 ('the Proposed Interconnection Directive').

Barriers to market entry

5.10   In looking at the market for telecommunications goods and services there are certain areas where limitations to competition arise, some of which may actually be caused by regulation. The principal limitations are discussed below.

Many barriers can exist which discourage potential competitors from entering a given market. These barriers can take many forms, such as high development and start-up costs (including the costs of obtaining funding from development agencies), lack of access to facilities such as network infrastructure, and over-regulation in the sector. If it is difficult to have new equipment technically approved for connection to a network, that will prevent new equipment being introduced. Difficulties may also arise in relation to encryption systems and intellectual property rights where there is a tension between an understandable desire to exploit a particular technological advantage and the desirability of competition. The potential problems in this area needed to be addressed. This has generally been addressed through measures such as the introduction of common technical standards and interfaces, homologation and the statutory right to connect to the network. This includes licensing; separation of operational and regulatory functions; interconnection and interoperability; dominant positions; radio frequency spectrum and site clearance; and administrative law.

Licensing

5.11   One of the major barriers to entry can be licensing. Limiting the number of licences which may be granted in a particular area has an obvious effect on the development of competition. Where fewer licences are granted, the incumbent PTT/TO is likely to face less competition. Concerns that arise out of the ways in which licences are issued in the member states have been expressed (for a discussion of the licensing framework in the UK, for example, see Chapter 6). As more and more competitive services are introduced in Europe harmonisation becomes increasingly important. The Commission's work on mutual recognition of licences goes some way to dealing with this important matter. However, what it does not address are the differing ways in which licences are granted within the EU by the National Regulatory Authorities (NRAs) or other relevant licensing bodies. Licensing procedures should be consistent with ONP principles (Council Directive 90/387/EEC on the Establishment of the Internal Market for Telecommunications Services through the Implementation of Open Network Provision (ONP) (OJ 1990 L 192/1) ('the ONP Framework Directive'; see para 5.34 *below*): that is, open, objective, non-discriminatory and transparent. In some member states a 'first come, first served' method of licensing is applied, assuming others, apart from the incumbent TO, can apply. While that might be 'objective', it is unsatisfactory for reasons similar to those voiced by developing countries in relation to access to radio frequency spectrum and orbital positions discussed in Chapter 2, para 2.39. It will be recalled from that discussion that the international community has moved towards an 'equitable approach' in relation to the allocation of scarce resources. Except where the number of licences that can be awarded is physically limited by objective factors such as the security of the radio frequency spectrum, it is expected that the Commission will make it difficult for member states to restrict the number of licences granted arbitrarily (see Consultation on Infrastructure, p 34 *et seq*). Likewise, it is contended that licensing of scarce resources should also be opened up to more than those who were fortunate to apply first, especially where only one licence is to be granted.

It is understood that, by a combination of measures foreshadowed in the Consultation on Infrastructure (see para 5.14 *below*) the Proposed Interconnection Directive (see para 5.9 *above*) and the ONP Committee's discussion document on a harmonised regulatory framework for licensing (see para 5.83 *below*) most of these concerns will be addressed.

5.12   Limited competitive tendering, where a small number of commercial operators are invited to tender and licences are awarded on objective criteria relating to the financial soundness, technical specifications and overall quality of the proposed service of the applicant, can also be a barrier to entry. This method has been widely used in Europe. It is clearly a step towards a liberalised regime, but at the same time does not fully achieve this as it envisages special rights to be granted to a limited number of operators. Other methods include award by lottery (assuming certain basic technical and financial criteria have been met) or by auction (where the financially stronger have the advantage and where the auction costs may be directed at the consumer). The need, therefore, to harmonise the EC law on this subject is acute and may well deserve the particular attention of DG IV.

It seems obvious that licensing should be fair, proportionate and open. Criteria for the award of licences should be objective, fair and known to all applying before the licence application. The decision-making process should be transparent and operated with the goal of furthering the EU's telecommunications policies and objectives. At the moment this would not appear to be the case throughout the EU.

The Commission has addressed this concern, in part, in Commission Directive 94/46/EC of 13 October 1994 Amending Directive 88/301/EEC in Particular with Regard to Satellite Communications (OJ 1994 L268/15) ('the Satellite Terminal Equipment Directive'). This amends the Terminal Equipment Directive, *inter alia*, to require member states to 'communicate [to the Commission] the criteria on which authorizations are granted, together with the conditions attached to such authorizations and to the declaration procedures for the operation of transmitting earth stations' and imposes an obligation to inform the Commission of any plans to introduce or change any licensing procedures (art 2). This is reinforced by the proposed measures referred to *above*. On-going work of the Commission is reflected in a discussion document XVI-A-1/b of 24 July 1995 issued for the ONP Committee, entitled *A harmonised regulatory framework for licensing* (the 'ONP Harmonisation Proposal') (see para 5.37 *below*). This document sets out the areas under consideration for any future harmonised regulatory framework for granting telecommunications 'authorisations'. Member states will be able to express their views informally before the final legislative process begins in the last quarter of 1995.

This also relates back to the issue of the separation of operational and regulatory functions.

In the Mobile Green Paper, it was proposed that the basic principles concerning access to radio frequencies should be those set out in the ONP Framework Directive. Allocation of frequencies should therefore:

(*a*)   be based on objective criteria;

(*b*)   utilise transparent procedures (published in an appropriate manner) which guarantee equality of access on a non-discriminatory basis. (p 46 of the Mobile Green Paper, English version.)

Separation of operational and regulatory functions

5.13 Whatever steps are taken by a member state to implement art 7 of the Services Directive, member states must separate telecommunications operational and regulatory functions. EC measures now refer to the separate regulatory office as an NRA, but the Commission considers that even this degree of separation has not occurred in at least five member states (the Services Directive Review, p 22 *et seq*). Regulators clearly need to have independence from the TO but ought also to have independence from government (which will vary from member state to member state), and at the very least, financial independence. Having the same government minister responsible for matters such as the ownership of the TO, the commercial exploitation of the public network, and the setting of technical standards somewhat stretches credibility (see *Francine Decoster* (C-69/91); and *Ministère Public* v *Annick Taillander* (C-46/90, ECJ Decisions of 27 October 1993)). This also links with the necessity for a clear regulatory framework for the European liberalised telecommunications environment and requires considerable involvement of the NRAs in ensuring an open access regime for interconnection, transparent licensing procedures and a fair, competitive environment. Effective administrative power ought also to be given to NRAs to ensure speed of justice.

Interconnection and interoperability

5.14 Ownership of the network infrastructure by the PTTs/TOs and connection to its infrastructure by competitors and interoperability of the connected networks are critical issues that must be answered in a way which will assist competitors to the incumbent TO. This means not only establishing the point at which the competitor may access the network and connect with other operators, but also setting the charges for doing so. The incumbent TO's inherent bargaining power gives it the ability to achieve the most favourable interconnect terms. At the very least, an incumbent TO which is able to delay interconnection through protracted negotiations is undermining a new entrant's pursuit of subscribers. The presence or absence of regulatory mechanisms or umpires may be critical in this context for the timely and commercially reasonable resolution of such deadlocks (see Chapter 12). This is probably the most important barrier to entry within Europe at the moment. As noted *above*, this is the subject of the Proposed Interconnection Directive; see para 5.9.

Dominant positions

5.15   The potential for abuse by the TOs of their dominant positions in the market for voice services and through ownership and control of the basic network infrastructure calls for close supervision. The EU has developed competition laws to prevent abuses of a dominant position, which are discussed at paras 5.40 and 5.42 to 5.43 *below*. Abuse can occur, other than in the areas already referred to, in the area of cross-subsidies, whereby a TO may improperly cross-subsidise some of its less profitable business from a profitable part of its business. This is of particular concern in vertically integrated companies, for example, where the TO is not only the network operator but also an equipment manufacturer supplying its operational side. This could lead to that TO's having a dominant position in the market for equipment, especially where it is also the sole purchaser.

Radio frequency spectrum and site clearance

5.16   As is already apparent from the discussion in Chapters 1 and 2, radio frequency spectrum is a scarce resource and access to it has important consequences for the introduction of new services, particularly pan-European or even global services, such as those for satellite personal communications (see Chapter 1, para 1.12, and para 5.61 *below*). Equitable access to radio frequency spectrum and to geostationary orbital positions has already been mentioned in Chapter 2. Equitable access to radio frequency spectrum in Europe, and the need for regulation to ensure fair allocation, remain critical.

Site clearance can be another barrier to entry. Obviously there is a necessity to avoid harmful interference especially around sensitive sites such as those used for military or aviation purposes. Some NRAs have introduced streamlined procedures for such clearances (for example, through the introduction of Codes of Practice) and joint studies are being undertaken between France and the UK to expedite such clearance, especially bearing in mind the volume of requests for clearance, and the need for such requests, especially for satellite news gathering (SNG), to be dealt with quickly.

Site clearance raises the even more important issue of the co-ordination of the allocation of radio frequency spectrum to ensure efficient use of radio frequency spectrum and development of services. There have been a number of EU-wide developments since the 1987 Green Paper to introduce pan-European services, such as those relating to the introduction of GSM (Council Directive 87/372/EEC of 25 June 1987 on the Frequency Bands to be Reserved for the Coordinated Introduction of Public Pan-European Cellular Digital Land Based Mobile Communications in the Community (OJ 17.7.87 L196/85) and ERMES (Council Directive 90/544/EEC of 9 October 1990 on the Frequency Bands Designated for the Coordinated Introduction of Pan-European Land Based Public Radio Paging in the Community (OJ 9.11.90 L310/28). However, there is obviously a need to co-ordinate this type of work in the context of international regulation on a wider scale with the work of the European Radiocommunications Committee of CEPT, which is recognised in current Commission proposals on radio frequency spectrum management (*Proposal for a Council Decision on the implementation by the Member States of measures concerning radio frequencies* (COM(93) 382); see para 5.87 *below*).

Administrative law

5.17   The award of licences and the allocation of radio frequency spectrum are administrative acts. Decision-making should be open and transparent. It should also be coherent. Parties whose rights are affected by any administrative decision should know why the decision was made and the nature of any rights they may have to challenge an unfavourable decision. Too often the law in the member states does not assist or is too uncertain to assist persons who are aggrieved by administrative acts. This is certainly true in the UK, where judicial review is expensive and not easy because decision-makers are not required to make public their reasons for decisions. Some EC legislation and proposals include a requirement that decision-makers state their reasons (see, for example, art 7 of the Mutual Recognition of Terminal Equipment Directive referred to in para 5.52 *below*; art 6 of the Satellite Equipment Directive referred to in para 5.53 *below*; and arts 7.2 and 12 of the Satellite Licensing Proposal, referred to in para 5.56 *below*). It is obviously outside the scope of this book to examine the jurisprudence on this subject. Suffice to say that the lack of such openness, and the lack of an adequate or uniform legal framework in the EU enabling aggrieved undertakings to challenge ill-founded administrative decisions, does not bode well for the development of true competition in Europe.

EC Legislation

5.18   It is convenient to consider, first, developments within the EU in telecommunications policy and regulation generally; secondly, those measures which relate to liberalisation in the satellite sector; and thirdly, EC legislation specifically related to the satellite sector.

Measures in relation to terminal equipment, the services sector and EC competition law (discussed in Chapter 4, paras 4.35 to 4.38 and in Chapter 8, paras 8.15 to 8.28) have been mentioned. The Commission's moves to liberalise the satellite sector and its proposals specific to satellites and guidelines on competition law are considered next. Lastly, other organisations of relevance in Europe are mentioned briefly.

As this work concerns the satellite sector, it should be noted at the outset that what follows is not intended to be an exhaustive discussion of all EC measures in the telecommunications sector. A more comprehensive list of measures relevant to telecommunications generally and satellite communications, in particular, appears in Appendix 2. Only a certain number of key measures considered relevant to the satellite sector are considered in detail.

The 1987 Green Paper

5.19   While there was EC legislation on telecommunications prior to 1987 (see Appendix 2), the main statement of the Commission's current telecommunication policy is in its *Green Paper on the development of the common market for telecommunications service and equipment* (COM (87) 290, 30 June 1987) ('the 1987 Green Paper').

The 1987 Green Paper did not deal specifically with matters relating to satellites (or, indeed, mobile communications). However, it established a basis for moves towards establishing a single market in the telecommunications sector and set the principles which are reflected in the Commission's current work in the satellite field. In short, it is the blueprint for harmonisation and liberalisation in telecommunications, and identified the following particular areas in the satellite sector for future consideration:

(*a*)   the development of the earth station market in Europe, in particular with regard to common standards;

(b)   the future development of space segments, in particular the relationships between EUTELSAT, national and private systems and the full use of the technological potential of the European Space Agency (ESA);

(c)   the development of international satellite communications, in particular with regard to INTELSAT and Inmarsat (1987 Green Paper (English version), p 191).

5.20   As will be recalled from the discussions in Chapter 4 on the ISOs and their reforms (Chapter 4, paras 4.43 to 4.54) and as appears *below* (para 5.22), it is interesting to note that as early as 1987 the Commission had begun to focus on the ISOs as an area for particular consideration.

The 1987 Green Paper set out three fundamental developments for EC telecommunications law and regulation, namely:

(*a*)   gradual opening to competition of the terminal equipment market (not merely for connection to the network, but also for the right to supply equipment in competition to the monopolist TOs);

(*b*)   acceptance by TOs of clear obligations to connect and provide access to cross-border service providers (crucial to the ability of others to utilise the existing network of the monopolist TO in order to compete); and

(*c*)   a clear separation of the regulatory and operational functions of TOs. (1987 Green Paper (English version), pp 184 and 185.)

The need for transparency in public procurement procedures was also recognised, as was the need to extend existing EU legislation on public procurement to the sectors excluded from Council Directive 77/162/EEC of 21 December 1976 Coordinating Procedures for the Award of Public Supply Contracts (OJ 15 .1.77 L13/1) and Council Directive 71/305/EEC of 26 July 1971 Concerning the Coordination of Procedures for the Award of Public Works Contracts (OJ 16.8.71 L185), so as to include the telecommunications sector (see para 5.38 *below*).

5.21   The conclusions of the 1987 Green Paper were taken further in *Council Resolution 88/C 257/01 of 30 June 1988 on the development of the Common Market for telecommunications services and equipment up to 1992* (OJ 4.10.88 C257/19) ('the 1988 Resolution'), which stated that the following points were major policy goals in the telecommunications field:

(*a*)   the creation of EU-wide network integrity, based on the principle of full interconnectivity between all public networks in the EU as an essential element for a common market in telecommunications services and equipment (thus emphasising the ability to access network infrastructure);

(*b*)   the creation of an open market for telecommunication services, particularly value-added services, including the rapid development of technical conditions, usage conditions and tariff principles for ONP (thus emphasising the need for 'openness');

(*c*)   the promotion of pan-European services so that European users can benefit from a wider range of better and cheaper telecommunications services. In the area of standards, this included the definition of common tariff principles and the encouragement of co-operation between network operators and others as far as compatible with EU competition rules (emphasising the benefits to consumers and recognising the potential for 'barriers to market entry' to potential competitors);

(*d*)   the development of the EU market for terminal equipment through the achievement of full mutual recognition of type-approval for terminal equipment, based on common European conformity specifications (thus extending the openness of standardisation of approval procedures for terminal equipment and taking a further step towards pan-European mutual recognition);

(*e*)   the development of a market in which TOs and other suppliers can compete equally, including the realisation of a clear separation of regulatory and operational functions and application of the competition rules of the Treaty of Rome to telecommunications (thus emphasising the need for equality and for the application of the competition rules of the EU); and

(*f*)   the continued development of EC measures with respect to common standards in the telecommunications sector. The Council welcomed the establishment of ETSI in this field (thus endorsing the establishment of ETSI as an independent standards institute, see para 5.93 *below*).

5.22   Significantly for present purposes, the 1988 Resolution also took up the need to develop EU policy in the field of satellites and called for:

> . . . a common position on satellite communications, so that this new information medium can develop in a favourable environment, taking account of the general rules of operation and exploitation of the network environment, as well as the competition rules of the Treaty and existing international commitments of member states. (para 10; p 257/3.)

It is not without significance that this Resolution refers to both the competition rules of the Treaty of Rome and the international commitments of the member states. This is a reference to the tension between the competition rules of the Treaty of Rome and international treaty obligations such as those which arise by reason of membership of the ITU or the ISOs which have been discussed in Chapter 4 (paras 4.23 to 4.38). All ministers voted in favour of this Resolution, although that might appear surprising in view of subsequent actions by certain member states and inaction by others.

The Terminal Equipment Directive (cited in para 5.8 *above*) was adopted shortly before the 1988 Resolution. The 1988 Resolution indicated that the aims of the Terminal Equipment Directive had been generally accepted by the member states (although, interestingly, it was later challenged, ostensibly by reason of its adoption under art 90(3)—see para 5.24 *below*). Following within a month of the 1988 Resolution were two further important directives: the first was the Services Directive and the second was the ONP Framework Directive.

These three directives marked the start of implementation of the basic objectives set out in the 1987 Green Paper and were the first stages in the legislative programme to liberalise network usage, the provision of competitive services, and the liberalisation of equipment supply and connection to the PSN.

Terminal Equipment Directive

5.23   The Terminal Equipment Directive aimed at achieving an EU-wide market for terminal equipment. It obliged member states to:

(*a*)   abolish all special or exclusive rights to import, market, connect, bring into service or maintain telecommunications terminal equipment (formerly enjoyed by the PTTs) (art 2);

(*b*)   ensure that users have access to new public network termination points (thus enabling connection of terminal equipment to the PSN) (art 4);

(c) ensure that independent standards bodies are established to draw up lists of technical specifications and type approval procedures, monitor their application and grant type approval (thus recognising that standard setting could of itself be a barrier to market entry and therefore needs to be carried out in an open and transparent way) (art 6); and

(d) ensure that customers can terminate, at a maximum of one year's notice, leasing or maintenance contracts for terminal equipment concluded when special or exclusive rights existed (thus allowing customers to avoid onerous contracts in situations where the TO still maintains its original monopoly) (art 7).

5.24   The Terminal Equipment Directive was amended following *French Republic* v *Commission of the European Communities* (referred to at para 5.8 *above*), when France and four other countries sought the annulment of certain provisions of this directive. In upholding the Commission's right to adopt the directive as part of its supervisory function under art 90(3), the court made a distinction between 'exclusive rights' and 'special rights' in deciding that the Commission was justified in requiring the withdrawal of exclusive rights, but the obligation to withdraw special rights was invalid as the Commission had failed to specify in the Terminal Equipment Directive the type of rights involved or in what way they contravened the Treaty of Rome. The ECJ therefore annulled art 2 of this directive in so far as it related to special rights. In other words the ECJ has permitted member states to grant what would otherwise be exclusive rights if held by a monopoly, to a limited number of TOs within their jurisdiction. Article 7 was also annulled as the member states were not privy to contracts between TOs and their customers. Council Directive 94/46/EC (the Services/Terminal Equipment Amendment Directive; see para 5.25 *below*) has required the abolition of exclusive rights, as further defined therein and requires the withdrawal of any 'special rights' which are in effect anti-competitive. This is discussed at para 5.69 *below*.

Services Directive

5.25   The Commission adopted the Services Directive under art 90(3). (This directive was previously adopted on 28 June 1989 and then revised and adopted on 28 June 1990.) Although initially the Services Directive did not apply to satellite services (see art 1(2)), it was still important as it set out the basic tenets of the Commission which were later applied directly to the satellite sector.

The Commission adopted Directive 94/46/EC of 13 October 1994 amending Directive 88/301/EEC and Directive 90/338/EEC in Particular with Regard to Satellite Communications (OJ 19.10.94 L268/15) ('the Services/Terminal Equipment Amendment Directive'). The directive specifically extended the Terminal Equipment Directive to cover satellite earth station equipment, and extended the Services Directive (see para 5.69 *below*) to include satellite communications services. The Article 90 Mobile Draft Directive also seeks to extend the Terminal Equipment Directive to cover 'mobile and personal communications services as well as mobile and personal communication systems' (see art 1: amendment to the definition of 'telecommunications services').

The objectives for the liberalisation of the satellite sector were set out in *Council Resolution 92/C8/01 of 19 December 1991 on the development of satellite communications services and equipment* (OJ 1992 C8/1) (based on the *Green Paper on a common approach in the field of satellite communications in the European Community* (COM(90) 490 final); see *below* at para 5.45). The Services Directive, as amended by the Services/Terminal Equipment Amendment Directive, now constitutes one of the central measures for liberalisation of the satellite sector (see para 5.69 *below*).

5.26 The Services Directive required member states to:

(*a*) abolish all exclusive and special rights for the supply of tele-communication services other than voice telephony (art 2);

(*b*) ensure that any operator is entitled to supply such services (art 2);

(*c*) ensure that conditions for access to networks are objective, non-discriminatory and transparent (art 4);

(*d*) ensure that there is no discrimination in the conditions of use or in the charges payable by service providers including TOs (art 6); and ensure that the granting of licences, the control of type approval and standards making, allocation of radio frequency spectrum and surveillance of usage conditions are separated from the TO in an 'independent' organisation (art 7).

Importantly, art 2 requires member states which impose licensing conditions or declaration procedures on liberalised services to ensure that 'such conditions are objective, non-discriminatory and transparent'. Furthermore, the directive aims to facilitate administrative or judicial review of such licensing procedure by requiring that 'reasons are given for any refusal, and that there is a procedure for appealing any such refusal'. This is similar to the provisions of art 6 of the Terminal Equipment Directive.

This directive, therefore, struck more directly at the heart of TOs' businesses and, hardly surprisingly, it was challenged in the ECJ by Belgium, Italy and Spain (see *Spain, Belgium and Italy v EU Commission*, joined cases C-271/90, C-281/90 and C-289/90. This case was decided in November 1992 and followed closely the decision on the Terminal Equipment Directive. The ECJ held that the Commission had acted properly in issuing the directive under art 90, but the court annulled those parts of the Services Directive which referred to 'special' (as opposed to exclusive) rights (see para 5.24 *above*).

5.27 Voice telephony is defined as 'the commercial provision for the public of the direct transport and switching of speech in real time between public switched network termination points, enabling any user to use equipment connected to such a network termination point in order to communicate with another termination point' (Services Directive, art 1(1)). The reservation is, therefore, very narrow and does not extend to leased circuit-based services without PSN connections or to services provided to any closed user group. What constitutes 'voice telephony' is important as it sets the limits of which exclusive or special rights have been retained and which have been abolished, and has already been the subject of litigation. This will ultimately become a question of fact to be examined by the relevant NRA. The burden of proof that a particular service falls within a reserved category lies with the NRA. However, the question of what is and is not reserved would be a question of EC law.

As noted in the 1992 Services Directive Review:

> A voice service may be reserved under national legislation *only* if it includes *all* of the elements of the Community voice telephony definition, ie it must be provided on a *commercial* basis to the *public* for the purpose of *direct transport* and *switching* of speech in *real time* between public switched network termination points.[7]

What is clear from the 1992 Services Directive Review is confirmation that the 'reserve' is to be 'interpreted narrowly' and is therefore very limited (p 16). To allow the NRA to consider what the applicant proposes to do when introducing a particular service, the NRA will require facts and details from the applicant. However, the Commission makes clear that there is a presumption of 'non-reserve' (therefore permitted) if the new service meets a current demand not met by existing telephony services. Importantly, the Commission states: 'If they are reserved, the burden of proof, as always, should fall on the Member State to justify such a restriction' (p 16).[8]

5.28   The Services Directive was particularly important as it set in place, in 1990, four dates by which certain goals were to be achieved:

(*a*)   31 December 1990 for the opening up of competition of all telecommunications services other than voice telephony and simple resale of capacity (art 4; see (*d*) *below*);

(*b*)   1 July 1991 for the establishment of an independent body (ie an NRA) to grant licences and supervise their conditions (art 7);

(*c*)   30 June 1992 for notification to the Commission of any licensing procedures for packet or circuit-switched public data services (art 3); and

(*d*)   31 December 1992 for the opening up of the market in simple resale capacity (art 3).

5.29   Initially, public voice telephony was excluded from the ambit of the Services Directive. The Commission considered that 'the opening-up of voice telephony to competition could threaten the financial stability of the telecommunications organizations' (Services Directive, recital 18). In 1992 the exception granted to voice telephony services was reviewed by the Commission. With the adoption of the 1992 Services Directive Review on 21 October 1992, the Commission launched a wide-ranging debate about the development of telecommunications in the EU up to the end of the present decade. The main aim of that consultation was to obtain the views of both European industry as a whole and of the main participants in the telecommunications sector on the issues raised in the 1992 Services Directive Review. It is apparent from the foregoing that the Commission's thinking has moved on to the extent that voice telephony (and infrastructure) will be fully liberalised in most member states on 1 January 1998, and in the meantime innovative voice services and closed user groups (see the discussion, *ibid*, pp 17 *et seq*) and the like will not only be permitted but encouraged, at least at the EU level. In particular, the 1992 Services Directive

Review offered four options for further action in telecommunications policy:

(*a*)   freezing the liberalisation process, ie maintaining the *status quo*;

(*b*)   introducing extensive regulation of both tariffs (in particular the surcharge in intra-EU tariffs) and investments at the EU level in order to overcome bottlenecks (such as tariffs, delays in offering new networks and services and a shortage of high speed links);

(*c*)   liberalising all voice telephony (including international calls inside and outside the EU and national calls);

(*d*)   an intermediate option of liberalising voice telephony to allow competition between member states.

5.30   After wide public consultation on the 1992 Services Directive Review, on 28 April 1993 the Commission issued another *Communication to the Council and the European Parliament on the consultation on the review of the situation in the telecommunications services sector* (COM(93) 159) ('the Services Directive Review Communication'). The Commission concluded that option (*d*) *above* was the best short-term option in conjunction with ONP regulation to ensure EU-wide interconnection and universal access to networks. At the same time, the Commission noted the need for a definition of 'universal service' obligations in the context of EU telecommunications services. The concept of 'universal service' is essential to ensure that a defined minimum service of specified quality is accessible to all users at an affordable price: *Council Resolution 94/C of 7 February 1994 on universal service principles in the telecommunications sector* (OJ 16.2.94, C48/ 1). Universal service is also relevant and is covered by the Proposed Interconnection Directive (see, for example, art 5 of the Proposed Interconnection Directive, referred to at para 5.9 *above*).

As noted above, the Council adopted the July 1993 Resolution in response to the Commission's Services Directive Review Communication. In the July 1993 Resolution, the Council gave its support (*inter alia*) to the preparation by the Commission of amendments to the EU regulatory framework in order to achieve full liberalisation of all public voice telephony services by 1 January 1998, subject to a derogation granting an additional transitional period of up to five years in the cases of Spain, Ireland, Greece and Portugal which have 'less developed networks'. The Council also considered that a major short-term goal for EC telecommunications policy was the adoption of legislative proposals in the field of ONP and satellites and the Commission proceeded accordingly.

5.31   As referred to in para 5.1 *above*, the December 1994 Resolution established the principles and proposed timetable for the liberalisation of telecommunications infrastructure and the establishment of open competition by 1 January 1998. This then became the subject of the Infrastructure Green Paper (Parts I and II) (see para 5.1 *above*). The consultation results were presented to the European Parliament and the Council on 3 May 1995. The Commission's *Communication to the European Parliament and the Council on the Green Paper on the liberalisation of telecommunications infrastructure and cable television networks* (COM(95) 158, 3 May 1995) ('the Infrastructure Communication'), sets out the Commission's proposals for the future regulatory framework for telecommunications and called for the preparation by the Commission of:

(*a*)   a draft directive amending the Services Directive with regard to mobile and personal communications, which is now the Article 90 Mobile Draft Directive; see para 5.9 *above*;

(*b*)   a Common Position on a proposal for a European Parliament and Council Directive for ONP voice telephony, which is now the *Amended Proposal for a European Parliament and Council Directive on the application of open network provision (ONP) to voice telephony*, (COM (94) 48 final) ('the Amended ONP/Voice Proposal');

(*c*)   a draft amendment of the Services Directive with regard to the full liberalisation of telecommunications infrastructure and services from 1 January 1998 (still to come).

These and other measures relating to the amendment of the ONP Framework Directive, and amendments to Council Directive 92/44/EEC on the Application of Open Network Provision to Leased Lines (OJ 19.06.92 L165/127) (the 'Leased Lines Directive'), are required to be in place by 1 January 1996. However, the Council of Ministers' failure, on 13 June 1995, to gain the agreement of member states to this timetable for liberalisation led to the Commission's announcement, on 19 July 1995, that it would issue an art 90 directive to force through the liberalisation of alternative infrastructure by the end of 1995.

While some may consider 1 January 1998 too far in the future for full liberalisation of voice telephony, it must be recognised that, if achieved, it would mark a significant success in the liberalisation policy of the Commission in view of the political and other obstacles that have been raised in implementing the 1987 Green Paper over the past six years. Likewise, the Amended ONP Voice Proposal and the Proposed Interconnection Directive are a considerable advance in EC telecommunications policy.

5.32   Another issue linked to liberalisation which was dealt with in the July 1993 Resolution and the 22 July 1992 Resolution is the importance of the development of trans-European networks (TENs) in the telecommunications field. The 1993 Resolution notes that 'increasing liberalisation in the [telecommunications] sector will be the most effective way to stimulate investment in trans-European telecommunications networks. . . . Liberalisation will open the way for further cooperative ventures between groups of operations in order to offer genuine pan European telecommunications services on an end-to-end basis' (see para 5.31 *above*).

Article 129 of the Treaty of European Union provides that 'the Community shall contribute to the establishment and development of trans-European networks (TENs) in the areas of transport, tele-communications and energy infrastructures'. The Treaty goes on to say that the Community shall establish guidelines concerning the objectives, priorities and measures envisaged in the sphere of TENs; shall implement measures to ensure the interoperability of networks and may support financial efforts by member states for projects of common interest identified in the guidelines (eg through feasibility studies and loan guarantees and interest rate subsidies). The Commission (DG XIII) intends to submit shortly a series of proposals for Decisions for the promotion of TENs in the telecommunications field concerning, in particular, ISDN, broadband communications networks and trans-European networks between Administrations. See, for example, the TENs Methodology Guidelines Proposal (para 5.1 *above*).

The fostering of a competitive and stable environment for the investment necessary to fund TENs highlights the necessity for open access to voice telephony, the availability of leased lines, interconnection on fair and reasonable terms, interoperability and harmonisation of the conditions of use of the PSN across Europe. The Commission has grasped this nettle and one can expect from the tone of the Infrastructure Communication and cognate matters that the Commission's implementation of measures will be direct and effective.

Likewise, the action plan which followed the Bangemann Report (see para 5.1 *above*) recognises the vital importance of continuing liberalisation and regulatory stability and encouragement for the development of the global information society in Europe (see the Information Society Action Plan). Similarly, the Commission's work on infrastructure liberalisation emphasises the need to synchronise the date of this liberalisation to 1 January 1998 (the 22 July 1992 Resolution as supplemented by *Council Resolution 94/C379/03 of 22 July 1994*, OJ 3.8.94 C209/1).

5.33   Before leaving the subject of the Terminal Equipment and Services Directives, it is worth noting that arts 6 and 7 require member states to separate operational and regulatory functions. Although NRAs have been established in most member states, the manner of implementation of these provisions is not clear in a number of them. To have a regulatory regime without an independent regulator does seem inconsistent with a liberalised telecommunications market. As noted in the Services Directive Review at p 22:

> This issue of the independence of the [NRAs] was raised in a number of preliminary referrals to the [ECJ] relating to Article 6 of [the Terminal Equipment Directive], which required Member States, as of 1 July 1989, to ensure that the fixing of technical standards as well as supervision of type approval, were carried out by bodies independent from public or private undertakings involved in the marketing of telecommunications equipment.

In the ECJ cases *Francine Decoster* and *Ministère Public v Taillander* (see para 5.13 *above*), the ECJ held that the French Government had not complied with art 6 of the Terminal Equipment Directive, as departments within the same P&T Ministry, were 'responsible for operating the public network, implementing the commercial policy on telecommunications, drawing up the technical specification, monitoring the application and granting type approval for terminal apparatus'. It then found that the P&T Ministry was an 'undertaking', because of its commercial activities, and was, therefore, bound by the directive.

Mere separation by administrative act will accordingly not of itself meet the requirements of both directives. The Commission has stated that, in its view, such a separation would comply only if it could be established that:

(*a*)   there is a 'real' separation;

(*b*)   there is financial independence;

(*c*)   personnel moving from the NRA to the operator were 'subject to special supervision' (the Services Directive Review, p 22).

But there remain the questions of what is real separation, how financial independence is to be achieved, and who will supervise the movement of staff. In the context of implementation of EC measures, as discussed in the July 1993 Resolution, the independence of the NRA and the extent of operational and regulatory separation are matters of continuing concern.

ONP Framework Directive

5.34   The ONP Framework Directive is a vital component in the creation of the single internal market for telecommunications and is aimed at preventing national telecommunications operators from abusing their positions as actual or former monopolists in preventing third party operators from gaining access to telecommunication infrastructure. Article 1.1 proclaimed that it 'concerns the harmonization of conditions for open and efficient access to and use of public telecommunications networks and, where applicable, public telecommunication services'. It set objectives to:

(*a*)   ensure that ONP conditions comply with three basic principles (these are the trinity of ONP) namely:

— they must be based on objective criteria;

— they must be transparent and published in an appropriate manner;

— they must guarantee equality of access, must be non-discriminatory and in accordance with EC law (art 3.1);

(*b*)   prohibit restrictions on access to the PSN or public telecommunications services (PTS) 'except for reasons based on essential requirements' (which are limited to security and integrity of the network, interoperability of services and data protection) (art 3.2);

(*c*)   prohibit any additional restrictions on the use of the PSN and/ or PTS except those special or exclusive rights 'which are compatible with [EC] law' (again this limits the exception of such rights to their compatibility with EC competition law) (art 3.3);

(*d*) draw up harmonised technical interface and/or service features to ensure ONP will carry the presumption that once complied with, the service provider and/or TO 'fulfils the relevant essential requirements' (necessary to ensure standards are not barriers to market entry) (arts 5.1 and 5.2);

(*e*) lay down a timetable for the Council to adopt specific directives establishing ONP conditions (to ensure the ONP programme continues to forward) (art 6); and

(*f*) establish an ONP Committee as an advisory committee to the Commission comprising representatives of the member states and chaired by a representative of the Commission to, *inter alia*, consult widely and deliver advisory opinions to the Commission (thus the ONP Committee, while only advisory, was the founding EU regulatory committee in telecommunications and was the forerunner of the Community Telecommunications Committee (CTC) referred to at para 5.81 *below*) (art 9).[9]

It will be appreciated that the Council recognised the importance of ensuring objective and non-discriminatory standards making and ONP conditions to ensure the creation of uniform conditions for use of the network, the creation of a fair and transparent tariff structure and the promulgation of common technical interface standards.

The directive did not require member states to limit TOs' special rights with regard to the provision of the network infrastructure, although it did lay down a timetable with a review period which roughly coincided with the Services Directive review timetable (see para 5.28 *above*).

5.35 A series of important measures has been enacted or proposed to implement logically the ONP principles for particular telecommunications services. These include *inter alia* the following:

(*a*) the Leased Lines Directive;

(*b*) *Council Recommendation 92/382/EEC of 18 July 1992 on the harmonised provision of a minimum set of packet-switched data services (PSDS) in accordance with open network provision (ONP) principles* (OJ 18.7.92 L200/1);

(*c*) the Amended ONP/Voice Proposal;

(*d*) Commission Decision 94/821/EU of 9 December 94 on a Common Technical Regulation for Attachment Requirements for Terminal Interface for ONP 64 kbit/s Digital Unstructured Leased Lines (OJ 29.12.94 L339/81); and (*e*)   the Commission's Proposed Interconnection Directive.

5.36   A proposal concerning ONP and voice telephony was first submitted by the Commission to the Council in September 1992. Following the entry into force of the Treaty on European Union on 1 November 1993, the European Parliament and the Council were unable to reach agreement on a joint text mainly on the issue of 'comitology' (see para 5.59 *below*), so the Common Position confirmed by the Council in June 1994 was rejected by the European Parliament in July 1994.

The Amended ONP/Voice Proposal has now been resubmitted with the articles relating to comitology excluded; the Commission has, however, largely maintained the remaining text which had effectively been agreed previously between the European Parliament and the Council at the conciliation meetings.

The Amended ONP/Voice Proposal is aimed at the harmonisation of the conditions governing the supply and usage of voice telephony services and networks within the EU. It also has another trinity of objectives which are to:

(*a*)   lay down the rights of users of voice telephony services in their relations with TOs;

(*b*)   improve access for all users, including providers of services, to the public telephone network infrastructure; and

(*c*)   encourage the Community-wide provision of voice telephony services.

As regards quality of service, billing and the supply of advanced voice telephony services, the Amended ONP/Voice Proposal, when implemented, will give the Commission power to check that member states have taken the required steps to attain the objectives laid down in it and if they have not, to take measures against them.

5.37   To understand how the Amended ONP/Voice Proposal will be presented, and presumably passed, it is only necessary to understand the significance of the Leased Lines Directive amending the Terminal Equipment and Services Directives, in particular with regard to satellite communications. Although this is dealt with *below* (see para 5.69 *et seq*), the important point is that the Leased Lines Directive requires the abolition of all exclusive rights granted for the provision of satellite services and any special rights to provide any telecommunication service covered by the directive. As noted in para 5.27 *above*, what constitutes 'voice telephony' is construed restrictively.

The Commission is currently discussing with the ONP Committee future harmonised licensing frameworks for telecommunications operators/service providers. Topics include widening the scope for general authorisations (as opposed to issuing individual licences) and their harmonisation throughout the Union. (See the ONP Harmonisation Proposal, para 5.12 *above*.)

In addition, the Commission is bringing forward the timetable for harmonised licensing frameworks, both through the follow-on work to the consultation on the *Green Paper on infrastructure liberalisation* and what is expected to be a Commission endorsement of the ONP Committee proposal.

Public procurement

5.38   Another area in which the EU has regulated TOs by legislation is the conduct of their procurement of services, supplies and works. As noted at para 5.20 *above*, the 1987 Green Paper referred to the need for transparency in public procurement in the telecommunications sector. This led the Council to adopt, on 17 September 1990, Council Directive 90/531/EEC on the Procurement Procedures of Entities Operating in the Water, Energy, Transport and Telecommunications Sectors (OJ 29.10.90 L297/1) ('the Utilities Directive').[10] This directive applies to 'contracting entities' which are either public authorities or undertakings or private operators with special or exclusive rights who provide or operate PSN or provide PTS. It followed an earlier directive which dealt with public procurement for other sectors, although the regime prescribed by the Utilities Directive is slightly less liberal than that for the other sectors.

The Utilities Directive rules apply to supply or works contracts made by contracting entities which exceed ECU 600,000 in value. 'Supply' contracts are essentially contracts for the supply of products or software services, while works contracts relate to building or civil engineering. It contains guidelines as to the technical specifications and standards which must be included in a contract and the procedures for the award of contracts. It also obliges TOs to publish annual notices to alert potential bidders of forthcoming procurement plans and contains provisions allowing tenders from non-European persons to be rejected in certain circumstances. This latter measure is aimed at bringing pressure on foreign markets to open up to European companies.

5.39   On 14 June 1993, the Council adopted a directive amending the Utilities Directive and extending the application of the procurement rules from supply or works contracts to contracts for 'the provision or operation of public telecommunications networks or the provision of one or more public telecommunications services (Council Directive 93/38/EEC of 14 June 1993 Coordinating the Procurement Procedures of Entities Operating in the Water, Energy, Transport and Telecommunications Sectors (OJ 9.8.93 L119/84)). This directive does not apply to contracts of an estimated value of less than ECU 600,000 as calculated in accordance with the guidelines for assessment of the value of such contracts set out in the directive. With the adoption of this directive, the EU's public procurement rules now have wide effect in the telecommunications sector, applying to both public entities and private operators with special or exclusive rights to have or provide a PTN or PTS.

EC competition law

5.40   Before considering the specific work of the Commission in the satellite sector, it is useful to give a brief description of EC competition law, the purpose of which is to ensure that undertakings compete with each other rather than collaborate to the detriment of their competitors and consumers. More and more of the industry specific measures of the *Commission's Communication on the full application of the competition rules in ensuring Commission policy* are enforced (see for example the Infrastructure Communication, para 5.1 *above*). As noted in the Proposed Interconnection Directive (p 5), the Commission recognises the great importance of the competition rules, but also recognises that in the transition to 'full competition' certain industry specific measures will be required and notes:

> In a perfectly competitive environment, the need for regulation would be limited to ensuring fair play, most probably *ex-post* application of the treaty competition rules, supported by *ex-ante* provisions aimed at satisfying certain public service goals and essential requirements. While the market is moving towards full competition, however, an appropriate *ex-ante* regulatory regime will be required to reduce the risk that existing players might use their strength to discourage new potential operators and service providers from entering the market.

Articles 85 to 95 of the EC Treaty set out the EC's competition rules. The two principal articles, which deal respectively with anti-competitive agreements and practices and abuse of a dominant position, are arts 85 and 86.

Article 85

5.41   Article 85(1) prohibits agreements and practices between undertakings which have as their object or effect (whether direct or indirect, actual or potential) the prevention, restriction or distortion of competition within the EU and which appreciably affect trade between member states. If an agreement violates the prohibition in art 85(1), it is void and unenforceable from the moment it is signed, or, at least, the offending provisions will be void if they are properly severable from the rest of the agreement.

The Commission recognises the value of collaboration between TOs which can play a major role in the development of a harmonious satellite system throughout the EU. However, it stresses that the application of arts 85 and 86 to research and development agreements and joint ventures is not precluded by virtue of the fact that such collaboration may have important benefits.[11]

Co-operation and joint venture agreements may be exempted under art 85(3) if they bring specific benefits, including, *inter alia*, the promotion of technological progress, which outweigh any detriment to competition. The Commission may be inclined to look favourably upon agreements involving collaboration in research and development as each satellite is, in effect, a prototype—its design and production being at great cost. However, in the *ASTRA* case (Commission Decision IV/32.74S Astra, 93/50/EEC of 23 December 1992 Relating to a Proceeding Pursuant to Article 85 of the EC Treaty, OJ 28.1.93 L20/23), described in more detail in Chapter 4, (para 4.34), the Commission decided that BT, in view of its financial position and its technical and commercial satellite know-how, had the necessary resources to enter the satellite market without the need for collaboration. The Commission found that the arrangements between BT and SES were prohibited by art 85(1). The *ASTRA* decision illustrates the point that collaboration arrangements may fall within art 85(1) and need individual exemption (see *below*) under art 85(3).

Article 86

5.42   Article 86 provides that any abuse by one or more undertakings holding a dominant position in a market within the EU or within a substantial part of it shall be prohibited as incompatible with the common market in so far as it may affect trade between member states. Such abuse may, in particular, consist in directly or indirectly imposing unfair purchase or selling prices or other trading conditions or limiting production, access to markets or technical development to the prejudice of competitors or consumers. Article 86 provides further illustrations of particular abuses.

There is no fixed market share which defines when a company or undertaking will be dominant. Much depends on whether a particular undertaking has sufficient power to operate, to a large extent, independently of its customers and competitors. In the case law of the ECJ, it is usually market shares in excess of 40 per cent which are regarded as capable of giving rise to a dominant position. Therefore, it is essential in this context to determine the structure of the market and the number and strength of the competitors within it.

Exemptions

5.43   If the parties are uncertain whether art 85 and/or art 86 applies to their arrangements, they may apply to the Commission for 'negative clearance', ie a declaration that the agreement does not fall within the competition rules. Furthermore, where the agreement is prohibited under art 85(1), the parties may apply under art 85(3) for an 'exemption' from the prohibition so that the agreements can be implemented. There is no like provision under art 86 for exempting abuses of a dominant position.

Other liberalisation in the satellite sector

5.44   Less than a month after the adoption of the 1988 Resolution (see para 5.21 *above*), on 26 July 1988, the Commission issued its *First communication on space: The Community and space: a coherent approach* (COM(88) 417) in which it was recognised that the EU was destined to play a broader and more active role in the international satellite sector, and that there was a need for a satellite policy incorporating technological, industrial, commercial, social and defence aspects. A number of action lines were proposed by the Commission and once those were established, the Commission began developing a Green Paper on satellite communications as its response to the Council's call for a common position on such matters.

The 1990 Satellite Green Paper

5.45   Although some details of the 1990 Satellite Green Paper have been discussed in Chapter 4, it is important to consider it further here as it has led to the various liberalisation steps and harmonisation of satellite communications measures recently adopted or currently under consideration, some of which have already been touched on.

The 1990 Satellite Green Paper was published on 20 November 1990. It embodied the EU's major policy in the satellite sector and was subsequently largely approved by the Council in *Council Resolution 92/C8/01 of 19 December 1992 on the development of the common market for satellite communications services and equipment* (OJ 14.1.92 C8/1) ('the Satellite Resolution') of 14 January 1992.

The Commission made four detailed proposals in respect of the regulatory environment, which are summarised on p 129 of the English version of the 1990 Satellite Green Paper, namely that:

(*a*)   earth segment should be fully liberalised: all exclusive or special rights should be abolished, including rights relating to receive-only terminals, subject to appropriate type approval procedures in cases where these are connected to the PSN; and transmit-receive terminals subject to the appropriate type approval and licensing procedures where these are justified for the implementation of the network integrity safeguards;

(*b*)   member states, in their capacities as parties to the constituent instruments of the ISOs, should be required to adopt measures which afford unrestricted access to space segment capacity. Such access would be subject to licensing procedures in order to safeguard any exclusive or special rights or regulatory provisions put in place by member states which are compatible with Community law. Access should be on an equitable, non-discriminatory and cost-orientated basis (see Chapter 4, para 4.27);

(*c*)   space segment providers should be given complete commercial freedom, including the freedom to market satellite capacity directly to service providers and users, subject to compliance with licensing procedures and conformity with Community law, in particular with the competition rules in the Treaty of Rome (see para 5.48 *below*), (Chapter 4 contains a detailed discussion of the 1990 Satellite Green Paper in relation to access to space segment);

(*d*)   there should be Community-wide harmonisation to facilitate the provision and use of Europe-wide services. In particular, there should be mutual recognition of licensing and type approval procedures, radio frequency co-ordination and the co-ordination of services provided to and from non-EU states.

5.46   As will be apparent, these four proposals reflect the reasoning behind the Terminal Equipment Directive, the Services Directive and the ONP Directive. In addition, the comments on access to space segment (see Chapter 4, para 4.27) relate to the satellite matters touched on in the 1987 Green Paper (see para 5.19 *above*).

The general goals of the 1990 Satellite Green Paper were endorsed by the Council in the Satellite Resolution. This resolution set out the following four points as major goals in satellite telecommunications policy:

(*a*)   harmonisation and liberalisation for appropriate satellite earth stations, including where applicable, the abolition of exclusive or special rights in this area, subject in particular to conditions necessary for compliance with essential requirements;

(*b*)   harmonisation and liberalisation as far as required to facilitate the provision and use of Europe-wide satellite telecommunications services subject, where applicable, to conditions necessary for compliance with essential requirements and special or exclusive rights;

(*c*)   separation in all member states of regulatory and operational functions in the field of satellite communications;

(*d*)   improved access to the space segment and access to the space capacity of intergovernmental organisations operating satellite systems and effective and accelerated procedures for the establishment of and access to separate satellite systems.

5.47   As regards points (*a*) to (*c*) above, the Council noted the intention of the Commission to propose the necessary measures to achieve these goals, including measures for the approximation of the laws of member states concerning satellite earth stations and the establishment of a harmonised regulatory framework for the licensing of satellite networks and satellite services. The Commission has subsequently produced proposals for both these measures and these are discussed in more detail (see paras 5.56 to 5.64 *below*).

As regards item (*d*), the Council invited member states to work towards:

(*a*)   the development of effective, non-discriminatory and accelerated procedures for the establishment of separate satellite systems;

(*b*)   the improvement and broadening of access to the space segments of intergovernmental organisations operating satellite systems, taking account of the special and exclusive rights for the provision of public telecommunications services and working along the following lines of action:

—   active participation of the member states within the intergovernmental organisations operating satellite systems to work towards that goal,

—   the development of effective procedures, eg along the line of Signatories Affairs Offices, as an initial step,

—   drawing up conditions for fair, non-discriminatory and transparent access to space capacity for earth segment operators.

As noted in Chapter 4, this invitation has not gone unanswered and the member states and ISOs have taken significant steps towards changing their co-ordination procedures to facilitate the establishment of other satellite systems (see Chapter 4, para 4.45) as well as altering the procedures for gaining access to space segment to facilitate improved access. For a further account of these changes, see Chapter 4, paras 4.43 *et seq*.

Competition Guidelines

5.48   While the 1990 Satellite Green Paper was being prepared in DG XIII and following its publication, DG IV was preparing a set of guidelines based on experience of the telecommunications industry and the applicability of EC competition rules to that sector. On 6 September 1991, DG IV published its *Guidelines on the application of EEC competition rules in the telecommunications sector* (OJ 6.9.91 C233/ 2) ('the Guidelines'). Although not binding, the Guidelines aimed to clarify the application of the Treaty of Rome's competition rules to the participants in the telecommunications sector and to emphasise that these rules, in particular arts 85 and 86 of the Treaty of Rome, apply fully to satellite communications (see the Guidelines, paras 122–128) and were directly relevant to the satellite sector.

The Guidelines recognised that agreements between TOs operating within international conventions (for example, the ISOs) may qualify for art 85(3) exemption if any adverse effect on competition is outweighed by benefits if, *inter alia*, it leads to technical or economic progress. The development of satellite services in the EU may fall within this category provided that the restrictions on the operations contained in the agreement are indispensable for the attainment of the beneficial objects, and that the other requirements of art 85(3) are satisfied.

5.49 Paragraph 126 of the Guidelines states that '. . . agreements between TOs concerning the operation of satellite systems in the broadest sense may be caught by Article 85'. The Commission's reasoning behind this is that TOs compete with one another for the provision of space segment capacity and up-linking facilities. As noted in Chapter 4, the ISOs are, in effect, conglomerations of national TOs. Therefore, the Commission believes that agreements between TOs operating within the ISOs may restrict competition, eg by pooling space segment capacity. Such agreements may restrict competition between themselves and reduce the ability of third parties to obtain satellite capacity and so limit their ability to provide telecommunications services in competition with the TOs. As a result, competition will be reduced and the consumer will suffer.

The Commission indicates in the Guidelines that such agreements between TOs are unlikely to qualify for an exemption under art 85(3) if the restrictions imposed reduce the ability of third parties to compete. The Guidelines also raise the possibility that such agreements might strengthen an individual or collective dominant position of the TO or TOs in contravention of art 86.

The Guidelines drew attention to the fact that agreements relating to up-linking between competing TOs may also restrict competition. The current wide choice of up-linking facilities in the modern telecommunications market led the Commission to conclude in the Guidelines that 'Community wide agreements providing directly or indirectly for coordination as to the parties' up-link provision are therefore caught by Article 85 (Guidelines, para 127, p 23). In addition, arrangements for the bundling of up-link and space segment capacity are almost certain to offend art 85(1) (see the *ASTRA* decision, *above*).

The Commission made it clear that it will scrutinise agreements between ISO signatories (see Chapter 4, paras 4.25 and 4.35), as well as other space segment providers, on a case by case basis, to ensure that their practices comply with the competition rules. If there is a danger that consumer choice is reduced, or that a TO's dominant position is strengthened, the Commission is not likely to approve the arrangement.

EC legislation specifically related to satellites

5.50   Since the 1990 Satellite Green Paper the Commission has been implementing the policy goals set out in it, as illustrated by the Satellite Resolution (see para 5.46 *above*). The mutual recognition of satellite earth station equipment has been achieved (see para 5.52 *below*) and there are currently three proposals at various stages of the legislative process covering mutual recognition of licences and satellite personal communications; these are discussed *below* at para 5.52. In addition, the Commission pursued a controversial policy in the area of transmission standards for High Definition Television (HDTV) which has recently been revised after much activity in the Council (see para 5.67 *below*). There is also Council Directive 89/552/EEC of 3 October 1989 on the Coordination of Certain Provisions Laid Down by Law, Regulation or Administrative Action in Member States Concerning the Pursuit of Television Broadcasting Activities (OJ 17.10.89 L298) otherwise known as the 'Television Without Frontiers Directive', which is discussed in detail in Chapter 7. Another proposal of relevance to satellite communications is Directive 93/83/EEC on the Coordination of Certain Rules Concerning Copyright and Rights Related to Copyright Applicable to Satellite Broadcasting and Cable Retransmission (OJ 6.10.93 L248/15) which is considered in detail in Chapter 8, para 8.29.

Controversy surrounded much of the Commission's work immediately following the 1987 Green Paper. Not all member states had the same views of the need or pace of change. Eight years later, member states still vary in their views on these matters. At times it does seem that some member states are highly reluctant to harmonise their laws in accordance with their EC Treaty obligations. Thus, the Commission's work in the satellite sector has shown in respect of mutual recognition of terminal equipment and, importantly, of licences (both discussed *below*) the need to abolish time-consuming member state-by-member state licensing, which hitherto has made it virtually impossible to introduce EU-wide satellite services. As discussed *below*, full mutual recognition has encountered considerable political problems in the EU. As a result, it would appear that harmonisation will be the main objective for the time being, with 'one-stop shopping' being a transitional solution. While this may be politically easier to achieve than full mutual recognition of licences, it should not be forgotten that harmonisation of 'essential requirements', for example, has yet to be achieved. Thus there is the possibility that some member states may impose conditions on satellite services as 'essential requirements' which are inconsistent with those imposed by other member states.

5.51 EC legislation introduced immediately after 1990 dealt only with the margins of the industry, eg the mutual recognition of satellite terminal equipment. Clearly, the terminal equipment area has been most successful. Although the Council recognised that a key factor in developing future EC regulatory policy was the 'implementation of the principle of mutual recognition of national licences and authorisations based on harmonized conditions . . .' (the July 1993 Resolution; see para 5.1 *above*), mutual recognition of licences, as discussed *below*, has stalled while the member states reflect on the practical implications of these seemingly logical steps in the Commission's overall progression from the 1987 Green Paper and the 1990 Satellite Green Paper. In the other major areas, the Services Directive, for example, amendments are, however, far-reaching.

Mutual recognition of earth station equipment

5.52 Directive 91/263/EEC of 29 April 1991 on the Approximation of the Laws of the Member States Concerning Telecommunications Terminal Equipment Including the Mutual Recognition of their Conformity (OJ 23.5.91 L128/1) ('the Mutual Recognition of Terminal Equipment Directive') was the successor to the Terminal Equipment Directive discussed *above* at para 5.23.

This directive laid down a mandatory mechanism for the complete mutual recognition of approval procedures for all terminal equipment, which is a natural consequence of harmonised equipment approval type procedures across the EU. Once equipment has achieved type approval in one member state by passing all the required tests, all other member states must accept the terminal equipment and allow it to be marketed and connected to the PSN within their jurisdiction.

Following the Mutual Recognition of Terminal Equipment Directive, on 29 October 1993 the Council issued Directive 93/97/EEC Supplementing Directive 91/263/EEC in Respect of Satellite Earth Station Equipment (OJ 24.11.93 L290/1) (the Satellite Equipment Directive) Relating to Mutual Recognition of Type Approval for Satellite Terminals. This was an important step, especially given the political controversy surrounding mutual recognition of licences generally (see para 5.56 *below*).

5.53   The purpose of the Satellite Equipment Directive was to implement the single market for satellite earth station equipment. It followed on from the 1990 Satellite Green Paper which recognised that at a global level, a new, high-growth market was emerging for point-to-multipoint private satellite networks based on the new very small aperture terminals, commonly referred to as VSATs, individually designed for each customer's need and often operated by third party service providers. The directive excludes from its ambit purpose-built satellite earth station equipment intended for use as part of the PSN of a member state.

The main effect of the directive, modelled on and supplementing the Mutual Recognition of Terminal Equipment Directive, is to allow earth station equipment which has been tested in one member state to be freely marketed in any other member state. Earth station equipment must, however, satisfy 'essential requirements' as under the Mutual Recognition of Terminal Equipment Directive. The Commission will identify the kinds of equipment for which common technical regulation (CTRs) is required and will introduce harmonised standards to implement the essential requirements, which will be transformed into CTRs, compliance with which will be mandatory. As will be apparent from the discussions in Chapters 1, 2 and 3 concerning the ITU and the work of its internal organs, especially the Radio Regulations Board and the Telecommunication Standardization Sector, these provisions follow closely the obligations and responsibilities of member states, eg in avoiding harmful interference, effective use of scarce resources (such as radio frequency spectrum and orbital positions), and licensing of transmitting stations. (See, for example, recitals (20) and (21).)

In the case of TVROs, the manufacturer may declare conformity of his terminals with the relevant CTR.

Under art 2.1, member states are required to take all appropriate measures to ensure that receive-only satellite dishes, not intended to be connected to the PSN, are put into service and used in conformity with 'national law compatible with Community law, only if it complies with . . . this Directive when it is properly installed and maintained and used for intended purposes.'

Unlike the position under the Mutual Recognition of Terminal Equipment Directive, however, approval under this proposal will not automatically confer permission to operate the equipment; that will require separate licensing (art 2.2). NRAs will retain both the right to license satellite earth stations within their jurisdictions and to administer the national type approval.

5.54 Article 4 distinguishes between satellite earth station equipment to be attached to the PSN and that which is not. Under art 4.1 the principle is that all such equipment will meet the same essential requirements of the Mutual Recognition of Terminal Equipment Directive. Articles 4.3, 4.4, 4.5 and 4.6 state that the essential requirements of art 4 of Directive:

(*a*)　in the context of transmit and receive equipment and effective use of the radio frequency spectrum, include the 'effective use of orbital resources and the avoidance of harmful interference' (art 4.3);

(*b*)　require that the electromagnetic compatibility of specific satellite earth station equipment is the same as art 4.4 of the Mutual Recognition of Terminal Equipment Directive (art 4.4);

(*c*)　require that satellite earth station equipment must meet the essential requirement of art 4.4 of the Mutual Recognition of Terminal Equipment Directive for interoperability with the PSN (art 4.5); and

(*d*)　(where satellite earth station equipment is intended to provide a service which the Council decides should be made available on a pan-European basis) include interworking requirements as determined in the procedure provided for in art 16 (art 4.6) (see also *below*).

Article 5.2 requires the Commission (using the art 16 procedure) first to identify the types of equipment for which common technical requirements are required with a view to communicating this to the relevant standardisation bodies. Secondly (after the standardisation body has proposed them), the corresponding harmonised standards implementing the essential requirements (referred to in art 4.2 to 4.5) shall be transformed into CTRs.

5.55 Chapter II sets out detailed procedures for the assessment of conformity to type. Once these procedures have been complied with and the satellite earth station equipment is assessed to have passed a type approval examination (sometimes called 'homologation'), such conformity will be recognised throughout the Community. All such equipment must be marked to denote its compliance with the envisaged directive (Chapter III). Article 16 sets out the procedure in relation to pan-European services referred to in arts 4.6 and 5.2 and in relation to the introduction of measures envisaged by the Approvals Committee for Terminal Equipment (see art 15) to set the necessary standards for such equipment. If there is no decision by the Committee, or if no opinion can be obtained, then the Committee may take the proposal to the Council, which can act by qualified majority. This becomes self-executing: if there is no action by the Council within three months of the matter being referred to it, the Committee can then act as though adopted.

Under Chapter IV, the Approvals Committee for Terminal Equipment, which was established by the Mutual Recognition of Terminal Equipment Directive (art 13(1)), is directed to assist the Commission in implementing the directive.

Member states were obliged to bring this directive into force by 1 May 1995.

Mutual recognition of licences

5.56 Mutual recognition of licences has had a chequered history. The issue is obviously politically sensitive; it has been the subject of debates about subsidiarity, as well as the mechanics of its implementation. For example, on 15 October 1992, the Commission produced a *Draft Proposal for a Council Directive on the mutual recognition of licences and other national authorizations for the provision of satellite network services and/or satellite communications services extending the scope of Directive 91/263/EEC* (Commission of the European Communities: DG XIII / 231 / 92 Rev 3EN). This was only one of a number of proposals. The most recent was a *Proposal for a European Parliament and Council Directive on a policy for the mutual recognition of licences and other national authorizations for the provision of satellite network services and/or satellite communications services* (COM(93) 652 final, OJ 4.2.94 C36/2 and (corrigendum) OJ 17.2.94 C49/16) ('the Satellite Licensing Proposal').

This proposal followed an earlier *Proposal for a Council Directive on the mutual recognition of licences and other national authorizations to operate telecommunications services, including the establishment of a single Community telecommunications licence and the setting up of a Community Telecommunications Committee (CTC) (OJ 25.9.92 C248/4).* (It is proposed to change the CTC's name to the European Tele-communications Council (ETC)).

Council Resolution of 22 July 1993 (OJ 6.8.93 C213/1) envisaged that mutual recognition of national licences and conditions based on harmonised conditions would be a key factor in the future develop-ment of EU telecommunications policy.

5.57   The purpose of the Satellite Licensing Proposal is to establish a single market in satellite services by setting up procedures whereby satellite network operators authorised to provide satellite network services and/or service providers authorised to provide satellite communication services in one member state will be al-lowed to provide satellite services throughout the EU without having to obtain individual licences or authorisations from the NRAs in the other member states. It also aims to harmonise, where possible, the licensing conditions to which similar service providers are subject in each member state. The proposal does not apply to the launch and operation of satellites.

The current regulatory position is such that operators and providers wanting to provide their services in more than one member state usually have to apply for licences in each member state in which they wish to operate. The proposal envisages an application proce-dure which is simple and flexible and will allow for rapid techno-logical development in the satellite sector, which is particularly trans-frontier in its operation.

5.58   Three licensing mechanisms are proposed under the Satellite Licensing Proposal:

(a)   the Commission, in consultation with the CTC (see para 5.81 *below*), may identify certain classes of satellite services where direct mutual recognition of licences can take place without prior harmonisation of conditions;

(b)   before such harmonisation of licensing conditions or mutual recognition without harmonised conditions, a 'one stop shop-ping' procedure based on that already *de facto* in place between the UK, the Netherlands, Germany and France, would be established, to simplify applications in more than one member state. A single co-ordinating service (yet to be determined) would deal with all appropriate NRAs. Licences would be issued or refused within six weeks. A conciliation procedure would be established and available to an aggrieved applicant. If this procedure does not produce any agreement, the Commission would decide whether to issue a licence on the basis of the relevant national licensing regime;

(c) harmonisation of licensing conditions in consultation with the European Committee for Telecommunications Regulatory Affairs (ECTRA, see para 5.88 *below*) and for the European Radio-communications Committee (ERC; see para 5.89 *below*) (within the framework of the Conférence Européenne des postes et télécommunications (CEPT; see para 5.87 *below*) whereby the Commission may request ECTRA to draw up harmonised licensing conditions for certain satellite service categories. Where appropriate this would be implemented in EU law by the Commission acting in consultation with the member states through the CTC.

5.59 The Satellite Licensing Proposal would make use of the CTC which is to be composed of expert representatives of the NRAs, and specifically constituted for the purposes of the implementation of the recognition procedures in the satellite field (arts 25 and 26). The CTC is based on the ONP Committee model, although it has been suggested that, given its regulatory nature, the CTC should be a regulatory committee under procedure III(*b*) of Council Decision 87/373/EEC of 13 July 1987 Laying Down the Procedures for the Exercise of Implementing Powers Conferred on the Commission (OJ 18.7.87 L197/33). A procedure III(*b*) Committee would enable the Council to review the decisions of the CTC, and an appeal to the ECJ would be open to aggrieved parties.

The NRAs will primarily handle the required frequency site co-ordination. In the case of failure to agree frequency and site co-ordination arrangements for satellite network services within six months of the NRAs being notified, any undertaking concerned may request the assistance of the Commission who may ultimately initiate the 'conciliation procedure' (arts 13–18).

The allocation and registration of subscribers' names, addresses and numbers are dealt with in art 19.

Articles 20 and 21 will require satellite network service providers to show that appropriate arrangements for access to space segment have been made and therefore that there is necessary satellite capacity, and that all technical requirements have been met.

Somewhat controversially, only those undertakings established within the EU, with no more than 25 per cent ownership by non-EU nationals, which are effectively controlled by EU nationals, will have the benefit of the proposed directive (art 27).

Given the comments in para 5.14 *above*, and the work of the Commission on interconnection generally (see para 5.9 *above* and Chapter 12, para 12.2), it is important to note that pursuant to art 28, NRAs will be empowered to intervene in interconnection disputes to ensure fair terms for interconnection 'in accordance with Community law'.

It will be interesting to see whether this proposal proceeds and, if so, whether it will do so by unanimous agreement of the member states. As it is made pursuant to arts 57(2), 66, 100A and 235 of the EC Treaty, it can be adopted by qualified majority. It will be subject to negative assent procedure with the European Parliament under art 189b of the Treaty of Union.

5.60   While there are obvious benefits to be gained if the proposal is implemented, even liberalised countries, such as the UK, will be mindful of subsidiarity and will resist any derogation from it, especially if NRAs' rights to issue, monitor and enforce licences are undermined. In its present form, the proposal envisages significantly affecting the UK Secretary of State's sole prerogative to issue licences under s 7 of the Telecommunications Act, and similarly under the Wireless Telegraphy Act (see Chapter 6, para 6.25), primarily because the proposal contemplates enforcement of licences issued by other member states in the UK. It is not clear therefore whether even in the UK this proposal will be approved.

Council Resolution on Satellite Personal Communications

5.61   On 7 December 1993 the Council adopted *Resolution C339/1 on the introduction of satellite personal communication services in the Community* (OJ 16.12.93 C 339/1).

The Resolution recognised the importance of the planned introduction and use of satellites for personal communications, and, in particular, the global characteristics of satellite personal communications services if provided through non-geostationary satellite systems, such as LEOS (referred to in Chapter 1, para 1.12) and their particular characteristics as they affect the European and international regulatory regimes. Given the global nature of these systems, their planned introduction will give the EU the much desired challenge of developing a forward looking, pro-active policy and regulatory system within the framework of co-ordinated EU action. The Council recognised the importance of developing an EU policy with regard to satellite personal communication systems and services that will build on existing EU policies in telecommunications, space, trade and mobile and satellite communications. To consider the many issues posed since the ITU WARC-92 Conference held in Torremolinos (World Administrative Radio Conference for Dealing with Frequency Allocations in Certain Parts of the Spectrum (WARC-92) Malaga-Torremolinos 1992 (ISBN 9261 046614) (see Chapter 2, para 2.43)), the Commission organised hearings in Brussels on 9–10 November 1992 on future activity in the field of personal communications (see Chapter 1, para 1.15).

5.62   The Resolution invited member states to work towards developing an EU policy in this area and an EU position in relation to third countries, in particular, within the context of the mJ and third countries. The Commission has undertaken a major study on satellite proposal communications networks (including LEOS) and the consequences for European telecommunications trade and industry. Satellite personal communications are a complex and somewhat controversial area.[12] Developments by the Federal Communications Commission (FCC) in this area in the USA (see Chapter 1, para 1.15) raise the question whether an allocation by the FCC would be, in effect, a global allocation of frequencies to US-based LEOS consortia. While such services would need to be co-ordinated with the ITU as well at the WRC to be held in Geneva in November 1995, it raises questions of the feasibility of one regulator being able to develop radio frequency assignment and standardisation models in isolation from those other regulators whose nationals may be affected by the introduction of a particular service, even on a seemingly domestic basis.

The Resolution, however, recognised the importance of co-ordination and planning in respect of the development of satellite PCNs and may lead to the development of certain objective licensing criteria, such as the requirement in GSM (see Appendix 3 for definition) licensing that Europe-wide 'roaming' be possible, which is achievable only by operating rigidly determined technical specifications. The drawback with such strict specifications is that they are not technology-neutral and the market tends to move faster than regulatory development which in turn could frustrate the application of technological advances.

Given that development of satellite personal communications is a global matter, there are important aspects to be considered, such as interconnection to existing terrestrial networks, international settlement and accounting rates, mobile satellite technical issues (including the availability of radio frequency spectrum) and the commercial viability of the present proposals. The *Communication from the Commission on satellite personal communications* (COM(93) 171 final, 27 April 1993), to which the Resolution was originally attached as a draft, identifies a number of areas where specific policies will need to be developed, including frequency management, regulatory, licensing and competition policy, standardisation, intellectual property rights, economic and industrial policy.

5.63 The Resolution invites member states to work towards an EU policy in respect of satellite personal communication systems. Although not significantly referred to in the Resolution, it is interesting to speculate whether satellite PCN for Europe on an EU-wide basis would be a TEN within Title XII of the Maastricht Treaty. The Resolution invited the Commission to:

(*a*) investigate the significance of satellite personal communications systems in the formulation of EU policies for telecommunications, space, trade, industry and regional development;

(*b*) define, in collaboration with member states, joint policy on the systems with co-operation of ESA in the determination of an effective joint policy on these systems aimed at enhancing the competitive position of the European space and related telecommunications industries;

(*c*) continue to monitor closely international developments, particularly the regulatory proceedings in the USA and to consult, where appropriate, with non-EU countries on the co-ordinated introduction of these systems at a global level;

(*d*) reinforce close co-operation with ETSI (see para 5.93 *below*), the ERC (see para 5.89 *below*) and the ERO (see para 5.90 *below*) in examining the related standardisation and frequency issues;

(*e*) set up a platform for strategic discussions among all interested parties from which detailed recommendations can be provided for the development of a coherent EU policy; and

(*f*) report regularly on the developments in this area and, where necessary, propose appropriate measures and / or actions.

5.64 Earlier versions of the Resolution had proposed positions consistent with bodies such as the ITU. However, this was replaced by inviting member states 'to make efforts towards developing as soon as possible a Community policy concerning satellite personal communications, and a coordinated position, in particular within the context of international organizations' (such as the ITU). Also omitted was the submission of proposals necessary for the harmonisation of conditions required for the licensing of networks and services, thus highlighting the sensitivity of some member states to such matters.

It should be noted that this acknowledges the need for co-operation between different regulatory jurisdictions mentioned earlier in this chapter. There are concerns about certain specific aspects of the LEOS proposals, especially regarding usage of radio frequency spectrum and protection of radio astronomy services in the 1610–1626.5 MHz band. These were issues discussed at WARC-92 and require further study by bodies such as the ITU and the ERC/ERO (see para 5.62, *above*).

European states need to come to their own views on the options for European and national policies and strategies before those are decided *de facto* by events elsewhere. For this reason, a Co-operation Group was recently established between the CEPT, the ERC (see paras 5.87 and 5.89 *below*), the FCC and the US National Telecommunications and Information Administration (NTIA).

Television without Frontiers

5.65   This directive is of great relevance to satellite television. Since it is the subject of extensive comment in Chapter 7, it will not be further covered here.

MAC Directive

5.66   EU policy on HDTV has a stormy history, although a lack of consensus within the Council in the past may now be giving way to a new policy more appropriate to meet relevant needs in the future.

On 11 May 1992, the Council issued its Directive 92/38/EEC on the Adoption of Standards for Satellite Broadcasting of Television Signals (OJ 20.5.92 L137/17) ('the MAC Directive'). The directive required the use of the 'MAC' family of standards for not fully digital widescreen, high definition format television transmission, which attracted criticism as a 'protectionist' measure because it benefited the major equipment manufacturers in Europe who had developed the MAC standards. With the increasing pace of change in broadcasting technology, however, the mainly analogue MAC standard was seen as likely to be overtaken by technical developments in digital technology in the USA. The adoption of MAC as a standard was therefore perceived as a retroactive step.

5.67 Following the MAC Directive, the Commission also produced a *Proposal for a Council Decision on an action plan for the introduction of advanced television services in Europe* (COM(92) 154 final OJ 1992 C139/3) (the 'Action Plan') which proved to be as controversial as the MAC Directive itself. The Action Plan essentially proposed an 850 million ECU subsidy for the launch or introduction of the D2-MAC and HDMAC transmission standards. After lengthy discussions the EU's telecommunications ministers failed to reach agreement on the Action Plan at their meeting of 15 November 1992, when it had been hoped that it would be endorsed, because of the objections of two member states. After a Telecommunications Council meeting on 15 December 1992 and the General Affairs Council meeting on 21 December 1992 failed to reach a compromise, the Commission announced in February 1993 that the Action Plan in its original form would have to be revised. The objective of promoting HDTV by subsidising the MAC standard would be replaced by the objective of the promotion of the 16:9 widescreen format.[13]

On 16 June 1993, the EU telecommunications ministers reached agreement on a nine-point 'Framework Agreement' for an action plan which was solely directed at promoting the 16:9 format, irrespective of the European television standard used and irrespective of the transmission method (terrestrial, satellite or cable) ('the Framework Action Plan'). The Framework Action Plan was put into effect following agreement on 16 June and translated into a full action plan which was annexed to the Council Decision of 13 July 1993. The objectives of the new action plan focus on achieving a critical mass of advanced television series in the 16:9 format and a significant and increasing volume of programming in the 16:9 format.

The objectives were therefore designed to contribute to market penetration of widescreen equipment.

With the Framework Action Plan now 'technology-neutral', it was clear that the directive itself would have to be changed. Accordingly, on 22 July 1993, the Council passed *Resolution 93/C on the development of technology and standards in the field of advanced television services* (OJ 22.7.93 C209/1). It invited the Commission, before 1 October 1993, to propose a revision to the MAC Directive taking into account, *inter alia*, 'the possible need to expand the scope to allow other standards, in addition to D2-MAC, to be used for the broadcast of not completely digital 625 line television services in the 16:9 format'. The Commission was also invited to produce a communication and possible proposal on digital television before 1 October 1993 containing, *inter alia*, a mechanism for achieving agreement on a common EU perspective on the development and needs of the market for digital television systems.

5.68 A new draft directive entitled *Amended Proposal for a European Parliament and Council Directive on the use of standards for the transmission of television signals (including repeal of Directive 92/38/EEC)* (COM(93) 556, OJ 18.12.93 C34, as amended by COM(94) 455, OJ 18.11.94 C321), repealing the MAC Directive, has now been adopted by qualified majority under the co-decision procedure.

The document contains a proposal to repeal the MAC Directive and replace it by a directive which meets the main criticism that the MAC Directive did not seek to promote consumers' interests, in particular in relation to the reduction in the use of wide-screen television receivers and hence their broad take-up. Thus the somewhat questionable restrictions in the MAC Directive have been dropped in favour of a much freer, market-oriented proposal.

The Council has also (in the July 1993 Resolution) invited the Commission to consider the advancement of digital television. The Commission's document, *Draft Council Resolution of 17 November 1993 on digital voice video broadcasting—a framework for a Community policy* (COM(93) 557 final) is its response.

The Services/Terminal Equipment Amendment Directive

5.69 As noted in para 5.25 *above*, the Services/Terminal Equipment Amendment Directive is now one of the cornerstones of the EU's liberalised satellite policy, extending the full force of the Terminal Equipment Directive and the Services Directive to the satellite sector. Significantly, given the problems with the ONP/Voice Proposal, the Commission used the powers conferred by art 90(3) of the EC Treaty to secure the passage of this measure.

Reciting the fundamental provisions of the Satellite Green Paper but in particular the necessity to abolish 'all exclusive or special rights ... subject to licensing procedures, as well as for the free (unrestricted access to space segment capacity)' (recital 1), it also refers to the need to abolish 'special or exclusive rights relating to the connection of satellite earth station equipment . . . to the switched networks operated by the telecommunications organisations' (recital 9).

The Commission makes clear that any exclusive right which restricts the development of satellite communications is incompatible with art 90 of the EC Treaty and therefore incompatible with art 86 (recital 14). It also looks at licensing or declaration procedures and says that they may be justified in the context of essential requirements but subject to the proportionality principle (recital 15).

5.70 The directive therefore extends the Terminal Equipment and Services Directives to satellites and proceeds to abolish all exclusive rights for the provision of satellite services (art 1.2 amending art 2 of the Terminal Equipment Directive). Article 12 also requires the withdrawal of all 'special rights which

(*a*) limit to two or more undertakings . . . otherwise than according to objective, proportional and non-discriminatory criteria, or

(*b*) designate, otherwise than according to such criteria, several competing undertakings . . .' .

'Special rights' are defined to mean 'rights that are granted by a Member State to a limited number of undertakings, through any legislative, regulatory or administrative instrument which, within a given geographic area' confers 'on any undertaking . . . any legal or regulatory advantages which substantially affect . . . any other undertaking to import, market, convert, bring into service . . . under substantially similar conditions . . .' (art 1.1).

'Exclusive rights' as defined in art 1 of the Terminal Equipment Directive are those 'that are granted by a Member State to the undertaking through any legislative, regulatory or administrative instrument, reserving it the right to provide a telecommunication service or undertake an activity within a given geographical area.

What can amount to 'essential requirements' is limited to 'security of network operations, maintenance of national integrity, and, in justified cases, interoperability of services, data protection and, in the case of satellite network services, the effective use of radio frequency spectrum and the avoidance of harmful interference . . .' (art 2).

5.71   The Commission has reiterated its restrictive view of what constitutes essential requirements in its Communication on Infrastructure and 'accepts that rights of way do not constitute a physical limitation on the possible grant of infrastructure licences and therefore cannot be used to justify *a priori* restrictions on licence numbers' (see para 5.70). The Services/Terminal Equipment Amendment Directive recognises that it cannot affect rights in respect of voice telephony (see art 2.2 amending art 2 of the Terminal Equipment Directive).

Importantly, in relation to ensuring transparency, openness and fairness of licensing or authorisations, the directive requires member states to:

(*a*)   communicate their criteria for granting such authorisations and their declaration procedures;

(*b*)   inform the Commission of any new or changed conditions or procedures;

(*c*)   ensure that any fees are objective, transparent and non-discriminatory;

(*d*)   inform the Commission of the criteria on which they are based and any changes to them and that they are published and easily accessible;

(*e*)   notify this information to the Commission nine months after the publication of the directive and the Commission will publish such information regularly.

(art 2 amending arts 2 and 6 of the Terminal Equipment Directive.)

5.72   In response to concerns about access to space segment (see *Communication from the Commission to the Council and the European Parliament on satellite communications: the provision of—and access to—space segment capacity*, COM(94) 210 final, 10 June 1994), member states are required, by art 3b), to abolish all restrictions on the offering of space segment capacity within their jurisdiction:

> Member States shall ensure that any regulatory prohibition or restriction on the offer of space-segment capacity to any authorized satellite ... operator are abolished, and shall authorize within their territory any space-segment supplier to verify that the satellite ... network in use in connection with the space segment of the supplier in question is in conformity with the published conditions of access to this ... capacity.

Article 3 is directed at the ISOs (see Chapter 4, para 4.30) and does not directly affect the position of signatories to the ISOs. The Commission is set to invoke the EC Treaty competition rules against the signatories if they exercise their commercial functions in any anti-competitive ways.

Article 4 gives member states nine months from the date on which the directive entered into force (8 November 1994), that is, until 8 August 1995, to supply all necessary information to the Commission. Obviously in enforcing this provision the Commission will have regard to proportionality.

5.73   Last, from the point of view of satellite television and, in particular, direct-to-home (DTH), recital 17 states:

> The provision of satellite network services for the conveyance of radio and television programmes is a telecommunications service for the purpose of this Directive and thus subject to its provisions. Notwithstanding the abolition of certain special and exclusive rights in respect of receive-only satellite earth stations not connected to the public network of a Member State and the abolition of special and exclusive rights in respect of satellite services provided for public or private broadcasters, the content of satellite broadcasting services to the general public or private broadcasters, the content of satellite broadcasting services to the general public provided via frequency bands defined in the Radio Regulations for both Broadcasting Satellite Services (BSS) and Fixed-Satellite Services (FSS) will continue to be subject to specific rules adopted by Member States in accordance with Community law and is not, therefore, subject to the provisions of this directive.

Thus there is a distinction between the services provided by the satellite operator as the conveyer of signals, that is, its telecommunication services, and the content of services. Content is outside the scope of this directive, but conveyance is clearly within its scope.

Access to space segment

5.74   On 22 December 1994, the Council adopted *Commission Proposal of 10 June 1994 to the Council and European Parliament on satellite communications, the provision of and access to space segment capacity* (COM(94) 210, OJ 31.12.94 C 379). This is an important development based on much work by the Commission, in particular DG XIII. It is discussed at length in Chapter 4, to which reference should be made.

Copyright relating to satellite broadcasting and cable retransmissions

5.75   After much debate, Directive 93/83/EEC on the Coordination of Certain Rules Concerning Copyright and Rights Related to Copyright Applicable to Satellite Broadcasting and Cable Transmission of 27 September 1993 (OJ 1993 L248/15) was adopted. This is dealt with extensively in Chapter 8.

Future action on satellite policy

5.76   The Services Directive, as amended, is the cornerstone of the liberalisation of all telecommunications within the EU and, therefore, the EEA and the six Central and Eastern European countries referred to *above* (para 5.2). Clearly the Commission will devote full resources to ensuring that it, the Terminal Equipment Directive, the ONP Framework Directive and the associated measures are implemented.

1 January 1998 is rapidly approaching and the Commission is well aware that much remains to be done by it and by the member states to achieve the liberalisation of voice telephony, not only of fixed but also of mobile and satellite services, and of infrastructure.

The Commission recognises that comparable access to third country telecommunication markets and the lifting of foreign ownership constraints on EU network operators and service providers requires, ultimately, multi-lateral solutions within the World Trade Organisation (WTO) forum. In the interim, pending the results of current WTO negotiations, the Commission considers it important for the Union to reserve its right to maintain conditions comparable to those currently in place in third countries with respect to market entry and the licensing of non-EU or EEA operators. Further, the Commission will continue to work towards a common Union position in international fora dealing with numbering and frequency allocation issues.

The emerging global approach to many regulatory issues, within the context of the G7 nations where many nations are now addressing the same regulatory and social issues, will necessarily see more co-operation internationally.

5.77   The US government is leading the way in this context. Vice President Gore presented his proposal for an international initiative at the ITU World Telecommunications Development Conference in

Buenos Aires in 1993 and outlined five core principles as the basis for a global information infrastructure (GII). These principles were:

(*a*)   private investment;

(*b*)   competition;

(*c*)   flexible regulation;

(*d*)   open network access;

(*e*)   universal service.

As a 'network of networks', the GII could enhance global economic growth and development while promoting broad social discourse within and between countries.

The US Administration further advised the US to join with other governments to implement regulations to facilitate new entrants to the telecommunications sector. In particular, the following are required:

(*a*)   interconnection among competing networks and service providers;

(*b*)   unbundling of bottleneck facilities of dominant network providers;

(*c*)   transparency of regulations and charges;

(*d*)   non-discrimination among network operators and between operators and potential users, including resellers

(Telecommunications Reports, 20 February 1995, p 11,12).

As will be apparent from the earlier parts of this chapter, the EU is now well down this road and continues to make measures across the four heads above in a logical and co-ordinated fashion. Indeed, the EC measures form a complex and comprehensive (yet integrated) package of legislation and regulation which, it is hoped, will ensure that the EU realises the world's largest single market for telecommunications closer to the end of this decade.

Taking account of these international developments and the emerging information society, the Commission recognises that the evolving regulatory framework must remain flexible to take account of constant development and must be consistent with the principle of subsidiarity. Such a framework should also ensure that new services in areas such as on-line education, health services, tele-shopping, video-on-demand and other leisure services are included within its scope. However, further consideration, consultation and study are required before these regulations can be formulated.

5.78   This work is already under way with the preparation of:

(*a*)   a Green Paper on corporate communications;

(*b*)   a Green Paper on the legal protection of encrypted signals;

(*c*)   a consultation Document on media ownership;

(*d*)   a Communication on the requirement for an internal market mechanism to ensure national proposals are transparent and comply with the principles of the internal market.

With reference to the future regulation of a converged telecommunications and media/content industry, the Commission has also identified a number of basic principles to assist in the coherent development of regulations for the converged industries. These include:

(*a*)   ensuring a clear distinction is made between 'carriage' of information over the physical infrastructure, and 'content'. The regulatory objectives may, accordingly, be quite different;

(*b*)   regulation should be technologically neutral;

(*c*)   a common approach to public service obligations should be applied to carriage and content activities.

The Commission has adopted a framework to introduce the global information society to Europe, but to achieve this all forms of barriers to entry, regulatory and other bottlenecks, and anti-competitive practices will need to be eliminated. Apart from these measures, a number of other specific measures can be expected to be adopted; they are neatly summarised in the Commission's Infrastructure Communication, set out *below*.

5.79   The following table contains a summary of the timetable for telecommunications liberalisation up to 1 January 1998 and gives the current measures in place or currently planned and their intended effects:

Date	*Liberalisation*	*Harmonisation*
Before 31.7.95	Draft amendment of Commission Directive 90/338/EEC with regard to mobile and personal communications	Common Position on proposal for a European Parliament and Council Directive for ONP Voice Telephony

Draft amendment of
Commission Directive
90/338/EEC with regard to
the full liberalisation of
telecommunications
infrastructure and services
from 1 January 1998

Before 1.1.96   Adoption of amendment to   Adoption of the proposal
                  Commission Directive   for a European Parliament
                  90/338/EEC with regard to   and Council Directive for
                  cable television networks   ONP Voice Telephony

                  Adoption of amendment of   Proposal for amendment of
                  Commission Directive   Council Directive
                  90/338/EEC with regard to   90/387/EEC (ONP
                  mobile and personal   framework directive) and of
                  communications   Council Directive
                                                92/44/EEC (ONP Leased
                                                Lines Directive)

                  Adoption of amendment of   Proposal for a European
                  Commission Directive   Parliament and Council
                  90/33/8/EEC with regard   Directive on the application
                  to the full liberalisation of of the principle of open
                  telecommunications   network provision to
                  infrastructure and services interconnection to public
                  from 1 January 1988   telecommunications
                                                networks and services

                  If required, proposals for   Adaptation of the current
                  appropriate measures to   proposals in the field of
                  give further effect to the   licensing
                  principles set out in the
                  Treaty (eg Articles 85 and
                  86), in particular, with
                  regard to interconnection
                  and access.

                                                Communication to the
                                                European Parliament and
                                                the Council on the
                                                preparations for a
                                                liberalised
                                                telecommunications
                                                environment, addressing in
                                                particular the issue of
                                                universal service.

                                                Communication to the
                                                European Parliament and
                                                the Council on directory
                                                information and directory
                                                services.

Before 1.1.97	Adoption of any measures required to give further effect to the principles set out in the Treaty, in particular in Articles 85 and 86.	Adoption by the European Parliament and Council of the measures set out above.
Before 1.1.98	Completion of implementation by the member states of the liberalisation measures set out above according to the timetables applicable.	Completion of implementation by the members states of the harmonisation measures set out above according to the timetables applicable.

Other European organisations concerned in satellite regulation and policy formulation

5.80   Below is a brief description of several EU Committees and other major European bodies and organisations concerned with satellite communications. It will be apparent from the discussion above that many of these organisations play important roles in respect of the development of European policy on satellite personal communications.

Community Telecommunications Committee

5.81   Article 16 of the *Amended Proposal for a European Parliament and Council Directive submitted by the Commission pursuant to art 189A(2) of the EC Treaty on the mutual recognition of telecommunications licences and other national authorisations for telecommunications services* (COM(94) final, 24 March 1994, OJ 1994 C108/6) ('the Amended Proposal for Mutual Recognition of Licences') envisages the establishment of the Community Telecommunications Committee (CTC). It is proposed to change the name of the European Telecommunications Council (ETC).

As noted at para 5.59 *above*, the CTC would comprise representatives of the NRAs of the community and would be chaired by a representative of the Commission. Article 17 sets out the procedure that the CTC is obliged to follow in assisting the Commission in the formulation of harmonised conditions for authorisations for the telecommunications services and common licensing conditions (see art 6). (The directive specifically excludes satellite services, which are covered by the (earlier) Satellite Licensing Proposal (see para

5.59 *above*). The CTC is able to consult PTOs, users, consumers, manufacturers, service providers and trade unions. In addition it would foster the exchange of information between and among the member states and the Commission pertaining to the development of telecommunications services authorisations (art 17).

Open Network Provision Committee

5.82   The Open Network Provision (ONP) Committee was created by the ONP Directive. It is composed of delegations from EU member states and observers from EFTA.

The purpose of the directive is to develop a harmonised regulatory framework for open and efficient access to and use of public telecommunications networks and services. It specifies that ONP conditions must comply with the following basic principles:

(*a*)   they must be based on objective criteria;

(*b*)   they must be transparent and published in an appropriate manner;

(*c*)   they must guarantee equality of access and must be non-discriminatory.

In addition, the directive identifies the three main areas to which harmonised conditions should apply: technical interfaces (including network terminations points); usage and supply conditions; and tariff principles.

Each step in the development of ONP is subject to consultation with the ONP Committee. The European Commission and the ONP Committee also take into account the views of a wide range of interested parties including the ONP consultation and co-ordination platform which contains representatives from interest groups.

European Union Telecommunications Committee

5.83   In the discussion document of the ONP Committee: *A Harmonised Regulatory Framework for Licensing* the European Commission proposed that a European Union Telecommunications Committee (EUTC) be established. This proposal is in fact very similar to an earlier proposal for a Community Telecommunications Committee (CTC). The Commission proposes that the EUTC will be composed of representatives of the National Regulatory Authorities of the member states and chaired by a representative of the Commission.

Its role would be to facilitate harmonisation of licensing procedures and conditions in Europe.

Council of Europe

5.84   The Council of Europe was established in May 1949. Its members now include all the member states of the EU, as well as Bulgaria, Cyprus, Estonia, Hungary, Iceland, Lithuania, Liechtenstein, Malta, Norway, Poland, San Marino, Slovenia, Switzerland, Turkey, Albania, Belarus, Bosnia-Herzegovina, Croatia, the Czech Republic, Latvia, Macedonia, Moldova, the Slovak Republic, Romania, Russia and Ukraine. The Council of Europe was founded to achieve a greater unity between its members, to facilitate their economic and social progress and to uphold the principles of parliamentary democracy and respect for human rights.

The activities of the Council of Europe are far-reaching and cover *inter alia*: human rights; social welfare; health; external relations; sport; education and culture; environment; regional planning and mass media.

The work programme of the Council of Europe has resulted in a number of European Conventions and Agreements. Member states and some non-member states generally harmonise and amend their own national legislation in the light of these conventions. For example, in March 1989 the Council adopted a European Convention on Transfrontier Television (European Convention on Transfrontier Television, Strasbourg 5.V. 1989, ISBN 92-871-1715-2). This Convention has been implemented into EC law and is dealt with in detail in Chapter 7. It is important to note that the work of the Council of Europe is quite distinct from that of the European Union institutions.

European Free Trade Association (EFTA)

5.85   EFTA is an association of non-EU countries (Austria, Finland, Iceland, Liechtenstein, Norway, Sweden and Switzerland). EFTA's main purpose is to administer the free trade between EFTA countries under the authority of the Stockholm Convention 1960 (Stockholm Convention establishing the European Free Trade Association, 4 January 1960; UK Treaties 30 (1960) (Cmnd 1026)). The EU and EFTA are now implementing their agreement on the creation of the European Economic Area. Under this, among other trade liberalising measures, the EFTA countries except Switzerland and Liechtenstein will introduce EC laws on telecommunications into their national laws, insofar as they have not done so already, and will apply EC competition law in their territories.

European Space Agency (ESA)

5.86   In 1962, six European countries (Belgium, France, Germany, Italy, The Netherlands and the UK) together with Australia formed the European Launcher Development Organisation (ELDO) to develop and build a launcher system independent of the great space powers of that time. Likewise, in 1962, ten European countries formed the European Space Research Organisation (ESRO) to undertake satellite programmes.

In July 1973 these two organisations decided to merge their activities and the principle of creating the ESA was laid. Ireland subsequently became a member.

On 30 October 1980 the ESA became a legal entity. The members now include Belgium, Denmark, France, Germany, Ireland, Italy, The Netherlands, Spain, Sweden, Switzerland and the UK, and, since 1987, Austria and Norway, and, most recently, Finland. Co-operation contracts in relation to some activities were signed with Canada in 1987.

The main task of the ESA is to provide for and promote co-operation among European states in space research and technology and their space applications, with a view to their being used for scientific purposes and operational space applications systems for exclusively peaceful purposes. The work programme of the ESA spans the following fields:

(*a*)   space education, documentation, studies of future projects and technological research work;

(*b*)   space science;

(*c*)   earth observation;

(*d*)   telecommunications;

(*e*)   man in space technologies, including the in-orbit station;

(*f*)   ground infrastructures;

(*g*)   space transport systems; and

(*h*)   microgravity research.

The ESA also co-ordinates its own work with the national programmes of its members in order that they may be integrated with
the European programmes to be conducted by ESA.

European Conference of Postal and Telecommunications Administrations (CEPT)

5.87   CEPT was formed in 1959. Its aim is to harmonise the links
between the members' Administrations in order to achieve harmonisation and improvement of their services and to create a dynamic
market in the fields of telecommunications and posts. It has 42
members which included the following countries: Albania, Austria,
Belgium, Bosnia, Bulgaria, Croatia, Cyprus, the Czech Republic,
Denmark, Estonia, Finland, France, Germany, Greece, Hungary,
Iceland, Republic of Ireland, Italy, Latvia, Liechtenstein, Lithuania,
Luxembourg, former Yugoslav Republic of Macedonia, Malta, Moldova, Monaco, The Netherlands, Norway, Poland, Portugal, Romania, San Marino, Slovenia, the Slovak Republic, Spain, Sweden,
Switzerland, Turkey, the UK, Ukraine, and Vatican City. CEPT
meets periodically, usually once every three years, and its rulings
are only recommendations and therefore not binding on its members.

In the past, CEPT has operated as an organisation to protect the
interests of the public network operators in the increasingly competitive European environment. At that time concerns were voiced
that the organisation may have been operating as a cartel. In 1990,
following intervention by the Commission, CEPT decided to abolish
its recommendation on the general principles for the leasing of
telecommunications networks and the establishment of international networks designed for private use.

Recognising the liberalisation of the telecommunications sector and
the fact that most CEPT countries had separated their sovereign/
regulatory tasks from their operational roles, CEPT underwent
reorganisation in 1990. CEPT now comprises an association of
regulators. European operators were separately organised on 12
May 1992 as the European Public Telecommunications Network
Operators Association (ETNO) to deal with their operational
needs.

In 1992 the entire structure of CEPT was altered so that CEPT
became the 'umbrella' for three separate committees, namely the
European Committee on Postal Regulations (CERP), ECTRA (see
para 5.88 *below*) and ERC (see para 5.89 *below*). Membership of CEPT

gives automatic membership of CERP, ECTRA and ERC. CERP, being responsible for regulating postal services, is not considered further. The European operators were separately organised in 1992 to form the European Public Telecommunications Network Operators Association (ETNO) which deals with the operational tasks.

CEPT is also a potential forum for Europe-wide radio frequency allocation, subject to the planning carried out by the ITU at various World Radio Conferences (WRCs). CEPT has now developed into a regulatory body having powers of sanction (as compared to the powers of the ITU—see Chapter 2).

European Committee for Telecommunications Regulatory Affairs (ECTRA) and the European Telecommunications Office (ETO)

5.88 ECTRA is one of three committees within CEPT (see para 5.87 *above*). ECTRA consists of representatives of NRAs (such as the Office of Telecommunications in the UK, see Chapter 6) with responsibility in telecommunications and meets approximately three times each year. The membership is the same as for CEPT.

ECTRA's terms of reference (adopted in 1990 by CEPT) are:

(*a*)   to consider telecommunications regulatory affairs in a European context;

(*b*)   to consider the development of common approaches in the legislative, regulatory and institutional fields;

(*c*)   to exchange views on issues of common concern to regulatory authorities in CEPT member countries;

(*d*)   to establish and maintain relations with bodies within and outside CEPT (such as operators, service providers, user groups and manufacturers) concerning questions of common interest; and

(*e*)   to take decisions on the results of the Committee's work.

After internal reports on licensing and declaration procedures and other matters, ECTRA decided in July 1993 to establish a permanent office known as the European Telecommunications Office (ETO) to deal with the technical aspects of harmonisation of licensing and numbering within Europe. The ETO became fully operational in February 1995 and is located in Copenhagen, Denmark, in the same building as the ERO.

As mentioned *above*, the Commission views ECTRA as one of the critical organisations in the development of the mutual recognition of licences and for harmonising licensing conditions. It is envisaged that the ETO will form an essential part of the 'one-stop shopping' procedure for licensing (see para 5.50 *above*) and to provide service providers with a means to have licence applications to a number of member states co-ordinated simultaneously. At the time of writing, this service is scheduled to commence in November 1995. The ETO will also carry out studies into European licensing and numbering schemes.

At the moment ECTRA does not have legal personality. Clearly if it is to be an active organ in the communications field, this issue needs to be settled. This contrasts with the ETO and the ERO which were created pursuant to a Memorandum of Understanding and, pending the signing of a relevant convention in each case, these organisations have been granted legal status in Denmark.

European Radiocommunications Committee (ERC)

5.89   The ERC is responsible for the development of European policy on radiocommunications and its membership comprises NRAs from the members of CEPT responsible for radio frequency spectrum, management and radio regulatory matters generally (such as the Radiocommunications Agency in the UK). Its main task is to develop radiocommunications policies and to co-ordinate frequency, regulatory and technical matters in this field. Also it is involved in the development of guidelines in preparation of ITU activities and conferences.

The ERC's work is currently carried out through three permanent Working Groups created by the ERC. The Committee also invites relevant organisations to participate as observers in meetings, and consults various interested parties before final approval of its Recommendations or Reports.

As noted at 5.16 *above*, it is the ERC which has the power to make decisions on matters relating to the efficient use of radio frequency spectrum which will be binding on CEPT member countries. Members of CEPT are asked to write to the ERC within two months of a decision being passed in order to confirm that they will comply with it.

This new ERC procedure commits countries to implementation and aims to avoid the criticism that the former resolutions of the ERC were unenforceable and that, therefore, policy should be made at EU level where directives may be enforced under the Treaty of Rome. At its meeting in November 1992, the EU Council agreed that this may be a preferred mechanism for European radio frequency allocation and withdrew two proposed frequency directives after ERC Decisions were adopted concerning the same frequency bands and system. Following this, on 10 September 1993 the Commission produced a *Proposal for a Council Decision on the implementation by the member states of measures concerning radio frequencies* (COM(93) 382, OJ 1993 C 266/11) which is designed to establish a formal procedure by which ERC Decisions will be recognised within the EU by ensuring that member states commit themselves to ERC decisions. On 7 December 1993 the Council of Ministers adopted conclusions supporting its November resolution and invited the Commission to sign a Memorandum of Understanding (MoU) and framework agreement with the ERC/ERO.

As a part of CEPT, the ERC has a wider membership than the 15 member states of the EU. One of the most important roles of the ERC in this respect is the co-ordination and harmonisation of radio frequency spectrum allocation in Europe. The European Commission has agreed to formalise the working arrangements between it and the ERC/ERO in respect of information exchange, co-ordination of activities and sharing resources pursuant to a MoU.

As well as the proposed MoU between the ERC and the European Commission, the ERC has also entered into MoUs with a number of other organisations including ETSI. Further MoUs are contemplated to create a formal mechanism for co-ordination between those bodies participating in ERC activities.

European Radiocommunications Office (ERO)

5.90   Established in 1991 as a permanent organ of CEPT, the main objective of the ERO is to assist the ERC to develop proposals for a European Table of Frequency Allocations for the band 29.7 MHz to 105 GHz. The ERO also acts as a focal point for identifying problem areas and new possibilities in the radiocommunications field. It is also busy developing proposals for long-term plans for future use of radio frequency spectrum on a European level. For example, it is presently developing a common European Table of Frequency Allocations, which should harmonise radio frequency management in Europe. To this end it liaises with NRAs, national frequency authorities, such as the Radiocommunications Agency in the UK and the

Commission and provides guidance for research studies and co-ordinates industry consultation meetings.

As to its legal status, an MoU defining the remit of the ERO has been signed by all member states and work is being carried out to formalise these arrangements under a Convention.

European Standards Committee (CEN)

5.91   The main aim of the European Standards Committee (CEN) is 'the implementation of standardization throughout Europe to facili-tate the development of the exchange of goods and services by the elimination of the barriers set by provisions of a technical nature'. Its work is very similar to that of the International Organization for Standardization (see para 5.96 *below*). CEN works closely with CENELEC and ETSI and, in common with those organisations, it maintains appropriate procedures to ensure liaison with European bodies which represent industry's and other relevant interests. The formal co-operation of these three organisations is organised through The Joint Presidents Group, the Joint Coordination Group and The Information Technology Steering Committee. The chair-manship of each Group and the Committee rotates yearly and during each year each organisation heads one of these bodies.

European Electrotechnical Standards Committee (CENELEC)

5.92   CENELEC is the European standards body in the electro-technical area. There are presently 18 member countries (Austria, Belgium, Denmark, Finland, France, Germany, Greece, Iceland, Republic of Ireland, Italy, Luxembourg, The Netherlands, Norway, Portugal, Spain, Sweden, Switzerland and the UK) and nine affili-ates (Croatia, Cyprus, Hungary, Poland, the Czech Republic, the Slovak Republic, Slovenia, Romania and Turkey). Most of CEN-ELEC's work involves preparing harmonised European standards from IEC's standards and the remainder involves the production of original standards.

CENELEC co-operates with ETSI (see *below*) and CEN, to achieve a coherent programme of the standardisation work which is required for the operation of the market and to ensure the coherence of the whole *corpus* of European standards.

In the area of information technology, CENELEC has been a major player in the development of Open Systems (OS) (Working with EWOS (European Workshop for Open Systems)) and functional standards. The main aim of EWOS is to develop OS profiles and corresponding conformance testing of specifications and forwarding them on to the International Standards Organisation or CEN so as to speed up the development of international and European standards.

European Telecommunications Standards Institute (ETSI)

5.93 CEPT was instrumental in setting up ETSI and ceded all its standardisation activities to the new body. ETSI was formed in 1988 and its role is to design standards in the fields of broadcasting, telecommunications and information technology.

At present ETSI draws its membership from the following countries: Austria, Belgium, Bulgaria, Croatia, Cyprus, Czech Republic, Denmark, Finland, France, Germany, Greece, Hungary, Iceland, Republic of Ireland, Italy, Luxembourg, Malta, The Netherlands, Norway, Poland, Portugal, Romania, Russia, Slovak Republic, Slovenia, Spain, Sweden, Switzerland, Turkey and the UK. There are also eight associate member countries. As at August 1995, the associate member states were: Andorra, Australia, Israel, India, Macau, Malaysia, Ukraine and USA.

All the members of ETSI must be established in the territory of a country falling within the geographical area of CEPT, and must demonstrate their interest in European standardisation in the field of telecommunications by compliance with the Statutes and Rules of Procedure of ETSI (Statutes of ETSI, art 6). Members need only be 'established' within Europe and need not necessarily be 'European', thus enabling Japanese and US manufacturers and service providers 'established' in Europe to become members. This is an important point, which is sometimes overlooked by those who often complain about 'Fortress Europe'. It goes some way to enable Japanese and US manufacturers to play some (however little) part in the process of setting standards in Europe. Representatives from the Commission and EFTA hold the status of special counsellors.

Structure

5.94 ETSI consists of:

(*a*) a General Assembly, consisting of representatives and members of ETSI which may be grouped in national delegations. The General Assembly makes decisions on the management of ETSI and meets at least twice a year;

(b)   a Secretariat, headed by a Director General who is the legal representative of ETSI. The Secretariat is responsible for the assignment of resources, relationships with external bodies (within the framework of the guidelines laid down by the General Assembly), and decisions of the Technical Assembly;

(c)   the Technical Assembly, consisting of the members of ETSI, is the highest authority within ETSI for the production and approval of technical standards;

(d)   Technical Committees, whose role is to develop and submit the proposals for draft standards to the Technical Assembly for approval. These committees are also the focus of the formulation of a harmonised European view for worldwide standards organisations, particularly the Standardization Sector of the ITU (see Chapter 2, paras 2.21 to 2.24); and

(e)   Project Teams, which are created by the Technical Assembly for specific tasks in limited time periods, and consist of small numbers of chosen experts.

National weighted voting applies in the General Assembly and the Technical Assembly, but the views of operators, manufacturers, users and research bodies should be taken into account by delegations in arriving at a view on how the votes are cast.

Procedure

5.95   Standards developed by the Project Teams and the Technical Committees have to be approved by the Technical Assembly in order to attain the status of European Telecommunications Standards. These are voluntary standards. It is then up to the national governments or the Commission to make them mandatory. This can be done by the method described in the Memorandum of Understanding on European Telecommunications Standardization (which outlines the procedure for CEPT to adopt) signed by the CEPT member countries.

Before a standard is issued by ETSI, it is approved and implemented according to a set procedure. This involves a 'standstill' period, public inquiry and approval by national weighted voting. Following approval of ETSI, it is the responsibility of the recognised national standards organisations to ensure that all conflicting national standards on that specific matter are withdrawn. ETSI is expected to liaise closely with international bodies, particularly those within the Standardization Sector of the ITU.

ETSI has a specific Technical Committee on Satellite Earth Stations (TC-SES). The TC-SES is the primary committee for co-ordinating the position of ETSI on the following issues:

(*a*) all types of satellite communication services and applications (including mobile);

(*b*) all types of earth station equipment, especially as regards Radio Frequency Interfaces and Network and/or User Interfaces; and

(*c*) protocols implemented in earth stations for exchange of information, for connection with network and/or user terminal equipment and for system management, control and monitoring functions.

TC-SES is particularly concerned with co-ordinating standardisation with outside bodies, such as the ISOs. It is presently working on standards, for example, to cover receive-only TV earth stations to FSS 10/11/12 GHz bands and data-receive-only stations in the same band. It is also working on standards for two-way VSAT earth stations to FSS 12/14 GHz bands and 6/4 GHz bands.

Most space segment providers have already issued specifications to be complied with by earth stations operating in their systems, for example, INTELSAT and EUTELSAT (see Chapter 4, paras 4.11 and 4.17). TC-SES does not aim to standardise every type of satellite system or equipment in Europe.

The main activities of TC-SES are:

(*a*) consideration of existing worldwide standards, with the objective of achieving the most convenient options for Europe. (An important application of such standards would be to establish the conditions for type approval of earth stations or equipment throughout Europe. As mentioned *above*, the Commission is likely to adopt such standards and incorporate them into its standardising directives);

(*b*) preparation of standards in anticipation of worldwide standards wherever particular, urgent European needs arise; and

(*c*) establishment, where possible, of a unified position of ETSI members as regards the work carried out by other standardisation bodies, with the aim of obtaining solutions reflecting European requirements.

215

ETSI is aware of the possibility that 'standards' are used either by TOs or by manufacturers as a means to delay or to stifle the introduction of new services or technology. ETSI actively works towards overcoming any such problems.

In relation to satellite PCNs (see paras 5.61 *et seq above*), both ETSI and the ERO have been working on addressing some of the issues concerning frequency allocation and technical requirements and ETSI has now submitted a draft report to the Commission covering these issues.

International Organisation for Standardisation

5.96   Based in Geneva, the ISO is a worldwide federation of national standards bodies from each member country (there are 100 members). The ISO's function is to promote the development of standardisation and related activities in order to facilitate the international exchange of goods and services and to develop co-operation in intellectual, scientific, technological and economic activities.

The ISO's work results in international agreements which are published as international standards.

International Telecommunication Union (ITU)

5.97   See Chapters 1, 2 and 3 for details of the ITU, in particular the work of radio frequency management and standardisation.

Conclusion

5.98   Clearly, the exercise by the EU of important legislative powers and policy formulation will continue, and will include consideration of the issue of direct access to the space segment of the ISOs and consideration of their constituent instruments (as discussed in Chapter 4, paras 4.23 to 4.54). The main issue is the pace of change. There is no doubt that the Commission has had, at least until now, a coherent telecommunications programme and has been following the blueprint of the 1987 and 1990 Green Papers. The proposals discussed all follow from these seminal works. The Commission is pushing ahead with the harmonisation of conditions in respect of VSAT networks in 14/12 GHz band (as well as those in 30/20 GHz band); SNG; mobile satellite services; satellite PCN and two-way radio-determination; and radio-location satellite services. However, it remains to be seen how, in practice, the member states implement their EU obligations and how soon pan-European satellite services can be introduced. The Review of the Services Directive shows the unsatisfactory nature of implementation of that directive in a number of member states.the sentiments of Council Resolution 93/C 213/01 of 22 July 1993 and DG IV on services, on the importance of ensuring full implementation of existing EC legislation and the EC legislation framework in anticipation of full liberalisation of voice telephony and infrastructure on 1 January 1998, which will necessitate properly funded NRAs which are independent and open, are to be endorsed.

---

1 This is subject to derogation for Spain, Ireland, Greece and Portugal of five years, and Luxembourg of two years).
2 Parliamentary Resolution A3-0113/93 of 20 April 1993 (OJ 31.5.93 C150/42) is also important as it called on the Commission in effect to push on with liberalisation of voice telephony and infrastructure.
3 Commission Directive 94/46/EC of 13 October 1994 amending Directive 88/301/EEC and Directive 90/388/EEC in Particular with Regard to Satellite Communications (OJ 1994 L268/15).
4 In respect of which arts 59 and 85 of the Europe Agreement are also relevant. See, for example, Council and Commission Decision 94/907/ECSC, EC, Euratom of 19 December 1994 on the Conclusion of The Europe Agreement between the European Communities and their Member States of the One Part, and Romania of the Other Part (OJ 31.12.94 L357/1) (published with full text of the Europe Agreement).
5 The Commission has produced a number of measures which concern the effect of telecommunications on the environment since 1973, including, eg Council Directive 89/336/EEC of 3 May 1989 on the Approximation of the Laws of the Member States Relating to Electromagnetic Compatibility (OJ 23.5.89 L139/19) which relates to the problem of electromagnetic disturbance produced by electrical and electronic apparati, and the Mutual Recognition of Terminal Equipment Directive which deals with issues such as user safety and protection of the public network from harm. For an excellent insight into the effect of telecommunications in the environment see *The Environmental Impact of Telecommunications* by John Salter, IBA, SBL Conference, New Orleans, 1993.
6 For an excellent discussion of the effect of the Services Directive on reserved services, see Bernard Amory, *Telecommunications Law in the European Communities, the New Regulatory Framework*, Heft 31992, EuZW p 75.
7 Ibid, p 14, for full discussion of each of these elements, see pp 14 *et seq.*
8 See the comments on calling card services as an example.
9 See dispute between Esprit Telecom de España SA and Telephonica SA. Esprit Telecom invoked the conciliation procedure under 12 of the ONP

Leased Lines Directive. This is an example of the effectiveness of the CTC's quasi-regulatory function.

10 Also note than on 25 February 1992 the Council adopted Directive 92/13/EEC Co-ordinating the Laws, Regulations and Administrative Provisions Relating to the Application of Community Rules on the Procurement Procedures of Entities Operating in the Water, Energy, Transport and Telecommunications Sectors (OJ 23.3.92 L76/14) ('the Utilities Remedies Directive'). This directive concerns the implementation of the Utilities Directive and requires member states to introduce into their laws efficient procedures to allow a review of procurement decisions taken by both public and private telecommunications operators providing a PTN or PTS within the ambit of the Utilities Directive and to put into place effective interim mechanisms to set aside unlawful decisions and infringements and to give parties adversely affected by the infringements a right to monetary compensation.

11 See *EC Notice concerning the assessment of co-operative joint ventures pursuant to art 85 of the EEC Treaty* (OJ 1993 C43/2); Bellamy and Child, *The Common Market Law of Competition*, 4th edn, Chapters 4 and 5; for an instructive example, see *Re the Agreement between Alcatel Espace and ANT Nachrichten-technik GmbH* OJ 1990 L32/19, [1991] 4 CMLR 208—a 10-year exemption under art 85(3) granted for arrangements relating to research and development and consequent exploitation of satellite communications equipment.

12 KPMG Peat Marwick: *Satellite Personal Communications and the Consequences for European Telecommunications, Trade and Industry* (1994).

13 '16:9' refers to the width:height ratio for new high definition television transmission.

6

UK Licensing and Regulation of Satellite Services and the Interception of Satellite Transmissions

Introduction

The UK licensing regime

6.1 A satellite service may need to be licensed in the UK under one or more of the following licensing regimes:

(*a*) the Telecommunications Act 1984 (TA) which covers the running and the connection of telecommunication systems, and the provision of telecommunication services;

(*b*) the Wireless Telegraphy Act 1949 (as amended) (WTA) which covers the licensing of the use of radio frequencies; and/or

(*c*) the Broadcasting Act 1990 (BA) which deals with the licensing of satellite television services and satellite radio services.

In this chapter, the licensing regimes mentioned *above*, as they apply to satellite services, are dealt with in outline. There will then be a brief reference to the Outer Space Act 1986 (OSA), and to UK regulations and laws relating to the interception of satellite transmissions.

Telecommunications Act 1984

Licences under the Telecommunications Act 1984

6.2   Under s 4 of the TA, the definition of a 'telecommunication system' covers:

(*a*)   an orbiting satellite (whether or not over the UK);

(*b*)   a satellite earth station; and

(*c*)   the radio circuit comprising the up-link or down-link between a satellite and an earth station.

The definition of 'telecommunication apparatus' includes apparatus forming part of either a satellite or an earth station which is used for transmitting, receiving or conveying any 'message' which is to be or has been conveyed by means of a telecommunication system.

The s 4 definition of a 'telecommunication service' includes:

(*a*)   any service consisting in the conveyance by means of a tele-communication system of:

(*i*)   speech, music or other sounds:

(*ii*)   visual images;

(*iii*)   signals serving for the impartation (whether as between persons and persons, things and things or persons and things) of any matter otherwise than in the form of sounds or visual images; or

(*iv*)   signals serving for the actuation or control of machinery or apparatus; and

(*b*)   any service consisting in the installation, maintenance, adjustment, repair, alteration, moving, removal or replacement of apparatus which is or is to be connected to a telecommunication system (eg components of an earth station).

Section 5 of the TA makes it a criminal offence:

(*a*)   to run a telecommunication system in the UK without a licence granted under s 7 of the TA. For this purpose a telecommunication apparatus in the UK which is not itself a telecommunication system is treated as if it were a telecommunication system if it is connected to, but not comprised in, a telecommunication system which is not in the UK (eg a receiving dish or earth station connected to a satellite) or if the telecommunication apparatus is connected to and comprised in a telecommunication system which extends beyond the UK (for example, where the satellite and earth station are treated as part of the same system);

(*b*)   to connect a licensed telecommunication system (for example, a satellite earth station) to another telecommunication system (eg a satellite) or to any apparatus without an authorisation under the licence under which the system is run; and

(*c*)   to provide any telecommunication service by means of a licensed system unless the service is so authorised.

There are certain exceptions to s 5. In the present context, the most relevant is an exemption in relation to receive-only apparatus to capture the transmissions of licensed broadcasts (s 6).

Licences are granted under s 7 of the TA and may be granted to particular persons ('individual licences'), persons of a class or description ('class licences') or all persons ('general licences'). If a person runs a telecommunication system and provides services which fall within the description of systems and services which are authorised to be run and provided under a class or general licence, that person is automatically authorised to run that system and to provide those services. The person must, however, connect the system only to the other systems connection to which is authorised by the relevant licence, and comply with other relevant obligations specified in the licence (see paras 6.6 and 6.7 and the Class Licence for the Running of Telecommunications Systems to Receive Messages from Earth Orbiting Apparatus, 3 February 1989).

The mechanics of regulation

Office of Telecommunications and the Department of Trade and Industry

6.3   The TA established an administrative body to supervise licensees and the processes of liberalisation and change to be introduced under the TA. The TA provided for the Secretary of State, currently the Secretary of State for Trade and Industry (also known as the

President of the Board of Trade), to appoint an officer to be known as the Director General of Telecommunications (the DGT) (TA, s 1 and Sched 1). The DGT is authorised to appoint such staff as he may think fit and this has resulted in the creation of the Office of the Director General of Telecommunications, better known as the Office of Telecommunications (OFTEL), a non-ministerial government department.

OFTEL's primary role is to assist the DGT in the exercise of the duties and powers given to him under the TA. The general duties of both the Secretary of State and the DGT are set out in s 3 of the TA. The primary duties are to exercise their licensing powers and functions under the TA in the manner best calculated to secure the provision of telecommunication services so as to satisfy all reasonable demands including, in particular, emergency services, public call box services, directory information services, maritime services and services in rural areas, and to secure that those by whom such services fall to be provided are able to finance their provision (TA, s 3(1)). Subject to that, they must exercise those powers and functions in the manner which is best calculated, *inter alia*, to promote the interest of consumers, purchasers and other UK users of the variety of services provided; to maintain and promote effective competition between persons engaged in 'commercial activities connected with telecommunications' in the UK; and to promote research into, and the development and use of, new technologies (TA, s 3(2)).

Section 7 provides that licences may be granted either by the Secretary of State after consultation with the DGT or by the DGT with the consent of or in accordance with a general authorisation given by the Secretary of State. In practice, no authorisation has been given to the DGT to grant licences and all licences are granted by the Secretary of State in consultation with OFTEL. Therefore, the primary responsibility for decisions to grant licences and for drafting them is with the DTI (Telecommunications and Posts Division). The DGT, however, is given the sole responsibility for modifying licence conditions under ss 12–15 and overseeing compliance with licence conditions under s 16 of the TA.

Section 12 empowers the DGT to modify the conditions of a licence granted under s 7 with the agreement of a licensee, and s 15 empowers him to make compulsory modifications over the objections of a licensee following an investigation by the Monopolies and Mergers Commission. Licence condition modifications do not affect the description of systems which a licensee is authorised to run, the connection he may make or the services he may provide.

Where the DGT is satisfied that there has been or is likely to be a contravention of a licence condition he is required to make an order which makes 'such provision as is requisite for the purpose of securing compliance with that condition' (TA, s 16). In addition to his advisory functions the DGT is given a number of general functions under Part III of the TA including the investigation of complaints (s 49) and certain functions of the Director General of Fair Trading under the Fair Trading Act 1973 (s 50).

There is no formal application procedure for licensing under the TA. Practical advice is that the person wishing to apply for a licence should contact both the DTI and OFTEL to open a dialogue. This should be followed by a formal letter requesting the grant of a licence which will need to be backed up by details of the proposed system and service and such other relevant information (including availability of finance) as the DTI or OFTEL may require.

Prior to 1988, the only operators allowed to connect their systems to satellites and hence to provide satellite services from the UK were British Telecommunications plc (BT) and Mercury. In 1988, however, Specialised Satellite Service Operator (SSSO) licences were granted by the Secretary of State to six operators for the provision of one-way point to multipoint satellite services in competition with the public telecommunications operators. The SSSOs were restricted in that they were allowed simultaneously to up-link from a maximum of only three sites.

The government's White Paper, *Competition and Choice. Telecommunication Policy for the 1990s* (1991 Cmnd 1461), which was published in March 1991, declared a policy of further liberalisation of the telecommunications market which resulted in, *inter alia*, the supplementation of the SSSOs by class licences. These authorise all members of a class to run telecommunications systems without the need to apply for an individual licence or to pay a fee. If an operator's system and services fall within the descriptions specified in the class licence then that system and those services do not have to be specifically licensed. As regards satellite services, two class licences are particularly relevant and they are dealt with *below* (paras 6.6 and 6.7).

British Telecommunications plc and the Signatory Affairs Office

6.4   BT is licensed under the TA as a Public Telecommunications Operator to connect its terrestrial systems to earth orbiting apparatus and to provide services by means of its systems when so connected. Hence, it is authorised to provide services via satellites. It is also the UK signatory to the International Satellite Organisations (ISOs) (see Chapter 4). Thus, BT was in the position of dealing directly with potential competitors in its administrative capacity as signatory and of dealing commercially with them as competitors. There were resultant concerns that BT might unfairly use its position as signatory to prevent or hinder the acquisition of ISO space segment by competitors, or that the information provided by competitors to BT in connection with applications for ISO space segment might not be treated as confidential and could be used by BT's operational arm for its commercial advantage. These concerns led to the 1989 statement of Sir Bryan Carsberg, the then DGT, relating to his *Review of British Telecom's Arrangements for the Provision of Space Segment*, published by OFTEL (see Chapter 4, para 4.31). The review concluded that the situation was clearly not appropriate in a new competitive climate because of the conflict between BT's commercial interests and its role as signatory. The result was a separation of regulatory and operational functions within BT. Signatory functions were transferred from British Telecom International's (BTI's) Satellite and Lines Directorate (an operational unit) to a new Signatory Affairs Office (SAO) within BTI's International Affairs Directorate. BT pledged that SAO staff would treat all commercial information in complete confidence and would release such information outside the SAO only on a 'need to know' basis to individual employees of BT who were named in a register.

The review also looked at and refined the amount of information which was required to be submitted by operators to obtain space segment capacity, and required BT's operational divisions to follow the same procedures as any other parties in ordering space segment capacity. The issue of BT recovering its costs in providing the signatory services was resolved by allowing BT to charge a seven per cent administration fee, *in addition* to the space segment utilisation charges of the ISOs, which would 'contribute to the costs incurred by BT in discharging the signatory function'.

OFTEL reviewed the SAO arrangements in 1993, publishing a consultation document, *The Operation of BT's Signatory Affairs Office and Competition in the Satellite Services Sector*, in July 1993, followed by a *Statement of the Director General of Telecommunications regarding the future of the Signatory Affairs Office* in February 1994. The questions of access to space segment and the SAO's current procedures are dealt with more fully in Chapter 4 (see paras 4.55 *et seq*).

British Approvals Board for Telecommunications

6.5   Under many licences granted pursuant to s 7 of the TA, it is a condition that apparatus connected to a telecommunication system be approved to be so connected. Apparatus should be approved by the Secretary of State (or, with his consent, the DGT) or by a person appointed to take over the responsibility by the Secretary of State (ss 22 and 25). Currently the appointee is the British Approvals Board for Telecommunications.

Satellite Class Licence

6.6   On 2 August 1991, the UK government issued the Satellite Class Licence (SCL). This licence authorises the running of satellite transmit and/or receive earth stations of any kind whether fixed, mobile or transportable. The SCL permits the provision of any kind of satellite service, whether one-way or two-way-point-to-point or point-to-multipoint including voice, data, vision or any other kind of 'message' for reception within the UK or any other overseas country. The SCL, however, contains an important restriction in that it does not allow 'messages' to be conveyed directly between an earth station and a public switched network (PSN) or to be sent indirectly to a PSN via another terrestrial system such as a private leased circuit. 'Messages' include speech, music, visual images and all other things referred to in s 4(1) of the TA. Earth stations may, however, transmit messages to be conveyed to the PSN by means of a satellite only if the connection to the PSN is by means of a system run under a TA licence which authorises connection to the PSN. Transmissions may be up-linked, for example, for reception by BT or Mercury who may convey the messages to the PSN under their own TA licences.

Self-provided System Licence

6.7   In addition to the SCL and the individual licences (see *below*), satellite operators may also operate satellite systems under the Class Licence for the Running of Self-Provided Telecommunication Systems granted by the Secretary of State under s 7 of the TA (SPSL). The SPSL authorises the conveyance of messages by way of a system covered by the SPSL provided that:

(*a*)   they are initially sent or are initially received, or both, by the licensee (that is, the person claiming the benefit of the licence) or a member of the licensee's group; and

(b)   neither the licensee nor any member of the licensee's group receives from any other person (other than the licensee or a member of the licensee's group) any financial benefit or advantage, whether direct or indirect, in respect of the provision of telecommunication services by means of or in relation to the system (SPSL, Sched 3, para 3).

Individual Licences

6.8   Service providers whose systems or services do not fall into the categories set out in the class licences, such as those who wish to connect directly to the PSN, must apply to the Telecommunications and Posts Division of the DTI for an individual TA licence.

Checklist for a person wishing to run a telecommunication system

6.9   The following is a basic guide to be followed in deciding whether a TA licence needs to be obtained:

(1)   Is the proposed system exempt from licensing (that is does it fall within one of the exceptions)? If so, no licence need be obtained.

(2)   Is the proposed system and are all the proposed services covered by an existing class licence? If so, no licence need be obtained provided that the restrictions and conditions of the class licence are observed.

(3)   If neither of the above apply, the person should consider applying for an individual TA licence.

Broadcasting Act 1990

General

6.10   Under the BA, both television and radio services provided from the UK must be licensed. It is a criminal offence to provide a television service without a licence (BA, s 13). Similar provision is made in respect of unlicensed radio services (s 97(1)). There are exemptions from the licensing requirements under s 13 for specified BBC-related satellite television services, such as BBC World Service

Television (The Broadcasting (Unlicensed Television Services) (Exemption Order 1994 (SI No 3172))).

Satellite television

6.11   As regards satellite television services, the BA created two categories of service which require a licence.

Domestic satellite service licence

6.12   A 'domestic satellite service' is defined as a television broadcasting service (that is, a service consisting in the broadcasting of television programmes) transmitted via satellite from a place in the UK using a frequency allocated by the UK for direct broadcasting by satellite ('an allocated frequency'), for general reception in the UK or in a prescribed country (mainly member states of the EU): see BA, s 43(1), The Broadcasting (Prescribed Countries) Order 1994 (SI No 454).

The reference to 'allocated frequencies' is to those frequencies allocated pursuant to the 1977 WARC–BS for broadcasting purposes (see Chapter 2, para 2.41). The BA makes the distinction between services transmitted from the UK on an allocated broadcasting frequency which are categorised as domestic satellite services, and services which are transmitted from the UK on non-allocated frequencies, in the FSS band, which are non-domestic satellite services (see *below*). There is currently no licensed domestic satellite service.

Non-domestic satellite service licence

6.13   A non-domestic satellite service is defined as a television service which consists in the transmission of television programmes via satellite which are either:

(*a*)   transmitted from a place in the UK otherwise than on an allocated frequency for general reception in the UK or any prescribed country (see para 6.12 *above*); or

(*b*)   transmitted from outside the UK or any prescribed country for general reception in the UK or any prescribed country if the programmes included in it consist of material provided by a person in the UK who is in a position to determine what is to be included in the service (ie a person who has some sort of editorial control) (BA, s 43(2)(*b*)).

In each case, the person who has to obtain the licence is the person who provides the programmes (and is in a position to determine what is to be included in the service). In the case of a non-domestic satellite service licence referred to in (*a*) *above*, if such a person is not in the UK, then the licence has to be obtained by the person who actually transmits the programmes (BA, s 43(3)), see also s 202(6)).

Licensing

6.14   Domestic and non-domestic satellite service licences are granted by the Independent Television Commission (ITC). Domestic satellite service licences are subject to a complicated and discretionary licensing procedure which is similar to that applying to terrestrial Channel 3 licences (BA, ss 44 and 45). Non-domestic satellite service licences, which cover all satellite television services which are currently provided, are available on payment of the relevant fee and satisfactory proof to the ITC that the licensee is in a position to comply with the licence conditions. The ITC may refuse to license a non-domestic satellite service only if it appears to it that the service would not meet the specified minimum requirements regarding programme content which are set out in s 6 of the BA and apply to all licensed services; these relate to good taste and decency, accurate and impartial news, responsible religious programming and subliminal advertising (BA, s 45).

As a consequence of being licensed under the BA, domestic and non-domestic satellite service licensees come under the regulatory authority of the ITC and as a result have to comply with the ITC's codes of practice which cover a range of areas such as programme content, advertising and sponsorship (see the following ITC publications, *inter alia*: *ITC Code of Advertising Standards and Practice*; *ITC Code of Programme Sponsorship* and *ITC Programme Code*). The various restrictions on programme content are further examined in Chapter 7.

Satellite radio

6.15   Satellite radio services are licensable as sound broadcasting services under the BA (BA, s 84(2)(*b*)).

General

6.16   In the case of satellite services, these are sound broadcasting services (other than those provided by the BBC) which are provided from the UK (BA, s 84(2)(*b*)(i)) or provided from outside the UK but using material provided by someone in the UK who has a degree of editorial control (BA, s 84 (2)(*b*)(ii)). They are deemed to be provided by the person in the UK providing material (if that person has a degree of editorial control) or otherwise the person transmitting the satellite radio service (BA, s 84(3)). In other words, they resemble non-domestic satellite services for television.

Licensing

6.17 Satellite radio service licences are available from the Radio Authority (RA). They are subject to basically the same licensing procedure as non-domestic satellite service licences (see BA, Part III for detailed provisions).

Licensable programme services

6.18 In some cases, where a satellite service is not licensable under any of the categories referred to *above* (in paras 6.11 to 6.15) (eg because it is provided from somewhere outside the UK), it may still be licensable as a 'licensable programme service' or as a 'licensable sound programme service' if provided with a view to being conveyed by means of a cable system in the UK (BA, Part I, Chapter IV, Part III, Chapter III). This will depend on whether the person providing the service has a place of business in the UK to bring it within the jurisdiction of the ITC or the RA.

Ownership

6.19 The granting of licences for domestic satellite services, non-domestic satellite services and satellite radio services is subject to ownership restrictions in respect of the persons who may hold licences. These are set out in Sched 2 of the 1990 Act and in orders made thereunder (principally the Broadcasting (Restrictions on the Holding of Licences) Order 1991 (SI No 1176), as amended by the Broadcasting (Restrictions on the Holding of Licences) (Amendment) Order 1993 (SI No 3199). They are more stringent in respect of domestic satellite services than non-domestic satellite services and satellite radio services. For example, licences for domestic satellite services cannot be held by non-EU persons (BA, Sched 2, Part II, para 1(1)(*a*) and (*b*)); this restriction does not apply to non-domestic satellite services (BA, Sched 2, Part II, para 1(2)). Paragraphs 6.20 to 6.23 *below* deal with the ownership restrictions relating to non-domestic satellite services and satellite radio services as these are the categories into which most commercial satellite broadcasting services will fall. In May 1995, the Government's proposals for a radical reform of the ownership restrictions were published in *Media Ownership: the Government's Proposals*, Cm. 2872. In the circumstances, it is not appropriate to consider those reforms in the present edition of his work.

General

6.20   Broadly, there are three areas where ownership of satellite television services is restricted by the BA: persons who may not hold licences, limitations on holding a number of licences and cross-media ownership between the press and the broadcasting sector. In each case it is important to understand the following terms of general usage (as defined in Part I of Sched 2 to the BA):

'Control' (in respect of a company) means owning or being beneficially entitled to 50 per cent or more of the equity share capital or voting power in the company, *or* power (through shareholding or voting power) to ensure the affairs of the company are conducted in accordance with one's wishes, *or* power (through corporate documents such as articles of association) to secure that the affairs of the company are conducted in accordance with one's wishes (BA, Sched 2, Part I, para 1(3)). The ITC applies a rule of thumb that anyone with an interest of more than 30 per cent has 'control' unless the contrary can be shown.

In *R v Radio Authority ex p Guardian Media Group* [1995] 1 WLR 334, the applicants successfully challenged the decision of the RA to approve a scheme of share ownership in respect of take-over arrangements which, so the applicants argued, would have resulted in a non-permissible accumulation of interests in radio licences under art 12(4) of the Broadcasting (Restrictions on the Holding of Licences) Order 1991. The applicants argued that the scheme would enable the company in question to secure that the affairs of a licensee would be conducted in accordance with its wishes on the grounds that the company in question was to hold 50 per cent of the shares in another company which was to own the company which itself held the radio licence, and that the other 50 per cent of the shares were to be owned by the merchant bankers of the company said to be exercising control. Schiemann J rejected this argument, holding that there were facts before the RA from which it could conclude that the scheme would not offend against the accumulation provisions, including the fact that the bankers would not be acting as mere nominees, and that the directors appointed by the bankers would have a duty under company law to act in the best interests of the company.

The interests of persons acting together 'in concert' are taken together for the purposes of establishing control (BA, Sched 2, Part I, para 1(5)). References to ownership of share capital or voting power apply whether ownership is direct or through a nominee (such as through holding an option which, under company law, amounts to having an interest held through a 'nominee') (BA, Sched 2, Part I, para 2(1)).

'Control' (in respect of a person other than a company) is the power (through the rules regulating the affairs of that person) to ensure its affairs are conducted in accordance with one's wishes (BA, Sched 2, Part I, para 1(1)).

'Associate' (in respect of a company) means a director of that company or a company that is a member of the same group as that company. Bodies corporate are treated as members of the same group if one is a parent and the other its subsidiary, or if both are subsidiaries of the same parent (BA, Sched 2, Part I, para 2(2) and 2(3)).

'Associate' in respect of an individual is a very wide concept including relations, business partners and companies of which the individual is a director (BA, Sched 2, Part I, para 1(2)).

In some cases the ownership restrictions apply not only to a licence holder but also to a person 'connected with' the licence holder, being a person who controls the licence holder (and any associate of that person), an associate of the licence holder, a person controlled by the licence holder or an associate of the licence holder (BA, Sched 2, Part I, para 3).

Disqualification

6.21   The rules relating to disqualification are complex and reference should be made to Sched 2, Part II of the BA to check the detailed provisions (particularly as in some cases the rules are extended to affiliates, associates and companies in which disqualified persons have interests). However, in very general terms the following categories of persons are disqualified:

(*a*)   local authorities (BA, Sched 2, Part II , para 1(1)(*c*));

(b)   bodies whose objects are wholly or mainly of a political nature (BA, Sched 2, Part II, para 1(1)(*d*));

(c)   religious bodies (BA, Sched 2, Part II, para 2), except that the ITC and the RA have the discretion to grant satellite licences if they are satisfied it is 'appropriate' (BA, Sched 2, Part II, para 2(2));

(d)   persons subject to 'undue influence' (BA, Sched 2, Part II, para 4); and

(e)   advertising agencies (BA, Sched 2, Part II, para 6).

There are also rules preventing the BBC and the Welsh Authority from holding licences and preventing publicly funded bodies from holding radio licences (BA, Sched 2, Part II, para 3 and 5).

Accumulations

6.22   The BA also contains detailed rules designed to restrict a person from building up a portfolio of licensed media interests that is contrary to the public interest.

In the context of satellite services, it is important to note that, where a person is licensed to provide a service made up of several channels, that person is deemed to hold a number of licences corresponding to the number of channels (BA, Sched 2, Part III, para 2(6)).

There are currently no restrictions on the number of licences to provide satellite services that one person may hold—but a maximum could be imposed by order (BA, Sched 2, Part III, para 2(2) and 2(3)) and, furthermore, a restriction on participation (as opposed to holding licences) may also be imposed (BA, Sched 2, Part III, para 4).

Subject to the above, the basic accumulation rules as they apply to satellite services are as follows:

(a)   both holders of a non-domestic satellite service licence and persons who run a satellite television service which is intended for general reception in the UK (but is not a non-domestic satellite service or a domestic satellite service) are restricted to holding no more than a 20 per cent interest in the holders of licences to provide national radio services, Channel 3 or Channel 5 television services and domestic satellite services, and *vice versa* (BA, Sched 2, Part III, para 6(2));

(*b*)   holders of satellite radio service licences are restricted to holding no more than a 20 per cent interest in the holders of licences to provide national radio services and Channel 3 or Channel 5 television services, and *vice versa* (BA, Sched 2, Part III, para 6(5)); and

(*c*)   holders of licences to provide satellite radio services on UK-allocated frequencies are restricted to holding no more than a 20 per cent interest in the holders of satellite radio services not provided on such frequencies, and *vice versa* (BA, Sched 2, Part III, para 6(6)).

There is provision for further restrictions to be imposed on accumulations of both satellite service interests and interests in local radio and local delivery services (BA, Sched 2, Part III, para 6(8)).

For the purposes of the rules outlined *above*, the restrictions also apply to 'connected persons' (BA, Sched 2, Part II, para 8).

Cross-media ownership

6.23   Part IV of Sched 2 of the BA includes rules relating to cross-media ownership between newspapers and broadcasting services. The BA itself does not impose these rules on satellite services although there is provision for the rules to be extended to satellite television and radio services (BA, Sched 2, Part IV, para 2(5)(*e*)). This has been done in respect of domestic satellite services (see the Broadcasting (Restrictions on the Holding of Licences) Order 1991 (SI No 1176), as amended (see para 6.19 *above*).

Proscription

6.24   Under Part X of the BA, there are provisions relating to satellite services that are not licensable in the UK but are, nonetheless, capable of being received in the UK (called 'foreign satellite services'). The Secretary of State is empowered, by order, to 'proscribe' foreign satellite services where the ITC or RA has notified the Secretary of State of a foreign satellite service which it regards as 'unacceptable' and the Secretary of State is satisfied that proscribing such foreign satellite service is in the public interest and does not breach any of the UK's international obligations (BA, s 177).

If a foreign satellite service is proscribed, it becomes an offence to undertake activities which assist the reception of the proscribed service, such as publishing listings of programmes or supplying reception equipment (see BA, s 178). However, it does not become illegal simply to receive the proscribed service.

To date, one service has been proscribed—Red Hot Television, a satellite television service transmitting principally pornographic material (see The Foreign Satellite Service Proscription Order 1993 (SI No 1024)). This service was encrypted and transmitted late at night but decoders were marketed in the UK and the satellite transmissions of the service were capable of reception in the UK. The circumstances of this proscription order were controversial as Red Hot Television was provided from The Netherlands and later Denmark, both member states of the EU. (For a further discussion of the *Red Hot Television* case, see Chapter 7, para 7.38.)

Wireless Telegraphy Act 1949 (as amended)

Licensing under the Wireless Telegraphy Act 1949

6.25   The use of radio frequencies is licensed under the Wireless Telegraphy Act 1949 (WTA). Section 1 of the WTA makes it an offence to establish or use wireless telegraphy equipment or apparatus without a licence. There is, however, provision under s 1(1) of the WTA for regulations to be made exempting certain classes of apparatus from the need to be licensed; this normally applies to types of apparatus which are not considered to have a potential for causing interference to licensed users. Exemptions already apply to receive-only terminals and exemptions are proposed for certain mobile terminals including Inmarsat C.

Licensing authority

6.26   Licences under the WTA are granted by the Radio-communications Agency (RCA). The RCA is an executive agency of the DTI which deals primarily with licensing under the WTA and all issues connected with radio frequency usage and interference in the UK.

WTA licences follow a standard form and the RCA has a straightforward approach to categorising services and licensing services. Under the newly liberated regime, there are four licence categories under the WTA covering fixed satellite services (see *below*).

Applications for any of the licences referred to *below* are obtained from the RCA Space Services Section. There is a common application form for a licence to establish an earth station, which is completed to establish which licence is the most appropriate to the service which is proposed.

Permanent Earth Station Licences

6.27   These licences are intended for large earth stations which are permanently installed and which are addressed to a satellite in the geostationary orbit. Very small aperture satellite terminal (VSAT) hub stations also operate under these licences. In order to obtain the licence, full site clearance and national and international co-ordination procedures are required. The annual fee per station is currently £12,000.

Transportable Earth Station Licences

6.28   These licences are intended to cover all transportable earth station applications such as satellite news gathering. Full clearance and co-ordination is not practical for such a transportable service but a rapid 24-hour 'fax' clearance procedure is operated by the RCA, which grants approvals on a 'no interference and no protection basis' for up to three months. The clearance procedure must be carried out prior to operation. A code of practice in order to avoid 'harmful interference' (see Site Clearance Manual Code of Practice Number 1, RA 172) has been prepared to guide operators on the procedures to be adopted in obtaining clearance and this can be obtained from the RCA. The licence fee for a transportable earth station licence is currently £8,500.

Very Small Aperture Terminal Licences

6.29   These licences will enable the licensee to operate any number of VSATs in any network configuration provided that up-links are confined to the non-shared frequency bands (14.0–14.25 GHz and 29.5–30GHz) to facilitate minimal co-ordination of the VSATs terminal. The annual fee for a VSAT licence is charged on an incremental block basis, calculated on the number of terminals in the network located in the UK.

Miscellaneous Earth Station Licences

6.30   This category covers services which do not fall within the scope of the other three licence categories. This could include earth stations involved in tracking, telecommand and control operations or earth stations addressable to non-geostationary satellites.

Receive-only apparatus for television and radio satellite services

6.31   The regulations most relevant to television and radio receiving apparatus are the Wireless Telegraph (Receivers) (Exception) Regulations 1989 (SI No 123), and the Wireless Telegraphy (Television Licence Fees) Regulations 1991 (SI No 436).

Outer Space Act 1986

6.32   The Outer Space Act 1986 (OSA) created a system of licensing and registration which arose out of the need to control and supervise increasing private sector space activity and to ensure that the government was able to fulfil its international obligations. In particular, these included The Treaty on Principles Governing the Activities of States in the Exploration and Use of Outer Space including the Moon and Other Celestial Bodies (27 January 1967) (see Chapter 1, para 1.33) and The Convention on International Liability for Damage caused by Space Objects (29 March 1972) (see Chapter 1, para 1.40) which exposed the government to liability for claims arising out of UK space activities, including those of private operators.

The Act applies to UK nationals, Scottish firms and bodies incorporated under the law of any part of the UK (OSA, s 2). They may not (subject to certain exceptions set out in s 3) carry out any of the following activities without a licence granted by the Secretary of State:

(*a*)   launching or procuring the launch of a space object;

(*b*)   operating a space object;

(*c*)   any activity in outer space (OSA, s 1).

These activities are administered by the British National Space Centre (BNSC). The BNSC is a combination of government departments and research councils whose main purpose is to develop and carry out government policy on outer space.

The Secretary of State may grant a licence 'if he thinks fit' (OSA, s 4(1)) but shall not grant a licence unless he is satisfied that the activities authorised by the licence:

(*a*) will not jeopardise public health or the safety of persons or property;

(*b*) will be consistent with the international obligations of the United Kingdom; and

(*c*) will not impair the national security of the United Kingdom (OSA, s 4(2)).

Five licences have so far been issued under the Act: three to Surrey University for OUSAT satellites and two to what is now British Sky Broadcasting Ltd, for the two Marco Polo broadcasting satellites. Before issuing a licence, the BNSC aims to satisfy itself as to:

(*a*) the operator's financial policies and technical capacity including financial details and a technical assessment of the proposal;

(*b*) the nature of the mission including the launch;

(*c*) safety aspects including emissions and radio transmissions;

(*d*) orbital parameters; and

(*e*) insurance for all phases: launch, operation and disposal.

Licences may contain conditions:

(*a*) permitting inspection by the Secretary of State of the licensee's facilities and testing of the licensee's equipment;

(*b*) requiring the provision of information to the Secretary of State about the launch, basic orbital parameters and anything else of relevance;

(*c*) requiring the licensee to conduct his operations in such a way as to prevent contamination of outer space or adverse changes in the environment of the earth, avoid interference with the activities of others and to avoid any breach of the UK's international obligations; and

(*d*) requiring the licensee to insure himself against liability incurred in respect of damage or loss suffered by third parties (OSA, s 5).

In addition to the above obligations on licensees, persons to whom the OSA applies must indemnify the government against any claims brought against the government in respect of damage or loss arising out of the activities to which the OSA applies (OSA, s 10).

As well as establishing a licensing regime, the OSA also provides that the Secretary of State must maintain a register of space objects (OSA, s 7). This is a response to the government's obligations under the Convention on Registration of Objects Launched into Outer Space concluded on 12 November 1974 (see Chapter 1, para 1.46). The 1986 Act provides that the Secretary of State may enter such particulars of such objects as he considers appropriate to comply with the international obligations of the UK. Under the OSA, any person may inspect a copy of the register on payment of an appropriate fee (OSA, s 7(3)).

Interception and unauthorised use of satellite transmissions

Introduction

6.33   The Radio Regulations (RRs) (see Chapter 3) make provision for ensuring that the laws of members of the ITU provide for measures to preserve the secrecy of transmissions which are not intended for general reception (RRs 1992–1994). The Convention Relating to the Distributing of Programme-Carrying Signals Transmitted by Satellite (Brussels, 21 May 1974) also makes provision for prohibiting the distribution of non-broadcast satellite transmissions without the consent of the transmitting organisation. However, few states are parties to the Convention and the UK is not a signatory. Article 10 of European Convention for the Protection of Human Rights and Fundamental Freedoms is also relevant (see paras 7.28 and 8.4).

In some states, laws of unfair competition may operate to prevent 'signal piracy', where no specific provision is made under domestic telecommunications laws. Satellite transmissions contain differing types of material, the unauthorised use of which may be detrimental to various commercial or other interests. These transmissions include pay-TV services, telecommunications traffic and other material, such as information derived from remote sensing activities. (See J A Ballard, *The Regulation of the Use of Information from Earth Observation Satellites*, International Bar Association, October 1991.) Since reception is not a copyright 'restricted act', copyright laws are irrelevant to the interception of communications. However, copyright does have applications in this field, where some further use is made of (broadcast) transmissions and/or of underlying material protected by copyright or related rights (see Chapter 8).

Statutory provisions

6.34   In the UK, the WTA, the TA and the Interception of Communications Act 1985 (ICA) contain provisions which may be applied so as to preserve the secrecy of, *inter alia*, certain satellite transmissions. The Copyright, Designs and Patents Act 1988 also contains provisions relating to encrypted satellite transmissions (see Chapter 8).

Under the WTA, it must first be asked whether equipment to receive satellite transmissions requires a licence under s 1, or is exempt from the requirements for such a licence. This has already been referred to in para 6.25 *et seq.*

Section 5(*b*) of the WTA creates two criminal offences in the following terms:

> Any person who . . .
>
> (*a*) . . .
>
> (*b*) otherwise than under the authority of [the Secretary of State] or in the course of his duty as a servant of the Crown, either—
>
> > (i) uses any wireless telegraphy apparatus with intent to obtain information as to the contents, sender or addressee of any message (whether sent by means of wireless telegraphy or not) which neither the person using the apparatus nor any person on whose behalf he is acting is authorised by the [Secretary of State] to receive;
> >
> > or
> >
> > (ii) except in the course of legal proceedings or for the purpose of any report thereof, discloses any information as to the contents, sender or addressee of any such message, being information which would not have come to his knowledge but for the use of wireless telegraphy apparatus by him or by another person
>
> shall be guilty of an offence.

These provisions are capable of applying to the reception and subsequent use of satellite transmissions. Satellite antennae and receiving equipment are 'wireless telegraphy apparatus'. The meaning of 'message' is less straightforward and is probably not the same as when used in licences granted under the TA, where 'messages' are capable of embracing all types of transmissions. Section 19(1)(*a*) refers to the 'conveying of messages, sounds or visual images . . .'. This might suggest that sounds or visual images are excluded from the meaning of 'messages', which is defined as 'including . . . any signal . . . warning or information . . . ' (s 19(4)).

A typical case was *Paul v Ministry of Posts and Telecommunications* [1973] Crim LR 322, where the defendant was successfully prosecuted for using a radio receiver to receive emergency fire brigade messages (see also *Francome v Mirror Group Newspapers* [1984] 1 WLR 892). In the authors' view, s 5(*b*) does apply to (at least to certain types of) telecommunications traffic, but it is unlikely to apply to transmissions including radio or television programmes. It must also be shown that reception of the transmission is not authorised by the Secretary of State. This means authorised within the meaning of s 1 (licensing of wireless telegraphy stations and apparatus). Accordingly, it must also be asked whether reception of the equipment is licensed under s 1 or (*quaere*) is exempt from requiring a licence: see, for example, SI 1989 No 123 (para 6.31 *above*), the explanatory note to which states that s 5(*b*) is left unaffected by this exemption.

The ICA was enacted in the light of the Home Office *White Paper on the Interception of Communications in the UK* (Cmnd 9438), which proposed changes in the law relating to telephone tapping following the decision of the European Court of Human Rights in the *Malone* case (see *below*). The ICA is capable of applying to certain types of satellite transmissions.

The statute prohibits 'the intentional interception of a communication in the course of its transmission by post or by means of public telecommunication system' (ICA, s 1(1)). It is a defence to show that the person concerned has reasonable grounds for believing that the person to whom or by whom the communication was sent has consented to the interception (ICA, s 1(2)(*b*)). A public telecommunication system is one so designated by the Secretary of State, being a system run by a Public Telecommunications Operator, for example, BT or Mercury (TA, ss 9 and 10). However, for the purposes of s 1(1), a communication which is in the course of its transmission otherwise than by a public telecommunication system is deemed to be in the course of its transmission by means of such a system if its mode of transmission identifies it as a communication which is to be or has been transmitted by such a system and has been sent from or is to be sent to a country or territory outside the UK (ICA, s 10(2)).

Receiving equipment for satellite transmissions is either not licensable under the TA (transmissions of specified broadcasting services) (s 6(2)(*c*)), or is likely to fall within the Class Licence for the Running of Telecommunications Systems to Receive Messages from Earth Orbiting Apparatus, 3 February 1989, issued pursuant to s 7 of the TA (see para 8.40).

The TA creates a number of further offences relating to the reception of (*inter alia*) satellite transmissions. The most important of these for present purposes is the dishonest obtaining of a service provided by means of a licensed telecommunication system with intent to avoid payment of any charge applicable to the provision of the service (TA, s 42). A similar provision is embodied in s 297 of the Copyright, Design and Patents Act 1988, relating to pay-TV services (see Chapter 8).

Common law and equity

6.35   It will be difficult to rely successfully on principles of common law and equity to prevent unauthorised interception and use of satellite transmissions (see *Malone v Metropolitan Police Commissioner* [1979] Ch 344). However, much depends on the type of transmission. In *BBC Enterprises Ltd v Hi-Tech Xtravision Ltd* [1990] FSR 217 (reversed on appeal on other grounds [1991] 2 AC 327, HL), Scott J rejected an argument that encrypted transmissions containing the BBC TV Europe television service were confidential. The learned judge said this:

> There is no confidentiality in the content of the . . . programmes as such. They are simply BBC programmes. The broadcasts are encrypted, but it is possible for Hi-Tech, and no doubt others, to decode the encryption. To do so is, in my judgment, no more a breach of confidence than it would be to decode a coded message placed in the columns of *The Times*. If an author chooses to place a coded message in a public medium he cannot, in my judgment, complain if members of the public decode his message. If the content, once decoded, does not qualify for protection on confidentiality grounds, the law of confidentiality is not, in my judgment, of any relevance. (p 237.)

In *Malone*, it was held that no confidentiality existed in respect of telephone conversations (pp 360–362, 375 and 376) and hence telephone tapping did not breach any duty of confidence which might arise (apart from contract). Telephone users are aware of the risks of being overheard by reason of extension lines, private switchboards and so-called 'crossed lines' and 'a person who utters confidential information must accept the risk of any unknown overhearing which is inherent in the circumstances of the communication' (p 376C): see however, *Francome* v *Mirror Group Newspapers*. The circumstances in which some satellite communications are sent may lend support to arguments that unauthorised interceptions may not be 'inherent'. In *BBC* v *Hi-Tech*, Scott J was prepared to accept the possibility of a duty of confidence where confidential information is transmitted. For a general commentary on the law of confidence see Gurry, *Breach of Confidence* and Chapter 13 of Clerk and Lindsell, *Torts*, 16th edn (Sweet & Maxwell 1989). Where the material in a satellite transmission is truly confidential, the law of confidence should be capable of providing protection. It may also be possible to use the so-called 'economic' torts to prevent unauthorised disclosure of the contents of satellite transmissions (see Chapter 15 of Clerk and Lindsell, *Torts*).

II

Legal and Regulatory Issues Relating to Satellite Television

7

Regulation of Programme Content

Introduction

7.1 Any broadcasting organisation is faced with the daily problem of ensuring that its service complies with the applicable rules relating to what types of material can and cannot be included in a television service. Most jurisdictions in the world impose some level of regulation on broadcasters in respect of programme content. For a satellite broadcaster the position can be rendered more difficult because it is quite likely that its television service will be received in a number of jurisdictions with different views on what may and may not be included in a television service. In Europe, steps have been taken to harmonise programme content rules. These steps will be discussed in detail later in this chapter, the purpose of which is to examine the general rules that apply to television services in Europe and to review the way in which these general rules have been implemented into the domestic laws of European countries, using the UK as an example.

European regulation

7.2 Current European regulation of programme content and harmonisation measures date back to 1989. This was the year when major European measures dealing with the issue of harmonisation of programme content regulation were adopted. In particular, in May 1989, the Council of Europe adopted the European Convention on Transfrontier Television (the Convention) (European Convention on Transfrontier Television, Strasbourg, 5 May 1989; HMSO Miscellaneous No 12 (1990) Cm 1068 (ISBN 92–871–1715–2)). In October 1989, the Council of the European Communities adopted Directive 89/552/EEC on the Coordination of Certain Provisions Laid Down by Law, Regulation or Administrative Action in Member States Concerning the Pursuit of Television Broadcasting Activities (OJ 17.10.89 L298/15) (the 'Television without Frontiers Directive'). Neither instrument applies to radio broadcasts.

The two instruments both deal with similar issues and include the same basic provisions. The Convention applies to all countries belonging to the Council of Europe. The members are: Andorra, Austria, Belgium, Bulgaria, Cyprus, Czech Republic, Denmark, Estonia, Finland, France, Germany, Greece, Hungary, Iceland, the Republic of Ireland, Italy, Latvia, Liechtenstein, Lithuania, Luxembourg, Malta, The Netherlands, Norway, Poland, Portugal, Romania, San Marino, Slovakia, Slovenia, Spain, Sweden, Switzerland, Turkey and the UK. 'Special guest status' has been granted to Albania, Belarus, Bosnia, Croatia, the Holy See, Moldova, Monaco, Russia and Ukraine.

Although the Television Without Frontiers Directive has already been implemented in the laws of most member states the Commission has indicated that it is unhappy with the way in which member states have done so. It is now taking steps to ensure that member states comply accurately with the terms of the directive. A Communication from the Commission to the Council and the European Parliament, COM (94) 57 final, 3 March 1994 (the Communication), contains the member states' reports on their implementation of arts 4 and 5 of the directive. The overall results emerging from the Communication are positive but there is some lack of transparency on the part of the member states in terms of methods used in compiling the figures for the reports. However, the Commission's view is that this first monitoring exercise has helped to clarify the scope of these articles. It has emerged that the majority of channels covered in the reports are economically able to present a 'majority proportion' of European works and at the same time achieve satisfactory audience ratings.

This chapter will concentrate on the directive rather than the Convention although, on points of particular interest, reference will be made to both instruments.

The Television Without Frontiers Directive

Introduction

7.3   Before examining the terms of the directive, it is worth reviewing the basis on which it operates. The principle of the directive is to set out minimum standards regarding programme content which member states are required to impose on broadcasters whose transmissions originate from their territories. Member states are free to impose more burdensome requirements.

However, provided that a broadcaster meets the requirements of the member state where the broadcast emanates, the principle of freedom of reception as between member states is to apply and other member states (even though their own requirements may be more onerous) may not restrict or prevent the reception of that broadcaster's service in their territory. According to art 25 of the directive, member states were obliged to bring into force relevant laws, regulations and administrative provisions necessary to give effect to the directive no later than 3 October 1991. This chapter will specifically deal with how the UK has implemented the directive into its domestic law.

The directive covers four broad areas:

(*a*)   promotion of programmes of European origin and programmes made by independent producers ('the quota provisions');

(*b*)   television advertising and sponsorship;

(*c*)   protection of minors; and

(*d*)   right of reply.

The directive also includes general provisions designed to give effect to the basic principle explained above and, in particular, defining where a broadcast originates for the purposes of the directive. This chapter deals first with the general provisions and then with the four broad areas identified above.

General provisions

7.4   The general provisions are set out in Chapter II of the directive, in particular arts 2 and 3.

Member states must ensure that television broadcasts transmitted by broadcasters under their jurisdiction or by broadcasters to whom they allocate a frequency or satellite capacity or who make use of a satellite up-link in their territory, comply with the domestic law of that member state relating to broadcasts to the public: art 2(1).

'Jurisdiction' is not defined, leaving member states free to designate which broadcasters they deem to be under their jurisdiction and which they do not. It is worth noting that member states will invariably decide that broadcasters who make use of a frequency allocated by their domestic authorities are under their jurisdiction, although this category is given in the directive as an alternative.

'Broadcaster[s]' is also not defined though it is fairly clear from the tenor of the directive and the definition of 'television broadcasting' that it is intended that the directive should apply to the originators of television programmes, that is, those who edit, put together and initially transmit the television service. Unlike the directive, the Convention does define broadcaster as 'the natural legal person who composes television programme services for reception by the general public and transmits them or has them transmitted, complete and unchanged, by a third party': art 2(*c*). Responsibility is placed on the 'transmitting Party' ('Party' meaning a member state of the Council of Europe) for ensuring compliance with the provisions of the Convention. As regards satellite transmissions, the transmitting Party is specifically defined as:

(i)   the Party in which the satellite up-link is situated;

(ii) the Party which grants the use of the frequency or a satellite capacity when the up-link is situated in a State which is not a party to this Convention;

(iii) the Party in which the broadcaster has its seat when responsibility under sub-paragraphs (i) and (ii) is not established. (art 5(2)(*b*).)

These definitions support the interpretation of the provisions of the directive given *above*.

The difficulty with both the directive and the Convention comes not when considering in which country a satellite up-link is situated or an allocated frequency or satellite capacity is used, but in the meanings of 'jurisdiction' (in the case of the directive) and a broadcaster's 'seat' (in the case of the Convention). Each of these terms would seem to suggest that a member state can apply its rules to a satellite broadcaster who does not up-link from that member state. This may lead to a conflict between member states as to the identity of the appropriate country for licensing of a service (see discussion on Red Hot Television in para 7.38 *et seq*). For example, a broadcasting company established in and having its administrative office in one member state may be held to be under that member state's jurisdiction or to have its 'seat' in that member state, but that broadcasting company may indeed up-link from another member state. In the reports contained in the Communication, few real difficulties in terms of conflicts, or absence of jurisdiction are revealed. However, this may be due to the fact that the reports relate to a period when broadcasting is still predominantly terrestrial based. The rapid rise of satellite channels is bound to reveal real problems of jurisdiction, affecting the operability of national regulation systems and hence of the directive itself, if common criteria on jurisdiction are not observed.

Implementation of the general provisions of the directive in UK law

7.5   The directive has been implemented in UK law, as far as the UK government is concerned, by the Broadcasting Act 1990 (BA) and the codes made under it by the Independent Television Commission (ITC), the body charged with the statutory duty of regulating independent television services.

In terms of establishing 'jurisdiction' for the purposes of UK law, the BA covers UK terrestrial broadcasters and satellite television services up-linked from the UK. It also reflects the intention that the directive should apply to the originators of television services by extending the ambit of the BA to services up-linking outside the EU to the extent that programmes included within the service consist of material provided by a person in the UK who is in a position to determine what is to be included in the service. Therefore, programme content originating in the UK but comprised in foreign television services can be regulated. The BA specifically declines jurisdiction over broadcasts originating in other EU member states.

Satellite television services are divided into 'domestic satellite services' and 'non-domestic satellite services' (BA, s 43) (see Chapter 6, paras 6.12 and 6.13).

All satellite services coming within the definitions must obtain and comply with the conditions of a licence from the ITC. Such broadcasters will be subject to the ITC Codes in accordance with their licences. The ITC has power to impose financial penalties, shorten a broadcaster's licence period and, in the last resort, to revoke licences where there are serious breaches of licence terms.

The promotion of programmes of European origin and programmes made by independent producers (the quota provisions)

Introduction

7.6 Rules imposing quotas on broadcasters for the inclusion of 'European works' and programmes made by independent producers in their services are set out in Chapter III of the directive.

The directive aims at maintaining and developing 'home-grown' programming throughout the EU. This objective is seen as desirable both as a means of fostering talent and creativity within the member states (with the concomitant influence on job and wealth creation) and as a means of maintaining strong European cultural identities. Chapter III also imposes a minimum quota obliging broadcasters to reserve at least 10 per cent of their transmission time for works originated by independent producers.

The European works quota

7.7 *The basic rule* The directive provides that 'member states shall ensure where practicable and by appropriate means that broadcasters reserve for European works . . . a majority proportion of their transmission time' (art 4.1).

The meaning of 'majority proportion' is open to debate, but the general view (in the absence of any particular rule in particular member states) is that it should be taken as referring to a simple majority (ie more than 50 per cent).

7.8 *Transmission time* The transmission time, the majority proportion of which is to be devoted to works of a European origin, is to be calculated by 'excluding the time appointed to news, sports events, games, advertising and teletext services' (art 4). The directive attaches much greater significance to the provenance of programmes not covered by this exclusion, having regard to the underlying objectives of the legislation, because they are adjudged to involve a much greater degree of creativity. It also makes the directive more onerous. Almost all news, sports events, games and advertising will originate in Europe; if a broadcaster were able to take them into account it would significantly reduce the burden of the quota requirements. However, this formulation does not allow for a neat demarcation of which programmes are included within 'transmission time' as defined. The status of current affairs programmes, documentaries, biographical films and nature programmes, for example, is by no means clear. It also seems somewhat inconsistent to exclude 'games' (which presumably refers to game shows) given the widely expressed concern about 'Americanisation' of European television programming; although it is probably the case that, while game shows may be based on American formats, they will originate in Europe.

7.9 *The meaning of 'European works'* The definition of 'European works' is obviously crucial to the practical effect of the quota requirement. Article 6 of the directive gives a complex definition of this term. The definition has been thought to be problematic and has aroused a good deal of discussion. The meaning given to each of the relevant terms will be finally settled only by detailed enactments in the member states or judgments of the ECJ. The definition is in line with (though vastly more complicated than) the definition of 'European audiovisual works' in the Convention. The Convention definition is: 'creative works, the production or co-production of which is controlled by European natural or legal persons' (art 2(*e*)), which is easily understood. It is interesting to note that the original proposal for the directive referred to a 'Community work'. The definition in the directive then became much more complicated—although there is a common view that the added detail has not made the directive any clearer than the Convention.

The meaning given to 'European works' in art 6 of the directive is: works originating from Member States of the Community, other European third states being party to the Convention or other European third countries. It appears works originate from member states and states being party to the Convention if they meet the requirements of para 2 of art 6 (see *below*). However, in this regard there is a lack of clarity; the drafting of the directive suggests that the requirement to meet the conditions of para 2 may be limited to non-EU Convention countries, pre-unified Germany not being part of the EU. However, the safer view is to take the drafting as meaning that para 2 applies across the board. Works originate from other European third countries (but not being member states or parties to the Convention) if they fulfil the conditions of para 3 of art 6 (see *below*).

Paragraph 2 of art 6 explains the meaning of 'originates' in respect of member states and European states being party to the Convention. The criteria appear to require both that the works must be 'mainly made with authors and workers residing in' the relevant states and that one of three stipulations regarding the production of the programmes is met. The three stipulations are as follows:

(*a*) they are made by one or more producers established in one or more of those States [ie Member States of the Community and European third states party to the European Convention on Transfrontier Television]; or

(*b*) production of the works is supervised and actually controlled by one or more producers established in one or more of those States; or

(*c*) the contribution of co-producers of those States to the total co-production costs is preponderant and the co-production is not controlled by one or more producers established outside those States (art 6(2)(*a*), (*b*) and (*c*)).

Works originating from other European third countries are works made exclusively or in co-production with producers established in either a member state or a European country with which the EU has concluded an agreement provided the works are mainly made with authors and workers residing in a European state (art 6(3)).

Where a work does not meet these criteria, works made mainly with authors and workers residing in the EU can be considered European works to the extent that their budgets have been funded by co-producers from the EU (art 6(4)).

7.10   These provisions are curiously drafted in that, ostensibly, the stipulation that the works must be 'mainly made' with 'authors and workers' residing in the requisite states is deemed to be satisfied if any one of the situations detailed in (*a*)–(*c*) applies. If this construction is correct, it would seem to render redundant the provisions referring to authors and workers. Most commentators, however, seem to regard the 'mainly made' provision as mandatory in itself, and the subsequent stipulations as additional compulsory requirements, that is, the works must be mainly made with authors and workers residing in one or more of the requisite states *and* comply with the provisions relating to production. Certainly, the drafting of para 3 of art 6 suggests that the 'workers and authors' and the 'production' criteria are separate and cumulative. Accordingly, the authors take the view that the text of the directive might be more easily understood by replacing the words 'provided that they comply' in para 2 of art 6 with the words 'and complying'.

The criteria for assessing compliance with the rule is left to be clarified in the various national laws introduced to implement the directive. Obviously, there is scope for varying interpretations. It has been suggested that the criteria will be based upon 'a head count, with different weights assigned to different classes of staff, from directors, to extras, to make-up artists' (J Howkins and M Foster, *Television in 1992: a Guide to Europe's New TV, Film and Video Business* (Coopers & Lybrand 1989)). For example, a single non-European, even the director or a lead actor, would probably not be sufficient to 'de-Europeanise' the production, but if all the lead actors are non-European this may well disqualify the production even though numerically most workers are European.

In the Communications to the Council and the European Parliament, the Commission notes that the national reports made no particular comments on this topic and therefore concludes that the application of art 6 poses no problem, apart from the possible misunderstanding that may have arisen in three instances. These concern TVZ in Denmark, VTM in Belgium, New Channel in Greece and the reference in art 5 to European works created by independent producers (see para 7.15). In these cases, the figures representing the proportion of European works from independent producers are higher than the proportion of European works, which seems impossible by definition. It is suspected that all independent productions could have been included in the figures, rather than just European ones as defined by art 6.

Despite the lack of comments from the member states, various failures are observed in meeting the requirements imposed by the directive. In the UK, which has the largest number of channels, a striking feature is the marked difference between the terrestrial broadcasters, which comfortably exceed the required proportion, and the satellite stations, some of which are well below the target. The main reasons advanced by the member states for such failures can be summarised as follows:

(*a*)   the situation of special interest or paying channels (catering for special interests or targeted at ethnic minorities or other specific categories of television consumers);

(*b*)   the situation of new channels;

(*c*)   the problem of the supply of European programmes liable to attract a large enough audience;

(*d*)   the volume of transmissions.

7.11   *Authors and workers*   The interpretation of 'authors' is likely to go beyond the strict English law interpretation (in the case of an audio-visual work such as a film, the 'author' has been taken to be the producer, although this position will change in late 1995 when the amendments to the Copyright, Designs and Patents Act 1988 will, for the first time under English law, mean that the director of a film is a copyright owner). The term 'author' will cover anyone involved in the creative side of the production, in so far as their role involves 'composition' of the overall work, such as scriptwriters, director(s), perhaps even composers of soundtracks.

'Authors and workers' do not have to be subjects of or domiciled in a particular state so long as they reside in a European country. 'Residence' is another undefined term. It will, obviously, have to be legal residence; it is likely to be determined by reference to a right of residence under immigration laws along with additional criteria seen as constituting actual residence. One method of determining residence would be for the individual member states to duplicate the criteria of their respective taxation authorities.

Another potential problem with the definition arises where 'workers' are themselves companies, such as 'loan-out' companies used by many highly regarded individual producers, directors and actors in the film and television field. The question arises whether 'residence' will be that of the individuals concerned or that of the company? One possible solution to this is that the credits will be deemed to be the determining factor. This is particularly likely in the case of works existing at the date of implementation. It is possible that the status of companies may be disregarded entirely, which would solve the problem of non-European actors or directors setting up European loan-out companies to meet the criteria of the directive.

7.12   *Production rules*   Works originating either from one or more member states of the EU or from one or more non-EU states which have signed the Convention must satisfy one of three conditions with respect to production.

The most straightforward of these alternatives is where the work has been made by one or more producers established in one or more of the requisite states. To be 'established' in any particular state, producers would either have to be incorporated in that state or be acting under its law. Subsidiaries could therefore be set up to enable a US company (eg) to qualify as an EU producer. The work could be made by a non-European producer as long as production is supervised and actually controlled by one or more producers established in one or more qualifying states.

A co-production with producers established in a non-EU/ Convention state (eg, Canada) would allow for the work to be classified as European, on condition that the co-producers established in the European state(s) contributed a 'preponderant' proportion of the total co-production costs and that the co-production was not controlled by one or more producers established outside the relevant European countries. 'Preponderant' is not defined. It must mean in excess of 50 per cent, although how much in excess is open to question.

A co-production which does not accord with the above stipulations but is made mainly with authors and workers residing in one or more member states will qualify as European 'to an extent corresponding to the proportion of the contribution of Community co-producers to the total production costs' (art 6(4) of the directive).

Finally, works originating from European countries which are neither member states nor signatories of the Convention may qualify as European if they are made exclusively by producers established in one or more such countries or in co-production with producers established in one or more member states, provided that the EU concludes agreements with those countries and the works concerned are mainly made with authors and workers residing in any European state. For example, unless the EU enters into an agreement with Poland, productions made by a US company's Polish subsidiary in a Polish studio would not qualify as European works.

7.13 *Further issues*   In view of the apparent stringency of the quota requirement it is important to take into consideration the further provisos and limitations on it.

Member states are obliged to reserve the majority proportion for European works only 'where practicable and by appropriate means'. This phrasing (coupled with other provisions *below*) should allow for considerable flexibility in the way in which member states require their broadcasters to meet the strict quota requirements. For example, an English-language broadcaster will have a strong argument as regards feature films that it is impracticable to show a majority of European works because the vast majority of English language feature films originate outside Europe. It would be impossible for the broadcaster of a commercial English language feature film theme channel to meet the quota.

Even outside the feature film field, in English language services, the inclusion of a high proportion of American or Australian produced material may also be justified by reference to practicality on the grounds of cost. In UK law, at least, there is good authority for the inclusion of cost considerations in the assessment of practicality. Current developments resulting in a massive increase in broadcasting activity and capacity will lead to increased competition for advertising and audiences which will restrict the money available to all broadcasters to make their own productions. In reality, broadcasters may well have little option but to buy in relatively cheap 'foreign' programmes in order to fill their schedules.

7.14 A further proviso is that the proportion must be achieved 'progressively' on the basis of suitable criteria. The broadcaster is entitled to take into account, when planning its schedules, its 'informational, educational, cultural and entertainment responsibilities to its viewing public' (art 4(1)). The Commission has recognised that it would be unrealistic to expect the quota to be achieved overnight, and that certain categories of European programming might be difficult to procure in sufficient numbers. The words quoted would appear to enable a broadcaster to put out non-European programming (even to a predominant extent) where European programming suitable for the broadcaster's particular audience is not available. Broadcasters may well be able to advance strong arguments that their projected audience profile dictates that, for example, predominantly American-produced programmes have to be shown. There is no indication in the directive of how, objectively, to assess what an individual broadcaster's particular audience might be. Broadcasters may therefore rely on their informational and entertainment 'responsibilities' to avoid being in breach of the quota. The 'cultural' argument will clearly be relevant for special interest channels aimed at particular ethnic groups: it would, of course, be very difficult to provide a commercial service aimed at Asian communities without using programming originating outside Europe.

Where European products of the requisite type are available but are of demonstrably lower quality, it may be open to broadcasters to argue that they are entitled to use a superior non-European product. In the long term, however, due to the stipulation that the 'majority proportion' requirement ought to be achieved progressively, this argument is likely to have increasingly less weight. It is envisaged that the quota will eventually become an absolute requirement in respect of services that cannot benefit from special treatment.

Finally, where a broadcaster operates more than one channel, it is likely that each channel will be considered separately from the point of view of quota requirements.

The independent works quota

7.15   Article 5 of the directive imposes, again 'where practicable' and subject to the same caveats as for the European works quota, an obligation on broadcasters to reserve at least ten per cent of their transmission time, excluding the time appointed to news, sports events, games, advertising and teletext services or, at the discretion of the member state, at least ten per cent of their programming budget, for European works created by producers who are independent of broadcasters. This proportion also has to be achieved progressively. Broadcasters must earmark an 'adequate' proportion of transmission time for recent works, which are defined as 'works transmitted within five years of their production'.

'Independent' is not defined, so that if member states do not choose to give detailed guidelines in their implementing legislation, it is possible that companies in effect controlled (whether by shareholdings or economic influence) by broadcasters could be commissioned as 'independent producers'. The Commission would be likely to disapprove of this, as the policy is clearly designed to foster diversity and new talent in programme making.

In the UK, the meaning of independent production has been the subject of intense debate because, unlike the definition of European works (where the UK regulatory authority has simply restated the provisions of the directive), subordinate legislation has been introduced to impose a definition. This debate is dealt with in more detail *below*.

Difficulties have been noted in the Communication in respect of the application of the 10 per cent rule in several member states because of the definition of 'independent producer'. There were those that ignored the definition proposed in the guidelines; other member states claimed to have had great difficulty in collecting data of this kind, or had not received any information at all for some channels. It is therefore not possible to present a clearer picture as to compliance.

Implementation of the quota provisions into UK law

7.16   *Which services are bound by the UK implementation provisions?*   The quota provisions in the directive were regarded by the Home Office[1] as being 'politically' binding but not legally binding on the UK government. In the Home Office's opinion this was the intention behind the directive. The quota provisions have been implemented by various means according to the category of broadcaster concerned:

(*a*)   as regards commercial terrestrial television, ss 16, 25 and 29 of the BA make it a condition of the licence for Channels 3, 4 and 5 (respectively) that 'a proper proportion of the matter included in . . . programmes is of European origin; and that in each year not less than 25 per cent of the total amount of time allocated to the broadcasting of qualifying programmes in the service is allocated to the broadcasting of a range and diversity of independent productions';

(*b*)   the Home Office has written to the BBC informing it pursuant to s 186 of the BA, that the European works quota and the independent works quota are directly applicable to the BBC;

(*c*)   domestic satellite services have to comply with the quota provisions: s 44(3) of the BA;

(*d*)   the provisions have yet to be extended to non-domestic satellite services by binding legal means. The non-domestic satellite service licence contains only a provision requiring the licensee to provide information to enable monitoring of the application of the quota provisions to be carried out. However, when a non-domestic satellite service licence is issued, a letter is sent out by the Department of National Heritage to the non-domestic satellite service provider which restates the provisions of the directive and stresses that they are to be achieved 'where practicable'. The guidance note intended to clarify the definition of European works in the directive is attached to the letters sent out. In addition, the ITC periodically contacts the satellite service providers requesting information as to the level of European programming on their services.

The BA gives the Secretary of State the power to make orders giving detailed guidelines in respect of the quotas and altering the percentage for independent productions.

How the provisions are applied

7.15   *The European works quota*   The ITC has issued a guidance note on the meaning of European works (ITC Guidance Note on Programme Definitions, *Programme Strands and European Programmes*, February 1991). Essentially, the note simply restates the terms of the directive.

Independent productions   The Secretary of State issued a statutory instrument on 18 June 1991 coming into force on 1 January 1993 with regard to independent productions (The Broadcasting (Independent Productions) Order 1991 (SI No 1408)). This has proved controversial in that it appears to prevent any person or body corporate who has a shareholding greater than 15 per cent in a broadcaster, or in whom a broadcaster has a shareholding greater than 15 per cent, from qualifying as an 'independent producer'. Somewhat surprisingly, the definition of 'broadcaster' is such that it applies to persons having interests in broadcasters anywhere in the world. In its Green Paper on Media Ownership, published in May 1995, the UK government proposed that the shareholding percentage be increased to 25 per cent, which proposal is expected to become law in 1996.

Cinematographic works

7.18   Article 7 of the directive provides that member states shall 'ensure that the television broadcasters under their jurisdiction do not broadcast any cinematographic work, unless otherwise agreed between its rights holders and the broadcaster, until two years have elapsed since the work was first shown in cinemas in one of the Member States of the Community'.

At first sight the provision seems very restrictive, especially compared with the theatrical window in the USA (6–12 months before pay-TV). It also represents an incursion of regulation into an area which has usually been governed in the past by private contractual agreement between the parties.

The wording specifically preserves the right for the broadcaster and the rights holders to negotiate a shorter period if they wish. Article 7 is likely, therefore, to have little practical effect.

The article also provides that the period between theatrical release and first television showing shall be one year where the film concerned is co-produced by the broadcaster.

The requirements of art 7 may be at odds with the current practice in some, if not most, member states. For example in the UK, although the contractual theatrical window is already normally (though not always) two years, calculation of this period runs from the first UK theatrical release, not the first showing in any member state.

Other provisions of Chapter III of the directive

7.19 *Language policy* Article 8 states that member states may 'where they consider it necessary' impose more stringent or detailed rules regarding all or some of the programmes put out by television broadcasters under their jurisdiction. These rules must be made in the interest of language policy and on the basis of 'language criteria'. (This is, of course, in addition to member states' freedom to impose a stricter framework generally, so long as the minimum requirements contained in the directive are complied with.)

7.20 *Exemption for 'local television broadcasts'* Article 9 gives immunity from all the provisions in Chapter III of the directive to 'local television broadcasts not forming part of a national network'. It seems highly unlikely that any satellite broadcasters would come within this definition, although the meaning of the term is not entirely clear. Conflicting interpretations have been put forward, though the conclusion of the 'Barzanti Report' seems logical (European Communities, European Parliament, Session Documents, 1987–8, Doc A 2 0246/87, p 31). This report said that local broadcasting stations would be exempt from the quota provisions; but to be considered as such, 'the stations must not broadcast across the national frontier'.

Likelihood of enforcement

7.21   The US television and film industry and government reacted with some hostility towards what they saw as the protectionist purpose of the directive. American officials alleged that it violated the General Agreement on Tariffs and Trade (GATT). European civil servants retorted that GATT concerned the supply of goods whereas television broadcasting was a service. In response to this controversy, the Council of Ministers of the EU promised that quota provisions would not be enforced against member states. The legal status of this declaration is unclear and it is far from certain whether the Commission would, in any case, agree to follow it. If this promise was adhered to, the part of the directive relating to quotas would merely serve as a policy document: intended to be politically binding but not legally binding.

Commission Vice President Martin Bangemann stated in October 1989 that failure to reach the quota goal 'would not be sufficient for the Commission to bring Member States to Court' for breaching the directive (Commission of the European Communities, *The Week in Europe* (WE 33/89—5 October 1989) (London Office)). Such an approach may be legally untenable, although under art 169 of the Treaty of Rome, the Commission does have discretion whether or not to bring proceedings before the ECJ against member states which have failed to implement directives. The Commission does not however have any discretion to authorise an entire system of regulation which violates EC law.

Recent proposals have, however, been developed to make the quota provisions more strictly enforceable (see para 7.46 *below*) and remain a point of contention between the USA and the EU.

Television advertising and sponsorship

General provisions

7.22   Chapter IV of the directive deals with television advertising and sponsorship. The rationale behind the provisions on advertising is to ensure that the interests of the consumer are fully and properly protected by specifying minimum rules and standards for broadcast advertising.

'Television advertising' is defined as 'any form of announcement broadcast in return for payment or for similar consideration by a public or private undertaking in connection with a trade, business, craft or profession in order to promote the supply of goods or services including immovable property or rights and obligations in return for payment' (art 1(*b*) of the directive). The definition in the Convention is somewhat wider in that it also covers public announcements intended to 'advance a cause or idea or bring about some other effect desired by the advertiser' rather than just to promote the supply of goods or services. The Convention, therefore, covers public service announcements, public information advertisements and advertisements for charities. For these categories as for the others, transmission time must have been given to the advertiser for remuneration or similar consideration. It is important to note that the provisions of the directive will typically not cover so-called 'home shopping channels' because in the case of these channels, payment is not specifically made to place adverts; the whole service is provided by the home shopping channel which will usually pay for its airtime (by way of, eg a transponder lease) whether or not it is transmitting programmes.

Prohibition against subliminal techniques and surreptitious advertising

7.23   Article 10 of the directive (which is very similar to art 14 of the Convention) provides that television advertising must be readily recognisable and must be kept 'separate from other parts of the programme service by optical and/or acoustic means'. Isolated advertising spots (which are covered in art 18; see para 7.25 *below*) must 'remain the exception'.

Article 10 also prohibits subliminal techniques and 'surreptitious advertising'. Surreptitious advertising is defined in art 1(*c*) as 'the representation in words or pictures of goods, services, the name, the trade mark or the activities of a producer of goods or a provider of services in programmes when such representation is intended by the broadcaster to serve advertising and might mislead the public as to its nature'. The use of the concept of intention obviously leaves it open to the broadcaster to argue that any such 'advertising' was inadvertent, although the directive does say that any such representation will be deemed to be intentional 'if it is done in return for payment or for similar consideration'. The Convention goes slightly further in prohibiting the 'presentation of products or services in programmes when it serves advertising purposes'. Arguably, the apparent removal of the element of 'intention' here means that inadvertent 'presentation' would be caught.

It is envisaged that member states will enact more detailed provisions to avoid potential loopholes.

Scheduling and amount of advertising

7.24   Article 11 of the directive sets out detailed provisions for the inclusion and spacing of advertisements in programme schedules.

Paragraph 1 of the article provides that advertisements must be inserted between programmes. However, it does allow advertisements to be inserted during programmes, provided that further conditions are met and that 'the integrity and value of the programme, taking into account natural breaks in and the duration and nature of the programme, and the rights of the right holders are not prejudiced'. This is extremely vague. The European Institute for the Media suggests that 'natural break' should be defined as 'a point in a programme where, even if there were no advertising at all, some interruption in the continuity would in any case occur',[2] for example, a change of scene in drama, between the acts in light entertainment or where the participants or topics change in factual programmes.

Paragraph 2 of the article stipulates that 'in programmes consisting of autonomous parts, or in sports programmes and similarly structured events and performances comprising intervals, advertisements shall only be inserted between the parts or in the intervals'. Although this requirement is framed as a restriction, it may offer scope for more advertising breaks than are permitted for other types of programmes (as detailed under paras 3–5). It may well be possible and desirable for the broadcaster to divide, for example, films and other programmes made for television into autonomous parts. The number and frequency of advertising breaks in American sport coverage suggest how this provision may be manipulated by broadcasters.

Paragraph 3 of the article states that 'the transmission of audiovisual works such as feature films and films made for television (excluding series, serials, light entertainment programmes and documentaries), provided their programmed duration is more than 45 minutes, may be interrupted once for each complete period of 45 minutes. A further interruption is allowed if the programmed duration is at least 20 minutes longer than two or more completed periods of 45 minutes'. The latter provision is highly likely to come into play in relation to feature films.

Paragraph 4 states that programmes other than those covered by the non-exhaustive list in para 2 should have gaps of at least 20 minutes between each successive advertising break within the programme.

Paragraph 5 prohibits the insertion of advertisements into any broadcast of a religious service. Where news, current affairs programmes, documentaries, religious programmes other than religious services, and children's programmes have a 'programmed duration' of less than 30 minutes they must not be interrupted by advertisements. If the programmed duration of any such programmes is 30 minutes or more, the general provisions apply.

There is some ambiguity in the duration specifications in paras 3–5 inclusive. *Prima facie*, the specified periods refer to periods of actual programme time. However, there was at an earlier stage of the debate some suggestion that the period should include the length of any advertising break. For instance, a 30-minute children's programme would commonly include 25 minutes actual programme time, though the next programme would commence 30 minutes after the start of the first programme so as to allow for the insertion of five minutes of advertising. The directive was amended at an earlier stage to include the phrase 'programmed duration'. This phrase is intended to indicate that the length of the advertising break is to be included in the specified period.

7.25   Article 18 of the directive, which is similar to art 12 of the Convention, lays down the maximum amount of advertising which can be shown as a percentage of the daily transmission time. The amount of advertising must not exceed 15 per cent of daily transmission time unless it includes 'forms of advertisements such as direct offers to the public for the sale, purchase or rental of products or for the provision of services', when the amount of advertising may be increased to 20 per cent of transmission time. Any such 'spot advertising' must not exceed 15 per cent of the total (though this is ambiguously drafted) in line with the general stipulation in art 10 that isolated advertising spots must remain the exception. In any event, the total amount of such spot advertising must not exceed one hour per day. This may, at first sight, suggest a problem for the 'home shopping' channels. However, as mentioned *above*, home shopping channels do not sell airtime for the placement of advertisements, they actually buy airtime as a 'channel' and then programme it with their own sales programming. Therefore, they should not be considered as advertising.

The European Institute for the Media has criticised the 15 per cent limit as too high and likely to lead to member states adopting this figure rather than the lower percentages prevalent at the time of the directive. A majority of members had previously agreed that the percentage should be fixed at 10 per cent. The Institute also considers that the directive should have provided for advertising to be spread evenly over the total daily broadcasting time by imposing a maximum of 15 per cent advertising in any one hour of broadcasting, so preventing any weighting of advertising time towards the lucrative evening prime time.

Content of advertising

7.26   Articles 12–16 of the directive are concerned with advertising content, although most of the points are already incorporated in one form or another in the national law of member states.

Article 12 sets out general principles which prohibit advertising of a discriminatory, offensive or anti-social nature. It provides that television advertising shall not:

(*a*)   prejudice respect for human dignity;

(*b*)   include any discrimination on grounds of race, sex or nationality;

(*c*)   be offensive to religious or political beliefs;

(*d*)   encourage behaviour prejudicial to health or to safety;

(*e*)   encourage behaviour prejudicial to the protection of the environment.

Again, the exact meaning of the terms used is unclear: this will have to be settled in the domestic laws of the various member states. The underlying policy, however, is clear.

The requirement that advertising must not prejudice respect for human dignity arises from efforts to ban advertisements which 'employ forms of expression which contravene respect for the dignity of women' (*Amended Proposal for a Council Directive on the coordination of certain provisions laid down by law, regulation or administrative action in Member States concerning the pursuits of broadcasting activities*; COM(88) 154 final; OJ 27.4.88 C110/3). There are no references to 'good taste' and 'decency' (concepts which are to be

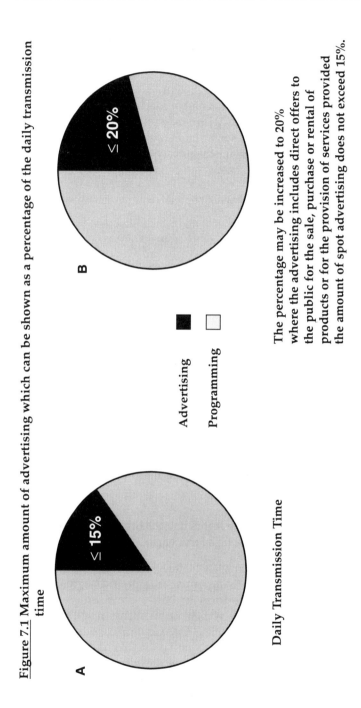

Figure 7.1 Maximum amount of advertising which can be shown as a percentage of the daily transmission time

A ≤ **15%**

B ≤ **20%**

Advertising

Programming

Daily Transmission Time

The percentage may be increased to 20% where the advertising includes direct offers to the public for the sale, purchase or rental of products or for the provision of services provided the amount of spot advertising does not exceed 15%.

found, for example, in the UK legislation), but it is thought that these are subsumed in 'human dignity'.

Sub-paragraph (*b*) refers not only to race and sex (which would be addressed by the laws of member states in all cases), but also to nationality as a ground of prohibited discrimination.

Sub-paragraph (*c*) requires that advertising must not be offensive to religious or political beliefs. If this provision is interpreted too widely in member states' implementing legislation, it could lead to a flood of complaints from aggrieved members of the public. Member states need to be careful to ensure that 'offensive' means something more than affecting a person's sensitivities.

The directive is given a 'green' hue by the inclusion of sub-para (*e*) prohibiting advertising prejudicial to the protection of the environment. It is uncertain how far-reaching the effects of this provision will be. Wallace and Goldberg, in an article entitled 'The EEC Directive on Television Broadcasting',[3] question whether, eg advertisements for cars with or without catalytic converters, would be caught by art 12, given this provision.

Prohibition and control of advertising of particular products

7.27   Articles 13, 14 and 15 of the directive cover the advertising of tobacco, alcohol and medicinal products and services. Article 13 imposes a complete ban on television advertising of cigarettes and other tobacco products. Article 14 prohibits the advertising of medicinal products and medical treatment which are available only on prescription in the member state within whose jurisdiction the broadcaster falls. The European Institute for the Media criticised the directive for not making all advertising dealing with pharmaceutical products subject to preliminary authorisation by a specialist body. It seems to the authors that this further qualification is unnecessary as all member states already have some such vetting procedure in place for advertising of this nature. In any case the Commission has published a Council Directive on the Advertising of Medicinal Products for Human Use (92/28/EEC, 31 March 1992, OJ 30.4.92 L113/13).

7.28   *Whether prohibitions compatible with European Convention for the Protection of Human Rights and Fundamental Freedoms*   It has been suggested that the provisions in arts 13 and 14 may not be compatible with art 10 of the European Convention on Human Rights and Fundamental Freedoms. The European Court of Human Rights has confirmed that advertising is commercial speech and is covered by the ordinary rules on freedom of expression. A report published in 1982 concluded that where an advertising ban is concerned 'the Commission has not considered the issue with reference to the restrictions permitted and clearly defined in art 10(2) of the Convention' (Mass Media Files No 1, Strasbourg 1982, 5 (ISBN 92–87100144). An opinion by A Lester QC and D Pannick QC which was published by the Marketing Commission of the International Chamber of Commerce (ICC) in October 1984, entitled *Advertising and Freedom of Expression in Europe*, expressed doubt as to the legality of restrictions on advertising in the light of art 10 of the European Convention on Human Rights. The Marketing Commission considers that states may not be able to justify such interferences as they will be 'unlikely to satisfy the burdens on them to show a pressing social need for the restriction'. States may be able to show that a particular restriction advances the public interest—particularly in the case of tobacco products, but a blanket ban may be hard to justify.

7.29   *Advertising for alcoholic beverages*   Article 15 sets out guidelines for television advertising of alcoholic beverages. In this context, 'alcoholic beverages' is thought to mean any beverage with an alcoholic content, whatever the degree of alcohol, including, *inter alia*, shandy, cider, beer and wine (Council of Europe, *Explanatory Report to the European Convention on Transfrontier Television*, D–MM (89)2, p 28, paras 166–7 ('The explanatory memorandum')). The directive states that advertising for alcoholic beverages:

(*a*) . . . may not be aimed specifically at minors or, in particular, depict minors consuming these beverages;

(*b*) . . . shall not link the consumption of alcohol to enhanced physical performance or to driving;

(*c*) . . . shall not create the impression that the consumption of alcohol contributes towards social or sexual success;

(*d*) . . . shall not claim that alcohol has therapeutic qualities or that it is a stimulant, a sedative or a means of resolving personal conflicts;

(*e*) . . . shall not encourage immoderate consumption of alcohol or present abstinence or moderation in a negative light;

(*f*) . . . shall not place emphasis on high alcoholic content as being a positive quality of the beverages.

As a drafting point, para (*a*) uses the words 'may not' whereas all the other restrictive provisions use the words 'shall not'. Some commentators have interpreted this as permissive but the authors conclude that this argument is incorrect, on the grounds that the directive is clearly intended to safeguard minors. The Convention (which contains very similar provisions in art 15) has slightly different phrasing as regards point (*a*); ' . . . no-one associated with the consumption of alcoholic beverages in advertisements should seem to be a minor' (The Convention, art 15(2)(*a*)). This would prevent advertisers from depicting youthful-looking persons consuming alcohol, though it is probable that such a ruse would be covered anyway as being advertising 'aimed specifically at minors'.

Advertisers face a difficult task even in complying with these minimum requirements, especially points (*c*) and (*d*), though (*d*) does refer to the relatively subjective question of a direct 'claim' rather than the more objective wording 'create the impression'.

Advertising and minors

7.30   Article 16 sets out standards with which television advertisements must comply in order to minimise adverse affects on minors. The explanatory memorandum to the original proposal for a Council directive makes it plain that these rules are formulated in relation to 'advertising which is explicitly addressed to them'.[4] The wording of art 16 does not make this clear, and *prima facie* the provisions apply to all advertising. The explanatory memorandum also makes it clear that the protection of young persons participating in the making of advertising is outside the scope of the directive, though indirect guidelines on permissible participation by minors is implicit in the wording of art 16.

The article states that television advertising:

> shall not cause moral or physical detriment to minors, and shall therefore comply with the following criteria for their protection:

> (*a*) it shall not directly exhort minors to buy a product or a service by exploiting their inexperience or credulity;

> (*b*) it shall not directly encourage minors to persuade their parents or others to purchase the goods or services being advertised;

(c) it shall not exploit the special trust minors place in parents teachers or other persons;

(d) it shall not unreasonably show minors in dangerous situations.

Point (*a*) is an extension of the general principle that advertisements shall not mislead the public. Presumably, a 'reasonable' depiction of minors in dangerous situations would involve some element of warning as in public information films.

Sponsorship

7.31   Article 17 deals with sponsorship. Sponsorship is defined in art 1(*d*) as 'any contribution made by a public or private undertaking not engaged in television broadcasting activities or in the production of audio-visual works, to the financing of television programmes with a view to promoting its name, its trade mark, its image, its activities or its products'. According to the explanatory memorandum, the original proposal did not define sponsorship because it was thought that 'the whole field of sponsorship is undergoing fundamental transformation' so member states should be left to define sponsorship in the light of current developments. However, it was later decided that though there should be flexibility, the limits of sponsorship ought to be defined in the interests of policy. The Convention has almost the same definition, though it refers to 'participation' by sponsors rather than to 'contribution'.

The article makes it clear that the responsibility and editorial independence of the broadcaster 'may in no circumstances be influenced by the sponsor'.

Sponsored television programmes must 'be clearly identified as such by the name and/or logo of the sponsor at the beginning and/or the end of the programmes'.

Sponsored television programmes 'must not encourage the purchase or rental of the products or services of the sponsor or third party, in particular by making special promotional references to those products or services'.

Article 17 prohibits sponsorship of television programmes by any person or body involved in the manufacture or sale of tobacco products or prohibited medicinal products and medical treatment.

News and current affairs programmes cannot be sponsored. In this context it seems that weather reports should not be considered either as news or current affairs.

General provisions and extension of or derogation from the rules laid down in the directive

7.32   Article 20 allows member states to lay down any conditions they think fit (so long as they comply with general Community law) in substitution for the provisions relating to scheduling and amount of advertisements outlined *above*, where the broadcasts concerned are 'intended solely for the national territory' and may not be directly or indirectly received in any other member state(s).

Article 21 specifically requires that member states must enforce the provisions of the advertising chapter by taking appropriate measures. This contrasts with the much vaguer wording obliging member states to ensure compliance with the quota provisions (see *above*).

Advertising directed specifically at a single state

7.33   The Convention contains a further provision in the area of the general regulatory framework for advertising in a particular state. Article 16 provides that ' . . . advertisements which are specifically and with some frequency directed to audiences in a single Party [to the Convention, that is, Member States of the Council of Europe and other States party to the European Cultural Convention] other than the transmitting Party shall not circumvent the television advertising rules in that particular party'. In other words, advertisements specifically directed at a country other than the one from which they are being transmitted must comply with the advertising rules of that country. This provision will not apply where:

(*a*)   the rules of the affected country 'establish a discrimination between advertisements transmitted by entities or by technical means within the jurisdiction of that Party and advertisements transmitted by entities or by technical means within the jurisdiction of another Party; or

(*b*)   the Parties concerned have concluded bilateral or multilateral agreements in this area'.

The economic objectives behind the restriction were held by the ECJ in *Bond van Adverteerders and other* v *The Netherlands State Kabelregeling* [1988] ECR 2085 not to constitute reasons of 'public policy' and therefore could not be grounds in EC law for refusing reception and transmission. However, this provision will still apply where relations between a member state and a non-member state which are both parties to the Convention are concerned.

The directive allows member states to impose stricter rules (both under the general 'catch-all' provision in art 3 and specifically subject to having considered the relevant factors, under art 19). It could be that this large element of 'home country control', coupled with the fact that under the directive, member states may not interfere with reception of signals from other member states, may lead, in the pan-European sector, to a degree of concentration of advertising revenue (and thus ultimately to a dominant number of television channels) in the member state with the most minimal controls over advertising.

As indicated, art 19 allows member states to lay down stricter rules for programming time:

> . . . so as to reconcile demand for televised advertising with the public interest, taking account in particular of:
>
> (*a*)   the role of television in providing information, education, culture and entertainment; and
>
> (*b*)   the protection of pluralism of information and of the media.

Implementation of the advertising provisions in UK law

7.34   Regulation of advertising in the UK is governed by the BA, the ITC Codes on Advertising Standards and Practice and Programme Sponsorship and the ITC Rules on Advertising Breaks. Terrestrial, domestic and non-domestic satellite services are all bound by these rules.

Section 8 of the BA obliges the ITC to ensure that licensees comply with the rules specified in and promulgated under the BA. A licensed service must not (among other things) include a programme which is sponsored by any person involved in the manufacture or supply of a product or service which the licensee is prohibited from advertising under s 9 of the BA. That provision obliges the ITC to draw up codes governing standards and practice in advertising and sponsorship, while prescribing advertisements and methods of advertising or sponsorship which are prohibited. The ITC is also under a duty to consult the Secretary of State with respect to classes and descriptions of advertisements which must not be included, and methods of advertising or sponsorship which must not be employed. The ITC has the power to direct broadcasters to exclude certain types and methods of advertising and sponsorship. The ITC can also give directions as to the scheduling and amount of advertising (BA, s 9).

Protection of minors

General provisions

7.35   Chapter V of the directive deals with the protection of minors. It consists of only one article—art 22.

The adoption of Community laws aimed at the protection of young people was felt to be essential because, although the relevant national rules in place at present can be justified, from the point of EU law, as being in the general interest, they still differ from one member state to another. This might have hindered the progress of transfrontier broadcasting. Article 22 is the only provision which entitles a member state to prohibit retransmission of a programme (see para 7.37 *below*).

By implication, the directive obliges Member States to set up procedures for the examination of programming material before it is broadcast. These procedures will most likely be self-regulatory and carried out within the broadcasting bodies themselves.

Article 22 states:

> Member States shall take appropriate measures to ensure television broadcasts by broadcasters under their jurisdiction do not include programmes which might seriously impair the physical, mental or moral development of minors, in particular those that involve pornography or gratuitous violence. This provision shall extend to other programmes which are likely to impair the physical, mental or moral development of minors, except where it is ensured, by selecting the time of the broadcast or by any technical measure, that minors in the area of transmission will not normally hear or see such broadcast.

The term 'minors' replaces the phrase 'children and young persons' in earlier drafts, but is not defined. The substitution was made because of the wide legal discrepancies across the member states in the dividing line between children and young persons. The problem has not been completely solved: for example in the UK there are differences in the age of minority between England and Scotland.

The article is ambiguously drafted and contains a number of separable points. It imposes an obligation on member states to avoid the serious impairment of the physical, mental or moral development of minors. This must be achieved by ensuring that broadcasters do not include programmes which might have this effect, in particular those involving pornography or gratuitous violence.

The provision extends to other programmes that are likely to impair the physical, mental or moral development of minors except where the risk of such effects is minimised by scheduling such broadcasts for times when minors 'will not normally hear or see such broadcasts' or where technical measures such as encryption are employed.

The article can be read as meaning that programmes that might seriously affect minors, particularly those involving pornography or gratuitous violence should never be shown, even at times when children are not likely to be watching. The second category of programming, namely programmes 'likely to impair the development of minors' (rather than seriously impair) can be shown subject to the scheduling restrictions. It is thought, however, that the sentence which allows broadcasting of such programmes subject to conditions designed to protect minors was intended to apply to the whole article.

In contrast to the provisions of the directive in this area, the Convention absolutely prohibits (in art 7) the transmission of any items of programme services which are indecent or pornographic, or which 'give undue prominence to violence'. This would apply to all programmes, regardless of the intended audience. The provision in art 7 of the Convention which is specifically directed towards protection of minors is much more clearly drafted than art 22 of the directive. It states that:

> ... all items of programme services which are likely to impair the physical, mental or moral development of children and adolescents shall not be scheduled when, because of the time of transmission and reception, they are likely to watch them.

Here the impairment must be probable and not just possible and the provision can be interpreted as permitting the transmission of all programme services (provided that they are not indecent or pornographic or violent) if they are transmitted in the evening after a certain hour. This idea of the 'watershed' is currently applied by UK terrestrial broadcasters.

Incitement to hatred

7.36   Article 22 of the directive concludes with a provision obliging member states to ensure that 'broadcasts do not contain any incitement to hatred on grounds of race, sex, religion or nationality'. The grounds of incitement are much wider than in the Convention, which merely requires that programmes must not contain any items 'likely to incite racial hatred', although 'likely' tends to widen the possible category of items.

It is curious that this provision is incorporated into an article designed to protect minors. The original proposal specifically obliged member states to ensure that broadcasts did not include material which might lead to the incitement of children and young persons to racial hatred. However, it seems that in the final version of the directive, this provision is intended to protect all viewers and not just minors. The drafting supports this interpretation as it contains the word 'also'.

Special powers to ensure compliance with article 22

7.37   Article 2(2) of the directive allows member states provisionally to suspend 'retransmission' of television broadcasts from other member states (under certain conditions) where those broadcasts have infringed the provisions of art 22. This is the only circumstance in which the directive allows member states provisionally to suspend the retransmission of broadcasts from other member states. The question arises whether the right to block 'retransmissions' entitles a member state to ban the sale or hire of decoders? It is understood that the Commission takes the view that decoders may be banned under art 2(2) (the Commission's stated position in respect of the *Red Hot Television* case, see *below*).

The limited right under art 2(2) does 'not apply to broadcasts intended exclusively for reception in states other than Member States, and which are not received directly or indirectly in one or more Member States'. Such suspensions are permitted where the following conditions are fulfilled:

(*a*) the broadcast coming from another member state 'manifestly, seriously and gravely infringes Article 22';

(*b*) the broadcaster responsible has infringed art 22 at least twice during the previous 12 months;

(*c*) a member state seeking to block retransmission has 'notified the broadcaster and the Commission in writing of the alleged infringement and of its intention to restrict retransmission should any such infringement occur again';

(*d*) no amicable settlement has been reached by consultation with the Commission and the transmitting state within 15 days of the written notification.

Any such suspension must be compatible with EC law. The Commission has the power to 'ask the Member State concerned to put an end to a suspension which is contrary to a Community Law, as a matter of urgency'.

This special provision is in addition to any civil, criminal or administrative action that the government of the member state may take against the broadcaster.

Article 2(2) is drafted in a very restrictive manner which will make it difficult to bring a case within its ambit. The result of this is that some observers believe that it will allow transmission of much 'detrimental material' which is too trivial to be dealt with by the 'last resort' procedure outlined. For example, the UK government has expressed concern about broadcasts from RTL—in particular *Veronique*, but it was considered that objections would have to be made at a political level, by making complaints through diplomatic channels to The Netherlands and Luxembourg and attempting to put pressure on UK-based shareholders of the channel.

7.38 However, the provisions have been applied in one case in the UK. This concerned the transmission of a 'hard-core' pornography service called 'Red Hot Television' from The Netherlands and later Denmark (both member states) which was capable of reception in the UK and in respect of which decoders were actively marketed to the UK.

After some debate regarding the position under the directive, the UK government eventually 'proscribed' the service under s 177 of the BA (see Chapter 6, para 6.24). The Dutch broadcasters of the service, Continental Television BVio, their UK marketing company, Continental Television plc, and its executive consultant, Mr Mark Garner, challenged the decision and order of the Secretary of State to proscribe the service in the English courts. But they failed to have the decision and order quashed before the proscription order came into force on 1 May 1993. The Divisional Court (*R* v *Secretary of State for National Heritage ex p Continental Television BVio* 23, 28 April 1993, unreported) decided to refer two questions on the interpretation of arts 2(2) and 22 of the directive to the ECJ pursuant to art 177 of the Treaty of Rome. The court also decided not to grant Red Hot Television an interlocutory injunction restraining the Secretary of State from implementing the proscription order (Foreign Satellite Service Proscription Order 1993 (SI No 1024)) pending the outcome of the reference to the ECJ. The decision not to grant an interlocutory injunction was upheld by the Court of Appeal on 28 April 1993. The result is that, although it is not an offence to receive Red Hot Television broadcasts in the UK, it is an offence in the UK, *inter alia*, to supply or offer to supply decoding equipment for Red Hot Television or to publish the times or details of programmes to be transmitted on Red Hot Television or to publish an advertisement promoting the channel (see further BA, s 178(3) and Chapter 6, para 6.24).

7.39 There were two key issues before the Divisional Court:

(1) Did art 2(2) of the directive empower the UK to take action against Red Hot Television, assuming that condition (*a*) of art 2(2) was fulfilled? (Red Hot Television admitted that the other conditions in art 2(2) were fulfilled.)

(2) If the answer to (1) was yes, was the Secretary of State entitled to conclude that Red Hot Television's broadcasts constituted a manifest, serious and grave infringement of art 22 so that condition (*a*) of art 2(2) was fulfilled?

On the first point the argument centred on the meaning of the word 'retransmission'. Red Hot Television argued that there was no 'retransmission' of its broadcasts in the UK, in the sense of re-broadcast by terrestrial broadcasts or rediffusion by cable. There was only direct reception from the satellite. Since art 2(2) itself made a distinction between 'reception' and 'retransmission', and since freedom to receive services was a fundamental right guaranteed by the Treaty of Rome, exceptions to which were to be construed narrowly, Red Hot Television submitted that the Secretary of State had no jurisdiction to make the proscription order. Only the broadcasting state, Denmark, had jurisdiction to control the initial broadcast of Red Hot Television by satellite. If the UK could restrict reception of satellite broadcasts to the UK, the purpose of the directive, the removal of restrictions on the freedom to broadcast across the European Community, would be frustrated.

The Secretary of State accepted that the literal wording of art 2(2) supported Red Hot Television's case, but argued that it should be given a wide purposive construction. One of the purposes of the directive was to protect the physical, mental and moral development of children. The need to protect children was the same whether the broadcasts were made directly by satellite or retransmitted by cable/terrestrial TV. Thus, 'retransmission' was to be understood as covering all technical means of retransmission and reception. To support this conclusion the Secretary of State produced a favourable letter from the Commission. He argued that, although the Commission's views were not a source of law in themselves, since the Commission was the body charged with enforcement of the directive, its views could be expected to carry weight with the ECJ.

7.40 In respect of the second point, the Secretary of State argued that art 22, on its literal interpretation, dealt with two categories of programme. The first category, which included programmes containing pornography, was banned outright regardless of the time of broadcast or technical measures aimed at preventing children from watching.

Red Hot Television contended that art 22 should be given a purposive construction; children could not be adversely affected by what they were unlikely to see. Since Red Hot Television broadcast after midnight and a decoder was necessary to view the channel, Red Hot Television argued that the Secretary of State was not entitled to decide that the conditions for controlling Red Hot Television's broadcasts under arts 2(2) and 22 had been satisfied.

The Divisional Court decided that it could not confidently resolve the first question without making a reference to the ECJ. As to the second question, the court stated that, if it had stood alone, it would have been inclined to decide it in favour of the Secretary of State, but since the answers to both questions were critical to the court's final decision both should be referred.

Both parties agreed that, as this case concerned EU rights, the court could grant an interlocutory injunction against the Crown (see *R v Secretary of State for Transport ex p Factortame (No 2)* [1991] 1 AC 603). They also agreed that damages would be an inadequate remedy (it being debatable whether the decision of the ECJ in *Francovich v Italian Republic* [1992] IRLR 84, that a member state could be held liable in damages for failure to implement a directive, extended to a breach by a member state of a directive) and that the cross-undertaking in damages was worthless (because the Secretary of State's action was aimed at protecting the public interest—loss to the public interest was not capable of compensation by damages).

Red Hot Television argued that, on the balance of convenience, an interlocutory injunction should be granted as it had a strong case which outweighed any alleged threat to the public interest. Further, Red Hot Television argued that the public interest arguments in this case were not strong; (1) children were unlikely to see Red Hot Television broadcasts; (2) the proscription order would not alter the risk to children, as reception was not banned; and (3) the Secretary of State had delayed for five months after he became aware of the existence of Red Hot Television before proscribing it.

7.41   The Divisional Court decided that no interlocutory injunction should be granted for three reasons:

(1)   Red Hot Television's broadcasts showed acts which were a criminal offence in England. Broadcasting such acts in England was also a criminal offence.

(2)   The moral welfare of children was more important than Red Hot Television's profits.

(3)   Red Hot Television's arguments were not sufficient to justify the court restraining the Secretary of State from acting in the public interest.

Red Hot Television appealed only against the refusal to grant an interlocutory injunction against the Secretary of State. It argued that the Divisional Court had failed to take into account the strength of its arguments on the two points of substantive law and the like-lihood of its winning in the ECJ in Luxembourg. The Court of Appeal decided that the Divisional Court had implicitly taken those matters into account. Glidewell LJ stated that because the Divisional Court had decided to refer the two points of substantive law to the ECJ, it must have decided that Red Hot Television and the Secretary of State's respective chances of winning were about equal and, in those circumstances, the Divisional Court was entitled to conclude that Red Hot Television's arguments based on its chances of success were outweighed by the Secretary of State's public interest arguments. In any case, the Court of Appeal decided that if it had set aside the Divisional Court's decision and exercised the discretion afresh, it too would have refused an interlocutory injunction. Both Glidewell LJ and Hirst LJ stated that they would have done so as they felt that Red Hot Television was 'substantially more likely to fail than succeed' before the ECJ.[5]

Both decisions demonstrate an underlying concern that, if the UK were to have no power to regulate broadcasts from other member states, the degree of permissiveness in the Community would be decided by the most liberal state. It will be interesting to see whether the ECJ sees this fear as valid or accepts such problems as the price of a Europe without internal barriers.

Implementation of the protection of minors provision in UK law

7.42   Provisions covering broadly the same areas as art 22 of the directive are contained in the BA and in the ITC Programme Code.

Although the provisions of art 22 do not appear to have been specifically implemented by the BA, it is worth remembering that s 188 gives the Secretary of State power to order the ITC to carry out any functions the UK government deems necessary to give effect to any international obligations of the UK.

Part VII of the BA applies the general law on obscenity, racial hatred and defamation to television programme services.

The ITC is obliged to 'do all that they can to secure' that every licensed service 'includes nothing in its programmes' which offends against good taste or decency or is likely to encourage or incite to crime or to lead to disorder or to be offensive to public feeling (BA, s 6(1)(*a*)). This is obviously much wider and less specific than the requirements of the directive.

The ITC is obliged to draw up a code giving guidance (*inter alia*):

> ... as to the rules to be observed with respect to the showing of violence, or the inclusion of sounds suggestive of violence, in programmes included in licensed services, particularly when large numbers of children and young persons may be expected to be watching

the programmes; . . . and as to such other matters concerning standards and practice for such programmes as the Commission may consider suitable for inclusion in the code. (BA, s 7(1).)

In considering what 'other matters' ought to be included in the code the ITC must have special regard to programmes in circumstances where 'large numbers of children and young persons may be expected to be watching the programmes' (BA, s 7(2)).

The ITC must also 'take account of such of the international obligations of the United Kingdom as the Secretary of State may notify to them' (BA, s 7(3)).

Right of reply

7.43   The final substantive provisions of the directive are contained in Chapter VI, art 23. A right of reply or equivalent remedies must be made available for 'any natural or legal person, regardless of nationality, whose legitimate interests, in particular reputation and good name, have been damaged by an assertion of incorrect facts in a television programme' (art 23(1)). Although nationality is irrelevant, the right can be exercised only by natural or legal persons resident or established in a member state. Statements of opinion would not give rise to the right. The particular form of the right of reply or equivalent remedies is left entirely to the discretion of member states, as is the procedure to be followed. Member states 'shall ensure that a sufficient time span is allowed and that the procedures are such that the right or equivalent remedies can be exercised appropriately by natural or legal persons resident or established in other Member States' (art 23(3)). The 'sufficient time span' presumably refers to the time within which an application should be made and the time within which any reply must be broadcast.

The broadcaster is not under an obligation to accept every application to exercise this right. Applications may be rejected if, *inter alia*, the exercise of the right of reply or equivalent remedies would involve a crime, would render the broadcaster liable for civil law proceedings or would transgress standards of public decency. The directive requires that judicial review must be available for decisions made under any procedure set up to consider applications for rights to reply (art 23(5) *above*). This does not mean 'judicial review' in the sense used in English law.

It is thought likely that several member states will not pass new statutes specifically implementing art 23 as they already have in place institutions which dispense equivalent remedies; for example, in the UK there are the Broadcasting Complaints Commission (BCC) and the Broadcasting Standards Council.

Implementation of the right of reply provision in UK law

7.44 Provisions covering the same area as art 23 have been implemented into the UK in the BA.

The ITC has power to direct a licensee to broadcast a correction or apology (s 40(1)). This power arises if the ITC is satisfied that the licensee has failed to comply with any condition of its licence. Form and timing of any correction or apology is at the discretion of the ITC, which is obliged to give the broadcaster a reasonable opportunity to make representations to it about the matters complained of (s 40(2)). The ITC also has the power to order a broadcaster not to show the offending programme again on any future occasion (s 40(4)). (These provisions are applied to satellite broadcasters by virtue of ss 44 and 45 of the BA.) This is obviously an indirect procedure whereby a correction or apology may be made in respect of somebody whose legitimate interest has been damaged by an assertion of incorrect facts, but only where this involves a breach of the broadcaster's licence conditions.

Section 143 of the Act sets out the functions of the BCC. The BCC shall:

> . . . consider and adjudicate upon complaints of:

> (*a*) unjust or unfair treatment in programmes; . . . or

> (*b*) unwarranted infringement of privacy in, or in connection with the obtaining of material included in . . . programmes.

Section 144 of the BA sets out the criteria and procedure for the making and entertaining of complaints to and by the BCC. *Inter alia*, complaints will not be entertained if the matter complained of is one in respect of which the affected person has a remedy by way of court proceedings or if it is frivolous. Section 145 sets out the detailed procedure for the consideration of complaints.

The BCC has power to direct the ITC to direct the licence holder to publish, in a specified manner and within a specified period, a summary of the complaint and the BCC's findings on the complaint (s 146). The licence issued by the ITC will include conditions requiring the licence holder to comply with any directions given by the ITC enabling it, in turn, to comply with any directions given by the BCC.

Prima facie, decisions made by both the ITC and the BCC in relation to 'right of reply' are susceptible to 'judicial review'. The grounds for judicial review under English law, however, are relatively narrow and may not tally with the Commission's concept of judicial review (see *R* v *BCC ex p Granada Television Ltd* (1993) *The Times*, 4 June).

The European Commission's attitude to member states' purported implementation

7.45 The Commission has reviewed the action taken by member states to implement the directive and has been less than impressed. As regards the UK, for example, it was reported in the *Financial Times* (16 November 1992, p 14) that Martin Bangemann, the Internal Market Commissioner, had written to the UK government complaining that the BA could obstruct the free circulation of television programmes in the EU. Specific objections made by Mr Bangemann relate to the BBC's licence, which he alleges imposes a discriminatory quota by requiring 'proper proportions of . . . programmes of British origin and British performance'. The Commission also objects to the BA because it alleges that foreign broadcasters would be obliged to obtain a licence from the ITC even if those foreign broadcasters had already obtained a licence in another member state. The authors do not agree with this reading of the BA. It seems quite clear that if a service is licensed in another member state, then it is not required to be licensed in the UK. The official attitude of the ITC is that if a satellite service from another member state complies with that state's licensing conditions the ITC and the UK government would have no right or desire to interfere with the retransmission of such service for a reception in the UK or to licence such a service in the UK. (See the discussion on Red Hot Television *above*.)

As a result of its continuing review of the implementation and operation of the directive, the Commission has developed a number of proposals to modify the directive.

Proposals to amend the directive

7.46   The first review of the terms of the directive, mandatory after five years from its implementation, is now under way. But the issue is so fraught that observers fear it could take up to four years for the Council to agree a strategy. The first new proposals, delivered on 22 March 1995, called for the broadcasting quotas to be made fully mandatory, and would extend the obligation on TV channels to show a majority of home-grown EU works on Europe's screens for a further ten years. The US Trade Representative called this proposal 'unacceptable' and a number of US film-makers hit out at what they saw as the 'intention of the Europeans to keep Americans out of their market'.

The passage of the proposals to implementation is likely to be difficult. The question of quotas is dividing the member states, with some ranged strongly against the new proposals to enforce the quotas more strictly. The Commission attempted to re-emphasise its stance on the issue and proposed in the second instance to change the current rules by deleting the words 'where practicable', which created a loophole which television stations could use to circumvent the law (the ECJ has had before it more than 30 cases dealing with the interpretation of 'practicable'), and by making the quotas mandatory but for ten years only. However, these proposals were not well received and observers expect little or no progress on this debate.

Hopes of toughening quotas faded further after a meeting of ministers in the last week of June 1995. France had hoped to use its EU Presidency to push forward a new version of the directive, aimed at boosting home-grown European film, but for the third time the scheme ran into opposition led by the UK and Germany. The Commission is now proposing to amend the directive in accordance with a request by the Council of Ministers for 'clear and well-defined rules on Governments' responsibilities towards broadcasters, the development of the European programme industry, respect for pluralism and protection for the public in relation to new services'. The issue of broadcasting quotas remains a continuing and fierce debate, and it is an open question whether the member states will reach agreement in the near future.

Conclusion

7.47   Programme content regulation remains in a state of flux; much will depend on short-term developments in implementing the directive and Convention together with the attitudes of national courts and regulators.

---

1 The functions of the Home Office with regard to broadcasting are now discharged by the Department of National Heritage.
2 Media Monograph No 8, 1987, *Towards a European Common Market for Television* (ISBN 0–948 195–12–6).
3 Wallace and Goldberg, *The Yearbook of European Law*, 'The EEC Directive on Television Broadcasting', 175–196.
4 Proposal for a Council Directive on the Co-ordination of Certain Provisions Laid Down by Law, Regulation or Administrative Action in Member States Concerning the Pursuit of Broadcasting Activities COM(86) 46 final, para 24; OJ 1986 C179.
5 The owners of RHTV have ceased to carry on business and will not be appealing to the ECJ as the deadline for appeal has now passed.

8

Copyright and Related Rights

Introduction

8.1 The focus of this chapter is the extent to which satellite transmissions are protected under copyright and related rights and the extent to which the transmission of sounds, visual images and other material may constitute activity restricted by such rights. An ancillary question is what liability attaches to and what protection is granted to cable operators and terrestrial broadcasters regarding the inclusion of satellite transmissions in their respective services. Furthermore, it is necessary to examine the protection given to encrypted and non-broadcast transmissions, whether forming part of a pay-TV service or otherwise.

The problems posed in the present context are special, in that whereas copyright protection is national by nature, satellite transmissions do not follow national boundaries. Accordingly, a variety of national laws may be relevant to determining the consequences in copyright law of a particular transmission. Moreover, the transnational nature of satellite transmissions renders them particularly amenable in Europe to the application of EC laws regarding competition and the free movement of services across national borders.

8.2 Satellite transmissions intended for direct-to-home (DTH) reception are not necessarily protected by copyright or neighbouring rights under national laws; nor is the inclusion of material protected by copyright necessarily a restricted act. The exceptions to protection or restriction usually arise in the case of transmissions made by Fixed-Satellite Services (FSS) satellite, because such transmissions were historically not regarded as broadcasts. Under the Copyright, Designs and Patents Act 1988 (the 1988 Act), copyright owners have the right to authorise or prohibit inclusion of their works in Broadcasting-Satellite Services (BSS) and in certain FSS transmissions. (See Chapter 1, para 1.18 for a general discussion of the distinction between these services, and Chapters 2 and 3 for more detail.) The practical effect of this legislation is to create copyright protection (and restriction) in respect of all satellite transmissions which are intended for direct reception by the general public. Protection against unauthorised interception and use of satellite transmissions which are not intended for direct reception by the public will arise from national telecommunications laws made pursuant to the International Telecommunication Convention (ITC) and the Radio Regulations (RRs) made thereunder; in the UK, the most significant legal restrictions arise under the Wireless Telegraphy Act 1949 (WTA), the Telecommunications Act 1984 (TA) and the Interception of Communications Act 1985 (see Chapter 6).

An associated problem with satellite transmissions is to identify the laws of the state or states which apply to the transmissions. This problem arises out of the language of the relevant international conventions relating to copyright, together with the practical difficulties associated with rival interpretations.

8.3 The rights of owners of copyright and related rights are protected internationally through a series of conventions and regional agreements, which signatory states have made part of their domestic laws typically by enacting legislation which extends rights arising under their domestic laws to persons incorporated, domiciled or resident in other signatory states and to satellite transmissions made from other contracting states. In this way, an interlocking system of protection is created by a series of international conventions, which deal with copyright and related rights, notably the International Convention for the Protection of Literary and Artistic Works, Berne, 9 September 1886, and thereafter revised (the Berne Convention), and the International Convention for the Protection of Performers, Producers of Phonograms and Broadcasting Organisations, Rome, 26 October 1961 (the Rome Convention). For example, the UK has given effect to its obligations under the Berne Convention by giving authors the right to authorise or prohibit the 'broadcasting' of their (qualifying) works, if the author is a citizen or subject of a country which is a party to that Convention (The Copyright (Application to Other Countries) Order 1993 (SI No 942), para 2(1)(*a*) and Sched 1) (see Appendix 1). The international system is not complete. States are entitled to make 'reservations' under relevant conventions and agreements and many have done so. Moreover, not all countries are parties thereto. A list of countries which are parties to relevant conventions is set out in Appendix 1. It is also notable that no international or regional agreement exists which relates to the protection of encrypted transmissions save for the rather limited provision made in the RRs and pursuant to the Satellite Convention 1974.

8.4 Articles 30–36, 59–66, 85 and 86 of the Treaty of Rome are of particular relevance to satellite transmissions, as are EC measures towards harmonisation of copyright and related rights, such as Directive 93/83/EEC on the Co-ordination of Certain Rules Concerning Copyright and Rights Related to Copyright Applicable to Satellite Broadcasting and Cable Retransmission of OJ 1993 L248/15 ('the directive'). EC laws affect satellite services in a variety of ways. For example, they often conflict with domestic laws of member states which restrict or prevent retransmission and reception of services originating in other member states; they also affect the extent to which broadcasters may properly obtain and enforce exclusivity in respect of the transmission of live events or pre-recorded audio-visual material, the extent to which rights may be licensed territorially, and also the prices and other licence terms which collecting societies may reasonably require.

As indicated in Chapter 7, art 10 of the European Convention for the Protection of Human Rights and Fundamental Freedoms is also relevant to satellite transmissions, because access to satellite transmissions is part of the wider right (under art 10(1)) of freedom of access to information. In *Autronic AG v Switzerland* 12 ECHR 485, the European Court of Human Rights held that reception of television programmes by means of a satellite receiver or dish fell within art 10(1) and that it was contrary to the rights laid down in that Convention for national laws to prohibit the use of receiving equipment for the purposes of receiving transmissions broadcast by telecommunications satellite. The proviso under art 10(2) was inapplicable, because although considerations as to the disclosure of confidential information were within the proviso, it did not apply because (among other things) the transmissions in issue were intended for reception by the public, and there was no risk of users of the receivers obtaining access to confidential telecommunications traffic.

International conventions and international and regional agreements

8.5 Satellite broadcasting by BSS/ DBS and FSS satellites falls within the scope of international conventions and regional agreements on copyright and related rights. The more difficult question is to identify the national laws applicable to these satellite transmissions.

The definitions used in the conventions and other relevant legal sources put forward a number of possibilities as to the applicable national laws. One theory is that broadcasting takes place in the transmitting and receiving states. Another theory (the so-called 'emission theory') is that broadcasting takes place in the state from where the signals are transmitted to the satellite. Each theory has its practical difficulties. The latter, because it presupposes that the 'emitting' state has adequate laws relating to copyright and related rights. The first theory causes potential difficulties, because (among other things) it requires a broadcaster to obtain consents in respect of each territory within the footprint of the satellite. In practice, this difficulty is lessened by the fact that collecting societies, which administer the bulk of the rights contained in a broadcast satellite transmission, represent foreign collecting societies (see generally SM Stewart, *Copyright and Neighbouring Rights*, 2nd edn; paras 7.59–70 and 12.35–7; see also Porter, *Beyond the Berne Convention/ Copyright, Broadcasting and the Single European Market*, and Sterling, *Intellectual Property Rights in Sound Recordings, Film and Video* (1992) paras 4.63 and 7.26).

The Berne Convention and the Universal Copyright Convention

8.6 The Berne Convention has had a number of revisions, the most important of which is the Paris Act (1971), which binds most of the signatory states. 'Broadcasting' is not defined in any version of the Berne Convention. The only relevant definition is to be found in the RRs of the ITC, which refer to a 'broadcasting service' as a 'radiocommunication service in which the transmissions are intended for direct reception by the general public' (art 28A). As indicated, this includes BSS/DBS broadcasts and FSS transmissions, where intended for general reception.

Pursuant to the Paris Act (and indeed the Brussels Act 1948), authors of literary and artistic works have the right to authorise the radio and television broadcasting of their works by satellite and the cable retransmission or rebroadcasting of their works, where this is undertaken by an organisation other than the original broadcaster (art 11 bis(1)). Signatory states are entitled to introduce compulsory licensing of these rights, but not so as to interfere with moral rights (as defined in art 6 bis) and such licensing must ensure that authors obtain 'equitable remuneration'. In the absence of agreement, this remuneration shall 'be fixed by a competent authority' (art 11 bis(2)). This would include the setting up of a tribunal to adjudicate where the parties are unable to reach agreement. However, broadcasting rights are typically licensed collectively and on a 'blanket' basis, because of the large number of rights required by broadcasters.

In certain countries art 11 bis(2) has provided the justification for national laws permitting the granting of non-voluntary licences. However, discussions have been taking place with a view to abolishing the possibility of such licences within a proposed protocol to the Berne Convention. There appears to be a broad consensus in favour of abolishing non-voluntary licences relating to (primary) satellite broadcasts. Whether abolition should extend to the elimination of non-voluntary licences in other cases, such as simultaneous and unchanged transmission by cable or by rebroadcasting, is less certain. In cases where countries have relevant non-voluntary arrangements in place, a transitional period of five years is proposed. The abolition of non-voluntary licences in the case of satellite broadcasts is highly arguably contrary to art 11 bis (2), given the transborder nature of satellite broadcasts and the limitation arising out of art 11 (bis) (2) that a non-voluntary licence can operate only in countries where they have been prescribed. Clearance of rights in a country of up-link where non-voluntary arrangements are in place can have the effect of creating a *de facto* non-voluntary licence in relation to countries in the satellite footprint where non-voluntary licences are not prescribed.

8.7   Broadcasters also need to record or 'dub' works for the purposes of broadcasting. Authors have the right to authorise recording under the Berne Convention (art 9). However, signatory states may introduce legislation to permit 'ephemeral recording', which satisfies three conditions. The recording must be transitory, made by the broadcasting organisation's 'own [technical] facilities' and must be made for the broadcaster's 'own broadcasts' (art 11 bis (3)). The terms of art 11 bis (3) permit states to allow ephemeral recording without remuneration. Provision is made for certain 'free uses' of works for reporting current events and other purposes (arts 10 and 10 bis).

The Universal Copyright Convention (Geneva, 6 September 1952 and thereafter revised) is less important in the present context. Article IV bis of the 1971 Paris revision makes provision for authors to be granted the exclusive right to authorise reproduction and broadcasting of their works. However, contracting states may make exceptions to these rights, provided that they do not 'conflict with the spirit and provisions' of the Convention and states must ensure that the exclusive rights granted create a reasonable degree of effective protection.

The Rome Convention

8.8   The Rome Convention provides for the protection of performers, phonogram producers and broadcasters in respect of certain recordings or 'fixations' and (re)broadcasting. WIPO is considering extending the rights created under the Rome Convention, but it is too early to say whether, or how, such amendments will be made.

Broadcasting is defined in the Rome Convention as 'the transmission by wireless means for public reception of sounds or of visual images and sounds' (art 3(f)). 'Rebroadcasting' means the simultaneous broadcasting by one broadcasting organisation of the broadcast of another broadcasting organisation (art 3(g)). This covers BSS/DBS and relevant FSS transmissions. Phonogram means 'any exclusively aural fixation [ie making of a recording] of sounds of a performance or other sounds' (art 3(b)).

Each state undertakes to grant 'national treatment' to performers, phonogram producers and broadcasters, provided that certain criteria are met (arts 4–6). For example, states agree to give such treatment to broadcasters where either the headquarters of the broadcaster are situated in another contracting state, or the broadcast is transmitted from a transmitter situated in another contracting state (art 6.1). However, states are entitled to make a reservation that they will grant national treatment only if both conditions are satisfied (art 6.2). The term 'national treatment' is currently the subject of debate. For the purposes of the Rome Convention it is defined as meaning the treatment accorded by the domestic law of the contracting state in which protection is claimed, to performers, phonogram producers and broadcasters who satisfy certain criteria by which they are linked to the applicable contracting state (art 2.1).

National treatment is subject to the protection specifically guaranteed, and the limitation specifically provided for in the Convention (art 2.2).

8.9   The Rome Convention does not require contracting states to create civil rights for performers. The protection to be granted to performers is to include the possibility of preventing the following relevant acts:

(*a*)   the broadcasting of their performances, save where the performance used in the broadcasting is itself already a broadcast performance or is made from a fixation (art 7.1(*a*));

(*b*)   the fixation of their unfixed performances (art 7.1(*b*));

(*c*)   the reproduction of a fixation of their performances, if—

  (i)   the original fixation was made without consent;

  (ii) the reproduction is made for purposes different from those for which the performers gave their consent;

  (iii) the original fixation was made in accordance with art 15 (ephemeral, private and certain 'fair use' recordings) and the reproduction is made for different purposes (art 7.1(*c*)).

Performers and others are also granted the right under the Convention to authorise or prohibit 'communication to the public'. This does not apply to cable (re)transmission in most cases. Where the relevant performers have consented to broadcasting, the domestic laws of the state where protection is claimed may regulate the protection created in respect of rebroadcasting, fixation for broadcasting and the reproduction of such fixations for broadcasting purposes (art 7.2(1)). The terms and conditions governing use by broadcasters of fixations made for broadcasting purposes (that is, ephemeral recordings) are to be determined by the laws of the state in which protection is claimed (art 7.2(2)). Accordingly, where a contract between a performer and a broadcaster is silent as to whether rebroadcasting is permitted, the performer is free to invoke relevant laws requiring the broadcaster to obtain the consent of the performer for the further use. However, statutory licensing is not permissible in any of the cases provided for in art 7.2(1), (2) (art 7(3)). Once a performer has consented to the incorporation of his performance in a visual or audio-visual fixation, art 7 has no further application (art 19).

8.10 Phonogram producers are to have an absolute right to authorise or prohibit the direct or indirect reproduction of their phonograms (arts 10, 11). However, where a published phonogram (or reproduction thereof) is used directly for broadcasting, a single equitable remuneration is to be paid by the broadcaster to the performers or to the phonogram producer, or to both. In the absence of agreement between the parties, domestic laws lay down the conditions as to the sharing of the remuneration (art 12). Neither cable relay of broadcasts nor rebroadcasting are protected. The contracting states are entitled to make a reservation so as not to grant the protection provided for under arts 10 and 11, or may make a reservation in respect of either broadcasting (or communication to the public) or in certain other ways (art 16.1(*a*)).

Broadcasters are to enjoy the right to authorise:

(*a*) the broadcasting of their broadcasts (art 13(*a*));

(*b*) the fixation of their broadcasts (art 13(*b*));

(*c*) the reproduction of—

(i) unauthorised fixations of their broadcasts;

(ii) fixations made in accordance with art 15 (fair dealing and other permitted uses), if the reproduction is made for different purposes;

(*d*) the communication to the public of their television broadcasts if made in places accessible to the public against payment of an entrance fee. The domestic laws of the state in which the protection is claimed may lay down the conditions under which this right is to be exercised (art 13(*d*)). This permits compulsory licensing.

The protection under art 13 excludes any right in respect of cable retransmissions. A contracting state may make a reservation in respect of the public performance right in (television) broadcasts. If it does so, the other contracting states are not obliged to grant the public performance right to broadcasters whose headquarters are in that state (art 16.1(*b*)).

The Satellite Convention 1974

8.11 The Convention Relating to the Distribution of Programme-carrying Signals by Satellite, Brussels, 21 May 1974 (the Satellite

Convention), applies to the unauthorised interception and use of programme-carrying signals from telecommunication satellites. The Convention does not apply where the signals emitted by or on behalf of the originating organisation are intended for direct reception from the satellite to the general public (art 3). Each contracting state undertakes to take adequate measures to prevent the distribution on or from its territory of any programme-carrying signal by any distributor for whom the signal emitted to or passing through the satellite is not intended (art 2(1)). Some contracting states have enacted civil rights to protect 'originators'. Others have enacted penal laws to create the protection envisaged under the Convention. The Satellite Convention has reduced in importance in the light of advances in technology, whereby broadcasters have been able to use FSS satellites for DTH satellite television transmission.

The European Agreement on the Protection of Television Broadcasts 1960 (1965, 1974, 1983, 1989)

8.12   This regional agreement (the European Agreement) was concluded through the Council of Europe, and preceded the Rome Convention by one year. It reflected the concerns of broadcasters through the European Broadcasting Union (EBU) about the unauthorised public performance in cinemas of their coverage of the Olympic Games in Rome in 1960: see also the European Agreement concerning Programme Exchanges by means of Television Films, Paris, 15 December 1958. The European Agreement does not apply to sound radio broadcasts and it was originally intended that the European Agreement would be of limited duration, pending the ratification of an international convention on neighbouring rights by the majority of members of the Council of Europe (art 13). However, when the Rome Convention was concluded, the protection accorded to broadcasters was lower than that created under the European Agreement. The agreement is still in force but is nevertheless under review. There are now six parties to it. They are the UK, France, Germany, Sweden, Norway and Denmark. The rights arising under the European Agreement are conferred on broadcasters constituted in the territory and under the laws of a contracting state or transmitting from such territory, in respect of their television broadcasts (art 1). 'Television broadcasts' are not defined. However, as indicated, BSS/DBS broadcasts and FSS transmissions intended for direct reception will qualify for protection.

The main additional rights provided for in art 1(a)–(e) of the European Agreement are:

(*a*)   cable retransmission of a broadcast or of any fixation of a broadcast;

(*b*)   still photographs;

(*c*)   an absolute right to authorise public performance, unless it is made the subject matter of a reservation which permits its limitation to a 'paying audience'.

The right to authorise the rebroadcasting, cabling or public performance of fixations or reproductions ceases once the broadcaster has authorised the sale thereof to the public (art 1(*e*)). This would typically apply to video releases of broadcast material.

However, states may make a number of reservations in addition to that relating to public performance, most significantly in respect of cable retransmission (art 3.1(*a*)). The right was amended in 1965 so as to limit the extent of the reservation. The revised art 3.1(*a*) entitles a contracting state to 'withhold the protection' in respect of cable transmissions 'as regards broadcasting organisations constituted in their territory or transmitting from such territory and restrict the exercise of such protection as regards broadcasts by broadcasting organisations constituted in the territory of another Party . . . or transmitting from such territory, to a percentage of the transmissions by such organisations which shall not be less than 50 per cent of the average weekly duration of the broadcasts of each of these organisations'. Contracting states may make a reservation for still photographs (art 3.1(*d*)).

The European Convention relating to Questions on Copyright Law and Neighbouring Rights in the Framework of Transfrontier Broadcasting by Satellite (1994)

8.13   The European Convention seeks to ensure that authors of literary and artistic works, performers and phonogram producers have rights in relation to the transmission of their works by satellite (by BSS satellite or by FSS satellite under conditions where direct reception is 'comparable' to reception of BSS satellite transmissions). The Convention is not yet in force. The following states have signed (but not yet ratified) the Convention: Cyprus, Luxembourg, Norway, San Marino, Spain and Switzerland.

The European Convention seeks to ensure uniformity of treatment by providing that relevant satellite transmissions are to be treated as taking place in the territory in which the transmission 'originates', which means the country where the broadcaster's transmission suite is sited. Further provision is made where the transmission suite is not sited in a state party to the Convention (see arts 2, 3).

Authors of literary and artistic works are to be protected in conformity with the Berne Convention (Paris Act, 1971), and rights for transfrontier broadcasting are to be acquired contractually (art 4.1). Limited provision is made for the situation where a broadcaster has made a collective agreement with a collecting society, to provide that rights owners who are not party to the collective agreement shall be deemed to be parties thereto, subject to specified preconditions (art 4.2). This does not apply to cinematographic works (art 4.3). Moreover, the European Convention does not extend to the complete, simultaneous and unchanged retransmission by terrestrial means of satellite broadcasts (art 6).

Performers and phonogram producers are to be accorded the minimum protection provided for under the Rome Convention (art 5.1). However, the rights of performers regarding fixation and reproduction of their performances are to be exclusive rights to authorise or prohibit such activity (art 5.2). Subject to specified exceptions, art 19 of the Rome Convention is not to apply, with the result that performers do not lose protection once they have consented to the fixation of a relevant performance (arts 5.3, 5.4). Where a phonogram has been published and is used for transfrontier satellite broadcasting, states which are party to the European Convention may make provision to ensure that a single equitable remuneration is paid by the broadcaster, to be shared between the phonogram producer and performer or performers in question (art 5.5).

Provision is made for transitional arrangements (art 13). Importantly, in their mutual relations, EU members which are also parties to the European Convention are to apply Community rules, and not the rules arising under the European Convention, save where there is no relevant regulation (art 9.1).

The TRIPS Agreement

8.14 The Agreement on Trade-Related Aspects of Intellectual Property Rights ('TRIPS') forms part of the Final Act embodying the Uruguay Round of GATT (15 April 1994), signed by 108 countries.

TRIPS makes general provision in respect of copyright, trade marks and patents, requiring signatories to grant specified minimum rights to 'nationals' of other signatories. The measures contemplated by TRIPS are with a view to (among other things) reducing distortions and impediments to international trade.

However, the obligations of signatories under TRIPS are not to affect the obligations which they may owe to each other under the Berne and Rome Conventions (among others) (art 2.2). Article 14 of TRIPS provides for the following rights. Performers are to have the right of preventing unauthorised broadcasts of their live performances, the fixation of their unfixed performances and any reproduction of such fixation (art 14.1). Phonogram producers are to have the right to authorise or prohibit the direct or indirect reproduction of their phonograms (art 14.2). Broadcasters are to have the right to authorise or prohibit the fixation of their broadcasts, the reproduction of such broadcasts and the rebroadcasting and communication to the public of their broadcasts (art 14.2). Limitations on such rights may be made to the extent permitted by the Rome Convention (art 14.). The rights accorded to performers are to last for 50 years from the end of the year of the performance; the rights of phonogram producers are to enure for 50 years from the end of the year of creation and broadcasters' rights are to last for 20 years from the end of the year in which the broadcast took place (art 1.5).

TRIPS differs from other copyright conventions in the requirements imposed on signatories with regard to enforcement of rights. Signatories are to ensure that particular enforcement measures are available under their domestic laws 'so as to permit effective action' against infringement (art 41). Those measures are to include not only injunctions and damages, but also specified 'prompt and effective provisional measures' including such as will 'preserve relevant evidence in regard to alleged infringement' (arts 44, 45, 50).

TRIPS is expected to enter into force on 1 January 1996 for so-called 'developed countries' and 'developing countries'; for 'least developed countries' a longer timetable is envisaged.

EC and competition law

Introduction

8.15   As noted in Chapters 4 and 5, EC law has a variety of applications to the provision of satellite services and ancillary or related services, eg in the field of programme supply. EC laws relating to competition and the free movement of goods and services across national borders are of particular relevance. Furthermore, there are important developments towards the harmonisation of national laws relating to copyright and related rights. Competition and other laws are also relevant to satellite services in the context of media concentrations. Some provisions of the EC Treaty (notably arts 85 and 86) may be used as defences and as causes of action in civil proceedings. The present chapter is intended as an overview of some of the more important issues in these fields: see, generally, Bellamy & Child, *Common Market Law & Competition*, 4th edn.

Consideration should also be given to national domestic competition laws. In the UK, the following are of potential relevance, namely the Restrictive Trade Practices Act 1976, the Fair Trading Act 1973 and the Competition Act 1980 (see Whish, *Competition Law*, 3rd edn (Butterworth, 1993)). Other statutes may contain matters relevant to the provision of satellite services; see, eg, s 39 and Scheds 2 and 4 of the Broadcasting Act 1990 (BA) (media concentrations and anti-competitive effects of networking on satellite broadcasters and others), the report of the Monopolies and Mergers Commission, *Channel 3 Networking Arrangements* April 1993, s 3 of the TA (duties of regulator, OFTEL, to ensure competition in telecommunication services) and s 144 of the 1988 Act (compulsory licensing of copyright where refusal to licence found to be anti-competitive).

In the UK, domestic competition laws do not give rise to private rights of action. However, the decisions of the Independent Television Commission and the Radio Authority under the BA, and OFTEL under the TA and other regulators are susceptible to judicial review. The basic grounds on which judicial review can be obtained are that a regulator's decision was based on an error of law, 'irrational', based on a breach of natural justice, defeated a 'legitimate expectation' or (where relevant) did not give reasons. For example, in *R v ITC, ex p TSW Broadcasting Ltd* (1992) *The Times*, 7 February, the House of Lords rejected an attempt by a disappointed applicant for a Channel 3 licence (terrestrial broadcasting) to show that the decision of the ITC to licence a rival bidder was irrational and defeated a legitimate expectation (see generally Wade, *Administrative Law*, 6th edn).

The free movement of goods and services

8.16   The cross-border nature of satellite transmissions attracts the application of those provisions of the EC Treaty which seek to ensure the free movement of goods and services across national boundaries. These provisions are arts 30–36 (goods) and 59–66 (services).

It is clear that television and radio broadcasting falls within the definition of services for the purposes of arts 59–66: eg Case 155/73 *Sacchi* [1974] ECR 409. The same is true of cable services (Case 52/79 *Procureur du Roi* v *Debauve* [1980] ECR 833) and telecommunications: *British Telecommunications* OJ 1982 L360/36 [1983] 1 CMLR 457, Case 41/83 *Italy* v *Commission* [1985] ECR 873.

Articles 59–66 have been applied to discrimination effected by the domestic laws of member states to transmissions originating from other member states, particularly in the field of advertising. In such cases, discrimination on grounds of nationality is prohibited. However, in the absence of harmonisation, arts 59 and 60 did not preclude national rules prohibiting the transmission of advertisements, provided that the rules were applied without distinction as regards the origin, whether national or foreign, of those advertisements, the nationality of the person providing the service, or his place of establishment (*Debauve*).

Harmonisation has taken place in the field of advertising and related fields: Council Directive 89/552/EEC of 3 October 1989 on the Coordination of Certain Provisions Laid Down by Law, Regulation or Administrative Action in Member States Concerning the Pursuit of Television Broadcasting Activities (see Chapter 7). However, where harmonisation has not taken place the principles laid down in arts 56 and 59 are applicable to all national laws which may restrict the movement of services transmitted by satellite across national boundaries (see also Case 33/74 *Van Binsbergen* [1974] ECR 1299; Case 352/85 *Bond Van Adverteerders* v *The Netherlands* [1988] ECR 2085; *Stichting Collectieve Antennevoorziening Gouda* v *Commissariaat voor de Media* (C–288/89) (1991) Transcript 25 July; Case C–211/91 *Commission* v *Belgium* (1993) OJ C22/7; *Vereniging Veronica* v *Commissariaat voor de Media* (1993) OJ C71/9).

8.17   Copyright and neighbouring rights also constitute potential restrictions on the free movement of broadcasting services across national boundaries. In Case 62/79 *Coditel* v *Cine Vog Films* [1980] ECR 881 (*Coditel 1*), the ECJ applied arts 59–66 to copyright, and in particular, to performance rights. The factual background to the case was as follows: Cine Vog were granted the exclusive right to show the film *Le Boucher* in Belgium for a seven-year period, subject to a television 'hold-back' provision of 40 months. Within the latter period, the film was televised in Germany pursuant to another exclusive licence and retransmitted in Belgium by a cable operator, Coditel.

In a reference to the ECJ, it was asked, *inter alia*, whether art 59 would be infringed by the enforcement of an exclusive grant of the performing right in a film where the contract territory was a member state, and where the defendant was seeking to retransmit a film which had been broadcast in another member state with the consent of the original owner of the copyright. Consent was relevant because, in other fields (for example sound recordings), certain copyrights were 'exhausted' once consent had been given to the marketing of physical copies.

The ECJ held that art 59 was subject to an implied reservation similar to that applicable under art 36 (measures justified on grounds of protection of industrial or commercial property). It also decided that the problems involved in the observance of a film producer's rights are not the same as those which arise in connection with literary and artistic works the placing of which at the disposal of the public is inseparable from the circulation of the material form of the works, as in the case of books and records. By contrast, a film belongs to the category of literary and artistic works made available to the public by performances which may be infinitely repeated and the commercial exploitation of which comes under the movement of services.

Accordingly, the 'specific object' of performing rights in films was held to consist in the right to receive a payment for each showing of the film. A television hold-back provision was consistent with that object, whether the means of exhibition was by television or cinema. However, this does not mean that copyright (or related rights) can be used as a means of arbitrary discrimination or a disguised restriction on trade between member states.

8.18   It may therefore be concluded that the territorial licensing of broadcasting rights is normally permissible under arts 59–66: (see para 8.20 *et seq* for the application of art 85 to territorial licensing). However, certain cable retransmission rights are to be subject to the requirement of exercise through a collecting society, as stipulated in the directive (see paras 8.29–8.38 *below*).

Articles 30–36 have a less prominent application to satellite services. However, they are of relevance to restrictions which may be imposed on licensee broadcasters and third parties (such as importers of decoding apparatus designed to enable members of the public to watch pay-TV services). It is suggested that both contractual restrictions on licensees regarding the export of decoders from the licensed territory and domestic laws affecting the manufacture, importation or commercial dealing in decoders are capable of falling within art 36, being justified on grounds of protection of industrial or commercial property: see also para 8.20 *below*. In *BBC Enterprises Ltd v Hi-Tech Xtravision Ltd* [1991] 2 AC 327, the defendants abandoned their 'euro-defence' based on art 34 to claims made under s 298 of the 1988 Act, which creates a statutory right in favour of broadcasters and others to authorise or prohibit the manufacture and commercial dealing in decoders. In *British Sky Broadcasting Group Ltd v David Lyons* [1995] FSR 357, Aldous J held that s 298 of the 1988 Act did not create a means of arbitrary discrimination or a disguised restriction on trade between member states. Leave to appeal was, however, granted.

EC competition laws

Article 85

8.19 Article 85(1) prohibits all agreements between undertakings, decisions by associations of undertakings and concerted practices which may affect trade between member states and which have as their object or effect the prevention, restriction or distortion of competition within the Common Market. Article 85(1) particularises (though not by way of limitation) a number of practices which are prohibited, including the fixing of purchase or selling prices or any other trading conditions, limitations or controls on production and markets, the sharing of markets or sources of supply, the application of dissimilar conditions to similar transactions with other trading parties (such as to render them at a competitive disadvantage) and making the conclusion of contracts subject to acceptance by other parties of unconnected supplementary obligations.

Any such agreement, decision or concerted practice is automatically void (art 85(2)), unless exempted (under art 85(3)). In order to qualify for exemption, the agreement, decision or practice must satisfy the following four conditions, namely that it:

(*a*) contributes to improving the production or distribution of goods or to promoting technical or economic progress;

(*b*) allows consumers a fair share of the resulting benefit;

(*c*) imposes on the parties only restrictions which are indispensable to the attainment of those objectives;

(*d*)   does not afford such undertakings the possibility of eliminating competition in respect of a substantial part of the products in question.

Article 85 has had a variety of applications in the fields of satellite services and programme supply and in areas relating to the technical provision of satellite transmission facilities. Parties to proposed arrangements which may fall within art 85(1) should give serious consideration to notifying the arrangements to the European Commission with a view to obtaining negative clearance (ie that the arrangements fall outside art 85(1) or art 86) or an exemption under art 85(3).

Article 85 and programme supply

8.20   Article 85 is mainly relevant to two situations. First, 'vertical' agreements between licensors of copyright and licensee broadcasters, which grant exclusivity for particular territories. Secondly, 'horizontal' arrangements between broadcasters which share access to programming. In both cases, the arrangements are capable of preventing, distorting or restricting competition between broadcasters and in other markets, such as film distribution.

8.21   *Vertical agreements*   In Case 262/81 *Coditel* v *Cine Vog Films SA* [1982] ECR 3381 *Coditel No 2*), the ECJ held that the mere fact that the owner of the copyright in a film has granted to a sole licensee the exclusive right to exhibit that film in the territory of a member state and, consequently, to prohibit, during a specified period, its showing by others, is not sufficient to justify the finding that such a contract must be regarded as the purpose, the means or the result of activity prohibited by art 85(1). The characteristics of the cinematographic industry and of its markets in the EU, especially those relating to dubbing and subtitling for the benefit of different language groups, showed that an exclusive television licence would not itself restrict, prevent or distort competition: at p 3401.

However, this does not mean that an exclusive licence is incapable of containing restrictions which infringe art 85(1). The ECJ concluded that it is for the national court to determine whether the manner in which the exclusive rights are exercised has the object or effect of preventing or restricting the distribution of films or distorting competition within the cinematographic film market: at p 3402; see also Case 258/78 *Nungesser* v *Commission* [1982] ECR 45, *Re the Application of United International Pictures BV* OJ 1991 L226/12.

In *Film Purchases by German Television Stations* OJ 1989 L284/36, the Commission considered an application for negative clearance or exemption under art 85 by a trade association of German regional broadcasters regarding agreements with a distributor for the exclusive showing of a substantial library of films on German television. The exclusivity provisions relating to the films were mostly for a 15-year period and precluded the grant of other licences, save for two pay-TV windows of up to one year in which 25 per cent of the films could be licensed to third parties for exploitation on pay-TV. The trade association was also granted a right of first negotiation in respect of further periods of exclusivity. The Commission took into account the increasing number of broadcasters who were in competition with one another, that the average licence periods were a few years only, and the large number of films which were the subject matter of the agreement. The arrangements were considered to be contrary to art 85(1). The Commission decided that the arrangements satisfied art 85(3), once substantial amendments had been made to them, so as to reduce the scope and duration of the exclusivity.

8.22   In the televising of football matches, the Commission has stated that exclusive arrangements between the English Football Association, the BBC and BSB (now BSkyB) fell within art 85(1), and in order to allow channels a fair chance to obtain access to football matches of general appeal, the duration of contracts should be limited to one football season (IP/93/614). The arrangements between BSkyB and the Football Association were of longer duration but were nevertheless exempted under art 85(3), because the long-term contract had been necessary to assist BSkyB to enter a developing market for satellite broadcasting direct to households.

In its *Twentieth Report on Competition Policy* (1991), the Commission concluded that:

> ...The granting of exclusive television rights is not itself anti-competitive; however, agreements whose scope or duration are excessive or which impose additional restrictions on the parties may be covered by Article 85(1) of the Treaty. In broadcasting, in particular, the Commission is careful to ensure that markets remain open and that programme access is guaranteed to all operators. (point 82.)

The present state of EC law is therefore that exclusive territorial licences are not in themselves contrary to art 85(1). However, they will be prohibited if they have the object or effect of distorting or restricting competition: see also *English Football League/London Week-end Television*, Ninth Report on Competition Policy (1980), point 116 (art 85(1) applied to exclusive rights to record football matches); *RAI/Unitel Twelfth Report* (1983) point 90 (proceedings regarding exclusive contracts for artistes).

8.23   There have been important recent decisions in the merger field in relation to television services. In Case IV/M 469 *MSG Media Services* OJ 1994 L364/1, the Commission blocked a proposed merger between Deutsche Telekom, Bertelsmann and a company in the Kirch group. The purpose of the proposed merger was to set up a joint venture company, MSG, to provide technical, business and administrative handling of mainly payment-based television services. (Kirch is the leading supplier in Germany of feature films and television programming.) The arrangements were found to be likely to eliminate potential competition which would otherwise exist between the joint venture partners, particularly in the field of digital pay-TV infrastructures and related services. The arrangements were also likely to give MSG a long-term dominant position in the market for technical and administrative services in pay-TV, particularly in regard to digital transmissions, because all entrants to the pay-TV market after digitalisation would find it necessary to take underlying services from MSG. The digital infrastructure services of MSG would strengthen an existing dominance of Kirch/Bertelsmann in the pay-TV market in Germany. The arrangements were also anti-competitive because of the effects of Deutsche Telekom's legal monopoly in the provision of cable infrastructure and the effects of the proposed merger on the planned deregulation of cable services in 1998.

Commenting on the *MSG Media Service* decision, the Competition Commissioner, Karel van Miert, stressed that the Commission:

> . . . is able and committed to . . . prevent the protection of future markets from competition. In principle, a joint venture like MSG is desirable because it is able to implement new technologies such as digital television. But the structural features of MSG would lead to a protection of the market for services as well as for digital pay tele-vision. The Commission is committed to leave future markets in the multi-media sector open to competition . . . ((1994) *Financial Times*, 10 May).

In two other relevant decisions the Commission cleared joint venture arrangements. In Case IV/M.140 *Kirch/Richment/Telepiu* OJ 1994 C189/6, the acquisition of joint control of Telepiu (a small Italian pay-TV service) by Kirch and Richmont was unobjectionable, because (among other reasons) neither had a significant market presence in Italy. In Case IV/M.0489, *Bertelsmann/News International/Vox* 6 September 1994, the sale of a 49.9 per cent stake in Vox, a German free access service broadcast on Astra, to News International, was approved. News International had no existing market presence in the relevant market for German television services. The Commission found that although Bertelsmann and News International had access to substantial quantities of programming, the sale was not likely to prevent access to this programming by rival television services. Decisions are awaited in further joint venture cases, *BSkyB/ MTV* and *VIP Pay TV*, the former for the operation of the satellite service, Nickelodeon, the latter for the establishment of joint selling arrangements for pay-TV services.

8.24   An ancillary question is whether restrictions on the supply of decoders in exclusive territorial licences, or exclusive agreements between broadcasters and manufacturers of decoders, fall within art 85(1). In the first case, it is unlikely, as long as the licence is not otherwise caught by art 85(1), because the restriction would be a necessary ancillary part of an agreement which is consistent with the objectives of the EC Treaty and does not offend art 85(1): Case 27/87 *Erauw-Jacquery* v *La Hesbignonne* [1988] ECR 1919.

In the case of an exclusive agreement between a broadcaster and a manufacturer, an exclusive arrangement in itself would not necessarily infringe art 85(1). In *BBC Enterprises Ltd* v *Hi-Tech Xtravision Ltd and Others*, *op cit* the defendants abandoned their defences based on art 85 relating to an exclusive agreement between BBC Enterprises and a manufacturer of decoders. The agreement was for less than five years, although it was disputed how much design and development of the decoders had been undertaken by the manufacturer.

8.25   *Horizontal agreements*   Restrictions on access to programmes may arise through arrangements between broadcasters, who agree to share programmes among themselves and to limit access to them to third parties.

In recent years, the Commission has examined certain activities of the EBU, which provided for the exchange of television programmes across the 'Eurovision' network by the state-owned broadcasters of EU and other European states. EBU membership is now open to television and radio broadcasters who provide, within the European Broadcasting Area (as defined by the RRs of the ITU), a licensed service of national character and national importance, and who are obliged to and do provide varied and balanced programming, and who satisfy other specified conditions (arts 3–7 of the EBU Statutes (1992)). Hence, commercial satellite broadcasters are largely excluded from membership. The activities of the EBU became of particular relevance to competition law in the light of the growth of commercial (satellite) broadcasters, who were ineligible for membership of the EBU. Particular attention has been given to the terms on which the EBU licences programmes to non-members. In avoiding the consequences of art 85(2), much has depended on the extent to which sub-licences could be granted to other broadcasters, and the terms thereof, including those relating to the timing of deferred transmissions and the amount of material that may be broadcast.

In its decision of 11 June 1993, the Commission approved a revised scheme promulgated by the EBU for the licensing to non-members of rights to sports programmes. The Commission also found that it was necessary for membership of the Eurovision system to be limited to public service broadcasters. All the relevant arrangements were cleared pursuant to art 85(3) subject to certain conditions, until 25 February 1998 (OJ 1993 L179/23).

8.26   In *Screensport/EBU Members* OJ 1991 L63/32, the Commission prohibited joint venture arrangements between the EBU and/or certain of its members with News International plc for the creation of the dedicated satellite sports channel, 'Eurosport'. A complaint was made to the Commission on behalf of a competing channel, 'Screensport'. The effect of the joint venture was to restrict access to the broadcasting of sports events, because the EBU and/or its members held exclusive rights to a substantial number of events. The Commission noted that non-members could acquire only limited access to EBU material through sub-licences, the priority for live broadcasting being given to EBU members and hence to Eurosport. The joint venture arrangements were within art 85(1) and were refused exemption under art 85(3) (see also Case T44/90 *La Cinq SA v EC Commission*; refusal of EBU to grant membership to broadcaster; application for 'interim measures'; NS *Eurosport Mark III* OJ 1993 C76/8).

Restrictions on competition in the supply of programmes may arise from arrangements other than those between broadcasters, for example by restrictions imposed on broadcasters by sporting bodies and others who hold exclusive broadcasting rights. Under art 14 of the UEFA rules, the footballing authorities of the various members agree with each other that they will authorise broadcasting of matches which they each control outside their respective territories, only if the relevant authorities of the receiving state have consented to the broadcast being shown in their territory. The right to withhold consent is not absolute, but is based on whether or not certain league or cup matches are being played on the same day.

These arrangements are directed at maintaining spectator attendances at matches. However, they probably fall within art 85(1). The question of whether or not the arrangements would be exempted should turn on whether the restrictions are unnecessarily wide, so as to fail to meet the third criterion imposed by art 85(3). In 1992, BSkyB obtained an injunction (based on alleged breaches of art 85(1)) to restrain the UK footballing authorities from acting so as to prevent it from televising the football match in Rome between the Italian club, Lazio and the English club, Tottenham Hotspur. The decision was largely based on 'balance of convenience' principles and does not reflect a decision that UEFA rule 14 does fall within art 85(1).

The European Commission is currently considering a complaint made by the satellite broadcaster MTV Europe against Video Performance Ltd (VPL) and IFPI, based on alleged infringements of art 85, arising from the collective licensing of music videos for pan-European broadcasting. MTV Europe criticises the arrangements because they prevent competition between record companies in relation to broadcast use of music videos. In March 1994 the Commission sent a Statement of Objections to VPL indicating the Commission's view that the arrangements infringed art 85(1) and would not qualify for exemption under art 85(3). The Commission can see no reason why the five 'major' record companies (being members of VPL) should preclude themselves from negotiating individually with MTV Europe.

The common feature of all these cases is the extent to which exclusivity prevents, restricts or distorts competition within art 85(1). As has been observed in relation to vertical agreements for programme supply, exclusivity is not necessarily prohibited under art 85(2). Most horizontal agreements will have great difficulty in satisfying the conditions in art 85(3).

Article 86

8.27   Article 86 provides that, *inter alia*, any abuse by one or more undertakings of a dominant position in the common market or in a substantial part of it shall be prohibited as incompatible with the common market in so far as it may affect trade between member states. Such abuse may, in particular, consist in directly or indirectly imposing unfair purchase or selling prices or other trading conditions, or limiting production, markets or technical development to the prejudice of consumers.

In the present context, art 86 has a limited range of possible applications in the field of copyright and related rights. These primarily relate to the activities of collecting societies, and the refusal of rights holders to grant licences to third parties for the broadcasting of programmes within the Community, either absolutely or on unreasonable terms.

Collecting societies typically enjoy a dominant position in the market for licensing the rights which fall under their control. (See, for example, *Re GEMA* OJ 1972 L134/15; [1971] CMLR D35; *Re GEMA (No 2)* OJ 1972 L182/24; [1972] CMLR D94). The dominant position of a collecting society will be abused where the society has imposed unfair prices or other trading terms. These issues were considered in Case 395/87 *Ministère Public* v *Tournier* [1989] ECR 2521, where the ECJ decided that differences between member states' royalty rates for the public performance of sound recordings would indicate an abuse if lower prices charged in other member states could not be accounted for by 'objective and relevant dissimilarities'. These would include differing legal, historical or cultural environments.

For example, in *Association of Independent Radio Companies Ltd* v *Phonographic Performance Ltd* (Ref/CT9/91) 26 February 1993, the UK Copyright Tribunal found that the rates sought to be charged for the (radio) broadcasting of sound recordings could not be criticised by reference to rates charged elsewhere in Europe. The tribunal found (at p 35) that:

> . . . the structure and the functions of the sound recording industry in each of the countries referred to are so different from those in the United Kingdom that no useful comparison can be made.

This finding relates to sound recordings and the right under consideration was the broadcasting copyright in sound recordings, in so far as it affects radio transmission. The *Tournier* case must also be seen in the context of the arbitration provisions of the directive which relate to the terms applied by collecting societies for the exercise of the cable retransmission rights (para 8.36).

8.28   Article 86 may sometimes be invoked where there has been an unreasonable refusal to license. A mere refusal to license without engaging in abusive conduct does not infringe art 86 (see Case 238/87 *Volvo A B v Eric Veng (UK) Ltd* [1988] ECR 6211). This is illustrated in Case T–70/89 *BBC v Commission* [1991] 4 CMLR 669 where the European Court of First Instance upheld the decision of the Commission, which had found that the BBC had abused a dominant position by unreasonably refusing to grant licences for weekly television listings, and directed that the infringement be brought to an end by licensing the listings on reasonable terms. In this case, the refusal of the BBC to grant licences of the copyright in the listings went beyond the specific subject matter of the right (the exclusive right to reproduce the protected work), thus stifling competition in a downstream market (programme listings), ancillary to the main (broadcasting) activities of the BBC. No appeal was made by the BBC from this decision. However, in *Radio Telefis Eireann v Commission* (T–69/89) [1991] II ECR 485, the European Court of First Instance came to similar conclusions with regard to the refusal by the applicant broadcasting company to license the reproduction of its advance weekly programme listings. An appeal against the decision was unsuccessful (95/C 137/05) notwithstanding the opinion of the Advocate General. The judgment is short and does not provide much assistance in resolving the difference between a 'reasonable' and an 'unreasonable' refusal to license.

Finally, in contrast to the foregoing, it is usually necessary to show 'objective justification' for a refusal to license an existing customer. The same applies to a refusal to supply save on unreasonable terms (see, eg, *Re National Carbonising Company Ltd* OJ 1976 L35; [1976] CMLR D82). These principles are capable of application to refusals to license existing, as opposed to prospective, users of material protected by copyright or related rights.

The Directive on Copyright and Related Rights in Satellite Broadcasting and Cable Retransmission Services

8.29   Directive 93/83/EEC on Copyright and Related Rights in Satellite Broadcasting and Cable Retransmission Services (OJ 1993 L 248/15) must be seen in the context of other moves to harmonise copyright and related rights and to improve the cross border movement of television services. The Commission's action in this field may be traced back to 1984, when it published its *Green Paper on the* *establishment of the Common Market for broadcasting, especially by satellite and cable, Television without Frontiers* (COM(84) 300).

A common market for such services could be established only through a series of measures designed to harmonise relevant rules and regulations and to apply the relevant provisions of the EC Treaty.

For example, national rules governing television advertising were creating major obstacles to the broadcasting of advertising across national frontiers. The development of satellite and cable technology would increase those distortions. Essentially, national rules were used to discriminate against foreign advertising. Other restrictions were present at the sponsorship level. Disparities in laws relating to the protection of minors were also noted. Approximation of these laws was seen as the necessary counterpart to the opening up of frontiers to broadcasting in the community (see Chapter 7).

A further field in which harmonisation was regarded as desirable was copyright. The legal situation was considered against the background of *Coditel (No 1)*. Following that decision, it was necessary to approximate the content of and limits on the exercise of certain copyrights. As *Coditel (No 2)* made clear, it was permissible to limit the exercise of copyright so as to prevent disguised restrictions on trade between member states.

8.30 The *Television Without Frontiers* Green Paper went on to examine the copyright issues raised by transfrontier broadcasting, particularly those posed by cable retransmission. The system worked well enough if the broadcaster secured the necessary cable rights, but problems would arise where cable operators needed to obtain rights from individual rights owners. Since cable transmissions are usually simultaneous with the originating broadcast, it would be difficult to secure rights individually. Usually the cable operator would not know the broadcaster's schedule until late in the day. Accordingly, the cable operator would be faced with having to obtain licences from numerous persons who would be difficult to identify, particularly at short notice. There was therefore the problem of 'the outsider', being the rights owner who either refused consent or could not be located. The problem arose in respect of satellite and terrestrial broadcasts. Collective negotiations were successful in the field of rights of producers of audio-visual works through the *Association Internationale Collective des Oeuvres Audio-visuelle (AGICOA)*, which negotiated with cable operators. However, 'the outsider' problem remained.

The Commission considered that collective licensing solved only part of the problem, because the collecting society could licence only rights that it represented. A second possibility was to introduce a system of statutory licensing. The exclusive right would be changed into one for equitable remuneration only. The injunctive right would therefore be neutralised. The statutory right could apply only to entire unchanged cable retransmissions, because of art 11 bis (2) of the Berne Convention, which requires, *inter alia*, that the moral rights of authors must not be prejudiced. Any legal measures also had to relate to simultaneous entire transmission, because subtitling and other alterations would affect, *inter alia*, other copyrights, or moral rights.

8.31   The Commission leant towards a statutory licence as its preferred solution. Doubts were expressed as to the compatibility of this approach with art 11 bis (2) of the Berne Convention, which stipulates that it is a matter for domestic legislation to determine the conditions under which broadcasting and cable rights are to be exercised.

The statutory licence has not found its way into the directive. However, it is significant that the Commission contemplated the establishment of an arbitration body (as envisaged by art 11 bis (2)) with the tasks not only of fixing remuneration, but also of ensuring uniformity of the criteria for remuneration and preventing distortions of competition. A sort of pan-European copyright tribunal was therefore envisaged. This idea has not been followed in the directive.

The directive also recognises the technical developments in satellite television transmission by FSS satellites and the disparities in copyright treatment of such transmissions under the national laws of member states, which could lead to distortions in competition. The crucial question was whether broadcasting was an act which took place in the country of the up-link alone, or whether it included the country of emission and / or all the receiving countries. The position was complicated. Different member states had different laws. For example, in November 1989 the Vienna Court of Appeals ruled that a German rights owner was not entitled to authorise a satellite broadcast from German territory into Austria, because under that law the copyrights of all countries 'in which the broadcast could be received' were relevant. This issue is still of considerable importance in relation to transmissions which are capable of reception outside the EU, and to those originating outside the EU where the deeming provisions of the directive do not apply.

The purpose of the directive is, therefore, to harmonise protection for owners of copyright and related rights in respect of satellite broadcasting, to ensure that this restricted act takes place in one country alone (so as to enable one-stop licensing) and to require owners of cable retransmission rights to exercise such rights, in so far as they relate to simultaneous, unaltered transmissions, through a collecting society.

Definitions

8.32 The following commentary is put forward as a guide to the main provisions of the directive. The directive contains certain basic definitions and provisions, which are fundamental to understanding the mechanism of the legal framework.

(1) 'Satellite'. This includes BSS/DBS BSS and FSS satellites, provided that the latter are used for DTH services: for example, BSkyB and other ASTRA services (art 1.1).

(2) 'Communication to the public by satellite'. This takes the place of 'broadcasting' and defines the relevant restricted act. It is defined as 'the act of introducing, under the control and responsibility of the broadcasting organisation, the programme-carrying signals intended for reception by the public into an uninterrupted chain of communication, leading to the satellite and down towards the earth (art 1(2)(*a*)).

The place from where a communication to the public (by satellite) is made is 'solely in the Member State, where under the control and responsibility of the broadcasting organisation, the programme-carrying signals are introduced into an uninterrupted chain of communication leading to the satellite and down towards the earth' (art 1(2)(*b*)).

In this way the directive fixes on the operational headquarters of the broadcaster, where the decisions regarding programme content and transmission are taken, ie where the signal passes through master control for onward transmission. This is important, because it limits the location of the restricted act to one country alone. Suggestions had been made that the act should be treated as taking place in the states where the broadcaster derives substantial revenues. This could have opened the way to the reintroduction of the 'footprint' theory by the back door.

It is also notable that the relevant country is not that where the up-link is situated (contrast s 6(4) of the 1988 Act). The country of up-link may have little to do with the commercial activities of the broadcaster and can change.

The definition also shows that the act does not include transmissions which are sent to the broadcaster from elsewhere, eg a musical event which takes place in another country and is relayed to the broadcaster in question. The insertion of advertising also arguably interrupts the chain of communication. Accordingly, the relevant country is the operational headquarters of the broadcasting organisation.

8.33   The restricted act of 'communication to the public' includes encrypted transmissions where decoders are made available to the public by or with the authority of the broadcasting organisation (art 2(*c*)). Therefore, transmissions to closed-user groups are excluded.

Provision is also made for the situation where signals are up-linked from a member state, but the operational headquarters of the broadcaster are outside the EU (in a state which does not grant exclusive rights to authorise the communication to the public of relevant material as provided for in arts 2 and 4). Here the restricted act takes place in the country of up-link. If there is no up-link in a member state, but a broadcasting organisation established in a member state has 'commissioned' the act of communication to the public by satellite, that act shall be deemed to have occurred in the member state in which the broadcasting organisation has its principal establishment in the EU (art 2(*d*)). In the present context, 'commission' is intended to apply to the situation where programmes are assembled within the EU and are sent in recorded form to broadcasting facilities outside the EU.

8.34   What of the position where transmissions are receivable within the EU, but there is no relevant link between the broadcasting organisation and a member state? Here, domestic laws will apply, so as potentially to render the broadcasting organisation liable in copyright in the state where the up-link takes place and in states where the transmissions are capable of reception (see para 8.5).

(3)   'Cable retransmission'. This means the 'simultaneous, unaltered and unabridged retransmission by a cable or microwave system for reception by the public of an initial transmission from another Member State, by wire or over the air, including that by satellite, of television or radio programmes intended for reception by the public' (art 1.3).

Accordingly, the insertion of local adverts or the subtitling or editing of programmes will take the transmission outside the ambit of the directive. Moral rights are also unaffected.

(4) The principal director of a cinematographic or audio-visual work is its author, or one of its authors. Member states may provide for others to be co-authors (art 1.5).

States such as the UK, which regard the producer as the author, will have to take account of this.

Substantive provisions

'Broadcasting' rights

8.35 Each member state undertakes to grant authors of copyright works the right to authorise or prohibit the communication of their works to the public by satellite (art 2). This effectively makes broadcasting by satellite a restricted act for the purposes of copyright. No compulsory licensing of this right is permissible (art 3.1). There is no provision that authors have the right to insist that the remuneration be stated in the agreement and must take account of all aspects of the broadcast. Previous drafts of the directive contemplated this additional protection.

Member states also undertake to ensure that for the purposes of communication to the public by satellite, performers, phonogram producers and broadcasters are protected in accordance with the relevant provisions of the Directive 92/100/EEC of 19 November 1992 on Rental Right and Lending Right and on Certain Rights Relating to Copyright in the Field of Intellectual Property (OJ 1992 L346/61) ('the Rental Directive') (art 4.1).

This means, *inter alia*, that performers are to be granted the right to authorise or prohibit the satellite broadcasting of their live performances. Satellite broadcasters' rights are also to be granted a neighbouring or 'related' right in their transmissions (art 8.1 of the Rental Directive).

Member states must also ensure that a single equitable remuneration is payable to phonogram producers and performers, where a satellite broadcaster uses a published phonogram or recording of such a phonogram (art 8.2 of the Rental Directive). The provisions of art 2.7 (production contracts authorising broadcasting) and art 12 (duration of rights) are to apply (art 4.3).

Derogation from the broadcasting rights of performers, broadcasters and phonogram producers may be made in respect of private use, fair use (eg reporting of current events) and dubbing for broadcasting purposes (art 10 of the Rental Directive).

However, this is the minimum protection necessary. Member states are at liberty to create greater protection for neighbouring rights owners; for example giving phonogram producers exclusive rights in respect of phonograms rather than merely the right to receive equitable remuneration (art 6).

Limited provision is made for the requirement in certain cases that authors exercise satellite broadcasting rights solely through a collecting society (art 3.2). However, the unrepresented rights holder has a power of veto and the restrictions imposed mean that collective licensing can usually be used only in the field of national broadcasting.

Cable retransmission rights

8.36   The remainder of the directive goes on to specify the ways in which the right of cable retransmission may be exercised by copyright owners and owners of related rights.

Cable retransmission rights in respect of programmes broadcast from other member states are to be exercised on the basis of individual or collective contractual arrangements (art 8.1). Hence, statutory licensing is not permissible. However, exception is made for schemes which were in operation or were expressly provided for by national law on 31 July 1991. These may be retained until 31 December 1997 (art 8.2). However, the cable retransmission right may be exercised only through a collecting society 'representing the professional categories concerned' (art 9.1). No proposal is made to exempt from copyright liability simultaneous, unaltered cable retransmissions of satellite broadcasts within the satellite footprint.

Where a rights owner has not 'transferred the management of his rights to a collecting society which manages rights of the same category', that society is deemed to be authorised to manage those rights. The concept of transfer of management would include mandates, licences and outright assignments. Where more than one society manages those rights, the owner can choose which one is deemed to manage his rights. The consequence of this is that the rights owner enjoys the same rights as would have arisen under the collective agreement. He is also entitled to claim these rights within a period to be fixed by the member state concerned, which must not exceed a period of three years from the relevant transmission (art 9.2; see also art 9.3). The provisions of arts 8 and 9 therefore constitute the preferred solution for the 'outsider' problem (see para 8.30). No exclusion is made for rights in films.

8.37   The requirement of collective licensing does not apply to broadcasting organisations in respect of rights in their own transmissions, irrespective of whether the rights concerned are its own or have been transferred to it by owners of copyright or related rights (art 10). This means that cable operators must secure individual licences from broadcasters in respect of the neighbouring rights of broadcasters in their own transmissions. It also applies where the broadcaster has cleared underlying cable rights in advance.

Provision is also made to facilitate rights acquisition by (collective) agreement. Mediators may be appointed between the parties to negotiations, who are to provide assistance with negotiations and to submit proposals to the parties (art 11). More importantly, member states undertake to create the necessary laws ensuring that the parties do not 'without valid justification' prevent or hinder negotiation regarding authorisation for cable retransmission (art 12.1; see also arts 12.2 and 12.3). It is also provided that the provisions of the directive are to be without prejudice to the regulation of the activities of collecting societies under national laws (art 13).

The meaning of art 12.1 is unclear. Unjustified prevention or hindering of negotiations could mean both refusing a licence and refusing to licence save on unreasonable terms. The mechanisms for negotiation provided for in art 12 therefore amount to an uneasy compromise between statutory licensing and negotiation. Hence, the directive provides little comfort for those seeking the establishment of a pan-European copyright tribunal.

Implementation and transitional provisions

8.38   Member states were obliged to bring the directive into force by 1 January 1995 (art 14.1). The UK has not yet done so, although it is expected to do so in the very near future. There is in existence a draft regulation which seeks to implement both the directive and the Rental Directive. Given the likely impact of new technologies (including the electronic delivery of copyright material), the Commission is to report on the application of the directive to the European Parliament, with a view to making further proposals to adapt the directive to developments in the audio and audio-visual sector (art 14.3).

Transitional provisions of the Rental Directive (art 13(1), (2), (6) and (7)) are to govern the rights granted to broadcasting organisations, performers and phonogram producers (art 7.1). Agreements concerning the exploitation of works and other protected subject matter which are in force on 1 January 1995 are to be subject to the provisions of arts 1.2, 2 and 3 as from 1 January 2000 if they expire after that date (art 7.2). Finally, where an international co-production agreement concluded before 1 January 1995, between a producer from a member state and one or more co-producers from other member states or third countries, expressly provides for a system of division of exploitation rights between the co-producers by geographical areas for all means of communication to the public, without distinguishing the arrangement applicable to communication to the public by satellite from the provisions applicable to the other means of communication, and where communication to the public by satellite of the co-production would prejudice the exclusivity, in particular the language exclusivity, of one of the co-producers or his assignees in a given territory, the authorisation by one of the co-producers or his assignees for a communication to the public by satellite shall require the prior consent of the holder of that exclusivity, whether co-producer or assignee (art 7.3).

UK law

Copyright subsistence and liability in respect of satellite transmissions

Introduction

8.39   Copyright protection and liability arise under the 1988 Act in respect of specified transmissions from BSS/DBS and FSS satellites. Under the Copyright Act 1956 (the 1956 Act), it was not clear whether copyright applied to FSS transmissions, because they were not usually intended for general reception, but for reception by cable operators or terrestrial broadcasters, who would distribute the transmissions to the public as part of their services. However, advances in technology for receiving equipment in the 1980s were followed by liberalisation of UK telecommunications laws. Until that time, transmissions from point-to-point satellites had been regarded as secret, amounting to telecommunication and protected as such under the WTA. Liberalisation took place with the decision announced in May 1985 to remove restrictions on reception by Satellite Master Antenna Television (SMATV) systems or directly by individuals or single sets of premises of programme services transmitted by low powered satellite. This was done by means of a so-called Television Receive Only Receiving Equipment (TVRO) licence issued under s 1 of the WTA.

The removal of these regulatory restrictions created a new situation for the purposes of copyright. The providers of FSS services (such as Sky Television, as it then was, now BSkyB) had been (arguably) under no legal obligation to obtain authorisations to include copyright material in their programme services. In practice, clearances were obtained for a number of reasons, notably for the sake of convenience and because such transmissions were primarily aimed at cable operators so that the programme provider would be 'authorising' (a restricted act) UK cable operators (within s 1(2) of the 1956 Act) to include protected material in their 'diffusion services'. However, the growth of the DTH market meant that FSS transmissions had a new audience and rights owners needed to be guaranteed the right to receive royalties not only in respect of cable retransmission, but also in respect of direct reception. Under the 1956 Act, it was not clear that rights owners had this entitlement.

8.40 The 1988 Act defines a (satellite) broadcast as follows:

> A 'broadcast' means a transmission by wireless telegraphy of visual images, sounds or other information, which:-
>
> (*a*) is capable of being lawfully received by members of the public; or
>
> (*b*) is transmitted for presentation to members of the public;
>
> and references to broadcasting shall be construed accordingly. (s 6(1).)

The primary definition of broadcasting under subs (1) does not expressly depend on whether or not the transmissions in question are intended for reception by the general public, in the manner specified in the RRs or the Rome Convention (art 3(*f*)). However, as will be seen, this is the rationale of the primary definition. The first limb of subs (1) covers DTH reception of satellite broadcasts, whether television or radio services. The statute creates the concept of 'lawful reception'. The circumstances in which satellite-delivered transmissions may be received are set out in the WTA and the TA and in the various exceptions, regulations and licences made thereunder.

The broad effect of the WTA and the TA is to render most FSS and BSS/DBS television services capable of lawful reception.

In the case of the WTA, the position is covered by the Wireless Telegraphy (Television Licence Fees) Regulations 1991 (SI No 436) and the Wireless Telegraphy Apparatus (Receivers) (Exemption) Regulations 1989 (SI No 123), made pursuant to ss 1 and 2 of the WTA (see Chapter 6).

The concept of 'lawful reception' is not exhausted by the regulations made under the WTA. Use of receiving equipment to receive the transmissions of a 'broadcasting authority' is not licensable under the TA (s 6(2)(c)). A 'broadcasting authority' means a person licensed under the WTA to broadcast programmes for general reception (s 6(5)). Where this exception does not apply, s 7 of the TA must be considered. On 3 February 1989, the Secretary of State granted a 'class licence' under s 7 of the TA, for the Running of Telecommunications Systems to Receive Messages from Earth Orbiting Apparatus. A licence granted under s 7 may be granted either to all persons, to persons of a class or to a particular person (s 7(3)). The licence is available to any person, except any public telecommunications operator and any person whose licence has been revoked. The licence is granted in respect of an applicable system, being receive-only satellite dish equipment.

8.41   All the receiving equipment comprised in the system must be situated on or within a single set of premises in single occupation; or on or within a single building; or where not so situated, situated within 200 metres of the single set of premises or single building to which the received transmissions are exclusively conveyed (Annex A/para 1; see also para 2). The class licence authorises the licensee to run systems to receive any satellite transmissions containing, *inter alia*, visual images, speech, music and other sounds (and signals serving for the actuation or control of machinery or apparatus) and to convey them from the receive-only satellite dish to the licensee's terminal equipment. Licensing of satellite services under the WTA and TA is dealt with in more detail in Chapter 6. A further question arises under s 6 of the 1988 Act, because subs (1)(*a*) does not make it clear whether the transmissions have to be lawfully capable of reception in the UK, or whether the 'public' referred to is only the UK public. A similar question arises in respect of s 6(1)(*b*). In *BBC Enterprises Ltd* v *Hi-Tech Xtravision Ltd* [1991] 2 AC 327 the House of Lords refused to limit the reference to 'persons . . . entitled' in s 298(2) of the 1988 Act to receive specified broadcasts to persons within the UK. There is no reason why lawful reception or the relevant public should be confined to the UK. It is significant that in *Hi-Tech*, the House of Lords was of the view that the BBC TV Europe service (transmitted by satellite across Europe in encrypted form, but not intended for reception in the UK) was a 'broadcasting service' for the purposes of s 298(1). Indeed, as a matter of statutory construction, it is probably not permissible to restrict the 'public' referred to in s 6 to members of the UK public alone.

8.42   This section must be read together with s 16(1)(*d*), which gives copyright owners the exclusive right to broadcast their works in the UK, and with s 6(4), which fixes the up-link as the place from where a satellite broadcast is made. The result is therefore that an FSS transmission is liable to copyright restriction and protection, if it is up-linked from the UK, even though it is intended for reception outside the UK.

In the context of satellite transmissions, the second limb of s 6(1) ('transmission for presentation to members of the public') includes satellite transmissions which are to be shown in public stadia and similar locations, such as sports events relayed to cinemas or pop concerts transmitted to sports grounds, for example the 'Live Aid' concert shown at Wembley Stadium. It would also include the transmissions of services which deliver live racing for presentation in betting shops via an FSS satellite.

Encrypted transmissions will qualify as broadcasts in the following circumstances:

> An encrypted transmission shall be regarded as capable of being lawfully received by members of the public only if decoding equipment has been made available to members of the public by or with the authority of the person making the transmission or the person providing the contents of the transmission. (s 6(2))

Encrypted transmissions will therefore be broadcasts if they are intended for reception by the general public. This is primarily aimed at pay-TV services, where the broadcaster funds his service by subscription, which is collected through the sale or hire of decoders. Section 6(2) does not make it clear whether decoders must be made available to any member of the public who wishes to subscribe to the service. However, any contrary interpretation would be difficult to sustain. An encrypted service would not be a broadcast service if the sender of the transmissions had made decoders available only to a section of the public, as when pricing information is sent to retail outlets of a chain store or members of a group of companies. These would be so-called 'closed-user group' transmissions. Again, it would be consistent not to limit the 'public' to the UK public.

8.43   A slightly different question is whether encrypted services directed at a section of the public (eg accountants, doctors, lawyers) qualify as broadcasts. Given the terms of s 6(2), such services probably qualify as broadcasts, where available to any member of the public who is willing to pay the subscription, although they are intended for reception only by a section of the UK public.

References to 'broadcasting' in the 1988 Act are relevant to whether a (satellite) broadcast attracts copyright and whether conduct amounts to committing the restricted act of broadcasting (s 16(1)(*d*)). In either case, such references include:

(*a*)   . . . the person transmitting the programme, if he has responsibility to any extent for its contents, and

(*b*)   . . . any person providing the programme who makes with the person transmitting it the arrangements necessary for its transmission. (s 6(3))

The first limb of the definition excludes carriers such as public telecommunication operators and others licensed to provide transmission facilities. Satellite broadcasters will fall within the second limb where they 'provide' the programmes to the carrier who transmits them. Both parts of the definition would have applied to DBS services licensed by the Independent Broadcasting Authority (IBA) pursuant to the Broadcasting Act 1981, under which the IBA was treated as the broadcaster. Accordingly, the IBA and the programme contractor would both have been regarded as broadcasters, the IBA because it satisfied the first limb of the definition, and the programme contractor because it satisfied the second limb. The successor to the IBA, the ITC, is not a broadcaster of satellite television programmes; similarly, the Radio Authority in the case of broadcast radio programmes.

The second limb of the definition in s 6(3) also falls to be considered in the context of so-called programme 'syndication', where a licensee of copyright material (eg music and sound recordings) uses transmission facilities to send the programming to a third party for distribution to an audience, by broadcasting or cable; or does so by delivering tapes of pre-recorded programmes. Is the 'syndicator' a 'person providing the programme who makes with the person transmitting it the arrangements necessary for its transmission'?

8.44   This question was considered by the Copyright Tribunal as a preliminary issue in *Reference No CT9/91, The Association of Independent Radio Companies Ltd & Others v Phonographic Performance Ltd* (unreported) 19 March 1992, where a syndicator, Unique Broadcasting Company Ltd, sought to intervene in the reference on the basis that it was entitled to a statutory licence to broadcast sound recordings under s 135A–C of the 1988 Act. Unique argued, *inter alia*, that it was a broadcaster within s 6(3). It financed the making of the programmes, in most cases by sponsorship, and then delivered the completed programme to the stations, usually in tape form. However, Unique occasionally acquired the right to a live broadcast from abroad and arranged for it to be taken by stations in the UK. On such occasions, the radio station simply took the feed and transmitted the programmes, relying on Unique to ensure that the programme content complied with the law.

The tribunal dismissed the argument that Unique was a broadcaster in the following terms:

> The definition of 'broadcast' in Section 6(1) of the 1988 Act read together with Section 6(3) makes clear . . . that Unique are not engaged in making broadcasts. In each case they neither transmit their programme nor make with the persons transmitting it the arrangements necessary for its transmission. They are simply suppliers of programmes to the stations. When they have sold a programme to a station, the station then broadcasts it as its own and is legally responsible for its content. The station and Unique cannot both be broadcasters of the one programme.

It is submitted that although the decision is correct on its facts, the reasons are open to criticism. Section 6(3) contemplates the possibility that two persons may be broadcasters for the purposes of copyright. Although Unique were providing the programmes, they were not making with the stations the arrangements necessary for the transmission of the programmes to the public, since the stations had already made those arrangements. The draft regulation implementing the directive contemplates the possibility that a person who 'commissions' the making of a broadcast is to be treated as though he were the broadcaster. However, this applies only where the up-link station is situated in a state outside the European Economic Area (EEA). Where the up-link station is within the EEA, the person operating the up-link is to be treated as the broadcaster (proposed amendment to s 6(3) and proposed new s 6A(2)(*b*), (3)(*b*)). However, for either of these possibilities to apply, it is necessary that the place from which a satellite broadcast is made be located in a country other than an EEA state and the law of this country must fail to give adequate protection in respect of copyright and performers' rights (proposed s 6A(1)). Subject to s 6A, the place from which a broadcast is made is the place where, under the control and responsibility of the person making the broadcast, the programme-carrying signals are introduced into an uninterrupted chain of communication including, in the case of a satellite transmission, the chain leading to the satellite and down towards the earth (proposed new s 6(4)). There is also a proposed definition of 'adequate protection' (proposed s 6A(4)). Finally, transitional provisions are proposed.

8.45   Under the present law, a satellite broadcast (whether FSS or BSS/DBS) is made from the place from which the signals carrying the programme material are transmitted to the satellite (s 6(4)). This is different from the provision of the directive that the transmission suite of the broadcaster will usually be the appropriate place from where the broadcast is made. An amendment will therefore have to be made to s 6. As indicated, it is proposed that a new s 6(4) will be introduced, replacing the existing s 6(4). It is interesting to note that in the BA, there is a slightly different mechanism for identifying the place from where a satellite television service is provided, for licensing purposes.

References in the 1988 Act to 'the reception of a broadcast' include reception of a broadcast relayed by means of a telecommunications system (s 6(5)); see eg ss 7(6) and 73(1) and reception and immediate retransmission of a broadcast in a cable programme service. Finally, references in the 1988 Act to a programme in the context of broadcasting are references to any item contained in the broadcast (s 6(3)).

Basic conditions for subsistence of copyright in satellite broadcasts and other subject matter

8.46   Satellite broadcasters must also obtain clearances in respect of copyright material which is included in their transmissions.

The 1988 Act grants protection and creates liability for the purposes of copyright in respect of transmissions up-linked from the UK or from another country to which the relevant provisions of the Act extend. This may include the Channel Islands, the Isle of Man or any colony (ss 6(4), 156 and 157).

In addition to the possibility of being extended elsewhere, the 1988 Act may also be 'applied' to other countries (s 159). The countries to which the relevant provisions of the 1988 Act (relating to copyright) have been applied are parties to relevant conventions or which otherwise give adequate protection under their law (s 159/Copyright (Application to Other Countries) Order 1993 (SI No 942) (see Appendix 1)). For example, if a satellite transmission were up-linked from France and were included in a terrestrial broadcasting service in the UK without the consent of the broadcaster, the broadcaster could bring proceedings against the UK broadcaster under the 1988 Act. This is because France is a party to the Rome Convention and because the relevant provisions of the 1988 Act have been applied to broadcasts up-linked from France.

The 'author' or maker of the broadcast is the first owner of the copyright in the transmission (s 11(1)). There is no restriction on the persons who may be entitled to be the first (or subsequent) owners of copyright in a satellite broadcast up-linked from the UK or another place to which the relevant provisions of the 1988 Act extend or where those provisions have been applied to another country, to relevant services up-linked therefrom (s 156). Accordingly, the relevant reservation made by the UK under the European Agreement on Television Broadcasts no longer applies. The reservation required a foreign broadcaster (in order to qualify for UK copyright protection) to be both constituted in the territory and under the laws of a contracting state and transmitting from that state. Qualification for protection under the 1988 Act is also fixed by reference to whether or not the maker of the broadcast or other 'work' was a 'qualifying person' at the 'material time'. The provisions of s 154 are particularly relevant to the ownership of other copyright works: see also s 155.

8.47   The copyright in a satellite broadcast expires at the end of the period of 50 years from the end of the calendar year in which the broadcast was first made. Copyright in a repeat broadcast expires at the same time as the copyright in the original broadcast. Accordingly, no copyright can subsist in a repeat broadcast made after the expiry of the copyright in the original broadcast. A repeat broadcast is a repeat of a broadcast previously made; by implication, by any broadcaster (s 14). The term of copyright in other works is as follows. For all other works except films and sound recordings, the term is the end of the period of 50 years from the end of the calendar year in which the author dies (s 12). For films and sound recordings, copyright expires at the end of the period of 50 years from the end of the calendar year in which the film or sound recording is made, or if there is a 'release' before the end of that period, 50 years from the end of the calendar year of release. Release means first publication, or televising, or in the case of a film or film sound track, when the film is first shown in public (s 13). However, all the above must be considered subject to Council Directive 93/98/EEC Harmonising the Term of Protection of Copyright and Certain Related Rights (the 'Term Directive').

The acts restricted by copyright

8.48   The satellite broadcaster is granted a bundle of exclusive rights under the 1988 Act which may be individually licensed or assigned. Equally, other rights owners (and other broadcasters) have the right to authorise or prohibit the broadcasting of their works by satellite, provided that the various basic requirements (as to subsistence of copyright) are satisfied.

These rights are limited to activity in the UK (or any other place to which the 1988 Act extends), because the 1988 Act does not apply to copyright restricted acts done outside the jurisdiction (*Def Lepp Music* v *Stuart Brown* [1986] RPC 273; see also para 8.55). Non-UK copyrights arise under the laws of the states where the applicable restricted acts take place. Accordingly, broadcasters must look to the copyright laws of other states where their transmissions are dealt with in an unauthorised manner outside the UK or any country to which the 1988 Act extends. For example, if a terrestrial broadcaster in Spain were to make an unauthorised retransmission of a satellite broadcast up-linked from the UK, the UK broadcaster would need to look to Spanish law for a remedy. Generally, countries which are parties to the Rome Convention should provide for such protection. However, copyright owners will be able to require clearance of their rights, where a satellite broadcast is made from a place in the UK or any country to which the relevant part of the Act extends (ss 6(4) and 157).

Satellite broadcasters and other copyright owners are given certain rights, which enable them to authorise or prohibit the following activity in the UK or in any country to which the 1988 Act has been extended. The most important of these are:

(*a*)   copying;

(*b*)   issuing copies to the public;

(*c*)   public performance;

(*d*)   (re)broadcasting;

(*e*)   inclusion in a cable programme service;

(*f*)   'authorisation' of any of the foregoing acts (s 16(1) and (2)).

Satellite broadcasters and other copyright owners are also given the right to sue for 'secondary infringement'. This will have relevance to unauthorised (video or audio) recordings of broadcasts and to the dubbing of works which goes beyond the statutory 'ephemeral right' (incidental recording for the purposes of broadcasting) (ss 22, 23, 24, 27 and 68).

8.49   *Copying*   'Copying' has a number of applications in the present context. First, 'dubbing' for the purposes of broadcasting, rebroadcasting (by a terrestrial or satellite broadcaster) or cable retransmission. The ephemeral recording right does not apply to the copyright in broadcasts, applying only to the underlying works (s 68).

Copying may also occur where third parties wish to make use of a still photograph of images included in the broadcast (s 17(4)). The effect of this subsection is to provide that a still image constitutes a 'substantial part' of a broadcast, which is a precondition for liability in copyright (s 16(3)(*a*). Copying of a satellite broadcast will also occur where a recording is made (for commercial purposes) in the UK of a broadcast which has been up-linked from a place in the UK and retransmitted by cable and thereafter copied. This is because references in the 1988 Act to the doing of an act restricted by copyright are taken to include the doing of the particular act directly or indirectly (s 16(3)(*b*)). Copying has also been held to occur where a work is displayed on a television monitor, being reproduced in a 'material form' (*Greyhound Services Ltd* v *Wilf Gilbert (Staffs) Ltd* [1994] FSR 723). This was a decision under the Copyright Act 1956, but it does raise the question whether the right to authorise or prohibit copying creates a right to authorise or prohibit reception of broadcast works.

8.50   *The issue of copies to the public*   The restricted act of issuing copies to the public (s 18) applies to the 'act of putting into circulation' relevant copies which have not previously been put into circulation in the UK or elsewhere. The main application of this right is in the field of video and photographs of still images included in the print media. The exclusive right does not apply to any subsequent distribution, sale, hiring or loan of the copies nor to any subsequent importation of the copies into the UK. The rights are exhausted once the copies in question have first been put onto the market. Accordingly, rental is not covered, so excluding videos of broadcasts to the extent of the copyright in the broadcast itself. Contractual mechanisms are necessary for these purposes; particularly in the case of recordings of live events, where there are no underlying copyrights.

8.51 *Public performance* Copyright owners also possess the exclusive right to authorise or prohibit the showing or playing of their works in public or the public performance thereof (ss 16(1)(*c*), 19). These restricted acts must be considered in the light of the act of inclusion in a cable programme service (see *below*). Playing or showing in public (or public performance) will typically occur where owners of pubs, clubs or other premises make the transmission available for listening or viewing in their establishments. The distinction is between performances which are public and those which are domestic or quasi-domestic in character (see generally *Copinger and Skone James on Copyright* 13th edn, paras 8.109–114).

However, where the viewers (or listeners) have not 'paid for admission', exclusive rights are not infringed in relation to the broadcast or cable programme or any sound recording or film included therein (s 72(1)). Other underlying rights are, though, unaffected. A viewer or listener is taken to have paid for admission to a place if he has paid for admission to a place of which the relevant establishment forms part, or if goods or services are supplied at prices which are substantially attributable to the viewing or listening facilities, or at prices exceeding those usually charged there and which are partly attributable to those facilities (s 72(2)). Payment for admission is deemed not to have taken place where the persons concerned are admitted as residents or inmates of the establishment, or are persons admitted as members of a club or society where payment is only for membership and the provision of facilities is incidental to the main purposes of the club or society (s 72(3)).

In each case, the person treated as playing or showing the broadcast in public is not the person responsible for 'sending' the transmission, ie the broadcaster (s 19(4)); see, however, s 6(1)(*b*). In the case of showings to guests in bedrooms of hotels and other institutions, it is necessary to consider whether the transmissions amount to the 'public' showing of broadcasts (see *Rank Film Production Ltd v Dodds* [1983] 2 NSWLR 553 and other cases cited in *Copinger*; see p 347 para 8.114). If the showing is not 'public', it is necessary to consider whether the activity amounts to inclusion in a cable programme service (see *below*). The showing of programmes in hotel and other similar bedrooms would amount to inclusion in a cable programme service, if not to showing in public: see s 7(2)(*d*) (the former exemption under s 48(3B) of the 1956 Act has not been re-enacted).

8.52 *Rebroadcasting and cable retransmission* A qualifying satellite broadcaster enjoys the exclusive right to authorise or prohibit the rebroadcasting of its transmissions. Typically, this covers terrestrial rebroadcasts of the original satellite transmission. This will include not only traditional broadcasters, but also local Microwave-Video Distribution System (MVDS) and other similar broadcasters, who broadcast within limited areas. The exclusive right also applies to rebroadcasting by satellite. Clearances will also be required for 'dubbing' the satellite broadcast (rather than the underlying works) for rebroadcasting purposes (see paras 8.48 and 8.49).

Satellite broadcasters and other copyright owners also have exclusive rights in respect of certain cable retransmissions. The exemption in respect of 'in-area' cable retransmissions does not apply to satellite (or encrypted) broadcasts (s 73(2)(*b*)). Accordingly, cable operators require clearances where they distribute programmes broadcast by satellite, even where the satellite footprint covers the entirety of their network area. However, they do not require clearances in respect of underlying works for in-area cable transmissions (s 73(3)(*b*)). In both cases, clearances are required to the extent that any part of the cable network falls outside the footprint of the satellite.

The 1988 Act provides a rather complicated definition of 'cable programme service'. The basic definition is:

> . . . a service which consists wholly or mainly in sending visual images, sounds or other information by means of a telecommunications system, otherwise than by wireless telegraphy, for reception—
>
> (*a*) at two or more places (whether for simultaneous reception or at different times in response to requests by different users); or
>
> (*b*) for presentation to members of the public. (s 7(1))

A 'telecommunications system' means a system for conveying visual images, sounds or other information by electronic means. 'Electronic' means actuated by electric, magnetic, electromagnetic, electrochemical or electromechanical energy (s 178). Again, there is no proper reason to limit the references to the 'public' to the UK public. None of the exceptions to the basic definition have any application to the typical situations in which satellite transmissions are distributed by cable.

8.53 Subject to one exception, all types of cable system are within the statutory definition, involving broadband and SMATV services. Master Antenna Television (MATV) systems are excluded, being no more than a means of delivering broadcast transmissions to areas where they would otherwise not be properly receivable, eg for geographical reasons (s 7(2)(*e*)). This provision also excludes liability for those operating cable systems which relay programmes to the cable operator or to broadcasters. It also operates to exclude the owner of the cable system, who makes his facilities available to the cable operator. Although the Secretary of State is enabled to provide further exceptions by statutory instrument (s 7(3),(4)), no relevant exception has yet been made.

An exception is made for:

> services where—
>
> (i)   all the apparatus comprised in the system is situated in or connects, premises which are in single occupation; and
>
> (ii) the system is not connected to any other telecommunications system,
>
> other than services operated as part of the amenities provided for residents or inmates of premises run as a business. (s 7(2)(*d*).)

The scope of the exception is not entirely clear. It is first necessary to identify 'premises which are in single occupation'.

8.54 Occupation has been held to have a variety of meanings, depending upon the statutory context in which it has appeared. For present purposes, it is reasonable to say that 'occupation' includes possession as its primary element, but it also includes something more. Legal possession 'does not of itself, constitute an occupation'; *per* Lush J, *R v St Pancras Assessment Committee* [1877] 2 QBD 581. Accordingly, pub visitors would not be 'occupiers', nor would members of social clubs which do not provide sleeping accommodation. But there is no reason why the owner or lessee of a pub (or less likely, of a club) should not be an occupier. Moreover, it is difficult to regard members of clubs and pub customers as 'residents' or 'inmates'. Therefore, such in-house systems would satisfy the definition of a cable programme service, because television programmes would be presented to members of the public within the meaning of s 7(1)(*b*).

Systems serving nursing homes, hotels or apartment blocks would qualify as cable programme services. Even if each separate room could be regarded as separate premises, the system in the premises is connected to the other parts of the cable system outside the premises and the service would be provided as part of the amenities of the institution. It is also arguable that any cable system which relays broadcast transmissions is 'connected' to the satellite or other transmitter: see s 4(2)(*b*) of the TA. In all the circumstances, s 7 (2)(*e*) has limited application. Where cable systems are taken outside the statutory definition by the exceptions set out in s 7, it is necessary to consider whether there is a playing or showing in public or public performance (see para 8.51).

The draft regulation implementing the directive proposes the creation of a new s 92A, to the effect that the exclusive right to authorise or prohibit inclusion of a relevant copyright (not broadcast) work in a cable programme service be exercisable only through a 'licensing body' in relation to simultaneous cable retransmission of a broadcast made from an EEA state. However, the restriction is not to apply where the broadcaster is the assignee of the cable right.

8.55   *Authorisation*   Satellite broadcasters and other copyright owners are also granted the right to 'authorise' others to exercise one or more of the restricted acts mentioned *above*. Authorisation means the grant or purported grant (express or implied) of the right to do the relevant act, whether the intention is that the grantee of the right should exercise it on his own account, or on behalf of the grantor (*Falcon* v *Famous Players Film Co* [1926] 2 KB 474, at 499 *per* Atkin LJ). Authorisation can relate only to restricted acts done in the UK or in another country to which the relevant part of the Act has been extended although the act of authorisation may take place outside the UK. In the context of satellite broadcasts, authorisation is mainly relevant to agreements between broadcasters and cable operators, where the former authorise the latter to include in their cable services films and other material protected by copyright.

8.56   *Secondary infringement*   A qualifying satellite broadcaster is also entitled to restrain 'knowing' dealing in 'infringing copies' of its broadcast transmissions. In the present context, this applies where an unauthorised third party possesses in the course of a business, sells or lets for hire, offers or exposes for sale or hire, exhibits in public in the course of a business or distributes one or more unauthorised videos of broadcasts, knowing or having reason to believe that the videos in question were infringing copies. The latter phrase means that the unauthorised recording must have been made in the UK, or if made outside the UK, the recording in question must have been or be proposed to be imported into the UK (s 27(1)–(3)). These provisions are also relevant where a broadcaster dubs a recording in circumstances where it cannot rely on the ephemeral right. The recording becomes an 'infringing copy', subject to the jurisdictional requirements referred to *above*.

As indicated, it must be shown that the alleged infringer knew or had reason to believe that he was engaged in deliberate wrongdoing. This test of knowledge is different from that which applied under the Copyright Act 1956 (see *Hutchinson Personal Communications Ltd v Hook Advertising Ltd* [1995] FSR 365; *LA Gear Inc v Hi-Tec Sports plc* [1992] FSR 121 and Laddie *et al, The Modern law of Copyright and Designs*, 2nd edn, paras 10.3–1.11). Under the Copyright Act 1956, a plaintiff had to prove knowledge. The test of 'reason to believe' is easier to satisfy and in broad terms is designed to catch the person 'who turns a blind eye'. The provisions as to secondary infringement are expressed to be (as they are in any event) subject to the provisions of arts 30–36 of the EC Treaty.

This will be relevant where a broadcaster has licensed the manufacture and/or sale of recordings in another member state.

Copyright in a broadcast is also infringed where a third party retransmits the broadcast by a telecommunications system (otherwise than by broadcasting or inclusion in a cable programme service), knowing or having reason to believe that infringing copies of the broadcast will be made by means of the reception of the transmission in the UK or elsewhere (s 24(2)). At first sight, this might appear to apply to the case of a person using satellite facilities up-linked from the UK for the purposes of rebroadcasting or cabling by third parties outside the UK. This is because the broadcaster will often dub the transmission prior to broadcasting it to his audience. However, the recording will be made outside the UK and it is unlikely that any steps would be taken to import it into the UK. Hence the recording will not be an infringing copy.

Restrictions on exclusive rights

8.57 *'Substantial part'*   In order to establish infringement of copyright in a satellite broadcast it is necessary to show that use has been made of a 'substantial part' of the broadcast (s 16(3)(*a*)). Under the 1956 Act, the copyright restricted acts in relation to (television) broadcasts applied to any sequence of images sufficient to be seen as a moving picture (s 14(6)). However, it is now provided that 'copying' will occur where a photograph is made of the whole or any substantial part of any image forming part of the broadcast (s 17(4)). A similar interpretation should therefore be given to the restricted act of issuing copies to the public (s 18(1)).

What is the position in relation to other exclusive rights, namely performance rights? In *British Broadcasting Corporation* v *British Satellite Broadcasting Ltd* [1988] 3 WLR 174, the defendants were satellite broadcasters who had made use of highlights of the BBC's coverage of the football world cup as part of their own sports news programme. Some excerpts varied between 14 and 37 seconds, and others were of approximately five seconds each. Each excerpt was shown a number of times per day and concentrated on significant events in a particular match, including goals scored. Subject to the defence of fair dealing (see *below*), the defendants accepted (at p 176H) that they had made use of a substantial part of the BBC's broadcasts. This concession was rightly made.

Under the 1988 Act, it is likely that the unauthorised use of any sequence of moving images would be use of a substantial part of the broadcast. Even though there is no provision equivalent to s 17(4) as regards performance rights, there is no reason why the use of a still image should not amount to a substantial part of the broadcast. Some support for this construction is to be found in the definition of 'programme' in the context of broadcasts, which includes 'any item' (s 6(3)).

Once it has been shown that use has been made of a substantial part of a satellite broadcast transmission, the next issue is whether the user can rely on the 'fair dealing' provisions of the 1988 Act or other exempting provisions thereunder. This question is also relevant where the broadcaster has himself made use of a substantial part of one or more copyright works in his broadcasts, including parts of other broadcasts. In order to show that use amounts to fair dealing, two basic elements must be established. First, that the relevant use of the broadcast or other work amounts to fair dealing and secondly, that such use falls within one or more of the specific enabling provisions of the 1988 Act.

8.58 *Fair dealing* The concept of fair dealing is impossible to define and is a question of degree and impression: see *Hubbard* v *Vosper* [1972] 2 QB 84, *per* Lord Denning MR at p 94. Fair dealing will depend on a number of factors, including the amount of material used. It may be relevant to consider trade practice, by taking into account what other broadcasters consider to be an acceptable amount to use from a copyright work (*Sillitoe* v *McGraw-Hill Book Co* [1983] FSR 545). It was formerly considered that use by a trade rival so as to attract customers could not amount to fair dealing (*Associated Newspapers Group plc* v *News Group Newspapers Ltd* [1986] RPC 515).

However, *BBC* v *BSB* showed that this was not necessarily so:

> The fact that the other broadcaster is a commercial rival of the copyright owner does not *ipso facto* take the case outside fair dealing. It is a factor and in some cases a very weighty factor, to be taken into account . . . Nor in my opinion, is a commercial rival seeking to build up its broadcasting business . . . in any worse position than a commercial rival already well established in the broadcasting industry . . . The building up of audience loyalty is no more an oblique motive than the retention of audience loyalty. (*per* Scott J at p 186D.)

In concluding that the use made was fair dealing, the judge took into account the fact that the excerpts were short in comparison with the duration of the matches, and that BSB could not be criticised for repeating the offending programmes in successive news reports over a 24-hour period, or for repeating each excerpt up to three times in each news report, or for taking the 'best bits', ie the goal-scoring sequences (at p 186E–H; see also *Time Warner Entertainments Co* v *Channel Four Corp & Anr* [1994] EMLR 1).

8.59   Fair dealing with a 'work' (which includes all types of copyright subject-matter, including other broadcasts), for the purpose of criticism or review of that or another work or of a performance of a work, does not infringe copyright provided that it is accompanied by a 'sufficient acknowledgement' (s 30(1)). This means an acknowledgement identifying the work in question by its title or other description and identifying the 'author' (including another broadcaster, where relevant), unless in the case of a published work it is published anonymously, or if the work is unpublished, the author cannot be identified by reasonable enquiry (ss 9 and 178). The author is to be distinguished from the copyright owner.

Consideration should also be given to acknowledgements in respect of underlying works.

Fair dealing with a 'work' (other than a photograph) for the purpose of reporting current events does not infringe copyright, provided that (save in respect of the reporting of current events by means of a sound recording, film, broadcast or cable programme) a sufficient acknowledgement is given (s 30(2),(3)). The material does not have to be 'current', provided that it is used for reporting current events (*Associated Newspapers Group plc* v *News Group Newspapers Ltd*). This provision was successfully invoked in *BBC* v *BSB* where use was

made of the broadcast material for a dedicated sports news programme, which was distinguished from a programme of football
analysis or review. The judge did not regard the fair dealing defence
before him as a 'borderline case'.

The ephemeral right may be exercised by broadcasters only if the
recording is used for no purpose other than broadcasting and is
destroyed within 28 days of being first used for broadcasting. If the
recording is used for other purposes, it is treated as an infringing
copy for such purposes, and for all purposes if it is not destroyed
within the statutory period (s 68).

8.60   *Other exemptions*   Copyright is not infringed by the incidental inclusion of protected material in a satellite broadcast. However, this does not extend to the use of musical works, or words
spoken or sung with music (s 31(1),(3)). Accordingly, copyright
liability does arise in respect of background music which is protected by copyright.

In certain circumstances, copyright may subsist in spoken words.
This could pose practical problems for broadcasters dealing with
interviews with politicians and others. The copyright could be used
to enable the speaker to require the broadcaster to edit out words
that he found to be embarrassing. Provision is made to avoid this
situation. Where any written or other record of spoken words is
made for the purpose of reporting current events, or of broadcasting
or including in a cable programme service the whole or part of the
work, it is not an infringement of any copyright in the words as a
literary work to use the record or material taken from it (or to copy
the record, or any such material, and use the copy), provided that
certain conditions are met. These are that the record is a direct
recording of the spoken words, the speaker did not prohibit (in
advance) the making or use of the recording, the recording did not
infringe any other copyright in the work and the use is made by or
with the authority of a person who is lawfully in possession of the
record (s 58). Accordingly, there is no need to seek and obtain
consent, merely to ensure that there has not been any relevant
prohibition.

8.61   Recordings of broadcasts may be made for private and domestic use for time-shifting purposes. Such recording neither infringes the copyright in the broadcast nor in the underlying works
(s 70). Still photographs may also be made for private and domestic use. This does not infringe the copyright in the broadcast or in
any underlying film (s 71).

Exceptions are made in favour of educational establishments (s 35). No infringement will occur in respect of acts done under statutory authority (s 50). Provision is made excepting the making and supply of recordings of broadcasts to the hard of hearing and handicapped people (s 74). Certain archival recordings may also be made (s 75).

Statutory licensing/the Copyright Tribunal

8.62   The 1988 Act contains a framework for the statutory licensing of copyrights, which is broadly confined to rights owned or administered by collecting societies. The statutory scheme is not appropriate for the licensing of pan-European broadcasts, even where services are up-linked from the UK. This is because non-UK copyrights are involved in the licensing of pan-European services. However, the scheme under the 1988 Act is at present relevant, eg in relation to encrypted services directed solely at the UK.

The basis of the statutory scheme is that persons or organisations who require licences, or do not wish to accept licence terms offered by the licensor, or, in some cases, require the extension of an existing licence, may apply to the Copyright Tribunal which may determine the appropriate royalty rate and other disputed terms. A statutory licence arises once the matter has been determined by the tribunal, save where an application is made before the expiry of a current licence (s 126(1)). The new statutory licence for broadcasting introduced by the BA in respect of 'sound recordings' does not apply to video (including music video) (ss 135A–G of the 1988 Act). However, it would apply to satellite radio services up-linked from the UK, subject to the comments made above in relation to jurisdiction.

The statutory framework applies to, broadly, two types of case (see also s 144). First, where a 'licensing body' operates or seeks to operate a 'licensing scheme' in which any user who falls within the scheme may exploit the licensor's copyright on terms specified in the scheme; eg a scheme applying to the dubbing and broadcasting/cabling within Europe of specified literary and musical works (ss 117–23). The second class of case arises where a licensing body is already in a 'one-to-one' contractual relationship with a user who wishes to continue exploiting the licensor's repertoire after the expiry (by effluxion of time) of its current licence (see *above*), or where the licensor has 'proposed terms' to a user. In both cases, the actual or prospective user may refer any disputed terms to the tribunal (ss 124–128).

8.63   The task of the tribunal is to decide upon licence terms which are 'reasonable in the circumstances'. In determining what is reasonable, the tribunal must have regard to all relevant considerations and must specifically take into account the availability of other licences or licensing schemes (as the case may be) and the terms thereof, and must ensure that there is no unreasonable discrimination between licensees (ss 129 and 135). In determining what is reasonable, the tribunal will have regard to, *inter alia*, the history of the dealings between the parties, and evidence of the value of the copyright to the licensee's business. Typical disputes between broadcasters and collecting societies concern the proper method of valuing the licensed copyright to the broadcaster. Sometimes a flat fee is appropriate; on other occasions a percentage of relevant revenue (eg *Independent Television Companies Association Ltd* v *PRS* PRT No 38/81 (unreported) 5 February 1982; *Association of Independent Radio Contractors* v *Phonographic Performance Ltd* CT 9/91 (unreported) 26 February 1993, and *Singapore Broadcasting Corporation* v *PRS* [1991] FSR 573). The tribunal may take into account royalty rates charged outside the UK, which will be useful in assisting the tribunal unless differences in royalty rates are attributable to objective and relevant dissimilarities. There is an interesting relationship in this context between the applicable provisions of the 1988 Act (ss 116–152) and art 86 of the EC Treaty. However, it is often difficult to show that royalty rates charged outside the UK are relevant; *Association of Independent Radio Contractors* v *Phonographic Performance Ltd*; see however, *Singapore Broadcasting Corp* v *PRS*. The tribunal must also take account of the level of payments for underlying rights and (where applicable) any extra audience served by cable operators which was not taken into account in determining the royalty charges payable for any broadcast transmission (ss 133 and 134). A failure to have regard to relevant criteria will amount to an error of law, which renders the decision of the tribunal susceptible to appeal (s 152). Similarly, taking into account irrelevant considerations will also amount to such an error (see, eg *Association of Independent Radio Contractors Ltd* v *Phonographic Performance Ltd* (unreported) 16 January 1986, decision of Harman J).

The draft regulation contains proposed amendments to the provisions in the 1988 Act relating to the tribunal, as necessitated by the directive (see Appendix C).

Remedies for infringement

8.64   Satellite broadcasters and other copyright owners have remedies available to them for infringement of their exclusive rights. The remedies include damages, injunctions, accounts and otherwise, as are available in respect of the infringement of any other property right (s 96(2)). This general right is defined in the ensuing provisions of the 1988 Act (ss 97–102) and is subject to the rules at common law and equity: see *Copinger and Skone James on Copyright*, 13th edn, Chapter 11.

Rights in performances

8.65   Performers and persons having 'recording rights' (usually record companies) are granted certain rights under Part II of the 1988 Act, known as 'rights in performances'. These rights are contemplated by the Rome Convention. Pending implementation of the Term Directive, the rights last until the end of the period of 50 years from the end of the calendar year in which the performance takes place (s 191). Restrictions are imposed on the transmissibility of these rights (s 192). The draft regulation also contains amendments to Part II of the 1988 Act. The amendments are made in the context of the Rental Directive. It is not appropriate to consider those proposals in this work, particularly as it is understood that they may be subject to significant revision. However, it is relevant to point out that the proposals do envisage the creation of a right to reasonable remuneration in respect of the broadcast use of licensed sound recordings (proposed s 184A).

Rights in performances apply to dramatic performances (including dance and mime), musical performances, the reading or recitation of literary works and performances of variety acts or similar presentations (s 180(2)(*d*)). The performances to which rights in performances relate are those given by citizens, subjects or residents of the UK, any EU member state or of any country (typically a party to the Rome Convention) which grants reciprocal protection and is designated as such, or performances given in any of the foregoing countries (ss 181, 206 and 208; the Performances (Reciprocal Protection) (Convention Countries) Order 1993 (SI No 943) (see Appendix 1)).

In the case of performers' rights, their consent (see s 193) is required for the recording (for broadcasting purposes) and/or broadcasting of the whole or any substantial part of their live performances (s 182). Their consent is also required for the broadcasting of recordings of performances, where the recording was made without the consent of the performers and where the broadcaster has reason to believe that no such consent has been given (s 183). This provision will require a close reading if and when the amendments proposed by the draft regulation are brought into force (see proposed s 184A and proposed amendments to the definition of 'recording' in s 180(2)).

8.66   The basic definition of a person who may own recording rights is any company incorporated under the laws of the UK, of any EU member state, or of any designated country which provides reciprocal protection, having a place of business at which substantial business is carried on in any of these countries, who is party to and has the benefit of 'an exclusive recording contract' or is an assignee of the benefit of such a contract. However, if the party to an exclusive recording contract (having the benefit thereof) is not such a person, his licensee (where licensed to make recordings of the relevant performances 'with a view to their commercial exploitation') or the assignee of such a licensee may own recording rights, provided that he is a person who satisfies the foregoing qualification requirements (ss 185(1)–(3), 206 and 208).

An exclusive recording contract is an agreement made between a performer and another person, whereby that other person has the sole and exclusive right to make recordings of one or more of the performer's performances 'with a view to their commercial exploitation', ie with a view to the recordings being sold, hired, shown or played in public (s 185(1),(4)).

A person having recording rights may prohibit the making of any recording of a live performance which is subject to an exclusive recording contract, provided that the performer has not given consent to the recording (s 186(1)). Where a recording of such a performance has been made without the consent of the person having recording rights or of the performer, the former may prohibit any broadcasting of the performance, provided that the performer has given no such consent (s 187).

Similar provisions to those relating to copyright apply to fair dealing and other permitted acts (Sched 2). The Copyright Tribunal is empowered to grant a statutory licence to (among others) broadcasters, where the identity or whereabouts of a performer cannot be ascertained by reasonable enquiry, or a performer unreasonably withholds his consent (s 190). Infringements of performers' rights are actionable as a breach of statutory duty and orders for delivery up may be made (ss 194, 195 and 197).

Moral rights

8.67   Certain persons are granted 'moral rights' under Part 1 of the 1988 Act. These consist of the right to be identified as author and the right to object to derogatory treatment (see generally ss 77–83, 87–89, 94, 95 and 103; see also s 85, right to privacy in respect of commissioned films and photographs). An infringement is actionable as a breach of statutory duty and the courts are empowered to grant injunctions restraining derogatory treatment unless an appropriate disclaimer is inserted in the broadcast (s 103).

Authors of copyright literary works (other than works intended to be sung or spoken with music) or of dramatic works have the right to be identified as such where such works are broadcast. The right also applies where adaptations of the works have been made (s 77(2)). Similar provision is made for authors of copyright artistic works, where visual images thereof are broadcast (s 77(4)). Film directors have the right to be similarly identified where copyright films are broadcast. The identification must be such as to bring the identity of the relevant person to the attention of the viewer and the identification must be clear and reasonably prominent (s 77(6) and (7)).

However, the rights have to be asserted in a specified manner as a precondition to their exercise (s 78). The rights are not infringed if the fair dealing or certain other exempting provisions would apply to exempt the broadcast use from copyright infringement, and the rights do not apply to any work made for the purposes of reporting current events (s 79(4) and (5)).

Authors and film directors of copyright works are also granted a statutory right to object to 'derogatory treatment' of their works. 'Treatment' essentially means any addition to, deletion from or alteration or adaptation of the work. Treatment will be derogatory if it amounts to a distortion or mutilation of the work or is otherwise prejudicial to the honour or reputation of the author or director (s 80(1) and (2)). The right does not apply to works made for the purposes of reporting current events.

Rights in encrypted transmissions

The international perspective

8.68   Some transmissions are encrypted so as to deliver by satellite and other means 'entertainment' and information services or confidential business communications. Many different encrypted services are 'up-linked' from a variety of states and are intended for reception either within the state where the up-link is situated and/ or outside it.

Entertainment services are encrypted as part of a 'pay-TV' service, often a film channel. Encrypted transmissions are also widely used to distribute confidential business information, such as new pricing structures from a corporate head office to retail branches. In addition, financial information services often require encryption, where the service is subscriber-based and is not funded by advertising.

The deregulation of national rules relating to the provision of satellite services is creating an expanding market in point-to-multipoint and two-way services. In order for this market to fulfil its potential, the secrecy of confidential transmissions must be preserved. The cross-border nature of satellite transmissions means that adequate legal protection of encrypted services cannot be based exclusively on national laws.

8.69   The need to protect encrypted transmissions from unauthorised reception is best illustrated by reference to pay-TV services. The difficulty usually arises where third parties decipher the encryption system and then manufacture decoders without the consent of the programme provider.

In the case of pay-TV services, the programme provider needs to retain control over the distribution and use of decoders in order to control the size and location of the audience, so as to collect money from viewers in order to fund the pay service and to remunerate rights owners, whose material has been included in the service. In the case of satellite-delivered services, potential viewers are spread across a number of different countries within the footprint of the satellite. The rights acquired by the broadcaster are usually limited by territory. Although the satellite footprint invariably extends beyond the licensed territory, the licensee will be authorised to supply decoders only within that territory. Difficulties arise when persons outside the licensed territory obtain or use decoders without the consent of the broadcaster or of the rights owners. (For the consequences in EC law, see paras 8.18 *et seq.*)

The following examples illustrate the transnational nature of the problem:

(1)   Pay-TV service A is up-linked from State Z and is intended for reception in States Y and Z. Unauthorised persons manufacture and sell in State Y decoders designed to enable persons to watch service A.

(2)   Pay-TV service B is intended for reception in territory X. Decoders are not issued outside that territory by the broadcaster, but the footprint of the satellite extends over most of Europe, including the UK. Service B is transmitted in English and subtitles are inserted at the cable head-ends in territory X. Service C is intended for reception in the UK and includes films which have been licensed to service B. Unauthorised third parties manufacture and distribute decoders in the UK designed to enable persons to watch service B.

The answers to these types of problem depend upon the terms of relevant national laws. However, such laws are often inadequate to assist aggrieved programme providers and rights owners.

8.70   France and the UK have enacted specific laws on the protection of encrypted programmes (see ss 297 and 298 of the 1988 Act; French *Code Pénal* art 429). In other EU member states, protection may be available under more general laws, in particular unfair competition and telecommunications; in the latter case pursuant to the ITU Convention and the RRs. The decision in *BSkyB Ltd and Others* v *Hi–Tech Innovative Electronics Ltd and Another* 19, 22 July 1993 (unreported) indicates that national copyright laws may be used to restrain the manufacture of and dealing in unauthorised decoders. The decision was interlocutory only and was based on an *ex parte* application. It was held to be arguable that UK copyright protection should be granted in respect of the decryption system used by BSkyB. Relief was also granted on the basis of s 298 of the 1988 Act.

However, the national laws referred to *above* are often insufficient to create adequate protection. Equally, the specific national laws designed to protect encrypted transmissions are of territorial application only. UK legislation contemplated the creation of a series of bilateral arrangements between states which create reciprocal protection for senders of encrypted services up-linked from the UK and other states in question (ss 298 and 299 of the 1988 Act). It would take many years to create a multilateral framework based on reciprocal arrangements.

The decision of the House of Lords in *BBC Enterprises Ltd* v *Hi-Tech Xtravision Ltd*, *op cit*, shows that national laws can be framed so as to provide some protection in respect of decoders supplied for use outside national boundaries. In that case, Hi-Tech were manufacturing decoders in the UK which were to be sold to customers abroad to enable them to receive the BBC TV Europe television service. The footprint of the satellite extended from the Azores to Turkey and from Spain to Scandinavia. Hi-Tech's customers were located throughout Europe. The House of Lords decided that an injunction should be granted to restrain the manufacture of decoders for use outside the jurisdiction.

8.71   In its discussion paper on copyright questions concerning cable and satellite broadcasts (*Broadcasting and the Internal Market*), November 1990; 111/F/5263/90 EN), the European Commission indicated that it proposed to give separate consideration to the necessary framework for the protection of encrypted services and noted that:

> If encryption is to be effective, however, both the satellite broadcaster and the owners of rights in the individual programme components must be protected against the decoding of signals using equipment which was not put into circulation by the broadcaster himself or by third parties acting with his consent. (para 4.3.2)

It will be difficult for dealers in unauthorised decoding apparatus to show that national laws directed at suppressing their activities infringe the provisions in the Treaty of Rome relating to the free movement of goods; see para 8.16.

It is suggested that a European convention for the protection of encrypted transmissions (and an EC Directive) would supplement to a significant degree the existing legal protection of encrypted services in and beyond Europe. The basic mechanism of the convention or the directive would be to require contracting or member states to grant appropriate remedies in respect of unauthorised decoders manufactured, imported, let on hire or sold within their territory. Such protection would be granted in respect of any service up-linked from within a relevant state or, alternatively, where the broadcaster or sender of the encrypted transmission had its real and effective establishment in such a state.

8.72 A convention should also address the so-called 'Filmnet problem'. This arose where films broadcast by Filmnet for reception in Scandinavia had negative effects on the potential audience in the UK of BSkyB for the same film. This was caused by the availability of unauthorised Filmnet decoders in the UK (see example (2) *above*). The Filmnet problem is clearly transnational in nature and merits treatment in a general convention on encrypted services. Specific UK legislation on the point should also be enacted by way of further amendment to the 1988 Act. Even though the protection granted under that Act against manufacturers of and dealers in relevant decoders can now be made available to services up-linked outside the UK (whether or not the receiver state has provided corresponding protection to services up-linked from the UK), it is unlikely that Filmnet and other broadcasters would have a sufficient commercial interest in bringing proceedings in the English courts since their rights do not extend to the UK. Accordingly, further legislation is necessary to enable the broadcaster which suffers the diminution in subscription revenue to bring proceedings.

UK law

8.73 Under the 1988 Act, rights in encrypted transmissions are conferred on:

(*a*) a person who makes charges for the reception of programmes included in a broadcasting or cable programme service provided from a place in the UK; or

(*b*) a person who sends encrypted transmissions of any other description from a place in the United Kingdom. (s 298(1).)

A broadcaster is likely to fall within the definition of a 'person who makes charges', even if the charges are made by a third party, eg where members of the public buy decoders from a third party, who accounts to the broadcaster for a proportion of the purchase price. A person falling within s 298(1) is entitled to the same rights and remedies as a copyright owner against any person who makes, imports or sells or lets for hire any apparatus or device designed or adapted to enable or assist persons to receive the programmes or other transmissions when they are not entitled to do so (s 298(2)(*a*)). Similar provision is made as to the publication of information calculated to enable or assist persons to receive the encrypted programmes or other transmissions. The word 'entitled' means 'authorised' (*BBC Enterprises Ltd v Hi-Tech Xtravision Ltd*). In *British*

Sky Broadcasting Group Ltd v *David Lyons* [1995] FSR 357, s 298 was held to be compatible with EC Treaty provisions relating to the free movement of goods (see para 8.18 *above*).

8.74   The following are, under the Act, criminal offences:

(*a*)   dishonest reception of programmes included in a broadcasting or cable programme service with intent to avoid payment (s 297(1)); see also s 43 TA;

(*b*)   importation, sale, or letting on hire of any 'unauthorised' decoder, being a decoder which will enable persons to avoid payment of the charges applicable to the reception of programmes included in a broadcasting or cable programme service which is provided from a place in the UK (s 297A).

An 'unauthorised' decoder in the context of s 297A is a decoder which will enable encrypted transmissions to be viewed in decoded form without payment of the fee (however imposed) which the person making the transmission, or on whose behalf it is made, charges for viewing those transmissions, or viewing any service of which they form part (s 297A(1)).

Provision is made for extending the application of ss 297 and 298 to transmissions sent from other countries (s 299(1)).

The terms 'broadcasting', 'programme', 'cable programme service' and related expressions have the same meaning as in Part 1 of the 1988 Act. Sections 297 and 298 also apply to ancillary telecommunication services (s 299(4)).

Conclusion

8.75   Rapid advances in satellite technology, particularly in the field of DTH satellite broadcasts, have had a considerable impact on the legal frameworks for copyright and related rights. Despite recent attempts to harmonise and modernise the law in these fields, technological developments are still ahead of legal measures and are likely to remain so in the near future.

III

Commercial Contracts in the Satellite Sector

9

Satellite Construction Contracts

Introduction

9.1   As in all industry sectors, the legal aspects of business in the satellite sector are both general and specialised. In broad terms, contracts are for services or equipment and the usual principles of commercial law and practice apply. A satellite construction or procurement contract will, therefore, resemble the procurement agreement for any other major item of industrial equipment.

However, being a specialised field, there are a number of key specialised legal provisions that one would expect to see in contracts relating to the various types of commercial transaction in the satellite sector. They derive from the special legal, commercial and technical characteristics of that sector and it is upon these special legal provisions that Chapters 9, 10, 11 and 12 will concentrate. These chapters do not purport to provide a comprehensive or exhaustive review of the provisions that would be present in the various contracts examined; they seek merely to highlight and explain those provisions that might be regarded as unusual for those not accustomed to negotiating contracts in this field.

This chapter deals with satellite construction or procurement contracts, being contracts normally made between the actual or prospective satellite system operator (the purchaser) and the satellite manufacturer (the vendor) for the construction and sale of the physical satellite itself often together with associated earth-segment equipment and support services.

Chapter 10 deals with satellite launch contracts, namely contracts between a satellite system operator wishing to launch a satellite and the provider of launch services. Chapter 11 deals with satellite transponder contracts, being contracts between a satellite system operator and a person wishing to use capacity on the satellite. Chapter 12 deals with interconnection contracts between any two satellite or terrestrial network infrastructure providers.

It should be stressed that the comments made in these chapters are based on the use of these contracts in the commercial field. The procurement of satellites and launch services and the use of satellite capacity does, of course, occur on a wide scale in the military and scientific fields—the comments below would be of limited relevance in these contexts.

Satellite construction contracts

General comments

9.2   Satellite construction contracts are a relatively recent development in legal terms, being a consequence of the rapid development in the commercial use of satellites. They derive from and are based upon commercial aircraft contracts. Many aspects of a satellite construction contract will be the same, in legal terms, as those of an aircraft construction contract. This chapter will provide an overview of the anatomy of a satellite construction contract and then move on to examine provisions that tend to be drafted in particular ways. First, however, the process of satellite procurement is worthy of a few words.

Satellite procurement

9.3   Normally, the process of satellite procurement begins with the prospective satellite purchaser putting together a set of specifications for the satellite that is needed. These will then be developed into an 'invitation to tender' or 'request for proposals' to be circulated to selected satellite manufacturers. It is wise to include in these invitations to tender or requests for proposals a form of the contract that the satellite purchaser will require. If this is done, each manufacturer will be able to submit a tender or proposal including not only all the technical and financial details relating to the satellite construction, but also amendments that it would require in order to agree the form of contract. This will allow the contractual amendments to be evaluated by the satellite purchaser's lawyers at the same time as the technical and financial evaluation takes place. The way a manufacturer deals with some contractual provisions can have a major impact if dealt with in a different way by other tendering manufacturers. For example, the transfer of risk provisions will have a tangible financial effect and bearing upon the question of who pays the insurance premiums (this is dealt with in greater detail *below*).

Once the evaluation procedure is completed and the successful tender selected, the existence of a pre-prepared contract and pre-existing amendments will mean that the final contract negotiations can be taken forward from a fairly advanced stage, thus streamlining the process of settling the contract.

Anatomy of a satellite construction contract

9.4 There is no settled and fast rule as to what should and should not be included in a satellite construction contract. However, set out below is a checklist of typical provisions some of which will be obvious, others less so. The list is not exhaustive but is a useful guide when drafting or reviewing a satellite construction contract. There follows a more detailed review of the particular provisions.

Checklist of typical provisions

9.5
- Scope of work
- Delivery schedule
- Provisions applicable during construction
- Inspection and acceptance
- Correction
- Risk and title
- Prices and payment
- *Force majeure* / excusable delays
- Patent and data rights
- Warranties
- Liability and indemnity
- Personnel and logistical support
- Changes
- Assignment
- Termination

- Language
- Notices
- Entire agreement
- Arbitration
- Governing law

Clause-by-clause review

Scope of work

9.6 These provisions detail the work to be done, equipment to be supplied and services to be provided. This is most often dealt with by reference to a technical schedule (deriving from the proposal originally put forward by the manufacturer) which will set out specifications and performance criteria for the satellite and associated ground segment equipment. Because the fundamental legal obligations of the manufacturer are dependent on the terms of the technical specification it is essential that the lawyers and engineers work together to ensure that the contract and the technical schedules are consistent and compatible. Too often the legal provisions of the contract and the technical schedules are developed entirely independently by lawyers and engineers, leaving a massive task of integrating the two (the task being so difficult that from some agreements it is clear that it has never been properly done). The services to be provided should include launch support and general support throughout the life of the satellite. Furthermore, if the satellite needs to be stored between its completion and launch, these provisions may include a requirement that the manufacturer store and/or maintain the satellite.

Delivery schedule

9.7 This provision is entirely dependent on what is negotiated by the parties. It should, of course, be remembered that many satellite construction programmes will be faced with a very specific deadline: the launch slot (that is, the date on which the launch is scheduled). Launches on any launch vehicle need to be reserved many months and often years in advance—therefore it is critical to put in place a delivery schedule which ties in with the arranged launch date. This should also deal with where (as well as when) the satellite, other equipment and software or documentation should be delivered.

Provisions applicable during construction

9.8   A purchaser will need to be in a position to scrutinise progress of the satellite construction programme: the availability of the satellite at a particular time will be crucial to both meeting the launch deadline and developing the purchaser's business through the use of the satellite once in orbit. As a satellite cannot be repaired once launched, both purchaser and manufacturer will wish to be as certain as possible that the satellite is being built on schedule and according to specifications. It is therefore customary for the purchaser to be given progress and status reports by the manufacturer throughout the construction period. It may also be useful to have prearranged review meetings. The purchaser should also seek access to the manufacturer's construction facilities and all data relating to the construction programme.

Inspection and acceptance

9.9   This procedure is, of course, crucial: in general terms the satellite cannot be altered once launched, and the manufacturer will want the purchaser to 'sign off' that the completed satellite meets its specifications. This procedure is also significant in respect of the transfer of risk (see *below*). A purchaser will normally want to undertake a pre-shipment review prior to the satellite leaving the manufacturer's premises and then finally accept the satellite once it is delivered to the launch site or (if relevant, and if not at the manufacturer's facilities) delivery of the satellite to the purchaser's designated storage facility. The manufacturer, by contrast, may want to achieve 'acceptance' at its own premises prior to shipment. There will also be different inspection and acceptance procedures for equipment other than the satellite itself and any associated software and documentation.

Correction

9.10   The inspection and acceptance procedure referred to *above* should include provision to correct or alter the satellite to conform to its specification. However, there may also be grounds for the satellite to be modified after acceptance. Satellites are normally taken from a series of basic designs and so there may be other satellites of the same series in use. If one of these satellites were to develop a problem requiring a modification to the basic design, it would be wise for the purchaser to oblige the manufacturer to make relevant modifications to its satellite at any time up to launch (whether before or after formal acceptance).

Risk and title

9.11   The purchaser will wish to ensure that it will obtain good title to all the equipment which is to be provided under the terms of the contract. This will normally be included as a fundamental warranty in the contract. It may be worthwhile separating this warranty from others: the manufacturers may have reasonable arguments as to why warranties should be tempered (see *below*) but they will not apply to the warranty on title.

The question of when title and risk should pass is open to negotiation. The financial consequence is obvious—who bears the insurance premiums? Risk and title in equipment other than the satellite will normally pass on final acceptance (which may well be after installation). There is no settled rule as to when title and risk in the satellite itself should pass. The critical point could be anywhere between shipment from the manufacturer's premises (either to the launch site or to storage) and launch of the satellite. As manufacturers often take on the responsibility of looking after a satellite during shipment to the launch site and preparing the satellite for launch, it is not unreasonable for title and risk to pass on launch. However, even this can be problematic. The question of when launch occurs can be difficult to settle and can have serious financial consequences. Launch could be deemed to occur on intentional ignition (ie ignition of the first stage engines of the launch vehicle provided that it is followed by opening of the table clamps (where they are used) with consequent release of the launch vehicle). However, some of the launch vehicles, such as Ariane, remain clamped to the ground for several seconds thereafter while the power builds up until the clamps are released (often referred to as 'clamps off'). This period can be the most expensive to insure in the satellite's life. Thus, the issue of who bears risk between intentional ignition and 'clamps-off' must be addressed if the satellite manufacturer will not take risk beyond intentional ignition.

Prices and payment

9.12   These provisions should fix the prices to be paid for the entire package of spacecraft, equipment and services. They should also set out the payment terms and any procedures for adjustment of the prices payable. Satellite construction has become a highly competitive business over the last 20 years. As a result, there is no standard approach to payment terms and schedules. Satellite manufacturers are becoming increasingly creative in putting financial proposals forward when submitting their tenders to prospective purchasers. The permutations are endless and range from a straight delivery payment to an option on the part of the manufacturer to acquire shares in the purchaser. In cases where the construction project has been put out to tender, the drafting of the prices and payment terms will be based on the financial proposal put forward by the manufacturer. Typical methods of dealing with payment terms include three schemes (which could be used separately or combined):

(*a*)   payments in instalments during the construction period;

(*b*)   a lump sum payment on acceptance;

(*c*)   payments during the projected life of the satellite on an instalment basis (often called 'incentive payments').

Incentive payments are, of course, particularly attractive to purchasers, because the payments are due to be made only when the satellite is in use and therefore capable of generating revenue for the purchaser.

The payment terms should include specific provisions relating to the adjustment of the prices payable (and / or the payment schedule) in the event of particular circumstances. These might be in addition to, or as an alternative to, remedies for breach of contract. For example, if there is a delay in the construction programme which results in the satellite being delivered too late to meet its scheduled launch date, the purchaser will be faced with the costs of cancelling and refixing the launch date—costs which might properly be taken into account in an adjustment to the purchase price.

Furthermore, if the satellite ceases to perform during its lifetime in whole or in part (which may well be as a result of a non-attributable fault), incentive payments should be cancelled or reduced *pro rata* to the reduction in the revenue-earning potential of the satellite. If there are no incentive payments there might instead be refunds if the satellite does not remain fully operational throughout its projected life.

Force majeure/*excusable delays*

9.13   It is not unreasonable to expect an appropriately drafted *force majeure* (sometimes described as 'excusable delays') provision in a satellite construction contract. However, in considering how the *force majeure* provision should work, it is important to bear in mind the financial consequences of delays (mentioned *above*) and to establish which of the parties agrees to bear what proportion of the associated costs (which may be distilled down to the question of who is liable to pay the relevant insurance premiums).

Patent and data rights

9.14   The purchaser will require the right to use all data and documentation provided to it in order to operate the satellite system after delivery. The manufacturer may, however, wish to temper this by imposing a duty of confidentiality and non-disclosure upon the purchaser. The purchaser will also need a licence (usually non-exclusive) to use all patents involved in the satellite and equipment delivered to it. Furthermore, the manufacturer should take on the obligation of resolving any patent infringement problem deriving from the use of third party patents in the satellite and associated equipment and should indemnify the purchaser against any liability occasioned by such an infringement.

Warranties

9.15   In addition to the warranty relating to title referred to *above*, other warranties typical of contracts for the supply of goods and services are appropriate. These include the following basic warranties:

(*a*)   satellite and equipment are free from defects and conform with specifications; and

(*b*)   services performed with skill and care.

The full extent of these warranties will be open to negotiation. In particular, the manufacturer may well wish to see relevant warranties limited in time for a period of, for example, 12 months from delivery. Furthermore, since a satellite cannot be repaired once launched, a manufacturer will normally insist that, with regard to the satellite itself, the warranty as to defects will apply only at launch and not thereafter.

Liability and indemnity

9.16 Most launch vehicle operators require a waiver of any claims which may arise as a result of damage to property or injury to personnel at the launch site. (It should be noted that, in English law, the Unfair Contract Terms Act 1977 operates to prevent parties from excluding liability for death or personal injury arising out of negligence (ss 2(1) and 26). This statute also contains other provisions relating to exclusion clauses. Other jurisdictions may have similar laws.) Subject to these considerations, if (as is usual) personnel and property of the manufacturer are to be at the launch site, it is wise for the purchaser to ensure that the manufacturer will agree to relevant waivers. It is also customary for the purchaser and manufacturer to indemnify one another for loss and damage caused by each of them to the other. In respect of liability for damage caused by the satellite, the manufacturer will normally expect this to cease upon launch of the satellite.

Personnel and logistical support

9.17 It may be that certain personnel of the manufacturer are critical to the purchaser's decision to do business with the manufacturer. If so, there should be a 'key man' clause dealing with the requirement that the manufacturer involve certain personnel in the project. Of course, the disadvantage of this for the manufacturer is manifest; it reduces his flexibility and could compromise his position with the relevant personnel.

As satellite construction programmes will normally be completed over a number of months (or even years) and the purchaser will want to send personnel to the manufacturer's facilities to review progress, it is customary for the manufacturer to provide the purchaser with an office and other logistical support (such as a telephone, facsimile and typing assistance) at its facilities.

Changes

9.18 As mentioned *above*, satellite construction programmes tend to be lengthy. They are also expensive. In addition to this, the satellite sector is somewhat volatile from a commercial point of view and the characteristics which may make a satellite attractive to its operator's customers one year may not do so the next. Accordingly, it is wise to put in the satellite construction contract an agreed procedure for modifying the technical specifications of the satellite, the applicable costs and associated adjustments to the delivery schedule. Obviously, this procedure needs to be reasonable and should not result in either party being obliged to do something it has not agreed to do. Equally, the procedure needs to be realistic in the context of genuine commercial pressures.

Assignment

9.19   There will normally be express provisions relating to the assignment of the benefit of the contract to supplement the normal contract law rules which apply.

There is no reason why the purchaser should not sell on the satellite, although the purchaser should not be able to avoid liability to make payments unless the manufacturer is satisfied that the assignee has the financial wherewithal to make remaining payments and therefore agrees to a novation. The manufacturer may also be subject to technology export rules which oblige it to ensure that the end recipient of the satellite and other equipment does not contravene these rules (see para 9.22 *below*).

Termination

9.20   Termination arrangements will always be open for negotiation. However, satellite construction contracts normally include provisions relating to:

(*a*)   termination on either side for breach by or insolvency of the other (where relevant, after due cure periods); and

(*b*)   termination on the part of the purchaser for convenience (normally coupled with an obligation on the purchaser to pay specified sums based on costs incurred by the manufacturer up to termination together with an appropriate premium. It is highly arguable whether the question of a penalty arises in these circumstances, at least under English law.)

The manufacturer may also wish to include in the contract a right to take over the construction of the satellite on a termination.

Language, notices, entire agreement, arbitration and governing law

9.21   These are all standard contract terms which do not require special explanation here save that it should be stressed, in a contract as highly technical as a satellite construction contract, it is essential to have an effective arbitration process: specialist experts are more likely to be able to understand and resolve a dispute than the courts.

Government approvals

9.22   Some governments (for example, the government of the USA) apply strict export rules in respect of high technology; these may apply to satellites. It should always be checked what rules apply in the country where the satellite is being constructed (if the satellite is to be exported) and, if necessary, the manufacturer should take on the obligation of obtaining any consents or approvals. There should also be a clear statement of what will happen if no such consent or approval is forthcoming within some defined time limit.

Conclusion

9.23   Properly administered, the process of agreeing a satellite construction contract should not be unduly complicated. If the major issues can be identified at an early stage, each side will be in a position to take a view on such issues in the context of the general benefits and burdens of the proposed contract. An interesting development in recent years is that the potential for satellites to be sold or otherwise dealt with (such as by way of charge) is being increasingly recognised. This is a growing area and one that is likely to become highly relevant to lawyers in the future. The key issue in the sale and purchase of an in-orbit satellite is the ability to take control of the satellite. The development of a market for in-orbit satellites has been accompanied by the growth of mechanisms for using in-orbit satellites as security for the raising of finance, or for securing existing debts.

10

Satellite Launch Contracts

General Comments

10.1 Satellite launch contracts are basically commercial contracts for provision of launch services by a satellite launching company, such as Arianespace in Europe. This chapter will provide an overview of the anatomy of a satellite launch contract and then move on to examine provisions that tend to be drafted in a particular way. First, however, the process of negotiating a satellite launch contract is worthy of a few comments.

Satellite launch services

10.2 At about the time that the process of satellite procurement begins, as outlined in the previous chapter, the purchaser of the satellite will need to consider choosing a launch services contractor and reserve a launch date for the satellite(s). Arianespace has already been mentioned, but there are a number of other companies specialising in the provision of these services. These include NASA, Lockheed-Khrunichev-Energia International Inc (the Russian launching company in which Lockheed Missiles and Space Company Inc now has an interest) and China Great Wall Industry Corporation.

Once the specifications for the particular satellite to be launched are known, it is useful for these to be put together and provided to the launch services contractor(s) by way of an invitation to tender or request for proposals, which can be circulated and subsequently returned to the purchaser by interested launch services contractors. Contracts can then be negotiated on the basis of the terms offered. Obviously, it is important that both the technical and financial details relating to the satellite launch and the technical interface with the satellite itself are correct. Also one would normally expect to receive amendments to the standard form of contract which will be submitted by the launch services contractor as with the satellite construction contract.

Anatomy of a satellite launch contract

10.3   These contracts have not yet become standardised. However, there are similarities between each satellite launch services contractor. In essence, one would expect to find the following main provisions in a contract for satellite launch services.

Checklist of typical provisions

10.4
- Services to be provided
- Launch schedule
- Launch schedule adjustments
- Contract price
- Payment
- Price adjustments
- Launch services contractor's obligations
- Re-flight or refund option
- *Force Majeure*/excusable delays
- Assignment
- Public release of information
- Limitation of liability
- Termination
- Insurance
- Government priority
- Compliance with government export requirements
- Licences, clearances and permits
- Handling of data
- Provision of post-launch, payload data
- Ownership of property
- Language
- Notices

- Entire agreement
- Arbitration
- Governing law

Clause-by-clause review

Services to be provided

10.5   The launch services contract will set out the contractor's obligations to perform all the tasks necessary to integrate the customer's satellite into the launch vehicle and any other associated services, and obviously to provide the launch services themselves.

What constitute the actual launch services will normally be defined in detailed technical annexes, which is why the lawyers, the technical advisers and the commercial negotiators need to work together carefully to ensure complete integration of the technical annexes with the text of the contract itself.

In relation to the services to be provided by the launch services contractor, care should be taken to make it clear whether the contract is for a dedicated or shared launch. This has a cost impact—shared launches are cheaper—but there is also a risk factor—shared launches can be riskier. Therefore, it is necessary to have clearly in mind which the particular customer wishes to have.

Launch schedule

10.6   The launch services contractor will publish from time to time a detailed list of its launch schedules. A launch slot is highly prized and therefore commercially valuable. However, launch service contractors do not engage in the sale of launch slots to potential customers and (as noted in Chapter 9, para 9.7) launches need to be reserved many months and often years in advance. Therefore, it is critical to put in place a launch schedule that ties in with the delivery of the satellite itself (see previous chapter).

Launch schedules can be worked out by reference to fairly complicated formulae, but it is fundamental to ensure that there is sufficient time between the completion of the construction of the satellite and the launch date for the satellite to be delivered to the launch site and for the necessary integration services and pre-flight tests to take place.

Postponement by the contractor

10.7   Postponements by the contractor can occur for various reasons. The most obvious one is where the launch services contractor suffers the unforeseen loss of a launch vehicle, which may then necessitate a lengthy delay in the satellite launch programme while the causes for the launch vehicle failure are examined and satisfactorily dealt with. Alternatively, delays can occur in civilian flights by reason of government priority.

Accordingly, the customer needs to have a clear right of rescheduling under which it can retain its position in the launch schedule and no other customer of the launch services contractor should have a preference or priority over this customer except in certain specified exceptional circumstances. Care should also be taken to make sure the payment schedule is amended to reflect the delay. Furthermore, the customer may want the right to terminate if the delay exceeds a fixed time limit, such as six months or twelve months.

Postponement by the customer

10.8   There may be reasons why the customer itself wishes to delay the launch. An obvious one is where delivery of the satellite is not going to meet the launch deadline. Customers will normally want to have this right and to limit their liability for the payment of any penalties to the launch services contractors in these circumstances. Different contractors seem to have different views on whether they are prepared to accept this. It is a matter for commercial negotiation.

Price/payment

10.9   Generally, fixed price quotations seem preferable and they should include applicable taxes. Again, this is a matter for commercial negotiation. However, the greater the risk accepted by the launch services contractor, the higher the price for the launch services.

Re-flight/replacement launches and refunds

10.10   Customers will always want the entitlement to ask for a re-flight or a replacement launch, if the initial launch is unsuccessful for any reason. In other words, if the satellite is lost or is otherwise a failure (see para 10.11 *below*), the customer will want to reschedule any replacement satellite as soon as possible. Customers may also want this right in the event that the launch is unacceptably delayed.

Generally, launch services contractors will accept that a replacement launch or reflight should be at no cost to the customer if that is required because of the loss of the first satellite. In other circumstances, normally the customer would have to pay the current price for launch of any replacement satellite lost at the initial launch.

Customers will want a re-flight/replacement launch to take place within a fixed period. Where there is no immediate replacement satellite to launch, then the re-flight option will need to take into account the necessity to build a replacement satellite.

Definitions of total loss/partial loss/constructive total loss

10.11   This is an area where the technical advisers are most important. They need to consider carefully the terms on which the satellite ceases to operate within the technical parameters that will be set out in the satellite construction contract. The technical specifications are therefore crucial.

Accordingly, customers will want to make clear that, if the satellite fails to meet the technical performance parameters because of damage to the satellite caused by the launch services contractor, this will amount to a total loss, partial loss or constructive total loss (whichever is appropriate) and give rise to a refund or other compensation.

Force majeure/excusable delays

10.12   Customers will want the payment schedule varied by any delays caused by *force majeure*/excusable delays. The customer may also want a right of termination after a specified period. Generally, see the comments on *force majeure* in Chapter 9, para 9.13.

Third party insurance/indemnity

10.13   Customers should ask launch services contractors initially to identify their proposals for insurance against damage or harm caused to third parties by the launch vehicle. In that regard, the launch services contractor should also submit proposals for indemnification of the customer in respect of any liability exceeding insured amounts or liabilities arising after the expiry of the insurance.

Termination

10.14 Launch services contractors normally should not be able to terminate otherwise than for non-payment by the customer of any sum due under the agreement and then only after a fixed cure period.

Government approvals

10.15 This is particularly important when dealing with the US government. Approval for the export of satellites from the USA must be obtained before the satellites can be delivered to the launch site. For launches within the USA this is not a problem. As noted in Chapter 9, para 9.22, the satellite manufacturer will normally deal with the export approvals for the satellite itself and the launch services contractor will want to make sure that the customer has taken all necessary steps to ensure that those licences and clearances that will be necessary to permit the launch to take place have been obtained and remain in force up to and including the time of the launch.

Launch risk guarantee

10.16 Launch services contractors sometimes provide a guarantee up to the amount necessary to cover partial loss, total loss or constructive total loss of the satellite. This may include consequential damages although launch services contractors are very reluctant to provide for this. That aspect can be dealt with by insurance.

Warranties and other provisions

10.17 As in any other form of contract, the warranties are important. Generally they should cover the following:

(*a*) that the launch services contractor will be in a position to provide a launch in accordance with the launch schedule;

(*b*) that the launch services contractor has a dedicated launch pad available for the particular launch;

(*c*) that the launch services contractor will perform any services with the highest possible level of skill and due diligence; and (*d*)   any goods to be supplied by the launch services contractor will be of the highest possible quality.

Limitation of Liability, Language, Notices, Entire Agreement, Arbitration and Governing Law

10.18   As regards provisions relating to language, notices, entire agreements, arbitration and governing law, see the comments in Chapter 9, para 9.21 and as regards limitation of liability, see the comments in Chapter 11, para 11.17.

Conclusion

10.19   As will be obvious from the foregoing chapters, it is important that the provisions of both the satellite construction contract and the launch services contract are consistent and in particular that there is consistency in relation to delivery schedules, risk and insurance, warranties and indemnities.

11

Satellite Transponder Contracts

General comments

11.1 Satellite transponder contracts are among the most common in the commercial satellite field. They are the legal basis on which a satellite operator provides satellite capacity to customers, either on a permanent or an intermittent basis. A satellite television operator will usually require a transponder on a permanent basis; some telecommunications operators require satellite capacity on a permanent basis; some businesses with Very Small Aperture (Satellite) Terminals (VSAT) systems (ie private satellite communication systems using relatively small receive/transmit equipment) will use satellite capacity on an intermittent basis; and some television operators will use capacity on an intermittent basis to transfer television programming from one location to another.

As noted in Chapter 4, obtaining access to space segment capacity is a relatively straightforward process when dealing with a private system: the customer and operator deal directly. In the case of space segment capacity on the systems of the International Satellite Organisations (ISOs), the position is more complicated and is currently in a state of flux, although progress is being made towards direct access for private parties to space segment capacity of the ISOs (see the general discussion on access to the ISOs' space segment capacity in Chapter 4).

11.2 All satellite operators have their standard form transponder contracts. As with other contracts in the satellite sector, transponder contracts are contracts for the provision of a particular service and usual commercial and legal principles apply. However, there are a number of specialised clauses that one would expect to find in transponder contracts and which are important both to the customer and the satellite operator.

In practice, the satellite operator is not able to control the content of the signal traffic transmitted from a satellite. Typically, therefore, a transponder contract contains a provision whereby the customer has an obligation to comply with all the relevant laws, policies or regulations. The applicable laws, however, can vary from contract to contract. They range from complying with all the laws, policies or regulations of *any* country within the footprint of a satellite, to where the customer must comply only with the laws, rules and regulations of the country from which the licensee transmits to the satellite and the laws of the country having jurisdication over the operation of the satellite. From the point of view of the satellite operator, the most favourable (and more normal) provision is the former one, where the customer must comply with all applicable laws, that is, the laws of all such countries where a signal is receivable.

11.3   In the context of transponder contracts, two separate issues must be considered. The first relates to which country has jurisdiction over the actual transmitting and receiving stations (the up-link and down-link stations) and the satellite itself. The second issue arises in the context of television transmissions, in respect of which laws are applicable to the content of the transmissions, especially where such transmissions are intended for direct reception by the general public, that is, direct-to-home broadcasting.

In relation to up-link and down-link sites, the Radio Regulations (RRs) of the International Telecommunication Union (ITU) provide that there should be no emission of radio waves without a licence by the government of the country where the transmitting station is located, and such licence must be in conformity with the provisions of the RRs (see Matte: *Aerospace Law, Telecommunications Satellites* (Butterworths 1982), p 68).

11.4   In relation to television transmissions from satellites, the obligation imposed in transponder contracts upon customers to comply with all laws and regulations of all the countries within the footprint of the satellite creates a much more difficult problem. There are two divergent theories as to how such a clause should be interpreted. In relation to radio broadcasting, a functional 'freedom of broadcasting' developed from 1937 onwards, when democratic states engaged in transborder radio propaganda broadcasting; at the end of the Second World War, 55 states were sending out political radio broadcasts in 40 different languages. As the receiving states did not protest against such transborder incursions, this led to a uniform state practice of acquiescence to transborder radio broadcasts. This was sufficiently general that, over a period of time, a customary rule of international law emerged—the principle of freedom of broadcasting (see Matte, *op cit*, p 68). However, it should be pointed out that this principle does not appear to apply to all specialised services transmitted by satellite. In particular, its application to direct broadcasting satellite services is controversial. The legal principles emerging from the work of the United Nations Committee on the Peaceful Uses of Outer Space (COPUOS), seem to indicate that the freedom of broadcasting principle does not apply to specialised satellite transmissions.

Some states have argued that the freedom of broadcasting principle should apply to satellite transmissions by relying on art 19 of the Universal Declaration of Human Rights ('the Universal Declaration') which states that:

> Everyone has a right to freedom of opinion and expression; this right includes the freedom to hold opinions without interference and to seek, receive and impart information and ideas through any media and regardless of frontiers.

In contrast, some states, fearing that uncontrolled international broadcasting by satellite will endanger their cultural, social, political and economic values have argued that there should be a prior agreement (prior consent) between the receiving and broadcasting or transmitting countries before television programmes are commenced by satellite, even if the service is not intended for reception in that country, but is nevertheless receivable there. This argument stresses the importance of 'national sovereignty' and the right of states to regulate broadcasting.

It has been argued that it is for each state to take whatever measures are necessary to prohibit or prevent reception of transmissions if such a state does not wish its citizens to receive there transmissions (*Autronic AG*, judgment of 22 May (12 ECHR 485)).

11.5   Attempts are still being made to reconcile the divergent principles of 'national sovereignty' and 'freedom of broadcasting', although increasingly the reality of transfrontier broadcasting by telecommunication satellites appears to be leading to a uniform practice of acquiescence by states, whereby it is up to the receiving state to take whatever steps are required to ensure that the un-authorised reception of radio communications is prohibited.

Within the EU, the question of transfrontier broadcasting has been dealt with by directive; provided transmissions meet the minimum requirements of the Television Without Frontiers Directive (89/552/EEC), then they should not be restricted by any member state of the EU (see the discussion in Chapter 7).

The two other important considerations for a customer who wishes to use satellite capacity are the price to be charged for the capacity, and the specifications (eg footprint and signal strength) of the capacity. Generally speaking, the transponder contract will be in a standard form; however, it should be ensured that the contract does at least include the performance criteria which the customer and operator have agreed.

Anatomy of a satellite transponder contract

11.6   Set out below is a checklist of typical provisions that might appear in a satellite transponder contract, together with a more detailed review of these typical provisions.

Checklist of typical provisions

11.7
- Specification
- Term/period of usage
- Charges
- Warranties
- Use of transponder
- Degradation and interruption
- Pre-emption
- Termination/effects of termination
- *Force majeure*/excusable delays
- Limitation of liability
- Subletting
- Indemnity
- Language
- Notices
- Entire agreement
- Arbitration
- Governing law

Clause-by-clause review

Specification

11.8   This provision will deal with the definition of the service that the satellite operator is to provide to the customer. It will normally refer to a technical schedule setting out the characteristics and capabilities of the satellite upon which the capacity is to be provided. The customer ought to require a minimum level of performance in terms of this satellite capacity. In the case of a telecommunications use between fixed points, this will be easy enough to establish because the strength of the satellite signals can be measured at those points. In the case of a television use, where transmission is being made over a wide area (the satellite's footprint), it may be useful to agree a set number of locations at which the satellite signal will be measured and where specific minimum performance levels will be required. Normally, from a customer's point of view, the locations chosen should be on the fringe of the satellite's footprint, where signal strength is most likely to falter.

Term/period of usage

11.9   In respect of permanent usage of satellite capacity (such as a television service), the term will normally be fixed, or the contract will be an annual or monthly 'extendable' contract. This may be varied if a customer is sharing the transponder on a permanent basis with another customer (which is not uncommon in the field of satellite television) so as to make it clear how the sharing arrangements will work (eg Customer A may have the capacity from noon until 8 pm daily and Customer B may have the capacity from 8 pm to 4 am daily).

In the case of intermittent use of the satellite capacity, this provision would need to set out how much capacity the satellite operator agrees to make available during what period.

Charges

11.10   The charges to be made will always, of course, be a matter for negotiation. Common schemes of charging include the following:

(*a*)   a fixed fee payable in advance (usually used in the case of permanent usage) if there is a fixed term;

(b)   a fixed fee in 'net present value' terms but payable in variable instalments over the term;

(c)   monthly or annual payments; or

(d)   charges calculated with reference to the amount of time that the satellite capacity is actually used—normally relevant to contracts for intermittent usage.

In any event, the charges should be subject to any refund or rebate provisions relating, eg, to degradation (see *below*).

Warranties

11.11   Normal contract warranties, such as fitness for purpose and merchantable quality, are of course relevant in this context.

Most satellite operators carry a number of competing services, whether telecommunications or television services. Thus, it is important for the satellite operator to make clear that it will provide no warranty that it will not allow its satellite to be used for services competing with that of its customer. In any case, such a warranty would be difficult to enforce, given its anti-competitive nature. In addition, since the satellite is in outer space and physically impossible to reach, the satellite operator will be reluctant to give any warranty relating to quality. However, it may not be unreasonable for the customer to ask the satellite operator to warrant that it will not do anything in its control (such as re-orientation of the satellite) to affect the quality of the service.

Use of transponder

11.12   The satellite operator may be under specific limitations as to the usage of the satellite and, accordingly, will want to impose on its customer limitations on the activities of the customer. These may cover the technical characteristics of the customer's usage and the content. The satellite operator may also impose on the customer an obligation to abide by all relevant applicable laws.

Degradation and interruption

11.13   'Degradation' is the term that is commonly used to describe a satellite's performance falling below the contractual standard. The customer may wish to have specific provisions which would include the right to a refund of money if performance falls below the minimum performance specification agreed between the parties, and, if the degradation persists, the right to terminate the contract. The satellite operator must ensure that liability in the event of a degradation in the performance of the satellite is limited. In particular, the satellite operator must make sure that it is not liable for loss of profits to the customer's business because the performance of the satellite is faltering. The satellite operator may also wish to provide that refunds for degradation apply only if degradation persists (either in one instance or cumulatively) for a period longer than a fixed minimum (such as one hour in any seven-day period).

The satellite operator should also ensure that it is empowered to interrupt the service that it provides for its customer in order to monitor and test the satellite, and for 'safety of the satellite' purposes. If the satellite is not eclipse-protected (that is, capable of avoiding interference during certain phases of the satellite's position in relation to other celestial bodies) then interruptions during an eclipse phase should also be allowed. By contrast, the customer may want to limit the amount of time during which its service can be interrupted by designating as degradations interruptions more lengthy or more frequent than a specified maximum. Furthermore, the customer ought to require the satellite operator, wherever possible, to interrupt its service at times best suited to the customer.

In terms of defining degradation, the satellite operator should make it clear that degradation will not be deemed to have occurred if the failure of the customer's signals to reach their destination is a result of a failure of the customer to provide the signals in the first place or, if the customer's signals are encrypted, a failure in the encryption system.

Pre-emption

11.14   In some circumstances where a customer is contracting for satellite capacity with a satellite operator, the service will be provided without reference to a specific transponder on the satellite. In other cases, a customer takes satellite capacity with reference to a particular transponder on the satellite. In this case, provision needs to be made for what should happen in the event that this particular transponder should fail while other transponders on the satellite (or, if the satellite operator's system comprises more than one satellite, on the system) remain available. In addressing this issue, it should be borne in mind that a satellite operator has the objective of keeping its system as full as possible (in order to maximise its revenues) thus leaving no spare capacity to cater for the failure of a transponder.

The satellite operator normally divides its customers into three categories:

(a)   those who have a right to stay on their transponder even if other transponders fail and have the right to be moved on to another transponder if their transponder fails;

(b)   customers who have the right to stay on their transponders even if other customers' transponders fail, but who are not entitled to be moved if their transponder fails; and

(c)   customers who may be moved off their transponders (with an appropriate refund) in the event that another customer's (who has a right to be moved) transponder fails.

It follows that there must always be as many customers in category (c) as there are in category (a). Furthermore, if the customer in category (a) wishes to move from one transponder to another seamlessly (so as not to affect its customer base), the transponders in question will need to operate in the same receive/transmit band and have the same polarization (this is particularly relevant if protection for one transponder is being provided by a transponder on another satellite in the satellite operator's system). The difference between the categories will normally be reflected in the price which the respective customers pay. The system of removing one customer to cater for the requirements of another is often referred to as 'pre-emption'.

Of course, in the event that the satellite operator's system does have spare capacity, it would be reasonable for customers to expect the satellite operator to use that capacity prior to implementing a pre-emption scheme.

Termination and effects of termination

11.15   Termination is normally available to both the satellite operator and the customer in circumstances where the other commits a material breach of the contract or becomes insolvent.

In addition, the satellite operator may wish to include a discretionary right to terminate the contract if the customer ceases to provide a service on the satellite for longer than a fixed maximum period. This is because an 'empty' transponder may have an adverse effect on the satellite operator's business; particularly in the television field, a satellite operator's system is often more attractive the more operational services it has upon it.

The customer should have the right to terminate the contract in the event of long term degradation (as discussed *above*).

Contract terms relating to termination by the customer normally include provisions for a refund of the balance of monies already paid (after making an allowance for time used prior to the termination) and a cancellation of obligations for further payment. The operator may try and withhold from this any amounts paid by it to third parties, allocated to the particular capacity used by the customer which are non-refundable (such as licence fees).

Contract terms relating to termination by the operator should provide for a termination payment equal to the amount still payable for the balance of the agreed contract period, although the operator may agree to refund all or part of this if it finds a replacement customer for the relevant capacity. A discount should be given for accelerated payment.

Force majeure/*excusable delays*

11.16   Provisions regarding *force majeure*/excusable delays are customary in transponder contracts. It is important, however, to ensure that matters which might constitute *force majeure* but which are otherwise dealt with in the contract are excluded. Generally, see the comments on *force majeure* in Chapter 9, para 9.13.

Limitation of liability

11.17   In some cases, the losses or damages at stake in the event of a problem under a transponder contract could be substantial. However, as it is usually accepted that the satellite itself is generally outside the scope of technical correction if it develops a fault, it is not unfair for an operator to limit liability (subject, of course, to applicable laws relating to exclusion of liability) to circumstances of gross negligence or wilful default and/or, to the extent permitted by applicable laws, to agree a fixed maximum level of damages that would be payable.

Indemnity and other provisions

11.18   As the operator has no control over the material transmitted by means of the capacity which is made available, it should seek an indemnity from the customer in respect of any liability arising out of the carriage of the customer's signals. In the case of a telecommunications service, this might include breach of rights in data. In the case of a television service, this might include defamation or copyright infringement. It may also be prudent for the operator to insist that the customer obtain adequate insurance to cover its potential liabilities. For provisions regarding languages, notices, entire agreement, arbitration and governing law, see comments in Chapter 9, para 9.21.

Digital Transmissions

11.19   Satellites designed to carry digital transmissions as well as, or instead of, analogue transmissions are becoming increasingly common. Particularly in the field of satellite television broadcasting, digital transmissions on a wide scale and in the direct-to-home market will soon be a reality. As digital transmissions require new or adapted reception equipment, it is not clear how successfully or rapidly the digital market will grow to take over from the existing analogue market. However, as the number of services that can be carried on a satellite are substantially increased by using digital, rather than analogue, technology, both satellite service providers and satellite operators are investing heavily in the promotion of digital transmissions.

The advent of digital technology affects a number of the typical provisions for transponder agreements that have been outlined *above*.

One of the major differences is that it is generally accepted that 'degradation' ceases to be relevant; either the service is available or not. If the digital transmission is deficient in some regard the service will be unavailable—there is no question of a weak signal generating a receivable but poor quality service. Availability of a service is therefore the only issue and it is normally determined by reference to the down-link signal having an agreed bit rate measured at particular locations. Satellite operators have to be careful to ensure that the customer's up-link signal is not deficient (ie that it has the correct bit rate).

Another major difference is that one digital transponder can carry a number of services (as opposed to analogue transponders, which can normally carry only one video service at once). Thus a digital transponder could be leased to one customer who would be entitled to use it for as many simultaneous services as the transponder capacity allows. Alternatively, the capacity on one transponder could be divided between several customers. The problem with the latter course of action is that the up-link signals to the transponder have to be woven together by a process known as 'multiplexing' and so all the customers will have to agree to use the same up-link. A satellite operator might be tempted to designate its own up-link facilities as appropriate in such circumstances, but this would be subject to competition law considerations.

Finally, in some cases, transponders can be used for either analogue or digital transmissions. A service provider may wish to have the option to switch between them (depending on how the digital market develops in its target territories). If this is technically feasible a satellite operator will not normally object (providing the price does not change), but will expect to be indemnified by the customer against any claims resulting from the switch from analogue to digital (or *vice versa*), for example by a person with analogue reception equipment who can no longer receive the service.

Conclusion

11.20   The above review gives an outline of the basic terms and conditions to be expected in a transponder contract. It is important to bear in mind that the 'bankability' of transponder contracts is also becoming increasingly important: for the satellite operator as a revenue stream against which to raise or secure financing, and for the customer as an asset to be used to generate revenue and against which to raise or secure financing. The review of portfolios of transponder contracts by banks, financiers and their lawyers is, therefore, becoming more common.

12

Interconnection Contracts

General comments

12.1 As telecommunications markets are transformed by liberalisation and, ultimately, deregulation, there will be a greater need to establish interconnection arrangements nationally, regionally and internationally between providers of telecommunications infrastructure and services, whether such infrastructure is satellite, wireless telegraphy or fixed line based. Satellite service operators are increasingly likely to require interconnection with other terrestrial telecommunications systems. This chapter explains why interconnection is important; considers some of the problems which may be encountered, together with some possible solutions; and provides an overview of the anatomy of an interconnection contract and an outline of an international roaming contract as a model relevant to satellite personal communications. While these contracts concern complicated technical matters, they are basically commercial agreements relating to the supply of telecommunication services.

Interconnection

12.2 The connection of two separate infrastructures for the transmission of telecommunications enables the users of one system to transmit and receive information from users of the other system and *vice versa*. In addition, as the European Commission has said in its *Proposal for a European Parliament and Council Directive on interconnection in telecommunications ensuring universal service and interoperability through the application of principles of open network provision*

(ONP) ('the Interconnection Proposal') (COM(95) 379) (see Chapter 5, para 5.14):

> Interconnection is seen as a key element in the future competitive environment, allowing new market entrants access to existing end-users, on a basis which will encourage increased investment and market growth in the telecommunication services sector, within a predictable and stable regulatory environment.

Apart from the economic and social benefits derived by users of the separate systems, the infrastructure owners and service providers should benefit from the increase in traffic. On the other hand, in the past it has been clear that the traditional monopoly infrastructure provider has seen interconnection with competitors as a threat to its business, allegedly leading to a reduction in income. New entrants tend to find it difficult to secure satisfactory terms of interconnection with an infrastructure provider which was previously the monopoly provider (see Chapter 5, paras 5.10 *et seq*); hence the need for regulatory safeguards to ensure that interconnection terms and conditions are fair and reasonable and based on the open network principles of transparency, objectivity and non-discrimination (see *below* and see Chapter 5 para 5.11).

12.3 Establishing a successful interconnection arrangement will require consideration of current and future commercial, service and technical requirements, objectives and criteria. Commercial matters will include establishing who owns, manages, maintains and pays for the point of interconnection between the systems and what the charge for carrying one another's traffic should be. Service matters include establishing whether a simple network interconnection for call conveyance is required, or whether ancillary network services such as operator services, directory enquiries and/or emergency services are also required. Given sufficient system sophistication and capability, consideration might also be given to introducing premium rate services such as 'freephone' and low call features and intelligent network functions. The technical criteria will determine the ability of each infrastructure to provide the agreed services and the point at which physical interconnection should occur. This has important effects on the design and construction of the new entrants' networks and therefore the location of points of connection and how traffic is routed have important competitive consequences.

Until there is effective competition between infrastructure providers, there will continue to be difficulties in obtaining satisfactory interconnection arrangements. For example, the previous monopoly infrastructure provider tends to exploit the new market entrant by recognising that without its infrastructure the new market entrant will not be able to connect its customers to the very much larger customer base of the previous monopoly infrastructure provider. Regulatory obligations must be brought to bear on the previous monopoly infrastructure provider to ensure that interconnection terms are fair and reasonable, and in particular that the price encourages effective competition between the parties. The result in the UK has been the establishment of fairly standard form contracts for interconnection with British Telecommunications plc (BT), and to a lesser extent with Mercury Communications Limited (MCL), at least for fixed network interconnection. While this may prevent conflicts between agreements, it has had the disadvantage of standardising prices. It has also meant that when groups such as the cable telecommunications industry negotiate *en bloc*, the need for consensus means decisions are taken at the speed and according to the agenda of the 'lowest common denominator' or worse, at that of the dominant undertaking.

12.4   Under UK law, infrastructure providers must negotiate terms of interconnection service; if agreement cannot be reached, the matter may be referred to the industry's National Regulatory Authority, the Office of Telecommunications, for determination. This approach is supported by the European Commission *Proposal for a European Parliament and Council Directive on the application of open network provision to voice telephony* (COM(94) 689 Final) which states that National Regulatory Authorities (NRAs) may intervene to set conditions which are non-discriminatory, fair and reasonable to both parties and offer the greatest benefit to all users. In addition, NRAs should have the right to ensure that contracts are entered into and implemented in an efficient and timely manner and that they include conditions as to compliance with relevant standards and with essential requirements and the maintenance of end-to-end quality. (NRAs must understand that delays in the negotiation of interconnect agreements are extremely detrimental to new operators and can adversely affect the establishment of effective competition in telecommunications markets).

Although a satisfactory regulatory environment appears to be being put in place in the UK to establish satisfactory terms of interconnection, difficulties continue to be encountered, as evidenced by the litigation between MCL and, *inter alia*, BT (*Mercury Communications Limited* v *The Director General of Telecommunications and Others*

(House of Lords, 9 February 1995)). After negotiations commencing in April 1992 which did not result in agreement as to the price to be charged for carrying each other's traffic, BT referred the matter to the Office of Telecommunications (OFTEL) for a determination. Following the determination in December 1993, MCL sought a court declaration on the construction of condition 13 of the licence granted to BT, as it was dissatisfied with the construction applied by OFTEL. It was not until February 1995 that the House of Lords allowed MCL to proceed with its request for a court declaration—the High Court and the Court of Appeal had refused to grant such a request to MCL. Similar difficulties have been encountered in New Zealand where Clear Communications appealed as far as to the Judicial Committee of the Privy Council (*Telecom Corporation of New Zealand Limited and Others v Clear Communications Limited* (Privy Council Appeal No 21 of 1994)) without any real solution of questions relating to the terms of, and the charges for, carrying traffic. In New Zealand, where there is no equivalent to OFTEL, the parties were obliged to take the matter to court to determine whether there had been a breach of the prohibition on the improper use of a dominant position. Effectively, competition law alone is relied on to provide a solution, although in most other jurisdictions some form of specific regulatory power of intervention will continue for some time.

12.5 In the UK, OFTEL, has now published the results of the consultation on its document (published December 1994), *Effective Competition: Framework for Action — A Statement on the Future of Interconnection, Competition and Related Issues* (Office of Telecommunication, December 1994). In OFTEL's summer statement, published in June 1995, it proposed the following changes to the UK regulatory framework:

1. moving towards an incremental cost basis for interconnection charges from 1997, away from the fully allocated costs method presently used by OFTEL;

2. that OFTEL step away from the detailed setting of some interconnection charges (to be examined as part of the pricing review for 1997);

3. a new licence condition for telecommunications operators aimed at preventing anti-competitive behaviour generally and providing for the more timely intervention of OFTEL where such behaviour occurs.

OFTEL will be examining the level of effective competition in the various sectors of the telecommunications market to determine when and at what pace it will move away from detailed regulation, placing greater reliance on general licence conditions and competition law.

Additionally, from 1997, OFTEL proposes to abolish ADCs (Access Deficit Contributions) which are charges required to be paid by an operator interconnecting with BT and which form the basis on which BT is permitted to recover the cost of providing network access to all persons who required it. (Exemptions are possible, as granted to MCL by OFTEL.)

All the above proposals will be the subject of further OFTEL consultation.

12.6   The European Commission's Interconnection Proposal (see Chapter 5 para 5.14) reflects the need for specific regulation in the absence of effective competition, in addition to the competition rules already provided by, in this case, the Treaty of Rome. Of relevance to dispute resolution is the suggestion that each party should have the right, if a dispute arises, to seek intervention. The intervention would be by a national regulatory body or a Community-level body, depending on whether the dispute is of a domestic or of a cross-border nature.

From these examples it can be seen that there is scope for disagreement, particularly as to charges for carrying traffic, the potential for extensive delays as a result of the unequal bargaining position between a new entrant and the dominant infrastructure provider and the inability of an external influence, whether an NRA or a court, to impose a satisfactory arrangement without such arrangement being subjected to further scrutiny by higher authorities or, simply, unsatisfactory.

On 25 August 1993 the National Competition Policy Review for the Heads of Australian Governments chaired by Professor Frederick Hilmer recommended that in the event of disagreement between prospective interconnecting parties, either party might seek binding arbitration by or under the auspices of the Australian Competition Commission. It may be that providing such a Commission with the power to bind the parties is what is needed, since in these circumstances experts in telecommunications would be making knowledgeable decisions in the interests of effective competition. Interestingly, under current Australian legislation, a determination by the regulator is taken to be an access agreement between the carriers who were parties to the determination, and may be enforced by each of them as if it were a contract between them.

The Interconnection Proposal provides a framework for interconnection which balances the rights and obligations of the interconnecting parties in accordance with their relative positions in the market so that, for example, those with significant market power would be assigned obligations (such as to publish price lists, and to have cost-oriented interconnection tariffs and transparent cost-accounting) aimed at compensating for the limited negotiating power of a new market entrant. The Proposal provides, in its final annexure, a useful list of provisions that are relevant to interconnection arrangements. Interestingly, it separates the issues into those that are to be settled by the relevant national regulatory authority and those that are to be agreed between the parties. Thus, for example, the allocation and use of numbering resources is to be under the control of the national regulatory authority, while the description of the interconnection services to be provided is left to the parties. The following section of this chapter deals with those parts of the interconnection arrangements that ordinarily the parties would negotiate.

Whatever the regulatory regime chosen for interconnection, a critical element remains the speed with which new entrants can obtain effective resolution of disputes. A regulatory regime backed by injunctive relief and an effective forum in which to bring an action for damages in respect of anti-competitive behaviour is essential.

Anatomy of an interconnection contract

12.7 Set out below is a checklist of the typical provisions contained in an interconnection contract. As has been mentioned *above*, the establishment of a satisfactory interconnection arrangement will require commercial, service and technical inputs. The checklist is followed by a clause-by-clause review. This provides a more detailed comment on the types of provisions which are common in such contracts.

Checklist of typical provisions

12.8

- Definitions and interpretation

- Commencement and duration
- Interconnection
- System alteration
- Standards
- Scope
- New services
- Forecasts and capacity
- Charges
- Payment
- Review
- Determination
- *Force majeure*
- Limitation of liability
- Dispute resolution

Clause-by-clause review

Definitions and interpretation

12.9   This clause tends to be one of the longest provisions of the contract and, possibly, one of the most important, in view of the fact that interconnection contracts often comprise a main body and a series of annexures, specifications and schedules all of which need to be put in an order of precedence for the purposes of interpretation of the relationship between the parties. Much of the terminology used is drawn from relevant telecommunications legislation. In addition, the numerous terms of art relating to interconnection are mentioned and defined. The mix of legal, technical and commercial input into the interconnection contract is clearly highlighted by this provision. Without each understanding the other's input, a satisfactory arrangement is unlikely.

Commencement and duration

12.10   Often each party to the contract can provide telecommunications infrastructure with the authority to interconnect only if it is licensed by the relevant NRA to do so. Thus, apart from the normal triggers for termination, it is important to ensure there is a provision entitling termination if either or both of the parties ceases to hold such a licence.

Interconnection

12.11   The primary obligation on each of the parties to the contract is to connect and keep connected its system with that of the other party at specified points of connection using specified types of connection with the responsibility for providing, installing, testing, making operational and maintaining all equipment on each party's side of the point of connection being, in the normal case, with such party. In view of their length and complexity, it is usual to annex the specifications for the points and types of connection, especially where there are a multitude of such points, as is likely with satellite personal communications systems.

System alteration and standards

12.12   Interconnection arrangements are long-term and it is not, therefore, surprising to find a provision that deals with alterations to one party's system that necessitates a change to the other party's system. Where such an alteration is anticipated and the other party might be affected, it will be necessary to ensure that any effect is accounted for by the affected party and paid for by the party making the system alteration. Of particular concern would be the need to protect the integrity and security of each party's system (see the discussion on essential requirements Chapter 5 para 5.70). Tied to the issue of system alteration is the need to apply agreed standards and operating guidelines which may have been established at a national, regional or international level. Parties should not be tied to a particular technology. New entrants, in particular, need to be able to take advantage of new technology and cost savings.

Scope and schedules

12.13   This provision would set out the level of service obligations established between the parties. Again, in view of their length and complexity, but also to allow for change over time, details of these services are often set out in schedules attached to the contract. The contract will need to define carefully whether the arrangement is for simple call conveyance, or whether it also extends to ancillary network services, such as operator services, directory enquiries or emergency services or, perhaps in the more advanced network environments, premium rate services such as freephone and low call features and intelligent network functions. In addition, the contract should set out the equipment and facilities that each party will provide or make available to the other.

Apart from establishing the services, equipment and facilities that will be made available, this provision is likely also to include details of what is not being provided. In particular, there is often agreement that reverse/transfer charge calls are not to be permitted. The main reason for this is that it disrupts the billing arrangement between the parties. This is supported by an obligation on each party to instruct its customers not to accept or agree to pay for reverse/transfer charge calls.

Forecasts and capacity

12.14 As already mentioned, the interconnection contract is likely to be in place for a long time and it should be possible to develop it as traffic flows vary. Thus, each party is obliged to provide the other with forecasts for traffic flows. While there is a sound basis for such a provision, it tends to result in the previous monopoly infra-structure provider having forecasts from all its competitors, and therefore an additional competitive advantage which might enable it to manipulate the market and, in particular, the charges payable for carrying traffic to and from its competitor's networks.

Charges and payment

12.15 Details of the charges payable and the method and timing of payment will vary according to the services and facilities being provided and the respective bargaining power of the parties. While the determination of charges will normally be the subject of bilateral or (in the case of satellite personal communications systems) multi-lateral negotiations, in the UK, OFTEL, as industry regulator, aims to achieve for competitors a 'level playing field' which would not otherwise exist. A standard interconnection agreement is on offer, which includes standard prices for services in respect of inter-connecting with BT. Negotiation, therefore, is severely limited.

Review and determination

12.16 Interconnection contracts are long-term agreements and it is of the utmost importance to have review and determination provisions under which unanticipated developments affecting a party's position can be fairly dealt with. The triggers for review are likely to be extensive and to include modification of either party's licence to operate (where relevant), and a material change in the law or regulation of operation, or some other material change which makes it necessary to amend the interconnection contract. While it may be necessary, on the occurrence of one or other of these triggers, for any or all of the terms of the interconnection arrangement to be amended, it is more than likely that the charge for carrying one another's traffic will need to change. In these circumstances it is likely that the matter would be referred to an independent arbitrator which, as mentioned *above*, could be a regulator or court of competent jurisdiction. In either case, the method of appointment of the arbitrator and his method of operation and determination will need to be set out in full to ensure that the determination is effective. In particular, the effective date of any amendment ought to be established. In the case of interconnection with BT, there is a further requirement that arises from the particular wording of BT's licence which requires the Director General to approve the terms of the review and determination provisions. The Director General has, therefore, *locus standi* subsequently to make a determination on any issue not agreed between the interconnecting parties during a review.

Force majeure

12.17   Normally neither party is liable to the other in the event of *force majeure*, but the considerations set out in para 9.13 of Chapter 9 will be relevant here as there.

Limitation of liability

12.18   As with all commercial arrangements, the limitation of each party's liability to the other is likely to consume a substantial amount of negotiating time. In the UK, though, BT is, by the terms of its licence, effectively entitled to require an indemnity for third party liabilities, damage to its system and loss arising from such damage which may result from the performance of the contract. This means that the normal bargaining position is somewhat established in advance. On the other hand, there is no reason why reciprocal or other arrangements should not prevail. These can vary from 'broad brush' provisions to detailed 'specific remedy for specific breaches' provisions. In either case, the law of the relevant jurisdiction may dictate that certain liabilities may not be excluded or capped.

Dispute resolution

12.19   Given the complex, industry-specific commercial and technical aspects of interconnection contracts, it is often sensible to include a provision to arbitrate rather than proceed to court. Any such provision should, however, allow the parties to continue to seek determinations from the national regulatory authority where that is part of the relevant regulatory system and, if the need arises, to obtain from a court interlocutory or other immediate relief that arbitration is unable to provide.

International roaming contracts

12.20   Increasingly, particularly for business purposes, there is a need for a subscriber to telecommunications services from an infrastructure operator in one country to gain access to equivalent services of another operator in another country. In other words, a person may wish to communicate with others despite his 'roaming' from one country to another, especially where satellite technology is used. To facilitate this, infrastructure and/or service providers in the relevant countries will need to establish international roaming contracts.

A roaming contract is made between two infrastructure and/or service providers and comprises the principal agreement, the general terms and conditions for international roaming and a set of annexures. While the principal agreement is a short 'frame agreement', set out *below* is a checklist of the main provisions contained in the general terms and conditions and the annexures. There follows a more detailed review of these provisions where they relate to roaming as against normal interconnection arrangements.

It is to be expected that international roaming contracts for satellite personal communications will probably be similar to those already coming into existence in Europe in relation to roaming for GSM networks. Indeed, as noted *above*, in terms of satellite personal communications, it is likely that these networks will interconnect not only with fixed networks, but also with mobile communications networks including GSM networks.

Checklist of typical provisions

12.21

- Scope of the contract
- Implementation of network and services
- Modifications

- Charging, billing and accounting

- Customer care

- Data privacy

- Fraud prevention

- Liability of the parties

- Suspension of services

- *Force majeure*

- Duration of the contract

- Termination of the contract

- Choice of law

- Arbitration

Clause-by-clause review

Scope of the contract

12.22   The parties will agree to establish international roaming between their respective networks and / or services. An agreed set of technical specifications and documents will be applied. Not surprisingly, the contract will be subject to any licence or rights and other national, regional or international binding regulations to establish and operate networks and / or services to which each party may be subject.

Network and services

12.23   The parties will need to agree on the level of service to be provided. Negotiators should expect to agree that the services which will be provided to roaming subscribers will at best be only those for which the roaming subscriber has subscribed in his 'home territory'; that when servicing a roaming subscriber that is outside his home territory the service provided to him will be the same as that provided to roaming subscribers from other territories; and that, while the level of service may differ from one country to the next, the levels of service provided to a party's own subscribers and to those of another country will not differ substantially. As liberalisation spreads and services become more sophisticated, there will be a need to modify the contract to account for these changes, so the contract should be drafted in a sufficiently flexible manner to allow modification of service by, for example, agreeing replacement annexures.

Charging and tariffs

12.24   The operator in the home territory will be responsible for payment of the charges for services rendered to its roaming subscriber, and the charges will be those stated by the country into which the roaming subscriber has ventured. A protection against abuse that should be provided to the operator of the home territory is that no payment need be made unless a subscriber identity authentication was provided at the time the call was made.

Customer care

12.25   A customer will have contracted with his home territory network and/or services provider, rather than the network and/or services provider in the territory in which he is roaming. Consequently, he should refer any issues regarding supply of information about roaming in another country, network and/or equipment faults, lost or stolen Subscriber Identity Module (SIM) cards and billing, to or though the home territory network and/or services provider.

Data privacy and fraud prevention

12.26   Usually parties agree to be responsible for compliance with relevant data privacy laws and regulations in their respective countries. Each party acknowledges that transfer of information may not be possible if that is the law of the relevant country. Each party is obliged to inform its subscribers that during roaming the storage, treatment and transfer of their personal data may be subject to regulation different from the regulation in their home territories. Normally the contract would contain a set of fraud prevention procedures and the parties would agree to co-operate in good faith regarding the procedures. Preferably, a similar arrangement should be applied to interconnection arrangements for all types of communications.

Liability

12.27   Given the international nature of the contract and assuming that there is only limited potential for liabilities arising, one would expect to have full recompense for non-payment of charges and, apart from loss or damage caused wilfully or through gross negligence, quite limited and capped liability.

Suspension of services

12.28   Services to all or any roaming subscribers should be capable of being suspended without liability to the other party to the contract, in circumstances, for example, where the suspending party would be entitled to suspend or terminate those services to its own subscribers. A party should also be able to suspend services to all roaming subscribers from countries other than its own by giving notice to the other party, although the other party should be given a right to terminate the contract if such suspension is to last for more than, say, six months. In addition, the contract should provide for a party to suspend access to the other country's services by its own roaming subscribers who are in that other country when, for example, the subscriber has not paid his charges.

Force majeure

12.29   As mentioned in previous chapters, in particular at para 9.13 of Chapter 9, a *force majeure* provision is to be expected, and the considerations outlined in para 9.13 would apply when settling the form of the provision.

Term and termination

12.30   The term should, as a minimum, reflect the time that will be required from a practical point of view to dismantle the physical connections made in pursuance of the contract. It may also reflect the level of cost incurred in setting up the connection. As regards termination, apart from the normal triggers for termination in an interconnection contract, arrangements should be capable of termination by written notice to the other party if roaming on either party's infrastructure becomes technically or commercially impracticable, and suspension of the service does not solve the problem, or there is an unacceptable level of unauthorised use which the other party is not capable of remedying within a set period from receipt of written notice to such effect.

Changes to the contract

12.31   While not having the same effect as the review and determination provisions in an interconnection contract to reflect changes over time, there should probably be an acknowledgement that it may be appropriate to change the contract in the light of experience. This is akin to the need to change the services to be provided, mentioned *above*. The provision would contemplate that the parties would enter into good faith discussions with a view to agreeing mutually acceptable modifications to the contract. This type of arrangement tends to reflect the international nature of the roaming contracts where solutions to problems encountered over time are dealt with in less proscriptive terms.

Choice of law and dispute resolution

12.32   Given the international nature of roaming, an applicable jurisdiction to govern the contract will need to be chosen. Normally this would be the law of one or other of the contracting parties. Also, the Rules of Conciliation and Arbitration of the International Chamber of Commerce will apply to dispute resolution and a place of arbitration will need to be appointed. For example, as already mentioned, the Interconnection Proposal suggests that international interconnecting parties would have the right to invoke a resolution procedure at Community-level in the case of cross-border disputes.

Conclusion

12.33   The establishment of a satisfactory interconnection contract between infrastructure providers requires commercial, service and technical input of a detailed nature. Each party will need to understand the other's input and its ramifications to ensure that the contract stands the test of time. The role of an external arbitrator, whether an independent regulator or a court, will be critical if effective competition is to be achieved, especially where a relatively small group of fixed network operators remains and is likely to remain for some considerable time dominant in their domestic markets, and even formidable players in the international telecommunication world.

IV

Appendices

Appendix 1

Parties to International Conventions and Regional Agreements, and Statutory Instruments Relevant to Satellite Communications in Europe

The Berne Convention (Status on 15 April 1995)

State	Date on which state became party to the Convention
Albania	6 March 1995
Argentina	10 June 1967
Australia	14 April 1928
Austria	1 October 1920
Bahamas	10 July 1973
Barbados	30 July 1983
Belgium	5 December 1887
Benin	3 January 1961
Bolivia	4 November 1993
Bosnia and Herzegovina	6 March 1992
Brazil	9 February 1922
Bulgaria	5 December 1921
Burkina Faso	19 August 1963
Cameroon	21 September 1964
Canada	10 April 1928
Central African Republic	3 September 1977
Chad	25 November 1971
Chile	5 June 1970
China	15 October 1992
Colombia	7 March 1988
Congo	8 May 1962
Costa Rica	10 June 1978
Côte d'Ivoire	1 January 1962
Croatia	8 October 1991
Cyprus	24 February 1964

State	Date on which state became party to the Convention
Czech Republic	1 January 1993
Denmark	1 July 1903
Ecuador	9 October 1991
Egypt	7 June 1977
El Salvador	19 February 1994
Estonia	26 October 1994
Fiji	1 December 1971
Finland	1 April 1928
France	5 December 1887
Gabon	26 March 1962
Gambia	7 March 1993
Georgia	16 May 1995
Germany	5 December 1887
Ghana	11 October 1991
Greece	9 November 1920
Guinea	20 November 1980
Guinea-Bissau	22 July 1991
Guyana	25 October 1994
Holy See	12 September 1935
Honduras	25 January 1990
Hungary	14 February 1922
Iceland	7 September 1947
India	1 April 1928
Ireland	5 October 1927
Israel	24 March 1950
Italy	5 December 1887
Jamaica	1 January 1994
Japan	15 July 1899
Kenya	11 June 1993
Lebanon	30 September 1947
Lesotho	28 September 1989
Liberia	8 March 1989
Libya	28 September 1976
Liechtenstein	30 July 1931
Lithuania	14 December 1994
Luxembourg	20 June 1888
Macedonia	8 September 1991
Madagascar	1 January 1966
Malawi	12 October 1991
Malaysia	1 October 1990
Mali	19 March 1962
Malta	21 September 1964
Mauritania	6 February 1973
Mauritius	10 May 1989

State	Date on which state became party to the Convention
Mexico	11 June 1967
Monaco	30 May 1889
Morocco	16 June 1917
Namibia	21 March 1990
Netherlands	1 November 1912
New Zealand	24 April 1928
Niger	2 May 1962
Nigeria	14 September 1993
Norway	13 April 1896
Pakistan	5 July 1948
Paraguay	2 January 1992
Peru	20 August 1988
Philippines	1 August 1951
Poland	28 January 1920
Portugal	29 March 1911
Romania	1 January 1927
Russian Federation	13 March 1995
Rwanda	1 March 1984
Saint Kitts and Nevis	9 April 1995
Saint Lucia	24 August 1993
Senegal	25 August 1962
Slovakia	1 January 1993
Slovenia	25 June 1991
South Africa	3 October 1928
Spain	5 December 1887
Sri Lanka	20 July 1959
Surinam	23 February 1977
Sweden	1 August 1904
Switzerland	5 December 1887
Tanzania	25 July 1994
Thailand	17 July 1931
Togo	30 April 1975
Trinidad and Tobago	16 August 1988
Tunisia	5 December 1887
Turkey	1 January 1952
United Kingdom	5 December 1887
United States of America	1 March 1989
Uruguay	10 July 1967
Venezuela	30 December 1982
Yugoslavia	17 June 1930
Zaire	8 October 1963
Zambia	2 January 1992
Zimbabwe	18 April 1980

TOTAL NUMBER OF STATES: 112

The Universal Copyright Convention
(Status on 1 February 1995)

State	Date on which state became party to the Convention	
	Text of 1952	*Text of 1971*
Algeria	28 May 1973	28 May 1973
Andorra	22 January 1953	—
Argentina	13 November 1957	—
Australia	1 February 1969	29 November 1977
Austria	2 April 1957	14 May 1982
Bahamas	13 July 1976	27 September 1976
Bangladesh	5 May 1975	5 May 1975
Barbados	18 March 1983	18 March 1983
Belarus	27 February 1973	—
Belgium	31 May 1960	—
Belize	1 December 1982	—
Bolivia	22 December 1989	22 December 1989
Bosnia and Herzegovina	11 February 1966	3 July 1973
Brazil	13 October 1969	11 September 1975
Bulgaria	7 March 1975	7 March 1975
Cambodia	5 August 1953	—
Cameroon	1 January 1973	1 February 1973
Canada	10 May 1962	—
Chile	18 January 1955	—
China	30 July 1992	30 July 1992
Colombia	18 March 1976	18 March 1976
Costa Rica	7 December 1954	7 December 1979
Croatia	11 February 1966	3 July 1973
Cuba	18 March 1957	—
Cyprus	19 September 1990	19 September 1990
Czech Republic	6 October 1959	17 January 1980
Denmark	9 November 1961	11 March 1979
Dominican Republic	8 February 1983	8 February 1983
Ecuador	5 March 1957	6 June 1991
El Salvador	29 December 1978	29 December 1978
Fiji	13 December 1978	—
Finland	16 January 1963	1 August 1986
France	14 January 1955	11 September 1972
Germany	3 June 1955	18 October 1973
Ghana	22 May 1962	—
Greece	24 May 1963	—
Guatemala	28 July 1964	—
Guinea	13 August 1981	13 August 1981
Haiti	1 September 1954	—

State	Date on which state became party to the Convention	
	Text of 1952	*Text of 1971*
Holy See	5 July 1955	6 February 1980
Hungary	23 October 1970	15 September 1972
Iceland	18 September 1956	—
India	21 January 1958	7 January 1988
Ireland	20 October 1959	—
Israel	6 April 1955	—
Italy	24 October 1956	25 October 1979
Japan	28 January 1956	21 July 1977
Kazakhstan	27 February 1973	—
Kenya	7 June 1966	4 January 1974
Korea	1 July 1987	1 July 1987
Laos	19 August 1954	—
Lebanon	17 July 1959	—
Liberia	27 March 1956	—
Liechtenstein	22 October 1958	—
Luxembourg	15 July 1955	—
Malawi	26 July 1965	—
Malta	19 August 1968	—
Mauritius	20 August 1970	—
Mexico	12 February 1957	31 July 1975
Monaco	16 June 1955	13 September 1976
Morocco	8 February 1972	28 October 1976
Netherlands	22 March 1967	30 August 1985
New Zealand	11 June 1964	—
Nicaragua	16 May 1961	—
Niger	15 May 1989	15 February 1989
Nigeria	14 November 1961	—
Norway	23 October 1962	7 May 1974
Pakistan	28 April 1954	—
Panama	17 July 1962	3 June 1980
Paraguay	11 December 1961	—
Peru	16 July 1963	22 April 1985
Philippines	19 August 1955	—
Poland	9 December 1976	9 December 1976
Portugal	25 September 1956	30 April 1981
Russian Federation	27 February 1973	9 December 1994
Rwanda	10 August 1989	10 August 1989
Saint Vincent and the Grenadines	22 January 1985	22 January 1985
Saudi Arabia	13 April 1994	13 April 1994
Senegal	9 May 1974	10 April 1974
Slovakia	6 October 1959	17 January 1980

State	Date on which state became party to the Convention	
	Text of 1952	*Text of 1971*
Slovenia	11 February 1966	3 July 1973
Spain	27 October 1954	10 April 1974
Sri Lanka	25 October 1983	27 October 1988
Sweden	1 April 1961	27 July 1973
Switzerland	30 December 1955	21 March 1993
Tajikistan	27 February 1973	—
Trinidad and Tobago	19 May 1988	19 May 1988
Tunisia	19 March 1969	10 March 1975
Ukraine	27 February 1973	—
United Kingdom	27 June 1957	27 September 1974
United States of America	16 December 1955	18 September 1972
Uruguay	12 January 1993	12 January 1993
Venezuela	30 June 1966	—
Yugoslavia	11 February 1966	3 July 1973
Zambia	1 March 1965	—

TOTAL NUMBER OF STATES: 96

The Rome Convention (1961)   (Status on 15 April 1995)

State	Date on which state became party to the Convention
Argentina	2 March 1992
Australia	30 September 1992
Austria	9 June 1973
Barbados	18 September 1983
Bolivia	24 November 1993
Brazil	29 September 1965
Burkina Faso	14 January 1988
Chile	5 September 1974
Colombia	17 September 1976
Congo	18 May 1964
Costa Rica	9 September 1971
Czech Republic	1 January 1993
Denmark	23 September 1965
Dominican Republic	27 January 1987
Ecuador	18 May 1964
El Salvador	29 June 1979
Fiji	11 April 1972
Finland	21 October 1983
France	3 July 1987
Germany	21 October 1966

State	Date on which state became party to the Convention
Greece	6 January 1993
Guatemala	14 January 1977
Honduras	16 February 1990
Hungary	10 February 1995
Iceland	15 June 1994
Ireland	19 September 1979
Italy	8 April 1975
Jamaica	27 January 1994
Japan	26 October 1989
Lesotho	26 January 1990
Luxembourg	25 February 1976
Mexico	18 May 1964
Monaco	6 December 1985
Niger	18 May 1964
Nigeria	29 October 1993
Norway	10 July 1978
Panama	2 September 1983
Paraguay	26 February 1970
Peru	7 August 1985
Philippines	25 September 1984
Slovakia	1 January 1993
Spain	14 November 1991
Sweden	18 May 1964
Switzerland	24 September 1993
United Kingdom	18 May 1964
Uruguay	4 July 1977

TOTAL NUMBER OF STATES: 46

The Phonogram Convention 1971 (Status on 15 April 1995)

State	Date on which state became party to the Convention
Argentina	30 June 1973
Australia	22 June 1974
Austria	21 August 1982
Barbados	29 July 1983
Brazil	28 November 1975
Burkina Faso	30 January 1988
Chile	24 March 1977
China	30 April 1993
Colombia	16 May 1994
Costa Rica	17 June 1982

399

State	Date on which state became party to the Convention
Cyprus	30 September 1993
Czech Republic	Under examination
Denmark	24 March 1977
Ecuador	14 September 1974
Egypt	23 April 1978
El Salvador	9 February 1979
Fiji	18 April 1973
Finland	18 April 1973
France	18 April 1973
Germany	18 May 1974
Greece	9 February 1994
Guatemala	1 February 1977
Holy See	18 July 1977
Honduras	6 March 1990
Hungary	28 May 1975
India	12 February 1975
Israel	1 May 1978
Italy	24 March 1977
Jamaica	11 January 1994
Japan	14 October 1978
Kenya	21 April 1976
Korea	10 October 1987
Luxembourg	8 March 1976
Mexico	21 December 1973
Monaco	2 December 1974
New Zealand	13 August 1976
Norway	1 August 1978
Panama	29 June 1974
Paraguay	13 February 1979
Peru	24 August 1985
Russian Federation	13 March 1995
Slovakia	Under examination
Spain	24 August 1974
Sweden	18 April 1973
Switzerland	30 September 1993
Trinidad and Tobago	1 October 1988
United Kingdom	18 April 1973
United States of America	10 March 1974
Uruguay	18 January 1983
Venezuela	18 November 1982
Zaire	29 November 1977

TOTAL NUMBER OF STATES: 51

The Satellite Convention 1974   (Status on 15 April 1995)

State	Date on which state became party to the Convention
Armenia	13 December 1993
Australia	26 October 1990
Austria	6 August 1982
Bosnia and Herzegovina	6 March 1992
Croatia	8 October 1991
Germany	25 August 1979
Greece	22 October 1991
Italy	7 July 1981
Kenya	25 August 1979
Mexico	25 August 1979
Morocco	30 June 1983
Nicaragua	25 August 1979
Panama	25 September 1985
Peru	7 August 1985
Russian Federation	25 December 1991
Slovenia	25 June 1991
Switzerland	24 September 1993
United States of America	7 March 1985
Yugoslavia	25 August 1979

TOTAL NUMBER OF STATES: 19

The European Agreement Concerning Programme Exchanges by Means of Television Films 1958

(Status on 1 July 1995)

State	Date on which state became party to the Agreement
Belgium	9 March 1962
Cyprus	21 January 1970
Denmark	26 October 1961
France	15 December 1958 (signature without reservation as to ratification)
Greece	10 January 1962
Ireland	5 March 1965 (signature without reservation as to ratification)
Israel	16 January 1978
Luxembourg	1 October 1963
Netherlands (including Aruba)	3 February 1967
Norway	13 February 1963
Spain	5 December 1973

State	Date on which state became party to the Agreement
Sweden	31 May 1961
Tunisia	21 January 1969
Turkey	27 February 1964
United Kingdom	15 December 1958 (signature without reservation as to ratification)

TOTAL NUMBER OF STATES: 15

The European Agreement on the Protection of Television Broadcasts 1960 (1965, 1974, 1983, 1989)

(Status on 1 July 1995)

State	Date on which state became party to the Agreement
Denmark	26 October 1961
France	26 June 1960 (signature without reservation as to ratification)
Germany	8 September 1967
Norway	9 July 1968
Sweden	31 May 1961
United Kingdom	9 March 1961

TOTAL NUMBER OF STATES: 6

The 1989 protocol was ratified or signed without reservation as to ratification by all parties except Belgium, which only signed the protocol, and Spain and Cyprus, which did not sign or ratify the protocol.

A notification of denouncement was made in 1989 stating that in accordance with art 13, no state may remain or become a party to the agreement as from 1 January 1990 if they were not also a party to the Rome Convention. Accordingly, Belgium, Cyprus, Spain and Turkey ceased to be parties to this Agreement.

The Copyright (Application to Other Countries) Order 1993 (SI No 942) (As amended by the Copyright (Application to Other Countries) (Amendment) Order 1994 (SI No 263))

Whereas Her Majesty is satisfied that provision has been or will be made—

(a) in respect of literary, dramatic, musical and artistic works, films and typographical arrangements of published editions, under the law of Uganda,

(b) in respect of sound recordings, under the laws of Bangladesh, Ghana, Malawi and Thailand,

(c) in respect of broadcasts, under the law of Malawi,

giving adequate protection to the owners of copyright under Part I of the Copyright, Designs and Patents Act 1988:

Now, therefore, Her Majesty, by and with the advice of Her Privy Council, and by virtue of the authority conferred upon Her by section 159 of the said Act, is pleased to order, and it is hereby ordered as follows:

1—(1) This Order may be cited as the Copyright (Application to Other Countries) Order 1993 and shall come into force on 4th May 1993.

(2) In this Order—

'the Act' means the Copyright, Designs and Patents Act 1988, and 'first published' shall be construed in accordance with section 155(3) of the Act.

2—(1) In relation to literary, dramatic, musical and artistic works, films and the typographical arrangements of published editions, sections 153, 154 and 155 of the Act (qualification for copyright protection) apply in relation to—

(a) persons who are citizens or subjects of a country specified in Schedule 1 to this Order or are domiciled or resident there as they apply to persons who are British citizens or are domiciled or resident in the United Kingdom;

(b) bodies incorporated under the law of such a country as they apply in relation to bodies incorporated under the law of a part of the United Kingdom; and

(c) works first published in such a country as they apply in relation to works first published in the United Kingdom;

but subject to paragraph (2) and article 5 below.

(2) Copyright does not subsist—

(a) in a literary, dramatic, musical or artistic work by virtue of section 154 of the Act as applied by paragraph (1) above (qualification by reference to author) if it was first published—
  (i) before 1st June 1957 (commencement of Copyright Act 1956), or
  (ii) before 1st August 1989 (commencement of Part I of the Act) and at the material time (as defined in section 154(4)(*b*) of the Act) the author was not a relevant person; or

(b) in any work by virtue of paragraph (1) above if—
  (i) a date is, or dates are, specified in Schedule 1 to this Order in respect of the only country or countries relevant to the work for the purposes of paragraph (1) above, and
  (ii) the work was first published before that date or (as the case may be) the earliest of those dates;

and for the purposes of sub-paragraph (*a*)(ii) of this paragraph a 'relevant person' is a Commonwealth citizen, a British protected person, a citizen or subject of any country specified in Schedule 1 to this Order, or a person resident or domiciled in the United Kingdom, another country to which the relevant provisions of Part I of the Act extend or (subject to article 5 below) a country specified in Schedule 1 to this Order.

(3) Where copyright subsists in a work by virtue of paragraph (1) above, the whole of Part I of the Act (including Schedule 1 to the Act) applies in relation to the work, save that in relation to an artistic work consisting of the design of a typeface—

(a) section 54(2) (articles for producing material in particular type-face) does not apply,

(b) section 55 (making such articles not an infringement) applies as if the words in subsection (2) from the beginning to 'marketed' were omitted, and

(c) paragraph 14(5) of the Schedule 1 (transitional provision) does not apply,

and subject also to articles 5 and 7 below.

3—In relation to sound recordings, article 2 above shall apply as it applies in relation to films, subject to the following modifications—

(a) sections 19, 20, 26 and 107(3) of the Act (infringement by playing in public, broadcasting or inclusion in a cable programme service and related provisions) apply only if—

(i)   at least one of the countries relevant to the work for the purposes of article 2(1) above is specified in Schedule 2 to this Order, or

(ii) the sound recording in question is a film sound-track accompanying a film.

4—(1) In relation to broadcasts, sections 153, 154 and 156 of the Act (qualification for copyright protection) apply in relation to—

(a) persons who are citizens or subjects of a country specified in Schedule 3 to this Order or are domiciled or resident there as they apply to persons who are British citizens or are domiciled or resident in the United Kingdom;

(b) bodies incorporated under the law of such a country as they apply in relation to bodies incorporated under the law of a part of the United Kingdom; and

(c) broadcasts made from such a country as they apply to broadcasts made from the United Kingdom;

but subject to paragraphs (2) and (3) and article 5 below.

(2) If the only country or countries relevant to a broadcast for the purposes of paragraph (1) above are identified in Schedule 3 to this Order by the words 'television only', copyright subsists in the broadcast only if it is a television broadcast.

(3) Copyright does not subsist in a broadcast by virtue of paragraph (1) above if it was made before the relevant date.

(4) Where copyright subsists in a broadcast by virtue of paragraph (1) above, the whole of Part I of the Act (including Schedule 1 to the Act) applies in relation to the broadcast, save that for the purposes of section 14(2) (duration of copyright in repeats)—

(a) a broadcast shall be disregarded if it was made before the relevant date, and

(b) a cable programme shall be disregarded if it was included in a cable programme service before the later of the relevant date and 1st January 1985;

and subject also to article 7 below.

(5) For the purposes of paragraphs (3) and (4) above, the 'relevant date' is the date or (as the case may be) the earliest of the dates specified in Schedule 3 to this Order in respect of the country or countries relevant to the broadcast for the purposes of paragraph (1) above, being (where different dates are specified for television and non-television broadcasts), the date appropriate to the type of broadcast in question.

(6) In respect of Indonesia and Singapore, this article applies in relation to cable programmes as it applies in relation to broadcasts, subject to article 5 below.

5—Schedule 4 to this Order shall have effect so as to modify the application of this Order in respect of certain countries.

6—Nothing in this Order shall be taken to derogate from the effect of paragraph 35 of Schedule 1 to the Act (continuation of existing qualification for copyright protection).

7—(1) This article applies in any case in which—

(a) a work was made before 1st August 1989 (commencement of Part I of the Act) and copyright under the Copyright Act 1956 did not subsist in it when it was made, or

(b) a work is made on or after 1st August 1989 and copyright under the Act does not subsist in it when it is made,

but copyright subsequently subsists in it by virtue of article 2(1), or 3 or 4(1) above.

(2) Where in any such case a person incurs or has incurred any expenditure or liability in connection with, for the purpose of or with a view to the doing of an act which at the time is not or was not an act restricted by any copyright in the work, the doing, or continued doing, of that act after copyright subsequently subsists in the work by virtue of article 2(1), 3 or 4(1) above shall not be an act restricted by the copyright unless the owner of the copyright or his exclusive licensee (if any) pays such compensation as, failing agreement, may be determined by arbitration.

8—The Orders listed in Schedule 5 to this Order are hereby revoked.

Schedule 1: Countries enjoying protection in respect of all works except broadcasts and cable programmes

(The countries specified in this Schedule either are parties to the Berne Copyright Convention and/or the Universal Copyright Convention or otherwise give adequate protection under their law.)

Albania
Algeria (28th August 1973)
Andorra (27th September 1957)
Argentina
Australia (including Norfolk Island)
Austria
Bahamas
Bangladesh
Barbados
Belgium
Belize
Benin
Bolivia
Bosnia-Herzegovina
Brazil
Bulgaria
Burkina Faso
Cameroon
Canada
Central African Republic
Chad
Chile
China
Colombia
Congo
Costa Rica
Côte d'Ivoire
Croatia
Cuba (27th September 1957)
Cyprus, Republic of
Czech Republic
Denmark (including Greenland and the Faeroe Islands)
Dominican Republic (8th May 1983)
Ecuador
Egypt
El Salvador
Fiji
Finland
France (including all Overseas Departments and Territories)
Gabon
Gambia

Germany
Ghana
Greece
Guatemala (28th October 1964)
Guinea, Republic of
Guinea-Bissau
Haiti (27th September 1957)
Holy See
Honduras
Hungary
Iceland
India
Indonesia
Ireland, Republic of
Israel
Italy
Jamaica
Japan
Kampuchea (27th September 1957)
Kazakhstan (25th December 1991)
Kenya
Korea, Republic of (1st October 1987)
Laos (27th September 1957)
Lebanon
Lesotho
Liberia
Libya
Liechtenstein
Luxembourg
Macedonia
Madagascar
Malawi
Malaysia
Mali
Malta
Mauritania
Mauritius
Mexico
Monaco
Morocco
Namibia
Netherlands (including Aruba and the Netherlands Antilles)
New Zealand
Nicaragua (16th August 1961)
Niger
Nigeria

Norway
Pakistan
Panama (17th October 1962)
Paraguay
Peru
Philippines
Poland
Portugal
Romania
Rwanda
Russian Federation (25th December 1991)
St Lucia
St Vincent and the Grenadines
Senegal
Singapore
Slovak Republic
Slovenia
South Africa
Soviet Union (27th May 1973)
Spain
Sri Lanka
Surinam
Sweden
Switzerland
Taiwan, territory of (10th July 1985)
Tajikistan (25th December 1991)
Thailand
Togo
Trinidad and Tobago
Tunisia
Turkey
Uganda (20th July 1964)
United States of America (including Puerto Rico and all territories and possessions)
Uruguay
Venezuela
Yugoslavia
Zaire
Zambia
Zimbabwe

Schedule 2: Countries enjoying full protection for sound recordings

(The countries specified in this Schedule either are parties to the Rome Convention for the Protection of Performers, Producers of Phonograms and Broadcastings Organisations or otherwise give adequate protection under their law.)

Argentina
Australia (including Norfolk Island)
Austria
Bangladesh
Barbados
Bolivia
Brazil
Burkina Faso
Chile
Colombia
Congo
Costa Rica
Czech Republic
Denmark (including Greenland and the Faeroe Islands)
Dominican Republic
Ecuador
El Salvador
Fiji
Finland
France (including all Overseas Departments and Territories)
Germany
Ghana
Greece
Guatemala
Honduras
India
Indonesia
Ireland, Republic of
Italy
Japan
Lesotho
Luxembourg
Malawi
Malaysia
Mexico
Monaco
Netherlands
New Zealand
Niger
Nigeria
Norway
Pakistan
Panama
Paraguay
Peru
Philippines

Slovak Republic
Spain
Sweden
Switzerland
Taiwan, territory of
Thailand
Uruguay

Schedule 3: Countries enjoying protection in respect of broadcasts

(The countries specified in this Schedule either are parties to the Rome Convention for the Protection of Performers, Producers of Phonograms and Broadcasting Organisations and / or the European Agreement on the Protection of Television Broadcasts or otherwise give adequate protection under their law.)

Argentina (2nd March 1992)
Australia (30th September 1992)
Austria (9th June 1973)
Barbados (18th September 1983)
Belgium (8th March 1968—television only)
Bolivia (24th November 1993)
Brazil (29th September 1965)
Burkina Faso (14th January 1988)
Chile (5th September 1974)
Colombia (17th September 1976)
Congo (18th May 1964)
Costa Rica (9th September 1971)
Cyprus, Republic of (5th May 1970—television only)
Czech Republic (1st January 1993)
Denmark (including Greenland and the Faeroe Islands) (1st February 1962 —television; 1st July 1965—non-television)
Dominican Republic (27th January 1987)
Ecuador (18th May 1964)
El Salvador (29th June 1979)
Fiji (11th April 1972)
Finland (21st October 1983)
France (including all Overseas Departments and Territories) (1st July 1961 —television; 3rd July 1987—non-television)
Germany (21st October 1966)
Greece (6th January 1993)
Guatemala (14th January 1977)
Honduras (16th February 1990)
Indonesia (1st June 1957)
Ireland, Republic of (19th September 1979)
Italy (8th April 1975)
Japan (26th October 1989)
Lesotho (26th January 1990)

Luxembourg (25th February 1976)
Malawi (22nd June 1989)
Malaysia (1st June 1957)
Mexico (18th May 1964)
Monaco (6th December 1985)
Netherlands (7th October 1993)
Niger (18th May 1964)
Norway (10th August 1968—television; 10th July 1978—non-television)
Panama (2nd September 1983)
Paraguay (26th February 1970)
Peru (7th August 1985)
Philippines (25th September 1984)
Singapore (1st June 1957)
Slovak Republic (1st January 1993)
Spain (19th November 1971—television; 14th November 1991—non-television)
Sweden (1st July 1961—television; 18th May 1964—non-television)
Switzerland (24th September 1993)
Uruguay (4th July 1977)

Schedule 4: Modifications

In respect of Indonesia—

(a) Subparagraph (c) of article 2(1) shall not apply except as applied by article 3(a) in relation to sound recordings, and

(b) in the application of article 4(3) above in relation to cable programmes by virtue of article 4(6), the relevant date is 1st January 1985.

Schedule 5: Orders in Council revoked

Number	Title
SI 1989/1293	The Copyright (Application to Other Countries) (No 2) Order 1989
SI 1989/2415	The Copyright (Application to Other Countries) (No 2) (Amendment) Order 1989
SI 1990/2153	The Copyright (Application to Other Countries) (No 2) (Amendment) Order 1990

The Performances (Reciprocal Protection) (Convention Countries) Order 1993 (SI No 943)

Her Majesty, by virtue of the authority conferred upon Her by section 208(1)(*a*) of the Copyright, Designs and Patents Act 1988, is pleased, by and with the advice of Her Privy Council, to order, and it is hereby ordered, as follows:

1 This Order may be cited as the Performances (Reciprocal Protection) (Convention Countries) Order 1993 and shall come into force on 4th May 1993.

2 The following countries are hereby designated as enjoying reciprocal protection under Part II of the Copyright, Designs and Patents Act 1988 (rights in performance)—

Argentina
Australia
Austria
Barbados
Brazil
Burkina Faso
Chile
Colombia
Congo
Costa Rica
Czechoslovakia
Denmark (including Greenland and the Faeroe Islands)
Dominican Republic
Ecuador
El Salvador
Fiji
Finland
France (including all Overseas Departments and Territories)
Germany
Greece
Guatemala
Honduras
Ireland, Republic of
Italy
Japan
Lesotho
Luxembourg
Mexico
Monaco
Niger
Norway
Panama
Paraguay
Peru
Philippines
Spain

Sweden
Uruguay

3 The Performances (Reciprocal Protection) (Convention Countries) (No 2) Order 1989 is hereby revoked.

Appendix 2

List of European Commission Documents

EC measures relevant to the field of telecommunications and satellite communications

Directive 71/305/EEC of 26 July 1971 concerning the coordination of procedures for the award of public works contracts ('the Public Works Directive'); OJ 16.8.71 L185/5 as amended by Directive 89/440/EEC of 18 July 1989; OJ 21.7.89 L210/1.

Directive 77/62/EEC of 21 December 1976; coordinating procedures for the award of public supply contracts ('the Public Supplies Directive') (OJ 15.1.77 L13/1 as amended by Directive 88/295/EEC of 22 March 1988; OJ 20.5.88 L127/1.

Council Directive 83/189/EEC of 28 March 1983 laying down a procedure for the provision of information in the field of technical standards and regulations; OJ 26.4.83 L109/8, as amended by Council Directive 88/182/EEC of 22 March 1988; OJ 26.3.88 L81/75; and Commission Decision 90/230/EEC of 3 May 1990 amending the lists of standardization institutions set out in the annex to Council Directive 83/189/EEC; OJ 18.5.90 L128/15; and Commission Decision 92/400/EEC of 15 July 1992 amending the lists of standards institutions annexed to Council Directive 83/189/EEC; OJ 6.8.92 L221/55.

Council Recommendation 84/549/EEC of 12 November 1984 concerning the implementation of harmonization in the field of telecommunications; OJ 16.11.84 L298/49.

Council Recommendation 84/550/EEC of 1984 concerning the first phase of opening up access to public telecommunications contracts; OJ 16.11.84 L298/51.

Council Resolution of 7 May 1985 on the new approach to technical harmonization and standardization; OJ 4.6.85 C136/1.

Commission Communication: White Paper on completing the internal market; COM(85) 310 final of 14 June 1986.

414

Council Directive 86/361/EEC of 24 July 1986 on the initial stage of the mutual recognition of type approval for telecommunications terminal equipment; OJ 5.8.86 L217/21.

Council Recommendation 86/659/EEC of 22 December 1986 on the coordinated introduction of the integrated services digital network (ISDN) in the European Community; OJ 31.12.86 L382/36.

Council Decision 87/95/EEC of 22 December 1986 on standardization in the field of information technology and telecommunications; OJ 7.2.87 L36/31.

Council Recommendation 87/371/EEC of 25 June 1987 on the coordinated introduction of public pan-European cellular digital land-based mobile communications in the Community; OJ 17.7.87 L196/81.

Council Directive 87/372/EEC of 25 June 1987 on the frequency bands to be reserved for the coordinated introduction of public pan-European cellular digital land-based mobile communications in the Community; OJ 17.7.87 L196/85.

Commission Directive 88/301/EEC of 16 May 1988 on competition in the markets in telecommunications terminal equipment ('the Satellite Terminal Equipment Directive'); OJ 27.5.88 L131/73.

Council Resolution of 30 June 1988 on the development of the common market for telecommunications services and equipment up to 1992; OJ 4.10.88 C257/1.

Commission Communication on the Community and space: A coherent approach; COM(88) 417 final of 26 July 1988.

Council Resolution of 27 April 1989 on standardization in the field of information technology and telecommunications; OJ 11.5.89 C117/01.

Council Directive 89/336/EEC of 3 May 1989 on the approximation of the laws of the Member States relating to electromagnetic compatability; OJ 23.5.89 L139/19.

Council Resolution of 18 July 1989 on the strengthening of the coordination for the introduction of the integrated service digital network (ISDN) in the European Community up to 1992; OJ 1.8.89 C196/04.

Council Directive 89/552/EEC of 3 October 1989 on the coordination of certain provisions laid down by law, regulation or administrative action in Member States concerning the pursuit of television broadcasting activities ('the Television Without Frontiers Directive'); OJ 17.10.89 L298.

Council Directive 89/665/EEC of 21 December 1989 on the coordination of the laws, regulations and administrative provisions relating to the application of review procedures to the award of public supply and public works contracts; OJ 30.12.89 L395/33.

Council Resolution of 21 December 1989 on the global approach to conformity assessment; OJ 16.1.90 C10/1.

Council Resolution 90/C 27/05 of 28 January 1990 concerning transEuropean networks; OJ 6.2.90 C27/8.

Council Resolution 90/C 166/02 of 28 June 1990 on the strengthening of the Europe-wide cooperation on radio frequencies, in particular with regard to services with a pan-European dimension; OJ 7.7.90 C166/4.

Council Directive 90/387/EEC of 28 June 1990 on the establishment of the internal market for telecommunications services through the implementation of open network provision ('the ONP Framework Directive'); OJ 24.7.90 L192/1.

Commission Directive 90/388/EEC of 28 June 1990 on competition in the market for telecommunications services; OJ 24.7.90 L192/10.

Commission Decision 90/450/EEC of 30 July 1990 setting up a joint committee on telecommunications services; OJ 24.8.90 L230/25.

Council Directive 90/531/EEC of 17 September 1990 on the procurement procedures of entities operating in the water, energy, transport and telecommunications sectors ('the Utilities Directive'); OJ 29.10.90 L297/1.

Council Recommendation 90/543/EEC of 9 October 1990 on the coordinated introduction of Pan-European land-based public radio paging in the Community; OJ 9.11.90 L310/23.

Council Directive 90/544/EEC of 9 October 1990 on the frequency bands designated for the coordinated introduction of pan-European land-based public radio paging in the Community; OJ 9.11.90 L310/28.

Council Decision 90/683/EEC of 13 December 1990 concerning the modules for the various phases of the conformity assessment procedures which are intended to be used in the technical harmonization directives; OJ 31.12.90 L380/13.

Council Resolution 90/C 329/09 of 14 December 1990 on the final stage of the co-ordinated introduction of pan-European land-based public digital mobile cellular communications in the Community (GSM); OJ 31.12.90 C329/25.

Notice 91/C 33/04 of 25 January 1991 to Member States laying down guidelines for operational programmes in the framework of a Community initiative for regional development concerning services and networks related to data communication (Télematique); OJ 8.2.91 C33/7.

Council Directive 91/263/EEC of 29 April 1991 on the approximation of the laws of the Member States concerning telecommunications terminal equipment, including the mutual recognition of their conformity ('the Mutual Recognition of Terminal Equipment Directive'); OJ 23.5.91 L128/1.

Council Directive 91/287/EEC of 3 June 1991 on the frequency band to be designated for the co-ordinated introduction of digital European cordless telecommunications (DECT) into the Community; OJ 8.6.91 L144/45.

Council Recommendation 91/288/EEC of 3 June 1991 on the coordinated introduction of digital European cordless telecommunications (DECT) into the Community; OJ 8.6.91 L144/47.

Council Decision 91/352/EEC of 7 June 1991 adopting a specific research and technological development programme in the field of communication technologies (1990–1994); OJ 16.7.91 L192/8.

Council Decision 91/353/EEC of 7 June 1991 adopting a specific programme of research and technological development in the field of telematic systems in areas of general interest (1990–1994); OJ 16.7.91 L192/18.

Council Decision 91/396/EEC of 29 July 1991 on the introduction of a single European emergency call number; OJ 6.8.91 L217/31.

Guidelines on the application of EEC competition rules in the telecommunications sector; 91/C 233/02 OJ 6.9.91 C233/2.

Council Resolution 91/C 325/02 of 18 November 1991 concerning electronics, information and communication technologies; OJ 14.12.91 C325/2.

Commission Communication—standardization in the European economy (follow up to the Commission Green Paper of October 1990); COM(91) 521 final of 16 November 1991.

Council Resolution 92/C 8/01 of 19 December 1991 on the development of the common market for satellite communications services and equipment; OJ 14.1.92 C8/1.

Council Directive 92/13/EEC of 25 February 1992 coordinating the laws, regulations and administrative provisions relating to the application of Community rules on the procurement procedures of entities operating in the water, energy, transport and telecommunications sectors ('the Utilities Remedies Directive'); OJ 23.3.92 L76/14.

Council Directive 92/38/EEC on the adoption of standards for satellite broadcasting of television signals ('the HDTV Directive'); OJ 20.5.92 L137/17.

Council Directive 92/44/EEC of 5 June 1992 on the application of open network provision to leased lines ('the Leased Lines Directive'); OJ 19.6.92 L165/27.

Council Decision 92/242/EEC of 31 March 1992 in the field of security of information systems; OJ 8.5.92 L123/19.

Council Decision 92/264/EEC of 11 May 1992 on the introduction of a standard international telephone access code in the Community; OJ 20.5.92 L137/21.

European Telecommunications Standards (NET)—Application of Directive 86/361/EEC; OJ 5.6.92 C143.

Council Resolution 92/C 158/01 of 5 June 1992 on the development of the integrated services digital network (ISDN) in the Community as a

European-wide telecommunications infrastructure for 1993 and beyond; OJ 25.6.92 C158/1.

Commission Communication: Towards cost orientation and the adjustment of pricing structures—Telecommunications tariffs in the Community; SEC(92)1050 of 15 July 1992.

Commission Communication: The European telecommunications equipment industry (the state of play, issues at stake and proposals for action); SEC(92)1049 final of 15 July 1992.

Council Recommendation 92/382/EEC of 5 June 1992 on the harmonized provision of a minimum set of packet-switched data services (PSDS) in accordance with open network provision (ONP) principles; OJ 18.7.92 L200/1.

Council Recommendation 92/383/EEC of 5 June 1992 on the provision of harmonized integrated services digital network (ISDN) access arrangements and a minimum set of ISDN offerings in accordance with open network provision (ONP) principles; OJ 18.7.92 L200/10.

Commission Communication to the Council and the European Parliament: The European Community and space: challenges, opportunities and new actions; COM(92) 360 final of 23 September 1992.

Commission Communication: 1992 Review of the situation in the telecommunications services sector; SEC(92)1048 final of 21 October 1992.

Directive 92/100/EEC of 19 November 1992 concerning rental rights, lending rights and certain rights to copyright in the field of intellectual property ('the Rental Directive'); OJ 1992 L346/61.

Council Resolution 92/C 318/02 of 19 November 1992 on the promotion of Europe-wide cooperation on numbering of telecommunications services; OJ 4.12.92 C318/2.

Council Resolution 92/C 318/01 of 19 November 1992 on the implementation in the Community of the European Radiocommunications Committee decisions; OJ 4.12.92 C318/1.

Council Resolution 93/C 2/05 of 17 December 1992 on the assessment of the situation in the Community telecommunications sector; OJ 6.1.93 C2/5.

Communication to the Council and European Parliament on the consultation on the review of the situation in the telecommunications services sector; COM(93) 159 final of 28 April 1993.

Council Resolution 93/C 213/01 of 22 July 1993 on the review of the situation in the telecommunications sector and the need for further development in that market; OJ 6.8.93 C213/1.

Council Decision 93/424/EEC of 22 July 1993 on an action plan for the introduction of advanced television services in Europe; OJ 5.8.93 L96/48.

Council Directive 93/83/EEC of 27 September 1993 on copyright and related rights in satellite broadcasting and cable retransmission services ('the Copyright Directive') OJ 1993 L248/15.

Council Directive 93/97/EEC of 29 October 1993 supplementing Directive 91/263/EEC in respect of satellite earth station equipment; OJ 24.11.93 L290/1.

Council Resolution of 7 December 1993 on the introduction of satellite personal communication services in the Community; OJ 16.12.93 C339/1.

Council Resolution 94/C 48/01 of 7 February 1994 on universal service principles in the telecommunications sector; OJ 16.2.94 C48/1.

Council Resolution 94/C 181/02 of 27 June 1994 on a framework for Community policy on digital video broadcasting; OJ 2.7.94 C181/3.

Europe's Way to the Information Society—an action plan: Communication from the Commission to the Council and the European Parliament and to the Economic and Social Committee and the Committee of the Regions; COM(94) 347 final, 19 July 1994.

Commission Directive 94/46/EC of 13 October 1994 amending Directive 88/301/EEC and Directive 90/388/EEC in particular with regard to satellite communications; OJ 19.10.94 L268/15.

Council Resolution 94/C 379/04 of 22 December 1994 on further development of the Community's satellite communications policy, especially with regard to the provision of, and access to, space segment capacity; OJ 31.12.94 C379/5.

Communication from the Commission to the Council and the European Parliament on the Consultation on the Green Paper on mobile and personal communications; COM(94) 492 final.

Communication from the Commission to the Council and the European Parliament on satellite communications: the provision of—and access to—space segment capacity; COM(94) 210 final; OJ 1994 C290/10.

Communication from the Commission to the Council and the European Parliament—The Consultation on the Green Paper on the liberalisation of telecommunications infrastructure and cable television networks; COM(95) 158 final of 3 May 1995.

Communication by the Commission to the Council and the European Parliament on the status and implementation of Directive 90/388/EEC on competition in the markets for telecommunications services; COM(95) 113 final.

Council Resolution 95/C 188/02 of 26 June 1995 on the further development of mobile and personal communications in the European Union; OJ 22.7.95 C188/02.

Proposed EC measures relevant to the field of telecommunications and satellite communications

Proposal for a Council Directive concerning the protection of personal data and privacy in the context of public digital telecommunications networks, in particular the integrated services digital network (ISDN) and public digital mobile networks; COM(90) 314 final—SYN 287 and 288, 13 September 1990; OJ 5.11.90 C277/12.

Proposal for a Council Directive on the frequency bands to be designated for the coordinated introduction of digital short-range radio (DSSR) in the Community; COM(91) 215 final—SYN 345, 12 June 1991; OJ 20.7.91 C189/14.

Proposal for a Council Directive amending Directive 90/531/EEC on the procurement procedures of entities operating in the water, energy, transport and telecommunications sectors; COM(91) 347 final—SYN 361, 6 November 1991, OJ 31.12.91 C337/1.

Draft Services Directive (OJ 31.12.91 C337/1) as amended; OJ 25.7.92 C188/21.

Proposal for a Council Resolution introducing a declaration of European interest to facilitate the establishment of Trans-European networks in the telecommunications domain; COM(92) 15 final; OJ 20.3.92 C71/12.

Amended Proposal for a Council Directive on the protection of individuals with regard to the processing of personal data and on the free movement of such data; COM(92) 422 final SYN 287, 16 October 1992; OJ 27.11.92 C311/30.

Proposal for a Council Directive on the mutual recognition of licences and other national authorizations for the provision of satellite network services and/or satellite communications services extending the scope of Directive . . . / . . . /EEC (DG X111/ 231/92 Rev 3EN).

Amendments to Proposal for a Council Regulation (EEC) introducing a declaration of European interest to facilitate the establishment of trans-European networks in the telecommunications domain; 93/C124/25; OJ 6.5.93 C124/16.

Commission Proposal for a European Parliament and Council Directive on a Policy for the mutual recognition of licences and other national authorizations for the provision of satellite network services and/or satellite communication services; COM(93) 652 final; OJ 4.2.94 C36/2.

Proposal for a European Parliament and Council Directive on the application of open network provision (ONP) to voice telephony; COM(94) 689 final of 1 February 1995.

Amended Proposal for a European Parliament and Council Directive on the mutual recognition of licences and other national authorizations for telecommunication services; COM(94) 41; OJ 10.4.95 C89/13.

Proposal for a European Parliament and Council Directive amending Council Directive 89/552/EEC on the coordination of certain provisions laid down by law, regulation or administrative action in Member States concerning the pursuit of television broadcasting services (Television Without Frontiers Directive); COM(95) 86 final of 31 May 1995.

Proposal for a European Parliament and Council Directive on interconnection in telecommunications—ensuring universal service and interoperability through the application of the principles of open network provision (ONP); COM(95) 379 of 19 July 1995.

Draft Commission Directive of . . ./ . . ./. . . 1996 amending Commission Directive 90/388/EEC regarding the implementation of full competition in telecommunications markets; 96/. . ./EC of 19 July 1995.

A harmonised regulatory framework for licensing—discussion document for the ONP Committee, European Commission, 24 July 1995.

Commission Proposal for a European Parliament and Council Directive on a policy for the mutual recognition of licences and other national authorizations for the provision of satellite network services and/or satellite communication services; COM(93) 652 final, OJ 4.2.94 C36/2.

Draft Commission Directive of . . . . 1995 amending Directive 90/388/EEC with regard to mobile and personal communications (95/. . ./EC) of 21 June 1995.

Green Papers of the European Commission relevant to the field of telecommunications and satellite communications

Commission Green Paper on the development of the common market for telecommunications services and equipment of 30 June 1987; COM(87) 290 final.

Commission Green Paper on a common approach in the field of satellite communications in the European Community of 20 November 1990; COM(90) 490 final.

Commission Green Paper on the development of European standardization —action for faster technological integration in Europe; COM(90) 456 final OJ 28.1.91 C20/1.

Commission Green Paper on mobile and personal communications; COM(94) 145 final.

Commission Green Paper on the liberalisation of telecommunications infrastructure and cable television networks—Part 1: Principles and timetable; COM(94) 440 final of 25 October 1994; and Part 2: A common approach to the provision of infrastructure in the European Union; COM(94) 682 final, 25 January 1995.

Appendix 3

Glossary of Acronyms

APC	Additional Plenipotentiary Conference
APP	Additional Plenipotentiary Conference
ARABSAT	Arab Corporation for Space Communications
BA	Broadcasting Act 1990
BABT	British Approvals Board for Telecommunications
BBC	British Broadcasting Corporation
BCC	Broadcasting Complaints Commission
BDT	Telecommunication Development Bureau of the ITU
BNSC	British National Space Centre
BSS	Broadcasting-satellite Services
BT	British Telecommunications plc
BTI	British Telecom International
CEN	European Standards Committee
CENELEC	European Electrotechnical Standards Committee
CCIR	Consultative Committee on International Radiocommunications
CCITT	Consultative Committee on International Telegraphy and Telephony
CEPT	Conférence Européenne des Administrations des Poste et des Télécommunications (The European Conference for Postal and Telecommunications Administrations)
CIS	Confederation of Independent States
COPUOS	Committee on the Peaceful Uses of Outer Space
COREPER	Committee of Permanent Representatives of the Member States
CTC	Community Telecommunications Committee
CTR	Common technical regulation
DBS	Direct Broadcasting-satellite Services
DG	Directorate General
DGT	Director General of Telecommunications
DMS	Designated Monitoring Station
DTH	Direct to Home

DTI	Department of Trade and Industry
EARC	Extraordinary Administrative Radio Conference
EBU	European Broadcasting Union
ECJ	European Court of Justice
ECTRA	European Committee for Telecommunications Regulatory Affairs
EEC	European Economic Community
EFTA	European Free Trade Association
EIRP	Equivalent Isotropically Radiated Power
ELDO	European Launcher Development Organisation
ENO	European Numbering Office
ERC	European Radiocommunications Committee
ERO	European Radiocommunications Office
ESA	European Space Agency
ESRO	European Space Research Organisation
ETC	European Telecommunications Council
ETNO	European Public Telecommunications Network Operators Association
ETO	European Telecommunications Office
ETSI	European Telecommunications Standard Institute
EUTELSAT	European Telecommunication Satellite Organisation
EWOS	European Workshop for Open Systems
FCC	Federal Communications Commission
FPLMTS	Future Public Land Mobile Telecommunication Systems
FSS	Fixed Satellite Services
GATT	General Agreement on Tariffs and Trade
GII	Global information infrastructure
GPS	Global positioning satellite
GSM	Special Mobile Group; and The Pan-European Cellular Digital Global System for Mobile Communication
GSO	Geostationary-satellite Orbit
GWARC	General World Administrative Radio Conference
HDTV	High Definition Television
HEOS	Highly Elliptical Orbiting Satellite
IBA	Independent Broadcasting Authority
IBC	Internal Broadband Communications
ICA	Interception of Communications Act
ICC	International Chamber of Commerce
ICT	International Court of Justice
IEC	International Electrotechnical Commission
IFRB	International Frequency Registration Board
IMF	International Monetary Fund
IMN	INMARSAT Mobile Number
INMARSAT	International Maritime Satellite Organisation

INTELSAT	International Telecommunications Satellite Organisation
ISO(s)	International Satellite Organisation(s)
ITC	Independent Television Commission
ITRs	International Telecommunication Regulations
ITU	International Telecommunication Union
LEOs	Low Earth Orbiting Satellites
LES	Land Earth Station
MATV	Master Antenna Television
MEOS	Medium Earth Orbiting Satellites
MIFR	Master International Frequency Register
MoU	Memorandum of Understanding
MSS	Mobile Satellite Service
MVDS	Microwave Video Distribution System
NMT	Nordic Mobile Telephone System
NRA(s)	National Regulatory Authority(ies)
OFTEL	Office of Telecommunications
ONP	Open Network Provision
OS	Open System
OSA	Outer Space Act
PSDS	Packet-Switched Data Services
PSN	Public Switched Network
PTN	Public Telecommunications Network
PTS	Public Telecommunications Services
PTT	Post Telegraph and Telephone
PTOs	Public Telecommunications Operator
RA	Radio Authority
RACE	Research and Development in Advanced Communications Technologies in Europe
RARC(s)	Regional Administrative Radio Conference(s)
RCA	Radiocommunications Agency
RHTV	Red Hot Television
RRs	Radio Regulations
RRB	Radio Regulations Board
RCB	Radiocommunications Bureau
SAO	Signatory Affairs Office
SCL	Satellite Class Licence
SCSCL	Single Community Satellite Communications Licence
SDR	Special Drawing Right
SES	Société Européene des Satellites
SMATV	Satellite Master Antenna Television
SNG	Satellite News Gathering
SPAG	Standards Promotion and Application Group
SPSL	Self-Provided System Licence
SSO	Satellite Service Operator
SSSO	Specialised Satellite Service Operator

TA	Telecommunications Act 1984
TC-SES	Technical Committee on Satellite Earth Stations
TEN	Trans European Network
TO	Telecommunications Operator
TRIPS	Trade-Related Aspects of Intellectual Property Rights
TTM&C	Telemetry, tracking, monitoring and command
TVRO	Television Receive Only Receiving Equipment
USAT(s)	Ultra Small Aperture (Satellite) Terminal(s)
VGE	Voluntary Group of Experts
VSATs	Very Small Aperture (Satellite) Terminals
WARC(s)	World Administrative Radio Conference(s)
WATTC	World Administrative Telegraph and Telephone Conference
WRC	World Radiocommunication Conference
WTA	Wireless Telegraphy Act 1949 (as amended)

Appendix 4

Footprints of the ASTRA Satellite System

The ASTRA Satellite System

Société Européenne des Satellites (SES) is a private company incorporated in Luxembourg. SES operates the ASTRA Satellite System which has broadcast television and radio channels throughout Europe since early 1989.

SES operates under a franchise agreement with the Grand Duchy of Luxembourg. The franchise runs until the year 2010, with the possibility for extension, and covers audiovisual services as well as possible new business applications. The Grand Duchy holds a 20 per cent interest in SES through two public financial institutions, while the rest of the equity capital comes from private international entities.

When SES was founded in March 1985 to set up the first privately owned satellite system in Europe, it focused on the needs of the European television viewer and the satellite TV programmer. SES introduced a new approach to satellite television: as a service and market orientated company, its aim is to offer entertaining and high quality packages of television channels and radio stations for the different European language markets, available on attractively priced and easy to install reception equipment.

ASTRA is a satellite system specifically designed to broadcast television and radio programmes across Europe. Currently, the services broadcast via ASTRA are transmitted using analogue technology whereas by autumn 1995, viewers will also be able to receive digital services.

The ASTRA Satellite System operated by SES currently consists of four co-located satellites: ASTRA 1A, launched on 11 December 1988; ASTRA 1B, launched on 2 March 1991; ASTRA 1C, launched on 12 May 1993 and ASTRA 1D launched on 1 November 1994. The satellites are co-located at 19.2° East in geostationary orbit. Another three satellites will be added to the system by 1997. Their capacity will be used for the transmission of digital services in Europe.

Today ASTRA is the only satellite system in the world to operate four satellites at the same orbital slot. The co-location of the ASTRA satellites at

19.2° East makes a total of 64 transponders available for reception from a single point in the sky. No other European satellite operator has been able to rival the number and variety of channels available via ASTRA over the same footprint area.

ASTRA viewers are able to pick up television and radio programming by installing a fixed satellite dish. The dishes are small (60 cm) and attractively priced. SES's communication efforts ensure that viewers understand the simplicity of the equipment needed: the dish antenna outdoors and the receiver indoors connected to the existing television set.

By closely collaborating with satellite equipment manufacturers, SES aims to ensure a smooth transition from the analogue to the digital era of satellite broadcasting. This way, digital-ready satellite dishes, when coupled with a digital receiver, will give the ASTRA viewer access to hundreds of new channels and services via ASTRA 1E, ASTRA 1F and ASTRA 1G.

At the beginning of 1995, more than 56 million homes (approximately 150 million people) were receiving television and radio programming via ASTRA. Some 20 million homes were watching programmes directly from the satellites through communal reception systems (SMATV) or direct-to-home (DTH) dishes. With this viewer base the SES/ASTRA Satellite System has established itself as the most successful television satellite system for DTH reception.

The ASTRA Satellite System concept has unique design features:

— footprints shaped to maximize European market coverage and increase flexibility for broadcasters;

— co-located satellites to ensure distinct programme bouquets transmitted in analogue and digital to viewers—by country, by language and by special interest;

— advanced satellite design providing intersatellite back-up;

— proven reliability of the ASTRA Satellite System and strong technical ground support services;

— professional marketing support.

Astra 1A

Antenna Diameter (cm) for Direct-to-Home (DTH) Reception (Indicative dish sizes, performance levels not guaranteed)

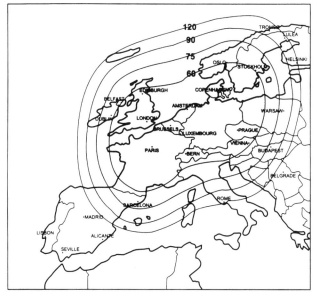

Horizontal Polarization Mode 1

Channel 1   11214.25 MHz
Channel 5   11273.25 MHz
Channel 9   11332.25 MHz
Channel 13 11391.25 MHz

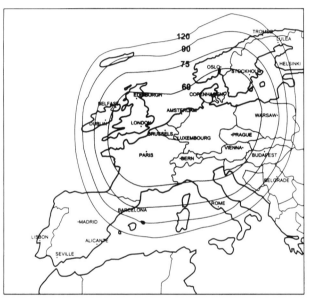

Horizontal Polarization Mode 2

Channel 3   11243.75 MHz
Channel 7   11302.75 MHz
Channel 11   11361.75 MHz
Channel 15   11420.75 MHz

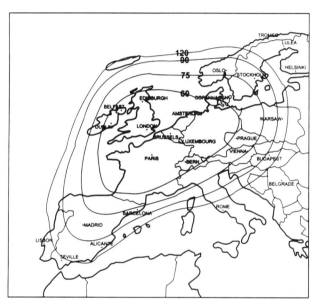

Vertical Polarization Mode 1

Channel 4   11258.50 MHz see footprints ASTRA 1C
Channel 8   11317.50 MHz
Channel 12 11376.50 MHz
Channel 16 11435.50 MHz

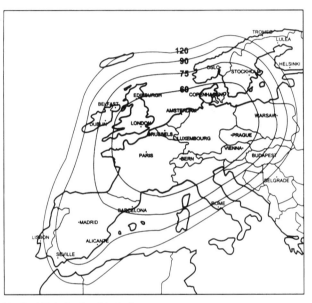

Vertical Polarization Mode 2

Channel 2   11229.00 MHz
Channel 6   11288.00 MHz
Channel 10   11347.00 MHz
Channel 14   11406.00 MHz

Astra 1B

Antenna Diameter (cm) for Direct-to-Home (DTH) Reception (Indicative dish sizes, performance levels not guaranteed)

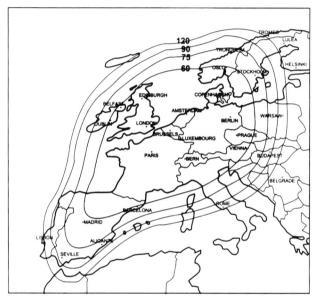

Horizontal Polarization Mode 1
Channel 17   11464.25 MHz
Channel 21   11523.25 MHz
Channel 25   11582.25 MHz
Channel 29   11641.25 MHz

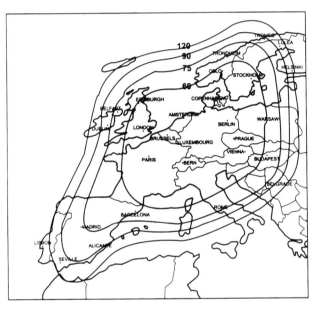

Horizontal Polarization Mode 2

Channel 19   11493.75 MHz
Channel 23   11552.75 MHz
Channel 27   11611.75 MHz
Channel 31   11670.75 MHz

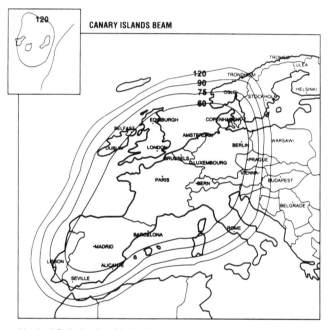

Vertical Polarization Mode 1
Channel 20   11508.50 MHz
Channel 24   11567.50 MHz
Channel 28   11626.50 MHz
Channel 32   11685.50 MHz

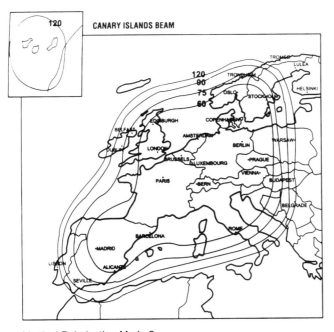

Vertical Polarization Mode 2
Channel 18   11479.00 MHz
Channel 22   11538.00 MHz
Channel 26   11597.00 MHz
Channel 30   11656.00 MHz

Astra 1C

Antenna Diameter (cm) for Direct-to-Home (DTH) Reception (Indicative dish sizes, performance levels not guaranteed)

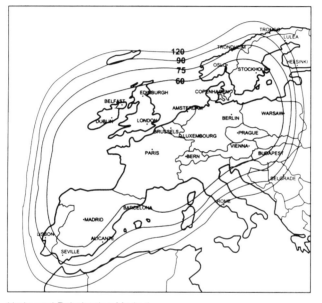

Horizontal Polarization Mode 1

Channel 33   10964.25 MHz
Channel 37   11023.25 MHz
Channel 41   11082.25 MHz
Channel 45   11141.25 MHz

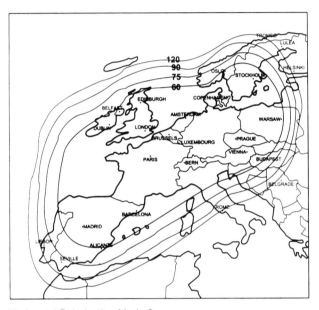

Horizontal Polarization Mode 2
Channel 35 10993.75 MHz
Channel 39 11052.75 MHz
Channel 43 11111.75 MHz
Channel 47 11170.75 MHz
Channel 63 10920.75 MHz

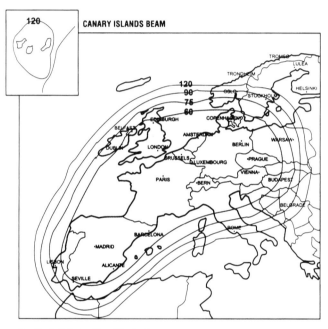

Vertical Polarization Mode 1

Channel 4   11258.50 MHz
Channel 36   11008.50 MHz
Channel 40   11067.50 MHz
Channel 44   11126.50 MHz
Channel 48   11185.50 MHz
Channel 64   10935.50 MHz

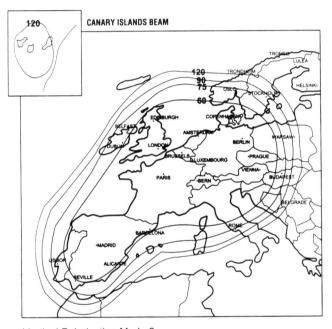

Vertical Polarization Mode 2

Channel 34 10979.00 MHz
Channel 38 11038.00 MHz
Channel 42 11097.00 MHz
Channel 46 11156.00 MHz

Astra 1D

Antenna Diameter (cm) for Direct-to-Home (DTH) Reception (Indicative dish sizes, performance levels not guaranteed)

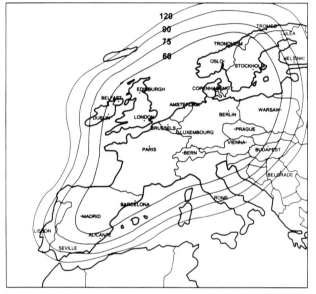

Horizontal Polarization Mode 1
Channel 49   10714.25 MHz
Channel 53   10773.25 MHz
Channel 57   10832.25 MHz
Channel 61   10891.25 MHz

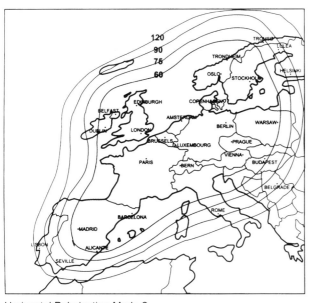

Horizontal Polarization Mode 2
Channel 51   10743.75 MHz
Channel 55   10802.75 MHz
Channel 59   10861.75 MHz
Channel 63   10920.75 MHz see footprints ASTRA 1C

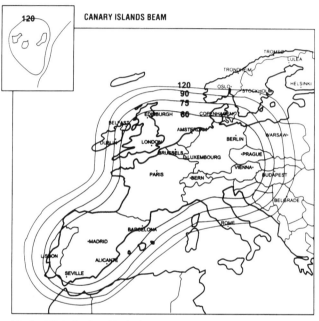

CANARY ISLANDS BEAM

Vertical Polarization Mode 1

Channel 52   10758.50 MHz
Channel 56   10817.50 MHz
Channel 60   10876.50 MHz
Channel 64   10935.50 MHz   see footprints ASTRA 1C

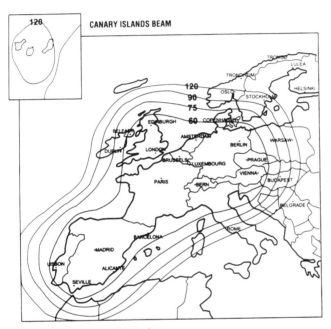

Vertical Polarization Mode 2

Channel 50   10729.00 MHz
Channel 54   10788.00 MHz
Channel 58   10847.00 MHz
Channel 62   10906.00 MHz

Index

445